The Arts of Japan

Creativity and Innovation

Front cover design by Lynn Kawaratani.

Back Cover: *Fujiwara Yasumasa Playing the Flute by Moonlight*, Tsukioka Yoshitoshi, 1883, color woodblock print triptych, Minneapolis Institute of Art, Public domain.

Key Issues in Asian Studies, No. 24
AAS Resources for Teaching About Asia

The Arts of Japan

Creativity and Innovation

Brenda G. Jordan

Association for Asian Studies, Inc.
825 Victors Way, Suite 310
Ann Arbor, MI 48108 USA
www.asianstudies.org

KEY ISSUES IN ASIAN STUDIES

"Key Issues" volumes complement the Association for Asian Studies' teaching journal, *Education About Asia*—a practical teaching resource for secondary school, college, and university instructors, as well as an invaluable source of information for students, scholars, libraries, and those who have an interest in Asia.

Formed in 1941, the Association for Asian Studies (AAS)—the largest society of its kind, with close to 6,000 members worldwide—is a scholarly, non-political, non-profit professional association open to all persons interested in Asia.

For further information, please visit www.asianstudies.org

Cataloging-in-Publication (CIP) Data is available from the Library of Congress.

This book is dedicated to Hiroshi,
my toughest critic and favorite cook.

About "Key Issues in Asian Studies"

Key Issues in Asian Studies (*KIAS*) volumes engage major cultural and historical themes in the Asian experience. *Key Issues* books complement the Association for Asian Studies' teaching journal, *Education About Asia*, and serve as vital educational materials that are both accessible and affordable for classroom use.

Key Issues books tackle broad subjects or major events in an introductory but compelling style appropriate for survey courses. Although authors of the series have distinguished themselves as scholars as well as teachers, the prose style employed is accessible for broad audiences. This series is intended for teachers and undergraduates at two- and four-year colleges as well as advanced high school students and secondary school teachers engaged in teaching Asian studies in a comparative framework and anyone with an interest in Asia.

For further information visit www.asianstudies.org.

"Key Issues" volumes available from AAS:

- *Modern Indian History* / Emily Rook-Koepsel
- *Japanese Government and Politics* / Lauren McKee
- *Shintō in the History and Culture of Japan* / Ronald S. Green
- *Indonesia: History, Heritage, Culture* / Kathleen M. Adams
- *The Philippines: From Earliest Times to the Present* / Damon L. Woods
- *Chinese Literature: An Introduction* / Ihor Pidhainy
- *The Mongol Empire in World History* / Helen Hundley
- *Japanese Literature: From Murasaki to Murakami* / Marvin Marcus
- *Japan Since 1945* / Paul E. Dunscomb
- *East Asian Societies* / W. Lawrence Neuman
- *Confucius in East Asia* / Jeffrey L. Richey
- *The Story of Việt Nam: From Prehistory to the Present* / Shelton Woods
- *Modern Chinese History* / David Kenley
- *Korea in World History* / Donald N. Clark
- *Traditional China in Asian and World History* / Tansen Sen & Victor Mair
- *Zen Past and Present* / Eric Cunningham
- *Japan and Imperialism*, 1853–1945 / James L. Huffman
- *Japanese Popular Culture and Globalization* / William M. Tsutsui
- *Global India ca 100 CE: South Asia in Early World History* / Richard H. Davis
- *Caste in India* / Diane Mines
- *Understanding East Asia's Economic "Miracles"* / Zhiqun Zhu
- *Political Rights in Post-Mao China* / Merle Goldman
- *Gender, Sexuality, and Body Politics in Modern Asia* / Michael Peletz

About the Author

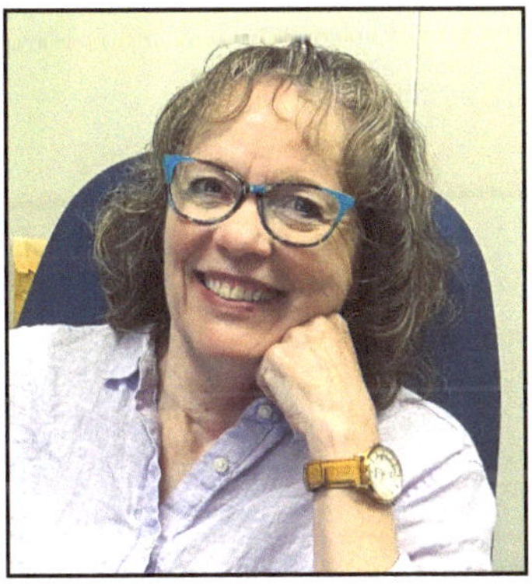

BRENDA G. JORDAN is a Japanese art historian specializing in Tokugawa-period paintings and woodblock prints. She received her PhD from the University of Kansas and was a Monbushō scholar at the University of Tokyo. She taught at Florida State University, University of Kansas, and Colorado College before joining the Asian Studies Center at the University of Pittsburgh in 2001. From 2008 to 2025, she was also the Director of the University of Pittsburgh's coordinating site for the National Consortium for Teaching About Asia (NCTA). Her publications include *Copying the Master and Stealing His Secrets: Talent and Training in Japanese Painting* (2003) and "Potentially Disruptive: Censorship and the Painter Kawanabe Kyōsai" in Hiroshi Nara, ed., *Inexorable Modernity: Japan's Grappling with Modernity in the Arts* (2007).

CONTENTS

Preface and Acknowledgments

This volume in the *Key Issues in Asian Studies* series focuses on the arts of Japan through the lens of creativity and innovation, drawing on current scholarship in the field. Since the arts are an integral part of any country's history, this volume also seeks to provide the context within which the arts flourished in Japan, from ancient times to the present.

Dissemination, adaptation, and the ability to change with the times are the hallmarks of a dynamic society. No culture advances without taking advantage of ideas and techniques from elsewhere. Japan's long history of innovation and creativity is an excellent example of this. Despite their deep respect for tradition, the Japanese have always adopted ideas and technologies from outside and then processed and restructured these cultural imports to develop entirely new styles and techniques. Certain themes crop up repeatedly in Japanese art, such as a heightened attention to nature and the seasons; humor and satire; and a fascination with the mysterious and strange (ghosts, demons, tricksters) dating back centuries. Certain aesthetic sensibilities also permeate the arts, from poetry and literature to painting and drama, including the appeal of things that are fresh and new, and a love of the understated and suggestive. Design elements such as asymmetry and use of negative space also play their part across a wide range of arts. Finally, technical skill, refinement, and production quality feature into this history and continue to be appreciated by Japanese today.

These factors in combination result in a pattern of art making that has a certain distinctive look or feel. The arts highlighted in this book, much like the art of the Italian Renaissance, Victorian England, or French Impressionism, have a flavor that is specific to a particular culture, time, and place. This book is intended to tease out some of these creative and innovative moments in the history of Japanese art and provide the reader with a foundation from which to learn more.

I owe a great deal to many people. Hiroshi Nara, Karen Gerhart, and Meg Taylor led the way with their scrupulous reading of the manuscript. Lucien Ellington, Jon Wilson, and David Kenley at the Association for Asian Studies encouraged me every step of the way. The National Consortium for Teaching About Asia (NCTA) educators Matthew Roberts, Angie Stokes, and Kachina Leigh offered insights from a K–12 teacher's standpoint. The Freeman Foundation, which funds the NCTA, provided me with years of experience in working with K–12 educators, informing the book's themes. The Asian Studies Center and the Japan Iron and Steel Federation endowment at the University of Pittsburgh generously provided grants to complete this work.

This book was a challenge to write, to say the least, since it attempts to cover thousands of years of history, and I was determined to include as much current research as possible. My apologies to my Japan studies colleagues for much that had to be left out in this short survey, but at the same time gratitude for the enormous amount of scholarship that has informed my approach to this book.

A Note to Readers

Japanese names appear with family name first and given name or art name (*gō*) second; sometimes the order is affiliation or studio name first, then art name. The art name is used thereafter (for example, Katsushika Hokusai, then Hokusai). Words such as "art," "architecture," and "painting" did not exist in Japanese prior to the late nineteenth century but are used here following current practice in both English and Japanese. The Japanese macron—for example, in *byōbu* (folding screen)—indicates a long vowel. When a word has been accepted into the English dictionary (for example, shogun and daimyo), the English spelling is used with a few exceptions (for example, Shintō). Dates given for historical figures often vary depending on the source, so readers might notice slight discrepancies.

Map of Japan

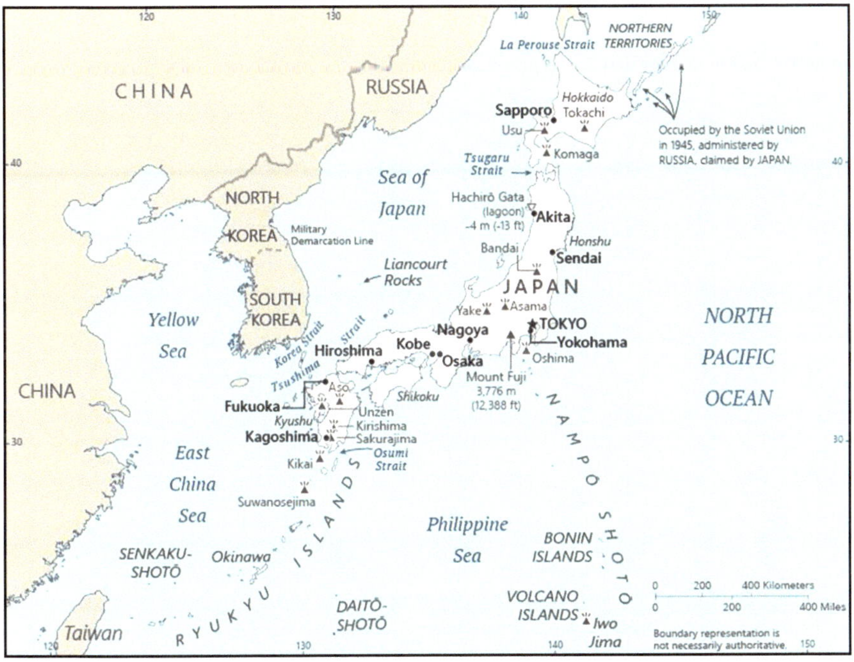

Map of Japan. From the World Factbook: https://www.cia.gov/the-world-factbook/static/maps/JA-map.jpg, Public domain.

1

The Most Ancient of Days

Jōmon, Yayoi, and Kofun Cultures

Thereupon, the two deities stood on the Heavenly Floating Bridge and, lowering the jeweled spear, stirred with it. They stirred the brine with a churning-churning sound; and when they lifted up [the spear] again, the brine dripping down from the tip of the spear piled up and became an island.

— Kojiki[1]

Like other cultures around the world, Japan has a creation myth that reflects its geography and climate. The archipelago now known as Japan—four main islands and thousands of smaller ones—is situated along the Pacific Ring of Fire, making it prone to earthquakes, tsunami, and volcanic eruptions. Three-quarters of its land is mountainous, and agricultural land is limited. Japan's natural beauty is striking and varied, from the snowy regions of the north to the semitropical southwest.

In 712 CE, when the *Kojiki* (literally, "Record of Ancient Things") was compiled and the creation myth recorded, the Japanese court was attempting to validate the rule of the Yamato emperors by proclaiming the sacred origins of the imperial family. Genealogies, myths, legends, folklore—all this and more went into the *Kojiki*, the earliest surviving book in Japan. Archaeological records in the form of clay figurines, ceramic containers, bronze bells, and imperial tombs provide us with physical evidence for the early development of Japanese culture. From these earliest of periods, there was both creative adaptation of things from abroad and innovation.

One of the oldest continuous pottery cultures in the world is that of the Jōmon, thought to have arisen around 13,500 BCE.[2] The name means "cord-marked" and was coined in 1877 by Edward Sylvester Morse (1838–1925), an American scientist and amateur archeologist. Traveling along the shores near Tokyo, he noticed shell middens that he suspected were left by early communities. Subsequent excavations of these areas revealed the pottery that we now call Jōmon.

The Jōmon people were semi-sedentary; they used stone tools and hunted and fished, but they also cultivated plants and trees, including the lacquer tree (*Toxicodendron vernicifluum*). They had contacts with the peoples of other Pacific regions, which led to their adoption of technologies alongside their own independent developments.[3] Two examples of technological adoptions are their use of wooden houses raised above the ground on posts and some evidence of rice cultivation.[4]

An important technological advance was the use of fire to harden clay for earthenware containers. Imagine the changes in diet that must have occurred when food that previously was only ever grilled could now be boiled in a vessel, other ingredients could be added, foods could be softened, and juices and nutrients weren't lost as they would be over an open fire. Fired wares also allowed for the storage of surplus food for longer periods.

The Jōmon people produced earthenware fired in open pits.[5] They used various tools to develop designs on the clay prior to firing, perhaps imitating the woven patterns of baskets.[6] The designs on pots created a textured surface, making them easier to handle when hot or wet. Designs might also have been social identifiers and expressions of wealth.[7]

Some of the most interesting and dramatic Jōmon ware comes from the Middle Jōmon Period (3650–2500 BCE)—a type called "flame pots" (*kaen doki*), made by building up large coils of earthenware clay. Potters used tools to smooth and shape both the outer and inner surfaces; these tools included cord-wrapped sticks that were rolled over the wet clay surface, shells used to press patterns into the clay, and bamboo or pointed sticks to create patterns. The pots were then fired outdoors in open pits at a temperature of no more than 900°C.[8]

These highly embellished pots vary in design, often reflecting different styles and approaches, suggesting a practice of experimentation and dissemination through exchanges among groups. Figures 1.1 and 1.2 demonstrate the variety of swirling patterns and pressed or incised patterns commonly seen on these pots. During the Middle Jōmon, ceramic pots also served as burial urns and lamps, as well as possibly having ceremonial uses.

Another type of earthenware appeared in the form of figurines, known as *dogū*. Their purpose seems to have been ritual, as most were apparently deliberately broken before burial. One of the best known of these figurines is the "Jōmon Venus" (Figure 1.3), found in the Tanabatake archeological site in Nagano prefecture. The Jōmon Venus is unusual in surviving mostly intact over the millennia. Her amply fleshed buttocks and stomach emphasize the contours of a woman's body, and her hair is elaborately arranged. Other *dogū* have large eyes with slits, small hands and

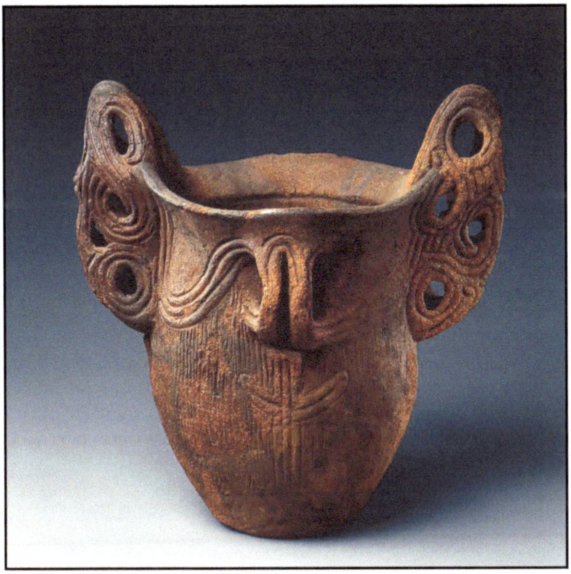

Figure 1.1: Deep vessel with handles, Jōmon period, earthenware with carved and incised decoration, Metropolitan Museum of Art, New York, Public domain.

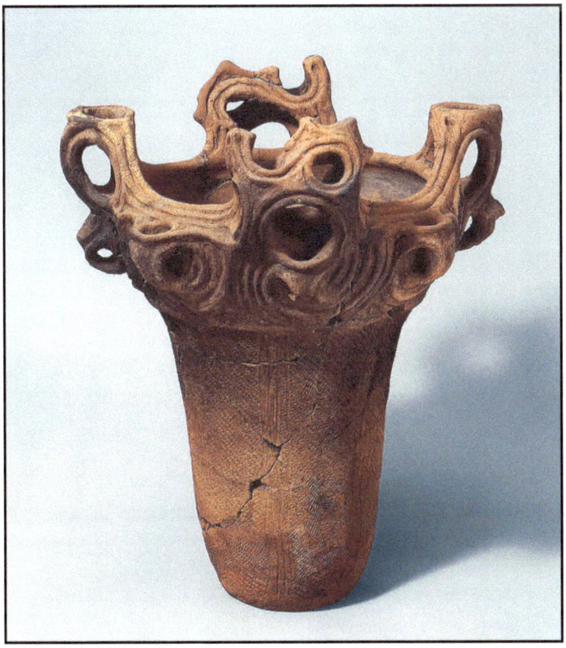

Figure 1.2: "Flame pot," Jōmon period, earthenware, Metropolitan Museum of Art, New York, Public domain.

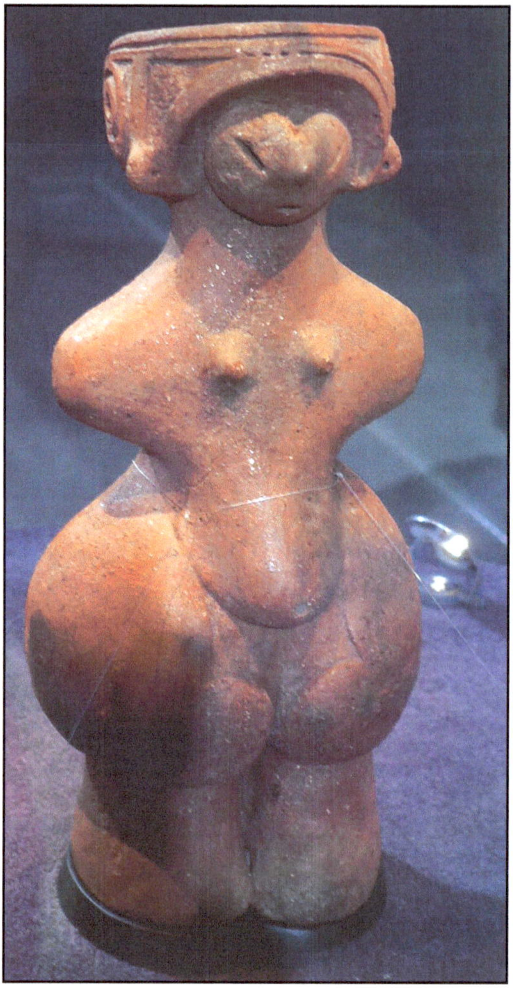

Figure 1.3: "Jōmon Venus" from the Tanabatake archeological site, Middle Jōmon period, earthenware, Togari-ishi Archeological Museum, Nagano prefecture, Wikimedia Commons.

feet, and are covered with designs that could indicate fairly sophisticated clothing and headdresses (Figure 1.4). Figurines such as monkeys, Japanese boars, shellfish, seals, and bears have also been found.[9]

During the Late Jōmon period (2500–500 BCE), potters' skills developed further. Their patterns on vessels were variations on a theme, more sophisticated and less flamboyant than Middle Jōmon ware. Other types of objects were also made in this period, such as detailed earrings fashioned from clay. Lacquer (*urushi*) was also used in the Jōmon, on objects such as bowls, coating them with

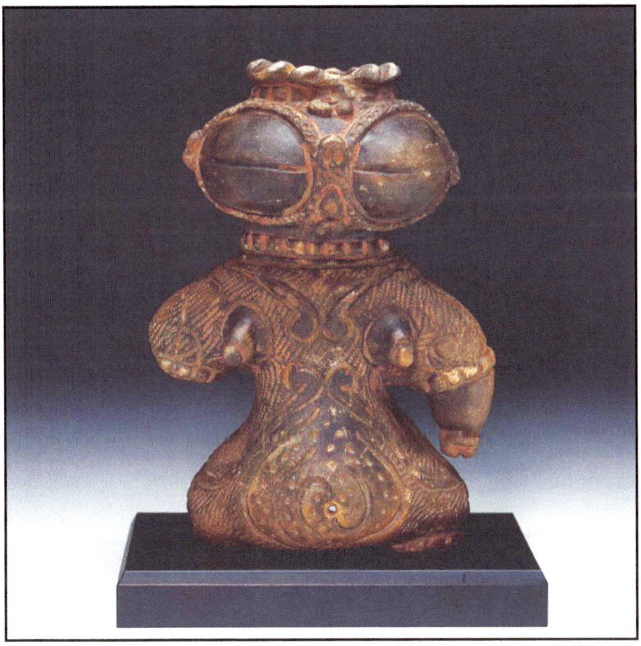

Figure 1.4: *Dogū* figurine, 1000–800 BCE, earthenware with traces of color, Minneapolis Institute of Art, Public domain.

red or black lacquer designs, making them waterproof. Discoveries at Late Jōmon sites such as Ondashi and Kamegaoka in northern Japan have led scholars to reevaluate the previous assumption that lacquer techniques were imported from China. Lacquer use in Japan may even predate that of Neolithic China.[10]

During the subsequent Yayoi period (300 BCE–300 CE), a different aesthetic sensibility appears.[11] This was a time when the influx of immigrants from the Korean peninsula and the shift to wet-rice agriculture were driving the dissemination of technology and cultural innovation. Metalworking and bronze technology were introduced from the continent, and silk weaving developed. This was also when settlements became larger and structures more complex, with raised-floor buildings that enabled rice to stay dry. These storehouses appear to have been the "sturdiest, most impressive and carefully constructed building[s]" in a village.[12] This type of architecture would later develop into the style associated with Shintō shrines.

Named after Hongō Yayoi-chō, the neighborhood in Tokyo where this earthenware was first discovered in 1884, Yayoi pottery is characterized by simplicity of design. The vessels are usually jar-shaped, as seen in Figure 1.5 from the Late Yayoi period. The technique of coiling clay to build a shape continued from Jōmon to Yayoi, but the pots' surfaces were smoothed and sometimes clay slip was applied, making the pottery more waterproof.[13] The Yayoi people spread from

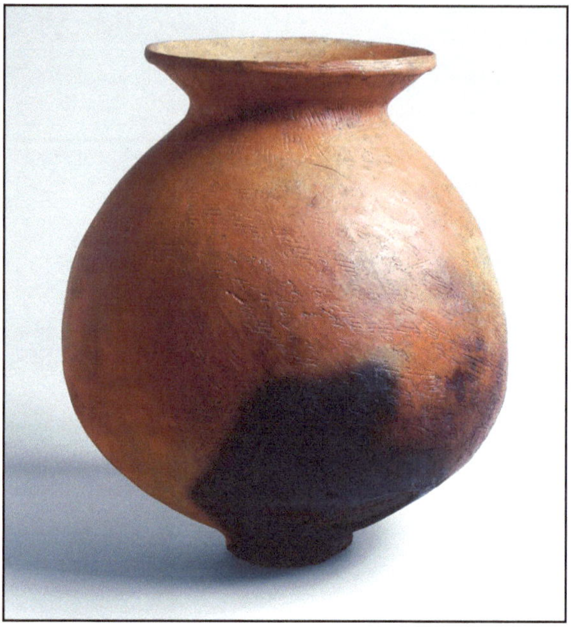

Figure 1.5: Yayoi jar, c. 100–300 CE, earthenware with incised decoration, Metropolitan Museum of Art, New York, Public domain.

the Kyushu region northeast into the main island of Honshu. They distinguished between vessels produced for ritual and those for daily use, as was the case in the later Jōmon. The Jōmon and Yayoi ceramic styles began to intertwine by the Middle Yayoi period (200 BCE–100 CE), with red-lacquered jars and designs of human faces that are stylistically similar to the earlier *dogū*.

As Yayoi society developed, leaders arose as heads of small chiefdoms. One such chieftain may have been a woman known as Himiko, one of a number of women rulers at the time. Himiko is mentioned in the third-century Chinese document *Wei Zhi* as the Queen of Yamatai. In 238–239 CE, written exchanges between the Chinese kingdom of Wei and Himiko designated her "a friend of Wei."[14] Himiko is said to have sent tributes of slaves and linen cloth to Wei, and in return, she received a hundred bronze mirrors and a gold seal, as well as textiles including silk and brocades. Thus, at this early period, fine textiles and metalworking were exchanged between the Japanese and Chinese.[15] As these small chiefdoms grew in number and social stratification, more earthenware was fired for ritual purposes. Some cylindrical pieces were around a meter high, and these may be precursors of the *haniwa* clay figures that appear in the Kofun period (second half of third century to the early eighth century).[16]

This period is also known for bronze bells (*dōtaku*), mirrors, and weaponry. The technology of casting bronze came to Japan from China via the Korean

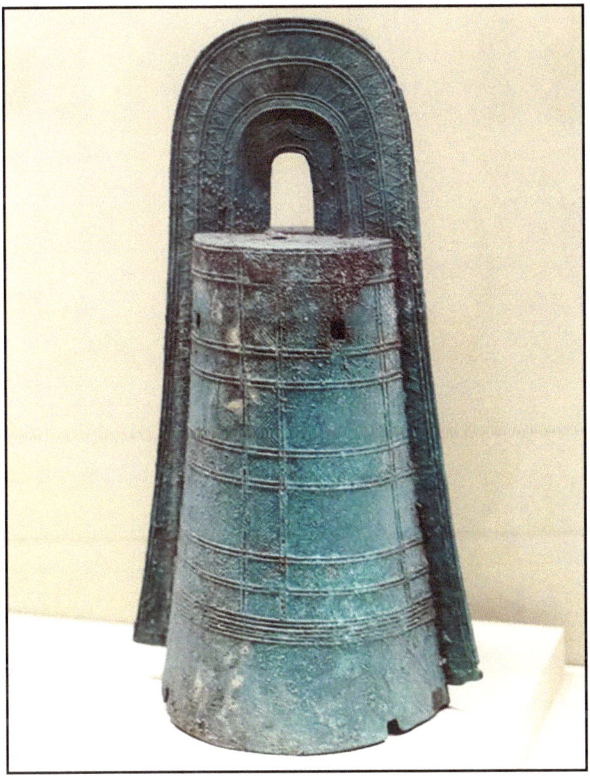

Figure 1.6: Bronze bell (*dōtaku*), first century BCE–first century CE, bronze, Minneapolis Institute of Art, Public domain.

peninsula (Figure 1.6). In Japan, stone and later clay was used to make molds, into which molten bronze was poured. Formed with intricate designs and likely used in rituals, *dōtaku* include scenes of human life and nature, such as hunters, herons, turtles, frogs, deer, and fish, all depicted in hairline relief within panels on the surface of the bells. Deer in particular came to be worshiped as messengers of the deities and subjects of the arts. Later bells are larger, as much as over a meter in height. The casting of bells died out in the late second century CE and was replaced by a surge of interest in bronze mirrors. The technique of bronze casting became integral to the development of Japanese visual and material culture.

In the second half of the third century, large-scale burial mounds began to appear throughout Japan, with many located in the areas of modern-day Osaka, Kyoto, and Nara. The Kofun period is named for these tombs, or burial mounds. The largest *kofun* is that of Emperor Nintoku; it dates to the Middle Kofun (end of fourth century–fifth century) and has the distinctive keyhole shape for which these tombs are known. The burial mound is 486 meters long; including the outside moats, the tomb is 842 meters in total length, 659 meters at its widest point, and rises to almost 40 meters at its highest point (Figure 1.7).[17] In the Late

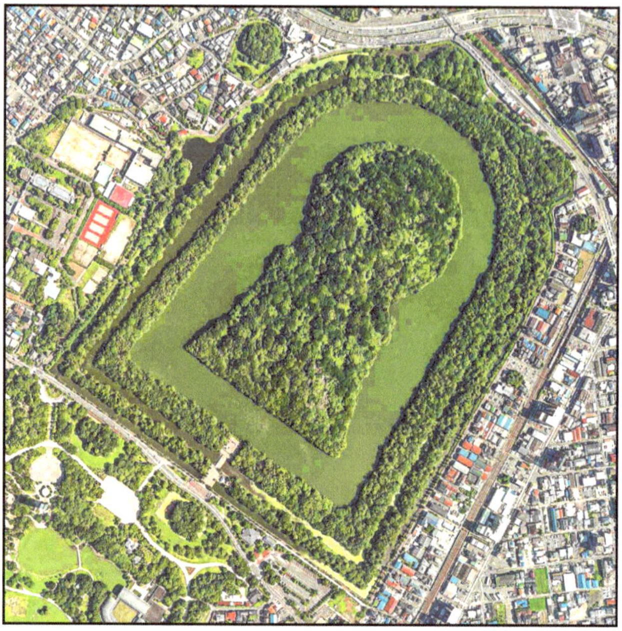

Figure 1.7: Tomb of Emperor Nintoku, fifth century, Sakai, Osaka, National Land Image Information, Japan.

Kofun (end of fifth century–end of sixth century), the huge keyhole-shaped tombs gave way to round and rectangular mounds, with stone burial chambers, some of which contained painted murals. These tombs were major engineering feats, and the skills developed would serve the Japanese well in the following centuries.

Most of the smaller tombs have been looted over the centuries, but some still contain evidence of wealthy and powerful rulers. In addition to wall paintings, there were gold and gilt-bronze ornaments, cut glass, gold crowns, swords, shoes, horse trappings and the like, all speaking to the power of the elite, as well as to the international exchange of ideas and technologies between cultures. For example, goldsmithing techniques came through the Silk Roads to China and then to Japan, while jade burial accessories crafted in Japan have been found in tombs of the elite on the Korean peninsula, and Japanese Umbrella Pine (*koyamaki*) was used for coffins in the tomb of King Muryeong (r. 501–523) and elsewhere.[18]

Terracotta *haniwa* are one of the most interesting artifacts from these tombs (Figure 1.8). *Haniwa* are figures that rise from cylindrical bases that were placed along tiers carved into the sides of the burial tomb mounds. The cylindrical form was likely developed from Late Yayoi vessels. Kofun *haniwa* represent a variety of objects and human figures: there are deer, a falconer with his bird, houses, boats, warriors, women, dancers, and jesters, to name a few. Some are solemn, but others could be described as playful. Why were they made? They may have been intended to appease the spirit of the deceased or had other shamanistic purposes.

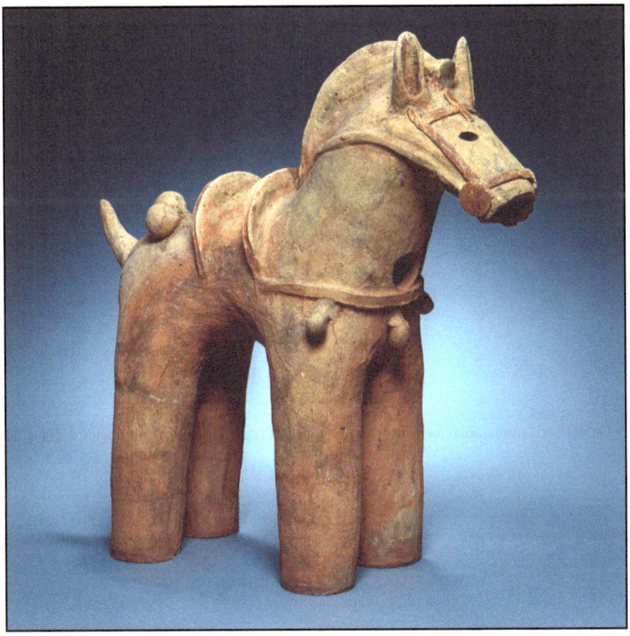

Figure 1.8: *Haniwa* horse, fifth–sixth century, earthenware with traces of pigment, Cleveland Museum of Art, Public domain.

The following centuries saw a burst of creativity and innovation, continuing from the previous cultural periods, with an increasingly stratified society, and exchanges between Japan, China, and the Korean peninsula, as well as the introduction of Buddhism and the corresponding response of Japan's native Shintō faith.

Notes

[1] *Kojiki*, trans. Donald L. Philippi (Tokyo: University of Tokyo Press, 1968), 49.

[2] The dates for the Jōmon period vary depending on the author or study; these dates are currently accepted, though provisional. See Nobuo Tsuji, *History of Art in Japan*, trans. Nicole Coolidge Rousmaniere (New York: Columbia University Press, 2019), 3.

[3] Sergey Lapteff discusses the relationship of Jōmon peoples with the continent in "Relationships between Jōmon Culture and the Cultures of the Yangtze, South China and Continental Southeast Asian Areas," *Japan Review* 18 (2006): 249–286, https://www.jstor.org/stable/25791304.

[4] Tsuji, *History of Art in Japan*, 3.

[5] A commonly repeated theory is that women were the primary producers of early pottery. See, for example, Tatsuo Kobayashi, edited by Simon Kaner with Oki Nakamura, *Jomon Reflections: Forager Life and Culture in the Prehistoric Japanese*

Archipelago (Barnsley, UK: Oxbow Books, 2004), 27, https://www.jstor.org/stable/j.ctv2p7j5rc; and Tsuji, *History of Art in Japan*, 10. Prudence M. Rice questions this assumption in "On the Origins of Pottery," *Journal of Archeological Method and Theory* 6, no. 1 (March 1999): 1–54; see page 10, note 8, https://www.jstor.org/stable/20177395.

[6] Kobayashi, *Jomon Reflections*, chap. 3, "The Appearance of Pottery," 19–50.

[7] Rice, "On the Origins of Pottery," 30 and 36–37.

[8] Department of Asian Art, "Jōmon Culture (ca. 10,500–ca. 300 B.C.)," *Heilbrunn Timeline of Art History* (New York: The Metropolitan Museum of Art, 2000–), http://www.metmuseum.org/toah/hd/jomo/hd_jomo.htm (October 2002).

[9] Tsuji, *History of Art in Japan*, 14.

[10] Tsuji, *History of Art in Japan*, 16.

[11] The word "aesthetic" refers to the study of beauty and/or the appreciation of beauty.

[12] William H. Coaldrake, *Architecture and Authority in Japan*, Nissan Institute/Routledge Japanese Studies (London: Routledge, 1996), https://doi.org/10.4324/9780203042830, 32–33.

[13] Department of Asian Art, "Yayoi Culture (ca. 300 B.C.–300 A.D.)," *Heilbrunn Timeline of Art History* (New York: The Metropolitan Museum of Art, 2000–), http://www.metmuseum.org/toah/hd/yayo/hd_yayo.htm (October 2002).

[14] From the *Wei Zhi* (*Shōki-hon*), translated in J. Edward Kidder Jr., *Himiko and Japan's Elusive Chiefdom of Yamatai: Archaeology, History, and Mythology* (Honolulu: University of Hawai'i Press, 2007), 16.

[15] Himiko is thought to have died in 247 or 248. Kidder, *Himiko and Japan's Elusive Chiefdom of Yamatai*, xii, 16–17.

[16] Tsuji, *History of Art in Japan*, 26. Tsuji defines the Kofun period as encompassing the Asuka, Hakuhō, and Nara periods covered in the next chapter.

[17] By way of contrast, the Great Pyramid of Giza is an average of 230 meters on each side of the base and had an original height of 147 meters. *Encyclopaedia Britannica Online*, s.v. "Pyramids of Giza," https://www.britannica.com/topic/Pyramids-of-Giza (accessed 2/23/2024); see also J. Edward Kidder Jr., "Nintoku, Tomb of Emperor," *Grove Art Online*, 2003, https://doi.org/10.1093/gao/9781884446054.article.T062565; also "Tomb of Emperor Nintoku (Daisen Kofun)," *New Golden Route*, https://www.westjr.co.jp/global/en/ticket/hokuriku-arch-pass/Explore_Japan/spot/osaka/tomb-of-emperor-nintoku-daisen-kofun/index.html (accessed 2/23/2024)

[18] Tsuji, *History of Art in Japan*, 33. Kwon Ohyoung, "Cultural Exchange and International Interaction in East Asia as Seen through the Tomb of King Muryeong," *Journal of Korean Art and Archeology* 2022, Vol 16, 13–23. https://www.ijkaa.org/v.16/0/13/4

2

An Opening of Eyes

Buddhism in the Asuka and Nara Periods

Buddha sits peacefully ruling over the universe
Buddha manifests himself in all the universe
Buddha is serene and shows himself in everything
Buddha's universe is vast and permeated with Buddha's laws

— Flower Garland Sutra[1]

The *Kojiki* tells of the quarrels between sibling deities, which seem to echo the conflict between a female ruler and a forceful male relative. Susanoo no Mikoto insults his older sister the Sun Goddess, Amaterasu Ōmikami, to the extent that she shuts herself in a cave, causing the world to go dark. The other deities dance and play music outside the cave, trying to lure her out. When Amaterasu appears at the mouth of the cave, they grab her and pull her into the open, whereupon light returns to the world.

Amaterasu is believed to have been adopted as the ancestral *kami* of the imperial Yamato rulers sometime between the fifth and seventh centuries.[2] She became a popular deity in Shintō, which often involves nature worship that was based on the belief that all things are potentially animate and to a degree sentient. Manifestations of nature (*kami*) harbor a divine presence and are worshipped accordingly. This worldview fosters a keen sense of seasonal changes, which has had considerable impact on the arts in Japan throughout history.

The word *kami*, although it is often translated as "god" or "spirit" in English, carries a sense of "above" or "superior." Things that induce a sense of awe were often understood as *kami* or are associated with them. There are said to be eight million *kami*, residing everywhere—in nature, in homes, and even in toilets.[3] The great Mt. Fuji is venerated as a *kami*, for example. Originally, however, *kami* were not thought to take human shape. This would change with the arrival of Buddhism to Japan.

Buddhism originated in India and spread throughout Asia, eventually reaching Japan by way of China and Korea. It has been described as "the world's first great missionary religion."[4] Founded in the sixth century BCE by the historical Buddha, Siddhartha Gautama, the faith emphasizes liberation from the endless cycle of rebirth and suffering. As Buddhism spread, numerous branches and schools developed, adding complexity and sophistication, and inspiring a range of artistic expressions. Buddhism's arrival in Japan in the sixth century, along with other cultural influences such as Daoism and Confucianism, as well as technological advancements, led to profound changes in the centuries that followed.[5]

The introduction of Buddhism was initially opposed by the Yamato rulers, who performed rituals for the *kami*; Buddhism threatened their power, and they argued that it would upset the local deities.[6] By the time of Emperor Yōmei (r. 585–587), however, Buddhist institutions were actively supported by the rulers, including emperors considered descendants of the Sun Goddess. This led to a proliferation in the construction of Buddhist temples as well as Shintō shrines.

The huge Izumo Shrine and the imperial shrine at Ise are but two of numerous Shintō shrines built with techniques still used today. Developed from the style

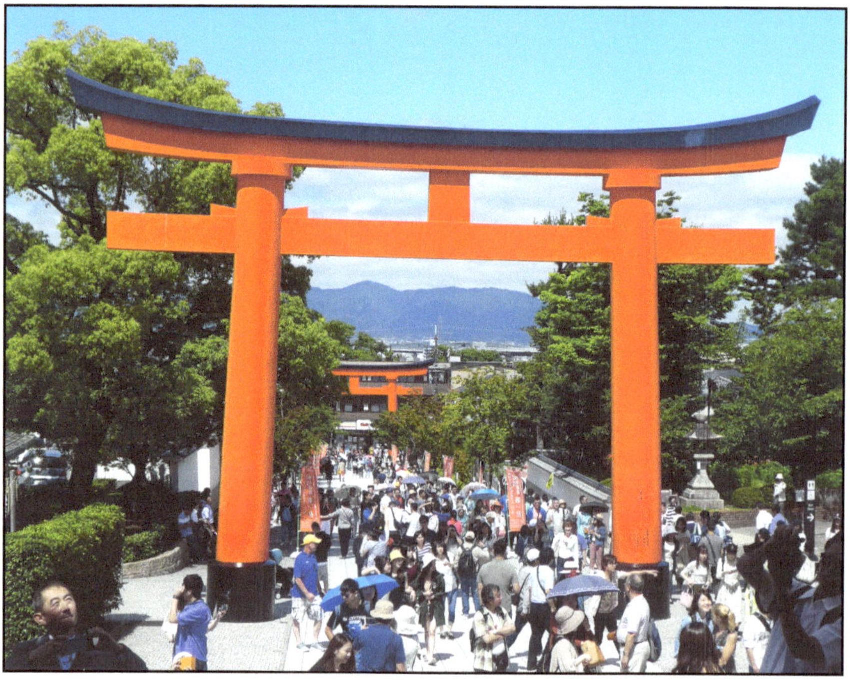

Figure 2.1: Fushimi Inari Taisha *torii*, Kyoto, wood gate with vermillion paint, photo by author.

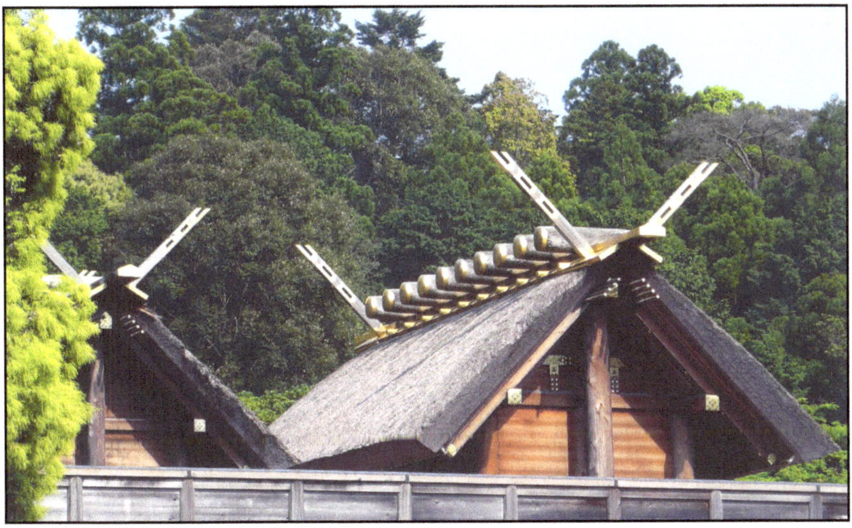

Figure 2.2: Ise Grand Shrine, Inner Shrine, Japanese cypress (*hinoki*) structure with thatched *kaya* roof, Mie prefecture, Wikimedia Commons.

of earlier storehouses, shrine architecture has numerous distinctive features. A *torii* ("bird perch") gate marks the transition into sacred space (Figure 2.1). The buildings that make up a shrine compound are situated asymmetrically. Taking Ise as an example (Figure 2.2), the main buildings are constructed using a post-and-beam technique without nails: a tenon (projecting pin) on one timber fits into a mortise (hole) on another. Boards set between posts create walls (bays), and verandas with railings surround the building. Other features include heavily thatched gable roofs that narrow dramatically as they rise, avoiding an overbalanced appearance; *katsuogi* (wood cylinders set crosswise along the roof ridge; also seen in *haniwa*, Figure 2.3); *chigi* (forked timbers); an emphasis on the horizontal; and unpainted wood, planed to a satin smooth finish.[7] Many shrines have been built in woods and in the mountains, using materials such as Japanese cypress (*hinoki*) and micanthus reed (*kaya*). Their construction allows for some degree of movement in earthquakes. The refined simplicity of shrine architecture and the reflection of nature in the chosen materials and sites have continued to be a dominant aesthetic throughout Japanese history.[8]

As early as the fifth century, Buddhist icons were filtering into Japan along with the courtly arts of China and Korea. During the Asuka (538–645) and Hakuhō (645–710) periods, Buddhist teachings and images flooded into the islands. The first Buddhist temple, Asukadera in Nara (609), was begun in 588 by a Korean group of six monks, two architects, a metalwork and casting master, four roofing specialists, and a painter. Soon after, Hōryūji, the oldest extant wooden temple building in the world, was constructed in 607. Destroyed by fire, Hōryūji was rebuilt in the late 600s (Figure 2.4). Its design follows a Chinese style of wooden

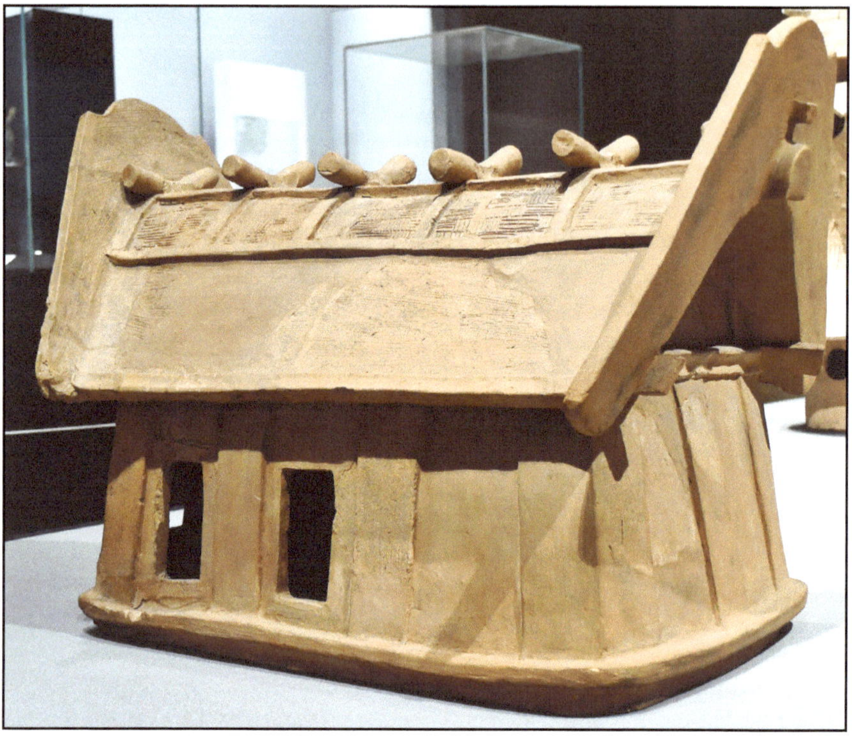

Figure 2.3: *Haniwa* house, early fifth century, terracotta, excavated from Chausuyama tomb, Akabori village, Sawa county, Gunma prefecture, Tokyo National Museum, Public domain.

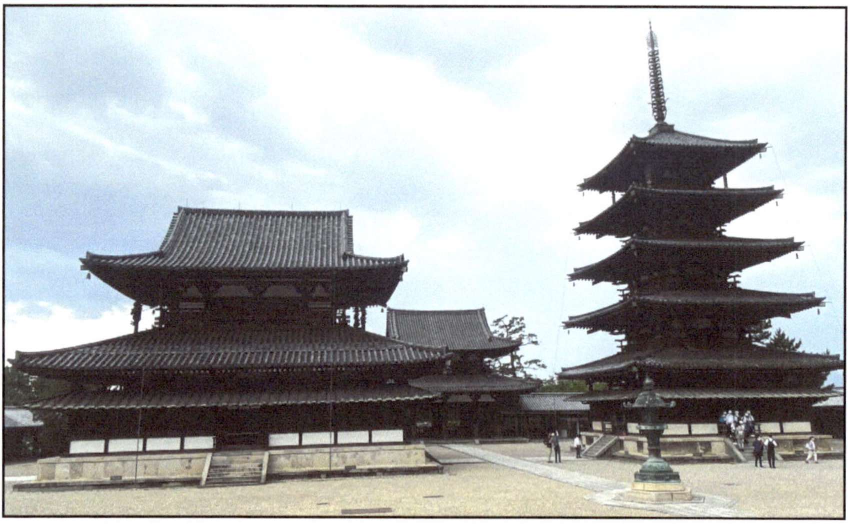

Figure 2.4: Hōryūji main hall and pagoda, Nara, post-and-lintel structure with tile roofs, late seventh century, photo by author.

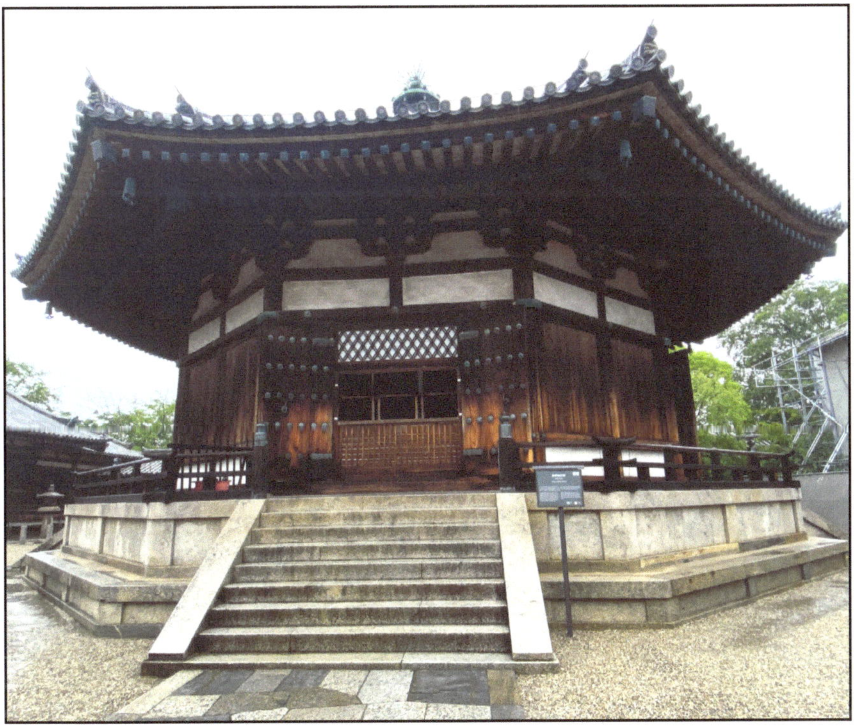

Figure 2.5: Yumedono Hall, Hōryūji, Nara, 1230 reconstruction of 739 hall, octagonal wooden structure with tile roof, photo by author.

temple construction but deviates from the Chinese model by placing the main hall (*kondō*, literally, "golden hall") and the pagoda (*tō*) side by side within the compound. Pagodas are relic halls; although their structure ultimately derives from the Indian stupa, the East Asian pagoda developed from the Chinese Han-dynasty (206 BCE–220 CE) tower.

Hōryūji and other temples of the period share several architectural features: double-terrace platforms on which the buildings sit, columns that have a slight convex curve in the middle of the column (entasis), heavy tile hip-and-gable roofs supported in part by wooden block plates at the tops of the columns, and wooden brackets decorated with cloud designs (Figure 2.5).[9]

These Buddhist temple complexes could not have been built without royal patronage. Empress Suiko (554–628) and her nephew and regent Prince Shōtoku (572–622) were active patrons of Buddhism, founding Hōryūji in 607. Inside the main hall is a bronze cast triad of the historical Buddha, worshipped as Sakyamuni (Shaka), and two accompanying bodhisattvas (*bosatsu*) (Figure 2.6). The triad is attributed to the sculptor Tori Busshi, a descendant of craftsmen from the continent. The figures reflect continental styles in the "waterfall" drapery of Shaka's robes, the decorative patterns of the mandorla (halo), the elongated proportions,

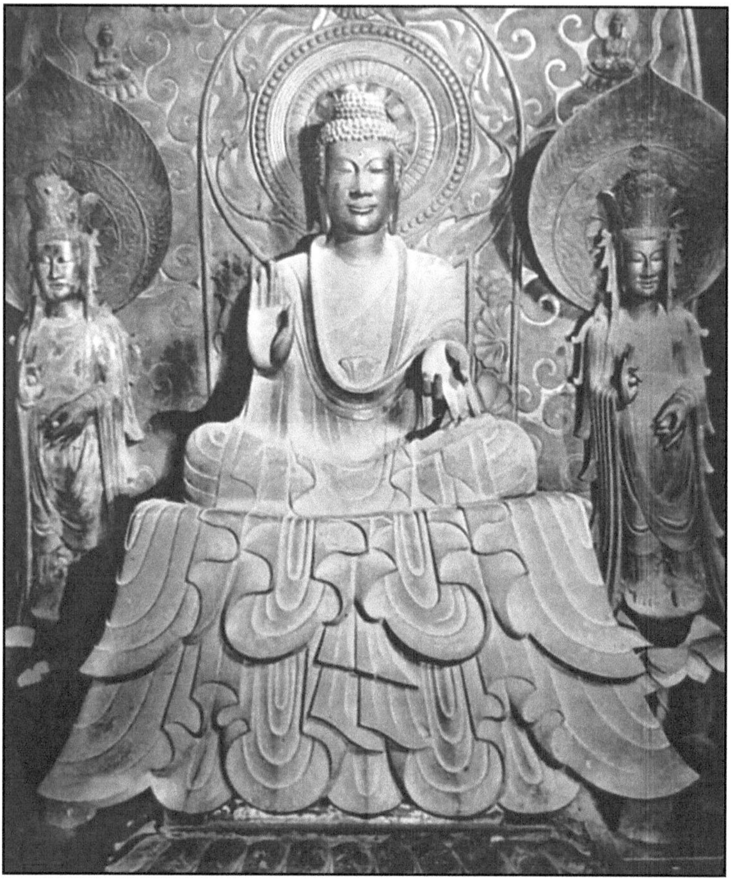

Figure 2.6: Shaka Triad, Hōryūji main hall, attributed to Tori Busshi, 623 CE, gilt-bronze, Wikimedia Commons.

the almond-shaped eyes, and Shaka's archaic smile.[10] The bronze casting method was a technical advancement for Japan: a wax model was encased in clay, and then the wax was melted away, leaving a clay mold for the molten bronze.

Royal patronage also gave rise to the Guze Kannon statue, recorded in 761 as being an image of Prince Shōtoku (Figure 2.7).[11] The figure, which holds a precious jewel, was carved from a single camphor tree and covered in gold leaf over a lacquer base. The statue's bronze coronet contains blue glass beads, and the wooden mandorla is a complex design of interlocking S curves, round jewels, and floral scrolls. Wrapped in silk and hidden for centuries as a *hibutsu* (secret Buddha), the statue was revealed in 1884 when the American art historian Ernest Fenollosa (1853–1908) visited the temple with the art critic Okakura Kakuzō (Tenshin; 1863–1913). Although the image reflects Chinese Northern Wei (386–534) styles, the facial features are specific to Japan and have been characterized as

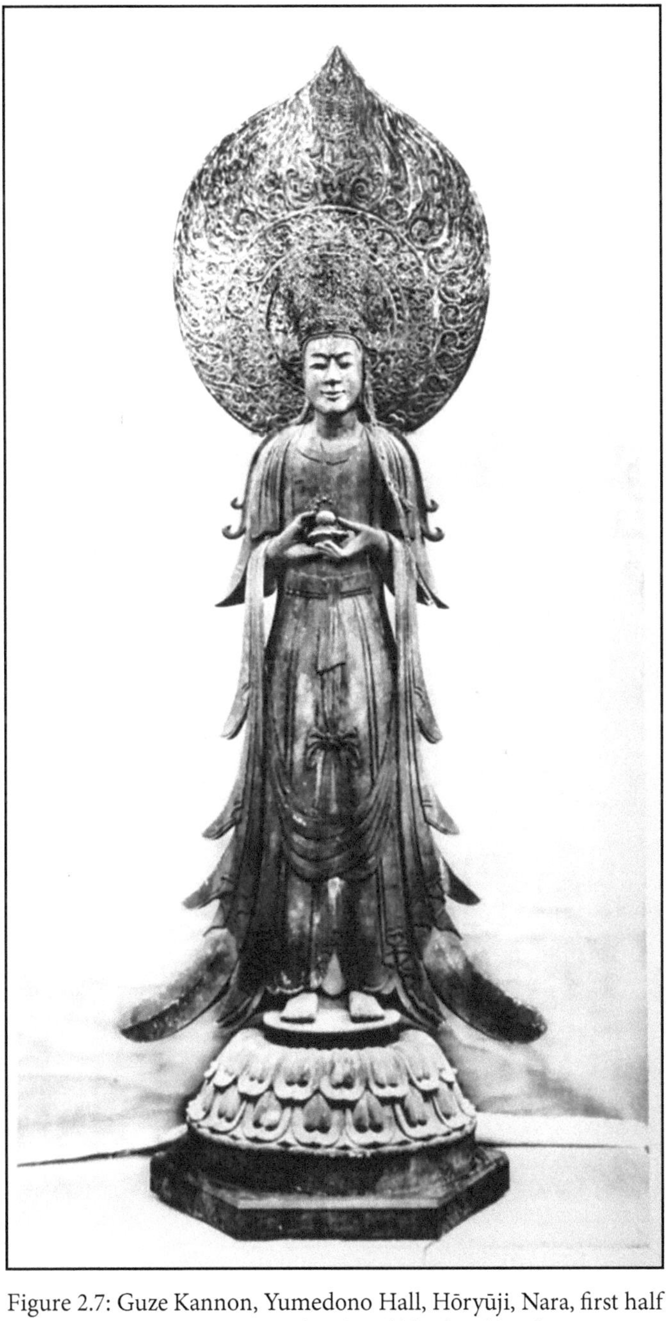

Figure 2.7: Guze Kannon, Yumedono Hall, Hōryūji, Nara, first half of seventh century, wood with gold leaf, Public domain.

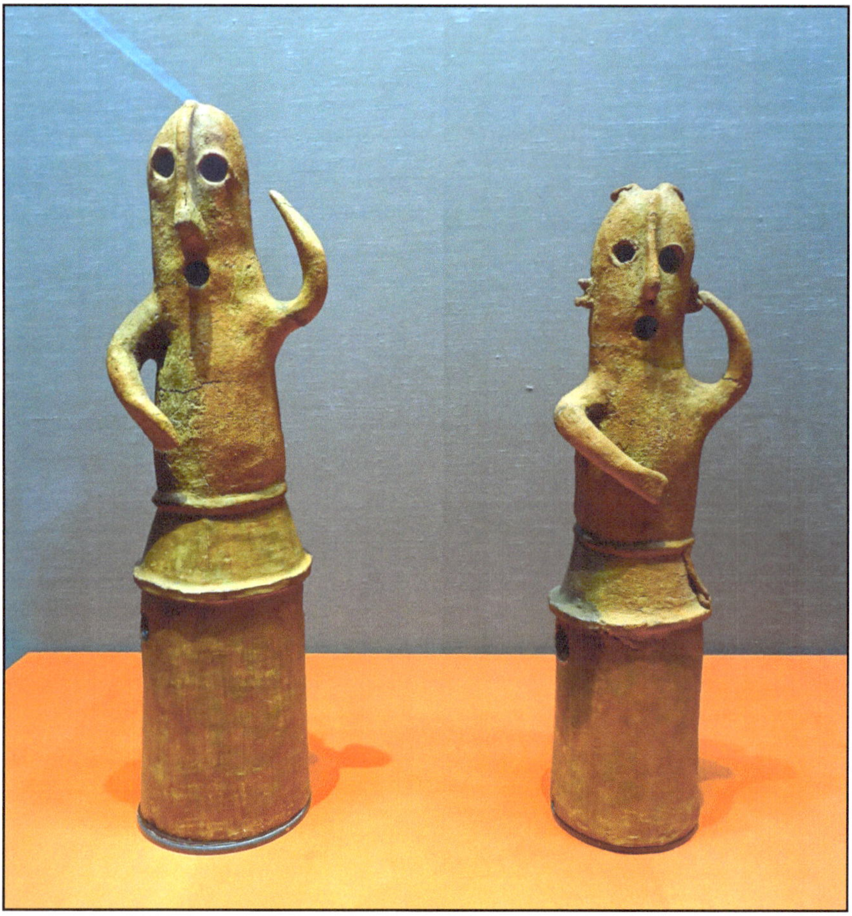

Figure 2.8: Two dancing *haniwa*, sixth century, terracotta, excavated from Nohara Tumulus, Kumagaya-shi, Saitama, Tokyo National Museum, Wikimedia Commons.

enigmatic. This inclination to weave foreign ideas and styles into a new expression would continue in Buddhist sculpture.[12]

Kofun-era *haniwa* exhibit a sense of playfulness in the form of whimsical images like the dancing figures in Figure 2.8. Playfulness and humor continued into the Nara period (710–794). Scribes and painters, perhaps bored or angry with their supervisors, hid graffiti inside Buddhist statues. Their subjects include caricatures of frogs and rabbits, cartoons of themselves, and floral motifs, mountains, and other references to nature.[13]

Some mention should also be made of the innovations in dry lacquer (*kanshitsu*) and clay modeling during this period. Records tell of a nearly five-meter-tall statue of Sakyamuni (668) made of dry lacquer at Daianji, a temple in

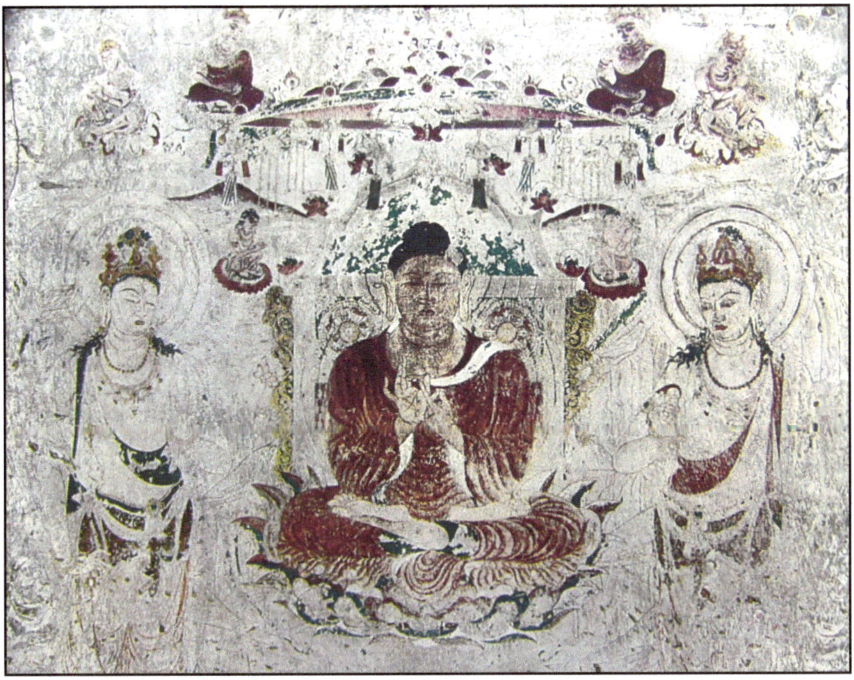

Figure 2.9: Amida Paradise from the *Pure Land Paradises of Four Buddhas*, late seventh to early eighth century, color on kaolin-covered plaster wall, Hōryūji, Nara, Wikimedia Commons.

Nara. Hollow dry lacquer (*datsu kanshitsu)* figures were made by covering a clay or earth model in lacquer-soaked linen and then drying it. Because the dry lacquer shrank, the interior material was removed and a wooden core inserted to prevent later distortion of the sculpture.[14]

Painted murals are also found in temples, such as the *Pure Land Paradises of Four Buddhas* in Hōryūji's main hall. The paintings were destroyed by fire in 1949, but photographs show a technique called "ironwire lines" (*tessenbyō*), in which brushwork is a consistent thickness (Figure 2.9). Bejeweled bodhisattvas in standing poses harken back to the *tribhanga* pose in Indian art, and the buddhas on lotus pedestals reveal the influence of early Chinese Tang-dynasty (618–907) cave paintings.[15]

Emperor Shōmu (r. 724–749)—at the encouragement of his queen-consort, Empress Kōmyō (701–760)—ordered temples, monasteries, and convents to be built throughout Japan. In 747, the emperor initiated a major engineering and architectural project by ordering the casting of a gigantic bronze statue of Vairocana, the Cosmic Buddha (Daibutsu). The statue was intended to protect the state during a period of plague and rebellion. A temple workshop of skilled artisans led by Kuninaka no Muraji Kiminaro, grandson of immigrants from

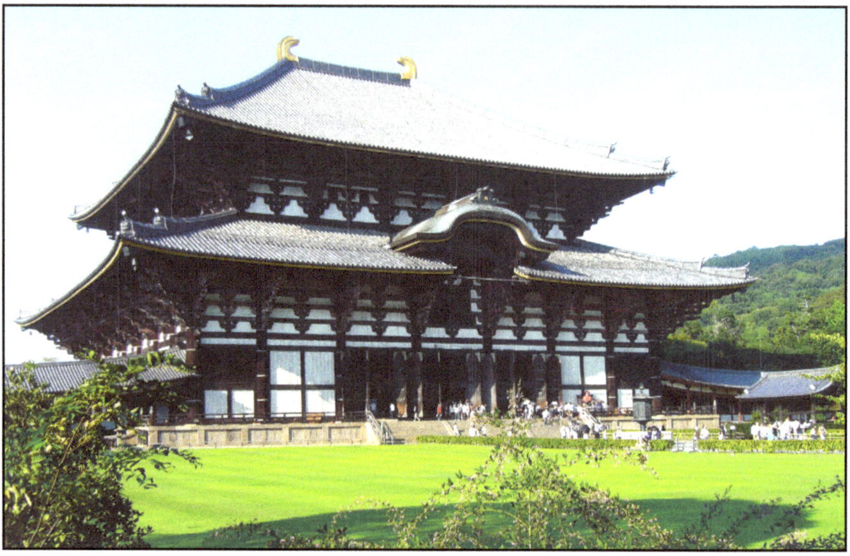

Figure 2.10: Main hall of Tōdaiji, Nara, 1688–1707 reconstruction, timber-frame structure, photo by author.

Baekje in Korea, began construction that same year. After great expense and numerous challenges, the statue was completed in 755 and housed in the main hall of Tōdaiji in Nara (Figure 2.10).

A spectacular "eye-opening" ceremony was held earlier, in 752. It is hard to imagine the size and grandeur of the original main hall and the Daibutsu—now much diminished after centuries of warfare and fires (Figure 2.11). The original gilded bronze statue was 16 meters high, and the great hall was 47 meters high and 86 meters long.[16] The construction of the temple itself required enormous coordination and effort: 227 site supervisors, 917 master builders, 1,483 laborers, and as many as 1,000 cooks worked to complete the massive complex.[17] To the south of the main hall, two seven-story pagodas stood, each 100 meters in height.[18] Thousands of monks, court and government officials, and visitors from as far away as China and India attended a ceremony that included flowers, colored banners, music, singing, and dancing. The Indian monk Bodhisena performed the eye-opening ceremony. It was a momentous occasion designed to unite Buddhism and the government.[19] The event also demonstrated that Japan was part of a broader Asian trade network.

When Emperor Shōmu died, the grieving Empress Dowager Kōmyō donated over 600 items to Tōdaiji, to be housed in the Shōsō-in storehouse. Included are treasures from Tang-dynasty China, the Korean peninsula, and items that reflect the styles of Persia, India, and southern Europe (Italy in particular). Functional and decorative textiles, bronze mirrors, musical instruments, Buddhist ritual implements, and folding screens are among the donated items that have been

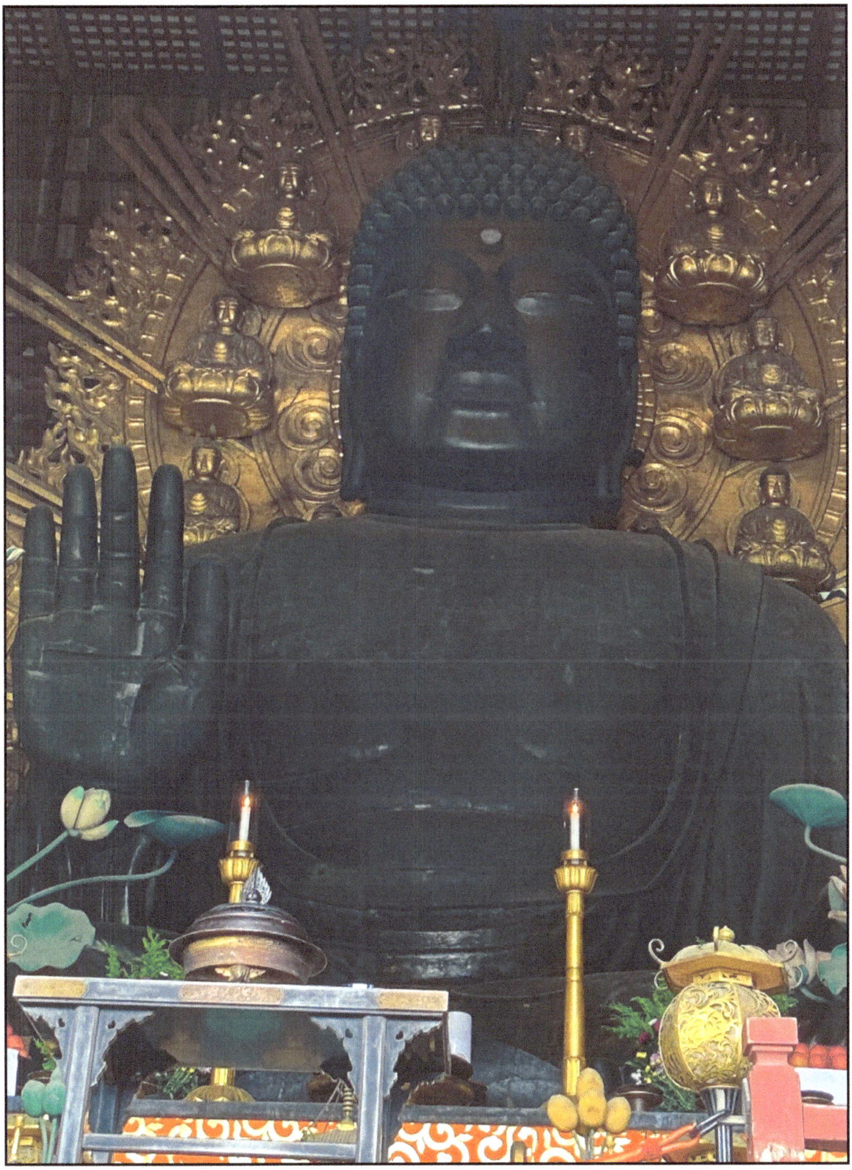

Figure 2.11: Daibutsu, original dates to 755; damaged and restored over the centuries, bronze, Tōdaiji, Nara, photo by author.

characterized as "unique in the world," and reflect the luxury items of the Chinese and Japanese courts.[20]

Advances in painting techniques occurred alongside the establishment of official government painting workshops. Master painters and their assistants produced underdrawings for Buddhist embroidery and textiles, for works such as

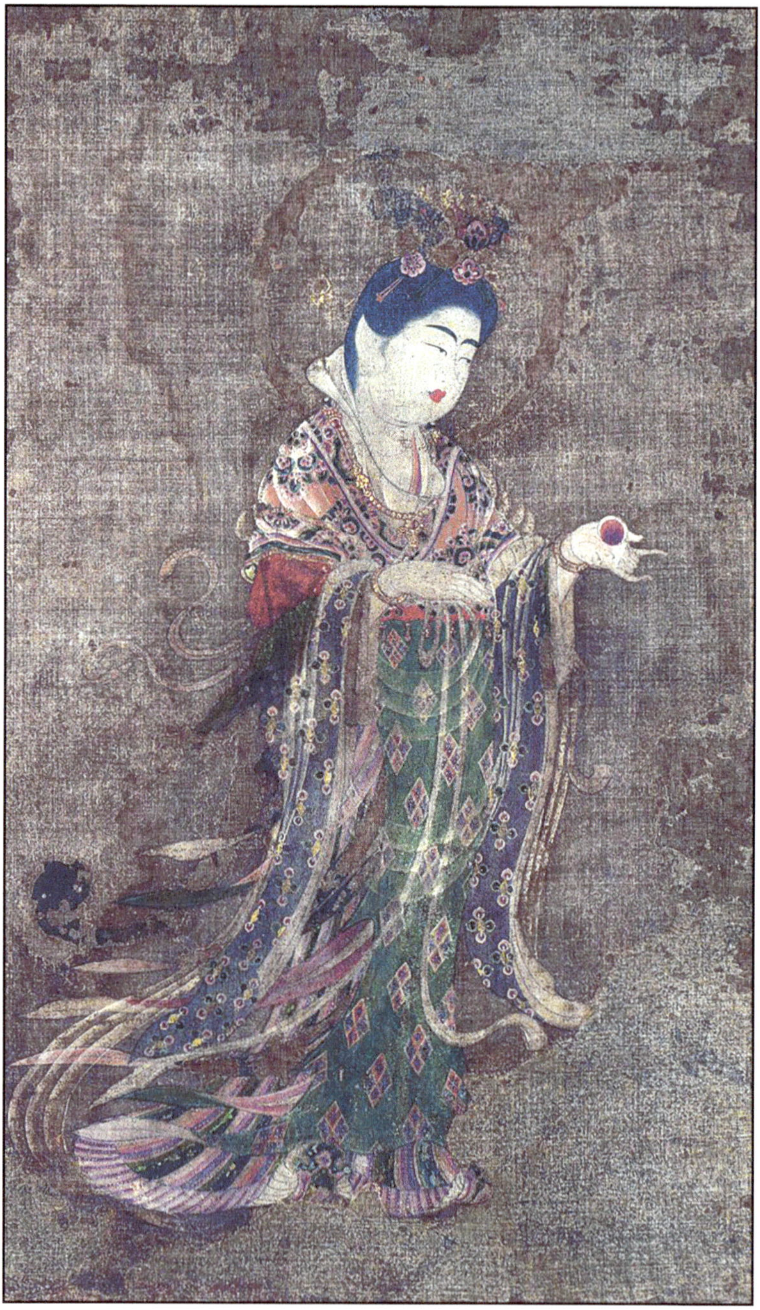

Figure 2.12: Kichijōten, eighth century, ink, color, and gold on hemp, Yakushiji, Nara, Wikimedia Commons.

large color embroidered tapestries and smaller silk or paper pieces. Among these is a painting of Kichijōten, a work on hemp held in Yakushiji, Nara (Figure 2.12). An Indian deity that was absorbed into Buddhism, Kichijōten became a deity of good fortune, the harvest, and fertility in Japan. She appears in this eighth-century painting as a plump, stylish Tang-dynasty court lady, resplendent in a richly patterned robe, floating scarves, and gold jewelry. Her rosebud lips, round face, and crescent-shaped eyebrows reflect the height of beauty for her time, and the "wish-granting jewel" in her left hand and the mudra (hand gesture) of charity of her right hand reveal her identity as Kichijōten. This painting further exemplifies Japan's interconnections within Asia and the selective assimilation of ideas and techniques from abroad.

Notes

[1] From the *Flower Garland Sutra*, translated by Eiji Suhara and Hiroshi Nara, in Tetsurō Watsuji, *Pilgrimages to the Ancient Temples in Nara* [*Koji Junrei*], trans. Hiroshi Nara (Portland: MerwinAsia, 2012), 56, 69.

[2] Norman Havens, "Shinto," in Paul L. Swanson and Clark Chilson, eds. *Nanzan Guide to Japanese Religions* (Honolulu: University of Hawai'i Press, 2006), 21.

[3] Akira Yamamoto, introduction to *Japanese Ghosts & Demons: Art of the Supernatural* (New York: George Braziller, 1985), 9.

[4] Charles Holcombe, *A History of East Asia: From the Origins of Civilization to the Twenty-First Century*, 2nd ed. (Cambridge: Cambridge University Press, 2017), 72.

[5] The Chinese writing system had already arrived in Japan by this time and would also have a major impact on Japanese culture.

[6] I am deeply grateful to Clark Chilson for his suggestions for these overviews of Buddhism and Shintō in early Japan.

[7] William H. Coaldrake, *Architecture and Authority in Japan*, Nissan Institute / Routledge Japanese Studies (London: Routledge, 1996), 41, https://doi.org/10.4324/9780203042830.

[8] For a discussion of the Ise and Izumo shrines from their beginnings to the late twentieth century, see Coaldrake, *Architecture and Authority in Japan*, chap. 2, "The Grand Shrines of Ise and Izumo."

[9] In their struggles to place Japan in world history and understand what it meant to be Japanese, architect Itō Chūta (1867–1954), philosopher Watsuji Tetsurō (1889–1960), and others cited entasis as one of the traces of Greek artistic influence on temples such as Hōryūji and Tōshōdaiji. See Hiroshi Nara, trans. Tetsurō Watsuji, *Pilgrimages to the Ancient Temples in Nara* [*Koji Junrei*], Introduction, ix-xxxiii and note 24, xxxi.

[10] The term "archaic smile" originally refers to Greek statuary and refers to this type of slight smile. The origins and meaning of the feature are unclear.

[11] According to the *Ledger of the Assets of the Tō-in at Hōryūji*. Nobuo Tsuji, *History of Art in Japan*, trans. Nicole Coolidge Rousmaniere (New York: Columbia University Press, 2019), 49.

[12] Seiichi Mizuno, *Asuka Buddhist Art: Horyu-ji*, trans. Richard L. Gage, Heibonsha Survey of Japanese Art, vol. 4 (Tokyo: Weatherhill, 1974), 69–72; Tsuji, *History of Art in Japan*, 49–51.

[13] Nobuo Tsuji, *Playfulness in Japanese Art*, Franklin D. Murphy Lectures, VII (Lawrence, KS: Spencer Museum of Art, University of Kansas, 1986), 17–20.

[14] Tsuji, *History of Art in Japan*, 59.

[15] *Tribhanga* is an ancient Indian pose in which the standing figure bends in three ways: the knees bend in one direction, countered by the hips in the opposite direction, and the shoulders and neck bend in the original direction.

[16] Coaldrake, *Architecture and Authority in Japan*, 74; Tsuji, *History of Art in Japan*, 77.

[17] Coaldrake, *Architecture and Authority in Japan*, 77. Coaldrake also notes that the monk Gyōki, as chief solicitor for the temple, recruited as many as 1.6 million volunteer laborers over the course of the project (78).

[18] For more about Tōdaiji in the Nara period, see Coaldrake, *Architecture and Authority in Japan*, 70–80.

[19] For further details see Tsuji, *History of Art in Japan*, 76–78, and Dorinda Neave, Lara Blanchard, and Marika Sardar, *Asian Art* (Pearson, 2015), 301–304.

[20] For the quotation "unique in the world," see Tsuji, *History of Art in Japan*, 86. For interesting discussions of the Shōsō-in's place in Japanese history, see Masaaki Itakura, "The Imperial Treasures of the Shōsōin and the Collections of the Tang Emperors," in *East Asian Art History in a Transnational Context*, eds. Toshio Watanabe and Eriko Tomizawa-Kay (Abingdon, UK: Routledge, 2019); Jun Hu, "Global Medieval at the 'End of the Silk Road,' circa 756 CE: The Shōsō-in Collection in Japan," in *Re-assessing the Global Turn in Medieval Art History*, ed. Christina Normore and Carol Symes (Amsterdam: ARC Humanities Press, 2018), 177–202; and Hiroshi Nara, "An Adoring Gaze: The Idea of Greece in Modern Japan," in *Receptions of Greek and Roman Antiquity in East Asia*, ed. Almut-Barbara Renger and Xin Fan (Leiden: Brill, 2019), 175–201.

3

The Blossoming of Courtly Culture

The Heian Period

In spring it is the dawn that is most beautiful . . .
In summer the nights . . .
In autumn the evenings, when the glittering sun sinks close to the edge of the hills . . .
In winter the early mornings. It is beautiful indeed when snow has fallen during the night, but splendid too when the ground is white with frost; or even when there is no snow or frost, but it is simply very cold and the attendants hurry from room to room stirring up the fires . . .

— Sei Shōnagon, *The Pillow Book*[1]

The Heian period (794–1192) dates from when the capital was moved to Heian-kyō (present-day Kyoto) in 794 CE, away from Nara's powerful temples and shrines. During the next four centuries, knowledge and technologies continued to be exchanged with the continent, though at a slower pace. In the capital the nobility, who numbered less than one percent of the population, created a uniquely Japanese cultural identity. A significant part of this identity was the way aesthetic sensibilities were woven into court life.

Certain aesthetic sensibilities had appeared earlier, as expressed in preferences for irregularity, refined simplicity, and unpainted wood seen in Shintō shrines. Courtiers accentuated these preferences with their love of the elegant, the restrained, and the subtly suggestive—encapsulated in the word *miyabi*. They were sensitive to the transitory nature of things, to aspects of nature, and cultivated a "splendor of longing."[2] But also predominant was the appreciation of things that were new, fashionable, interesting and fresh.

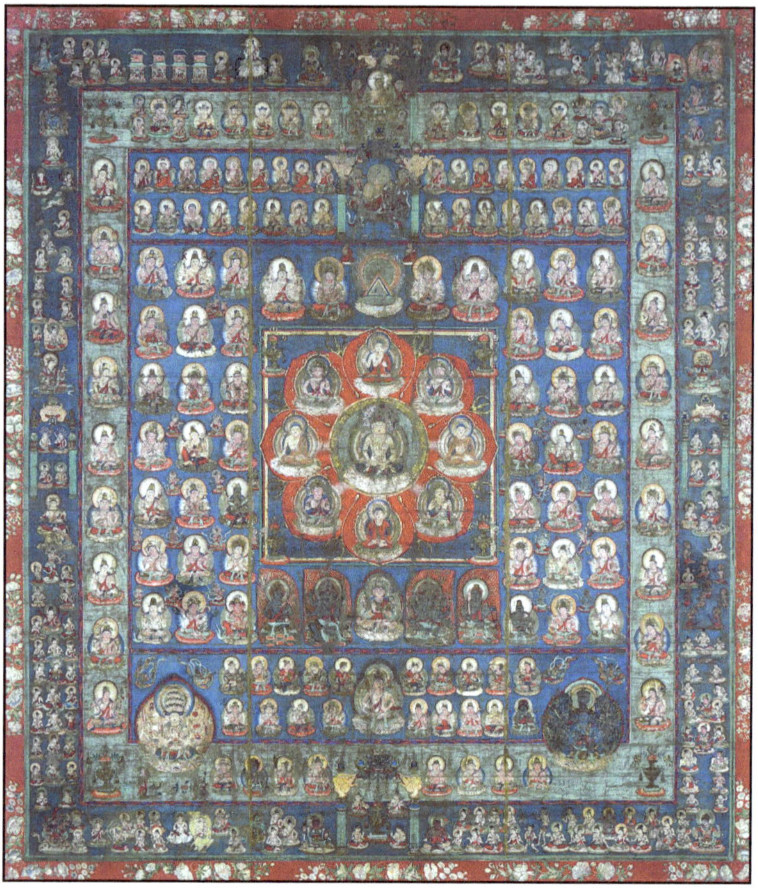

Figure 3.1: Sai-in Mandala (Womb World Mandala), second half of ninth century, hanging scroll, color on silk, Tōji, Kyoto, Wikimedia Commons.

Japanese envoys to Tang-dynasty China returned with a wealth of knowledge and materials, including a more systematic approach to Esoteric Buddhism (Mikkyō), which had a profound impact on both Buddhist practice and the arts. The monks Saichō (767–822) and Kūkai (774–835) introduced Tendai and Shingon, respectively. Esoteric Buddhism focused on secret teachings, emphasizing mysticism, symbolism, and incantations. Visual images were considered crucial in transmitting the teachings, and thus paintings took on a larger role in Buddhist practice than had been the case in earlier periods.[3] One of the most popular of the deities represented was Fudō Myō-ō, considered a manifestation of Dainichi Nyorai (the Cosmic Buddha), a wisdom king and fierce temple guardian. As will be seen, Fudō Myō-ō became an important deity for the military class as well as a protector of the nation.

Also important in Esoteric Buddhist rituals were large paintings of the Mandalas of the Two Worlds (also called Womb World Mandala and Diamond

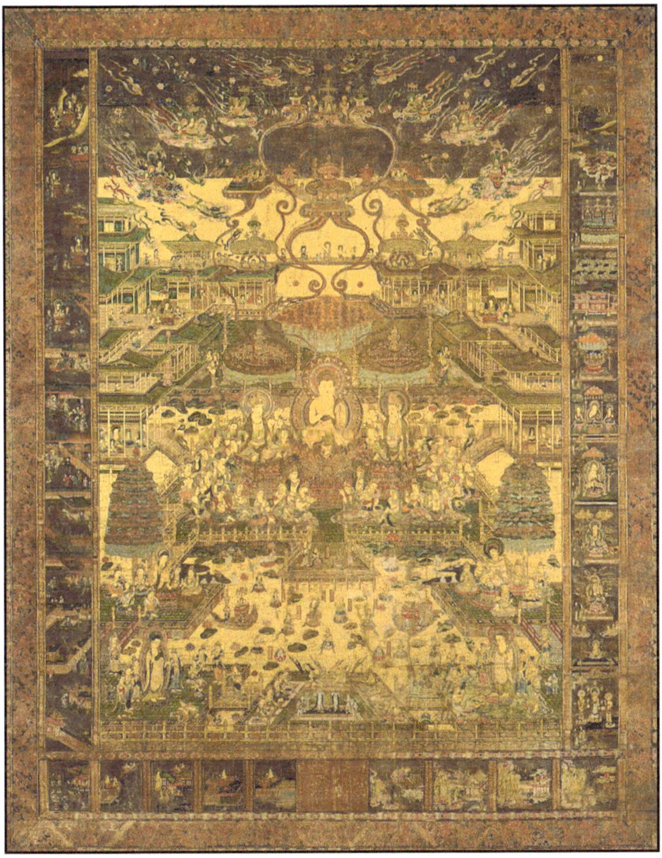

Figure 3.2: Taima Mandala, fourteenth century, hanging scroll, ink, color, and gold on silk, Metropolitan Museum of Art, New York, Public domain.

World Mandala), which had been introduced from China.[4] The Sai-in Mandala (Figure 3.1) is 185.1 x 164.3 cm.; a different mandala that Kūkai brought back from China was five meters high and four meters long. In these paintings, Dainichi Nyorai (Sk: Mahāvairocana) would typically be positioned at the center with various deities arranged around him. Mandalas were used to guide a worshipper through a ritual, serving as a guide to meditation. The paintings were brought to the temples for each ritual and thus frequently rolled and unrolled, hung up and then taken down. Due to their large size and this repeated use, they often became damaged, with paint flaking off and the silk backings being torn; as a result, most of the extant mandala date from the tenth century or later. Another type of mandala was a representation of the Pure Land of Amida, as seen in the Taima Mandala (Figure 3.2), rendered, like other mandala, in ink, color, and gold on silk.[5]

Buddhist sculpture also changed. Icons in what is called the Jōgan style (Figure 3.3) were carved from a single block of wood (*ichiboku-zukuri*), with the

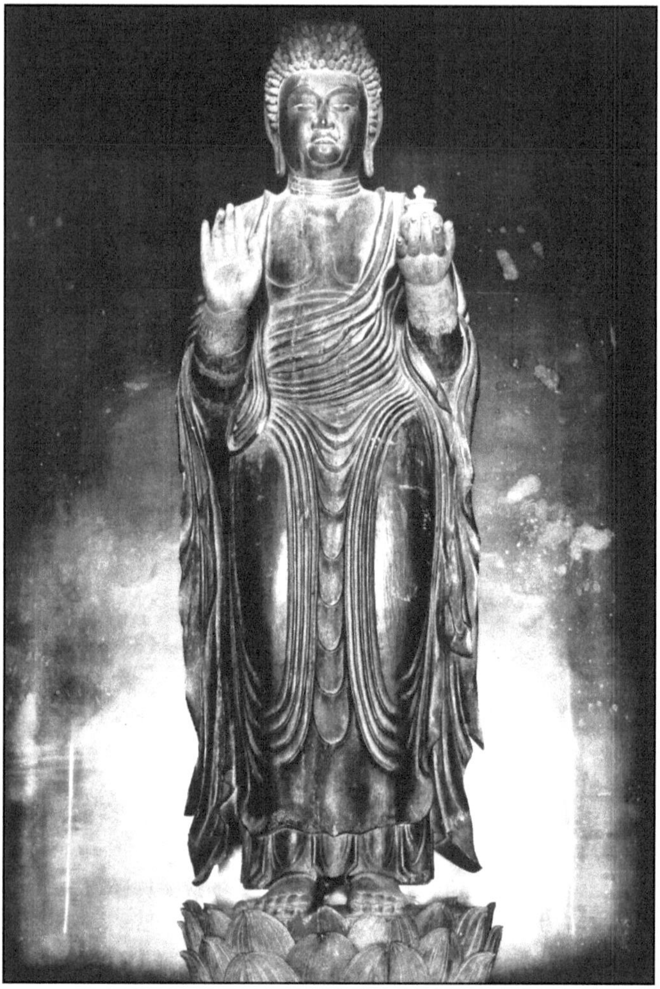

Figure 3.3: Yakushi Nyorai, early ninth century, wood, Jingoji, Nara, Wikimedia Commons.

tool marks visible in the deeply incised carving. Sculptors carved drapery in a wave or fold pattern called *honpa*. Using a technique introduced from China, the wood was then left untreated, allowing for the scent of aromatic woods such as nutmeg-yew (*kaya*) to permeate the air. These figures also contrasted with those of earlier periods in being symmetrically balanced, columnar, and standing fully erect.

Another type of Buddhism, Pure Land, was disseminated during the tenth and eleventh centuries and, like Shingon and Tendai, was practiced by the nobility. Pure Land is the most popular form of Buddhism in Japan today. In this practice, the goal is to be reborn after death into the Pure Land (Western Paradise) of

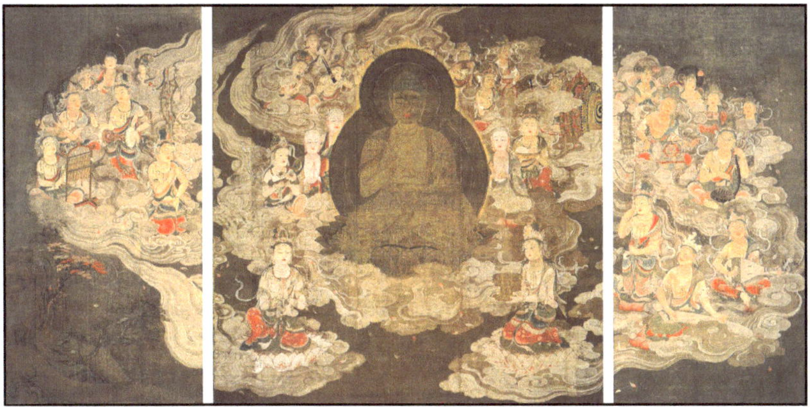

Figure 3.4: *The Descent of Amida*, twelfth century, triptych of hanging scrolls, ink and color on silk, Yūshi Hachimankō Jūhachi Ka-in, Mt. Koya, Wikimedia Commons.

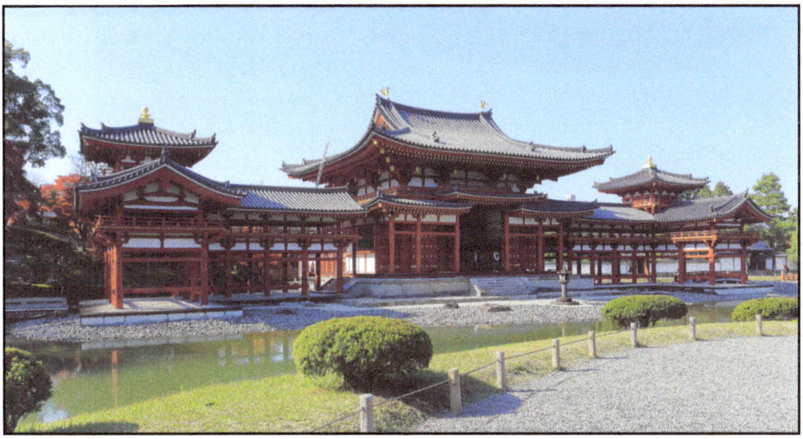

Figure 3.5: Phoenix Hall, Byōdō-in, 1053, timber-frame building with tile roof, Uji, Kyoto prefecture, Wikimedia Commons.

the Buddha Amida (Sk. Amitabha), where one awaits final enlightenment.[6] The Pure Land is described as filled with birdsong, flowers, trees laden with jewels, music, and the newly reborn emerging from lotus blossoms. For the nobility who considered their world the best of all worlds, to be welcomed into this paradise by Amida on a large lotus blossom was the best of all rebirths.

Rebirth in the Pure Land could be facilitated by looking upon a painting known as a *raigō* while reciting the *nenbutsu*. The *nenbutsu* is an invocation of the name of Amida as a form of meditation.[7] The dying also used the chant in their final hours, facing a *raigō*, and sometimes holding threads that linked their hands to the painting. *The Descent of Amida* (Figure 3.4) is an example of a large *raigō*:

Amida, surrounded by his retinue and musicians playing instruments, descends toward the believer in a swirl of clouds. Autumn foliage appears in the lower left, a reference to Japanese scenery and the seasons.

Courtly aesthetic sensibilities were integrated into Esoteric and Pure Land practice. The nobility believed that in 1052 the world was entering *mappō*, the final stage of the Buddhist dharma (law or teachings), when people could no longer achieve enlightenment through their efforts alone. This belief led them to dedicate buildings to Amida and his Western Paradise. The Byōdō-in and its Phoenix Hall (Hōō-dō) in Uji, an important temple site south of Kyoto, was consecrated in 1053 (Figure 3.5). Until the late twelfth century, Pure Land Buddhism was part of Tendai, but the Phoenix Hall in the complex was designed primarily to be a recreation of Pure Land belief in the Western Paradise on earth.[8] Architecturally, the Phoenix Hall has a hip-and-gable roof and was designed with corridors that

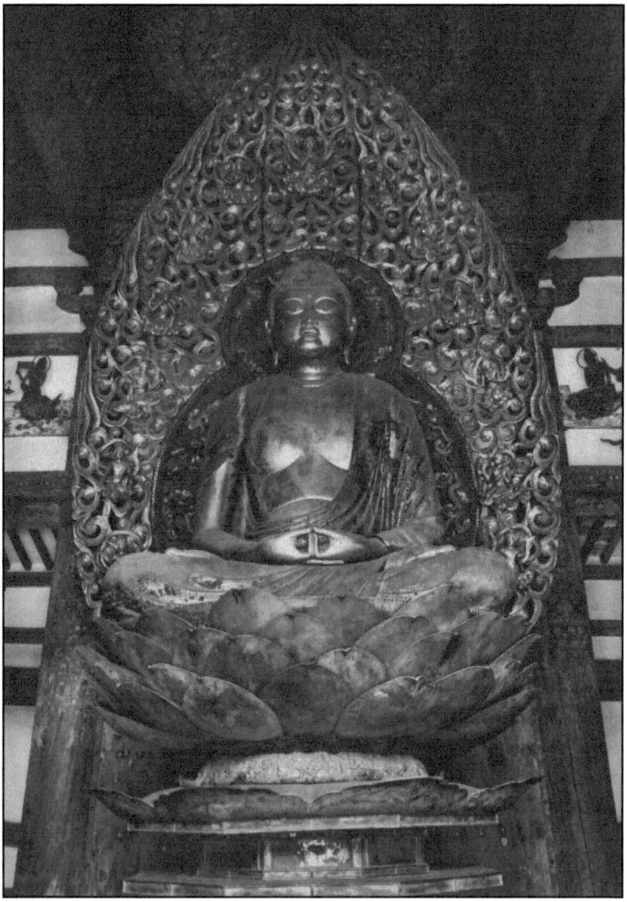

Figure 3.6: Amida Nyorai at Phoenix Hall, Jōchō, 1053, Japanese cypress with gold leaf, Byōdō-in, Uji, Public domain.

connect a central hall to wings, resembling the phoenix bird in flight. A skirt roof around the central hall gives the impression that it is a two-story building; the corridors and turrets have very low second stories. Inside, gold leaf predominates in images, canopies, and mandorlas. Mirrors in the ceiling reflected light from the garden pond in front of the building.

Master sculptor Jōchō (d. 1057) carved the main deity, a gilded Amida Nyorai (Figure 3.6) who sits in meditation amid sumptuous surroundings. Fifty-two bodhisattvas seated on clouds surround Amida on the hall's tie beams. Colored panel paintings of the nine cycles of rebirth on the doors and lower walls add to the overall splendor. Tendai elements are included in the iconography, such as Amida's concentration mudra (hand gesture) and the appearance of Dainichi on Amida's mandorla.[9] This mandala is like those discussed above (Figures 3.1 and 3.2), but in a fully architectural form. The layout and construction were a new way of rendering the Western Paradise.[10]

Jōchō used Japanese cypress for the Amida in a new technique called *yosegi-zukuri* (joined-wood construction). This technique used smaller trees and joined carved blocks of hollowed wood to create the main parts of a statue. It had numerous advantages over the Jōgan style of carving a single block of wood, as the statues were lighter weight and more resistant to cracking. The technique also allowed for faster production as carvers could work on several parts concurrently.

The Phoenix Hall also represented a move toward a more native Japanese architectural style (*wayō*), with deep eaves and embellished details in the brackets and elsewhere. Domestic aristocratic architecture took on a more specifically Japanese character with the development of *shinden-zukuri*. In this style, residences were designed around a south-facing building, with annexes to the east and west, all linked by covered walkways (Figure 3.7). A garden was designed south of the main building, with a pond and fishing pavilion.[11] Materials included cypress bark for roofs, plaster walls, bamboo blinds (*sudare*) to partition interior space, raised wooden floors, and curtains and screens to further subdivide interiors.

New literary forms also grew out of the highly refined and cultured world of the Heian court, facilitated by the *kana* writing system. Both women and men wrote using Chinese characters but the development of two phonetic writing systems, collectively called *kana*, made it possible to write in the vernacular.[12] Women of the court were particularly active in this type of literary writing.[13] Three well-known examples are Murasaki Shikibu's *The Tale of Genji* (*Genji monogatari*; early 11th century), the world's first psychological novel; Sei Shōnagon's witty and often acerbic *The Pillow Book* (*Makura no sōshi*; c. 1010); and the *Kagerō Diary* (*Kagerō nikki*; 954–974).[14]

Poetry and writing were crucial in romantic relationships, as a person's skills were considered reflective of their character and education. Writing was an art in itself, and the combination of image and text or text over a decorative background was a characteristic feature of these communications (Figure 3.8). Courtiers wrote

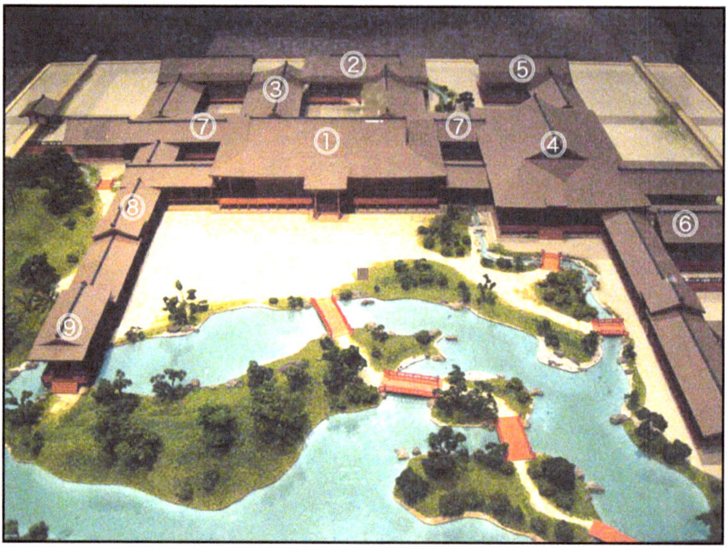

Figure 3.7: *Shinden-zukuri* architectural style, miniature model of the Higashi Sanjō-dono in Kyoto, Wikimedia Commons.

letters and poems to one another on fine papers, with embellishments such as overlapping colored papers, sprinkles of gold and silver, and colored paintings underneath the writing. Waka poetry, consisting of lines of 5-7-5-7-7 syllables, was the means of communication between lovers. Nature echoes the melancholy emotions of the writer in the following example by the poet Ono no Komachi, a court lady:

hana no iro wa	The color of the flowers
utsuri ni keri na	has faded—in vain
itazura ni	I grow old in this world,
waga mi yo ni furu	lost in thought
nagame seshi ma ni	as the long rain falls.[15]

Literature was both written and illustrated on handscrolls (*emaki*). A handscroll is a long horizontal sheet of paper or silk that is rolled around a dowel. It is made of numerous joined sections and is opened only a section at a time, from right to left, resulting in an intimate form of reading, as only a few people can view it at a time. A classic example is *The Illustrated Scrolls of the Tale of Genji* (*Genji monogatari emaki*; first half of the twelfth century), which illustrates each chapter of the book with three or four key scenes, alternating with text (Figure 3.9). Called *onna-e* (women's painting; also called *tsukuri-e* "produced paintings"), this style emphasizes facial features such as slits for eyes and hooks for noses (*hikime kagibana*), and "blown-away" roofs (*fukinuki yatai*) with scenes depicted from a bird's-eye view. Architectural features shown include the bamboo blinds, curtains, and screens, and the verandas and gardens of the *shinden-zukuri* style.

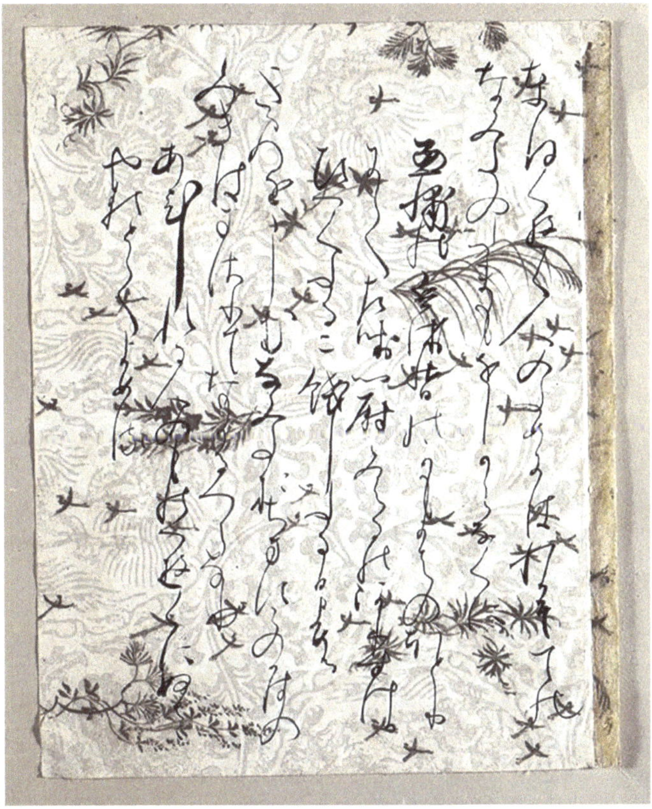

Figure 3.8: Page from the *Tsurayuki Anthology*, vol. 2, *Ishiyama-gire*, attributed to Fujiwara Sadanobu (1088–1156), 1112, ink on assembled dyed paper decorated with silver and gold, Minneapolis Institute of Art, Public domain.

Also apparent in these scrolls are the twelve-layer robes worn by women of the court, consisting of multiple layers of silk in different colors and designs. A woman's beauty and taste were reflected in her choice of colors and textures, including her attention to appropriate seasonal designs and colors. These garments and those for men were difficult to clean and bathing was rare, so both men and women used incense and perfumes to disguise body odors. Aesthetic sensibilities also drove the taste in makeup and hairstyles. Men and women alike used powder to whiten their faces, and women applied rouge and painted their lips to achieve a rosebud effect (as in the Kichijōten painting). Women also plucked their eyebrows and painted in brows higher up on the forehead as well as blackening their teeth. Long, silky black hair was highly valued in a woman. Some of these practices lasted well into the early twentieth century. The forerunner of the modern kimono now appeared as "a plain white undergarment hidden beneath the multiple strata" of robes.[16]

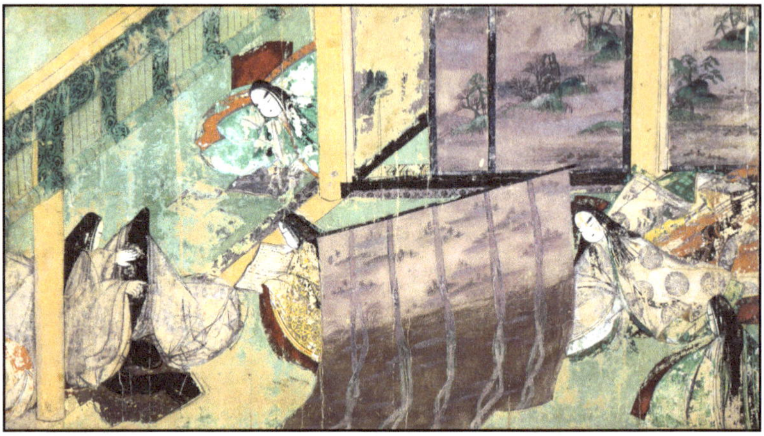

Figure 3.9: *Illustrated Scrolls of the Tale of Genji*, scene from the "Azumaya" chapter (chapter 50), first half of twelfth century, handscroll, ink and color on paper, Tokugawa Art Museum, Wikimedia Commons.

Other important examples of illustrated handscrolls from this period are the *Illustrated Scrolls of the Courtier Ban Dainagon* (*Ban Dainagon ekotoba*; attributed to Tokiwa Mitsunaga; Figure 3.10) and the *Illustrated Scrolls of the Legends of Shigisan* (*Shigisan engi emaki*; Figure 3.11), both believed to be from the second half of the twelfth century. These scrolls, known as *otoko-e* (men's paintings) feature dynamic brushwork, witty scenes, powerful and dramatic scenes of fire and grief, and real-life observations of human bodies and actions.

The four monochrome ink *Scrolls of Frolicking Animals* (*Chōjū jinbutsu giga*) span the years from the late Heian to the early thirteenth century. The quickly applied brushwork illustrates scenes such as a frog Buddha statue being worshiped by a monkey priest, frolicking deer, rabbits, frogs, and foxes, some wearing the black headdresses of courtiers, and other caricatures that suggest satire (Figure 3.12). Indeed, the word *giga* (caricature) is used for this playful, satirical expression. Significantly, these late twelfth-century illustrated handscrolls incorporate action, changes of scene for narrative development, and theatrical images that eight centuries later, "form the basic elements of contemporary Japanese animation

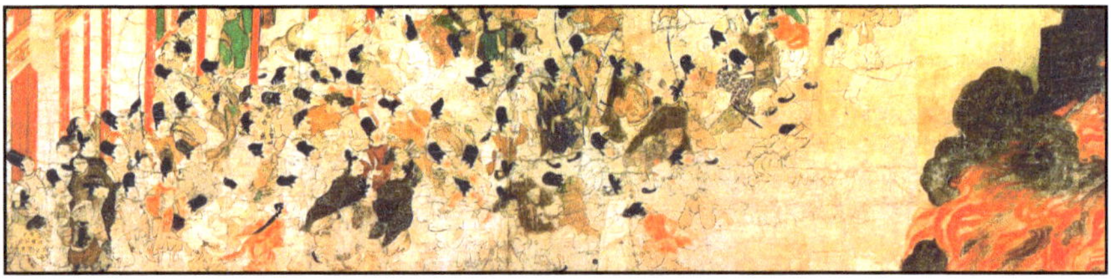

Figure 3.10: *Illustrated Scrolls of the Courtier Ban Dainagon*, attributed to Tokiwa Mitsunaga, second half of twelfth century, color and ink on paper, Idemitsu Museum of Art, Wikimedia Commons.

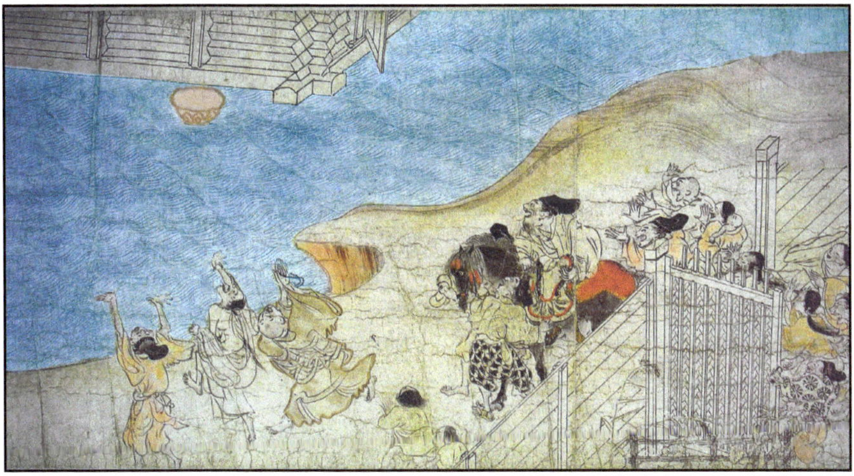

Figure 3.11: *Illustrated Scrolls of the Legends of Shigisan*, second half of twelfth century, handscroll, ink and color on paper, Chōgosonshiji, Nara prefecture, Wikimedia Commons.

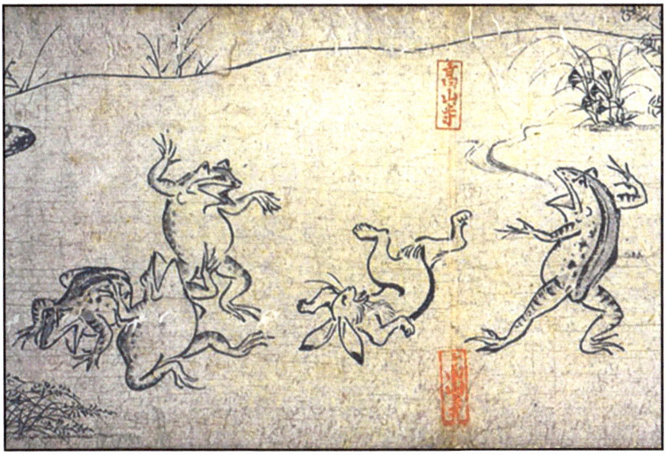

Figure 3.12: *Scrolls of Frolicking Animals*, detail of wrestling frogs from the first handscroll, twelfth century, ink on paper, Kōzanji, Kyoto, Wikimedia Commons.

(anime)."[17] Various kinds of *giga* continued to be produced into the Tokugawa period (1603–1868) and were the forerunners of not only anime but also manga.

Buddhist themes gained in popularity in late Heian, especially paintings of the six Buddhist realms (*rokudō*): hells (*jigoku*), hungry ghosts (*gaki*), beasts (*chikushō*), fighting warriors (*ashura*), humans (*hito*), and celestials (*ten*). The *Hells Scroll* (*Jigoku zōshi*), for example, depicts the various hells where humans

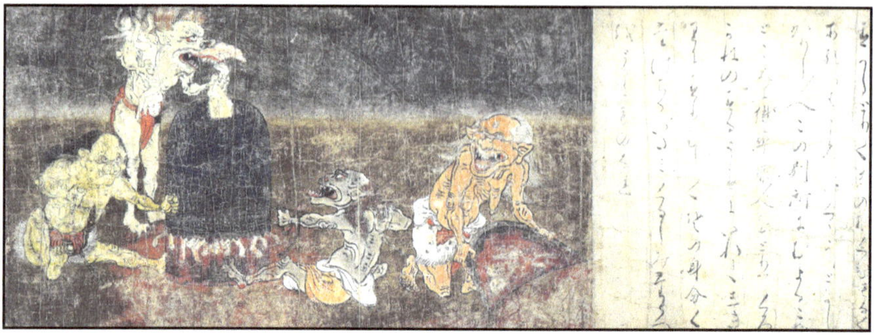

Figure 3.13: Scene from the *Hells Scroll*, twelfth century, handscroll, ink and color on paper, Nara National Museum, Wikimedia Commons.

are punished for crimes committed during their lifetimes (Figure 3.13). The painters hold nothing back. The guilty fall into pits filled with feces and are eaten by maggots; others are forced to hold a wooden box of flaming hot iron; still others are burned by the flames of a fire-breathing giant cockerel; and in one hell, the guilty endure burning sand raining down on them, are boiled in a bronze vat, or are thrown into a pool of pus and stung by bees.

There were also depictions of human suffering, as in the *Scroll of Hungry Ghosts* (*Gaki zōshi*), in which wandering ghosts are pictured with extended stomachs and emaciated bodies, a familiar image during the periodic famines (Figure 3.14). Also notable is the *Scroll of Afflictions* (*Yamai no sōshi*), which represents ailments such as insomnia, colds, visual impairments, decaying teeth, and lice, among other things. In these paintings Buddhist messages intertwined with the observance of social customs and realities of life at that time.

In the late tenth century, the term *yamato-e* appeared for paintings of Japanese scenery, including famous places (*meisho*), in contrast to *kara-e* (Chinese paintings). The door panels of the Byōdō-in, heavily damaged, are rare

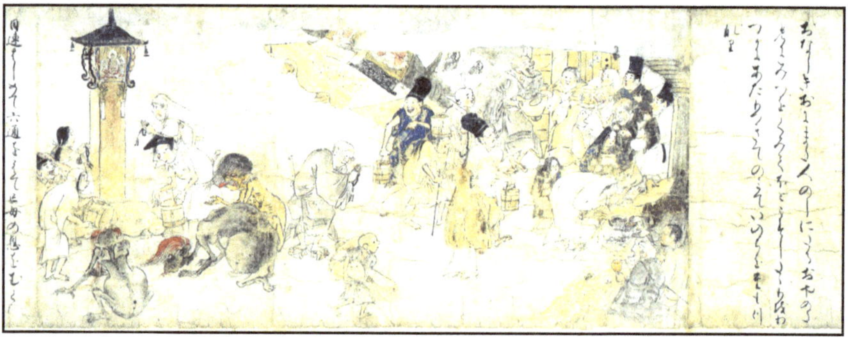

Figure 3.14: *Scroll of Hungry Ghosts* (detail), twelfth century, handscroll, color on paper, Tokyo National Museum, Art Collection/Alamy Stock Photo.

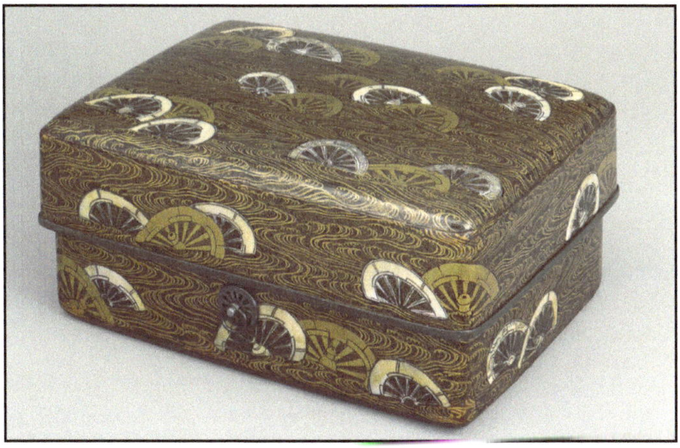

Figure 3.15: Lacquered wood case with design of carriage wheels in a stream, twelfth century, *maki-e* and mother of pearl inlay, Tokyo National Museum, Wikimedia Commons.

extant examples of *yamato-e*. A significant feature of the style is a keen sense of the seasons. Spring is typically represented with plum and cherry blossoms and warblers; summer with rice planting and cormorants; fall with autumn grasses, the moon, and deer; winter with snow and mountain villages. This focus on seasonal variations would continue to permeate paintings and poetry throughout Japanese history.

Finally, artisans of the late Heian period used the *maki-e* lacquer technique brought from Tang China to incorporate more pictorial subjects such as plovers, sparrows, carriage wheels in water, iris, and other scenes of nature. Figure 3.15 shows the use of this technique with its distinctly Japanese expression. *Maki-e* literally means "sprinkled pictures" and is produced by painting lacquer designs on the surface of a piece and then sprinkling gold and gold-alloy powders with silver on top to create lavish designs. Mother-of-pearl inlay was also added. Although these techniques originated in China, the innovations in Japan surprised the Chinese when they saw imported wares. They reportedly believed that the inlay technique, for example, was a specialty of Japan.[18]

Notes

[1] Ivan Morris, *The Pillow Book of Sei Shōnagon* (New York: Columbia University Press, 1991), 21.

[2] See Norma Field, *The Splendor of Longing in the Tale of Genji* (Princeton: Princeton University Press, 1987).

[3] Nobuo Tsuji, *History of Art in Japan*, trans. Nicole Coolidge Rousmaniere (New York: Columbia University Press, 2019), 97.

[4] Richard K. Payne, "The Ritual Culture of Japan: Symbolism, Ritual, and the Arts," in *Nanzan Guide to Japanese Religions*, ed. Paul L. Swanson and Clark Chilson (Honolulu: University of Hawai'i Press, 2005), 240–241 and William M. Bodiford, "The Medieval Period, Eleventh to Sixteenth Centuries, *Nanzan Guide to Japanese Religions*, 174–175.

[5] For more on Esoteric Buddhism in the visual arts, see Tsuji, *History of Art in Japan*, 95–105, and Payne, "The Ritual Culture of Japan," 235–256.

[6] The hope of rebirth in the Pure Land had existed as early as the seventh and eight centuries, but the Heian period dissemination of the Tendai vision was a particularly significant development. Tsuji, *History of Art in Japan*, 125.

[7] The invocation often cited of *Namu Amida Butsu* became standard later, in the fifteenth century. Other forms of the *nenbutsu* were used during the Heian period. Payne, "The Ritual Culture of Japan," 242.

[8] For more, see Mimi Hall Yiengpruksawan, "The Phoenix Hall at Uji and the Symmetries of Replication," *Art Bulletin* 77, no. 4 (December 1995): 647–672.

[9] Yiengpruksawan, "The Phoenix Hall at Uji," 657–659.

[10] Yiengpruksawan, "The Phoenix Hall at Uji," 649.

[11] The eleventh-century gardening manual *Sakuteiki* reveals the reliance on nature imagery in literature and poetry for garden and pond design. See Wybe Kuitert, *Themes in the History of Japanese Garden Art* (Honolulu: University of Hawai'i Press, 2002).

[12] For the use of *kana* by Heian men, see Gustav Heldt, "Writing Like a Man: Poetic Literacy, Textual Property, and Gender in the 'Tosa Diary,'" *Journal of Asian Studies* 64, no. 1 (February 2005): 7–34.

[13] High-ranking Heian women had greater social status and more legal rights than in other periods. Women's status and legal rights varied by period and even within cultural periods. For more, see Haruko Wakita and Suzanne Gay, "Marriage and Property in Premodern Japan from the Perspective of Women's History," *Journal of Japanese Studies* 10, no. 1 (Winter 1984): 73–99.

[14] The work of women authors later influenced many aspects of Japanese culture, from paintings to modern anime and even music groups. For an overview of Japanese literature, see Marvin Marcus, *Japanese Literature from Murasaki to Murakami*, Key Issues in Asian Studies (Ann Arbor: Association for Asian Studies, 2015); also Haruo Shirane, ed. *Traditional Japanese Literature: An Anthology, Beginnings to 1600* (New York: Columbia University Press, 2007).

[15] Shirane, *Traditional Japanese Literature*, 128.

[16] Liza Dalby, *Kimono: Fashioning Culture* (New Haven: Yale University Press, 1993), 12.

[17] Tsuji, *History of Art in Japan*, 167.

[18] Tsuji, *History of Art in Japan*, 183.

4

The Rise of the Samurai

The Kamakura Period

The Jetavana Temple bells
ring the passing of all things. . . .
The arrogant do not long endure:
They are like a dream one night in spring.
The bold and brave perish in the end:
They are as dust before the wind.

—*The Tale of the Heike* [1]

Unrest and social changes in the late Heian period culminated in one of the most consequential events of Japan's history, the Genpei War of 1180–1185. From his stronghold in the east, Minamoto Yoritomo (1147–1199) challenged the powerful Taira clan led by Taira Kiyomori (1118–1181) from his headquarters in the capital. The two great armies battled one another intermittently for five years. Eventually, the Taira were forced west and south until they were pushed to the farthest tip of the main island of Honshu. There, in a climatic naval battle at Dannoura, Yoritomo's younger brother Yoshitsune (1159–1189) defeated the Taira. As the outcome became clear, Taira warriors and family members threw themselves into the sea, and the child emperor Antoku (1178–1185) was carried to a watery grave by his grandmother Taira no Tokiko.[2]

Having won the war, Yoritomo remained in his headquarters at Kamakura near present-day Tokyo, and in 1192 received the title *Sei-i tai-shōgun*, commonly shortened to *shōgun* (shogun). There, he established a military government (*bakufu*). This was the beginning of the Kamakura period (1192–1333), during which a class system developed, with military lords (daimyo) presiding over various ranks of samurai vassals, all of whom served the shogun. The military would rule Japan until 1868.

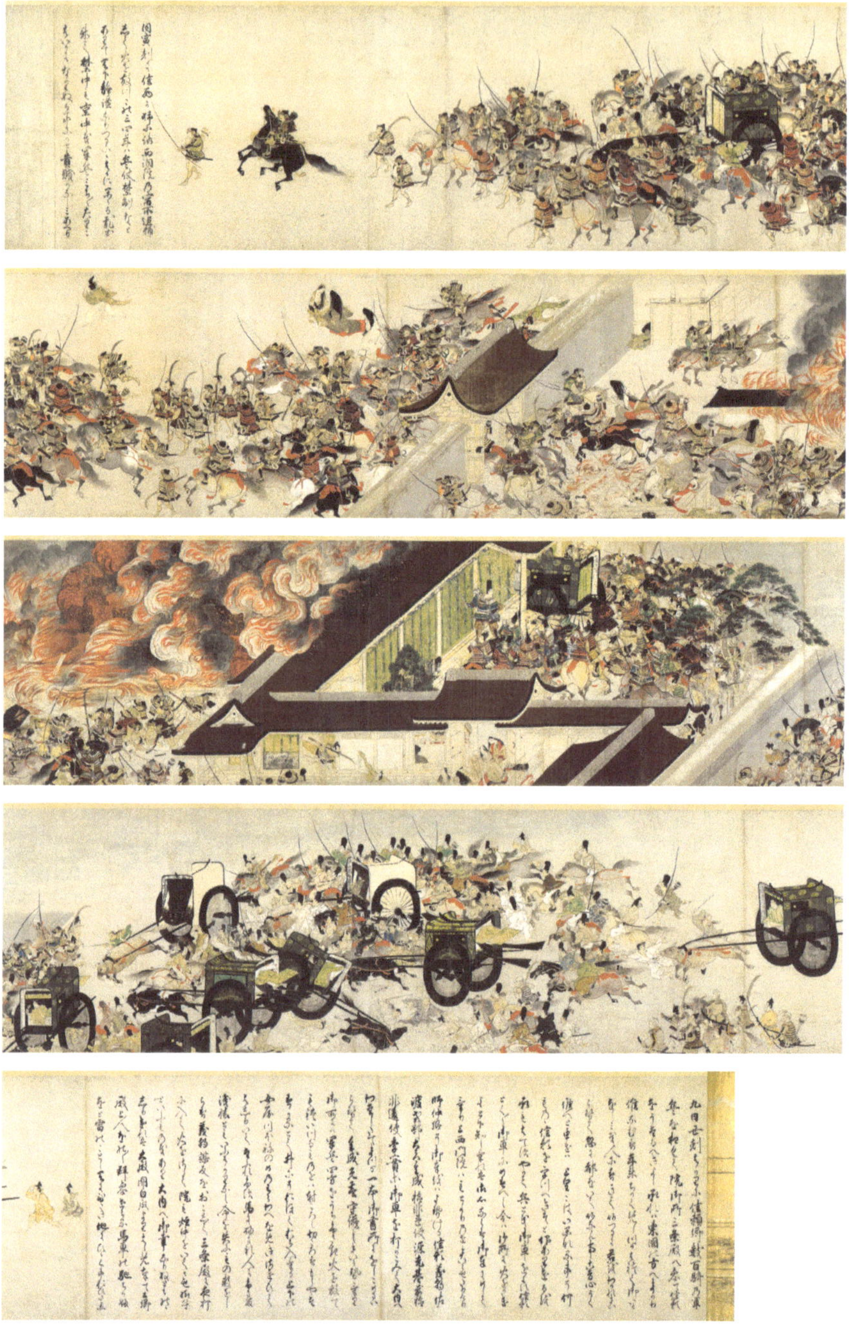

Figure 4.1: *Night Attack on the Sanjō Palace*, from *Heiji monogatari emaki*, second half of thirteenth century, handscroll, ink and color on paper. Photograph © 2026 Museum of Fine Arts, Boston.

The Tale of the Heike (*Heike monogatari*) recounts human dramas during the Genpei War, presenting a strong contrast to the courtly elegance of the earlier masterpiece of Japanese literature, *The Tale of Genji*. Many versions of the tale exist, some intended to be read and some to be performed.[3] Hugely influential, *The Tale of the Heike* has inspired the visual arts, literature, and drama for centuries, even to the present.[4] An earlier battle is represented in the *Tale of Heiji* scrolls (*Heiji monogatari emaki*; late thirteenth century), in which the Minamoto (aka Genji) forces attack the Kyoto palace of retired emperor Go-Shirakawa (1127–1192), who was allied with the Taira (aka Heike), burning the Sanjō Palace to the ground in 1160 (Figure 4.1).[5]

The historian Saburo Ienaga describes this style of scroll as "entirely new," "something like watching a silent movie" because the action develops progressively as the scroll is unrolled.[6] Introductory text is followed by a long series of images, rather than the alternating text and picture of the *Genji* scrolls. Stylistic links with Heian handscrolls like the *Genji* scrolls include the viewpoint from above (bird's-eye view in this case) and the use of diagonal thrusts. The architecture depicted is traditional *shinden-zukuri* style, with dark cypress roofs and buildings linked by corridors and verandas.[7] What is new, however, is the focus on drama and action as well as renderings of horror and human tragedies, the destructive power of fires, and a sense of the impermanence of all things—trends that emerged in the latter half of the twelfth century.

Myths surround the samurai (*bushi*), valorized much as cowboys are in the American West.[8] Samurai behavior, technologies, and culture changed over time; they were not always the loyal and honorable warriors depicted in modern media. Depending on the era, samurai life and military prowess varied. In the Kamakura period, warriors fought on horseback and used bows and arrows, as well as pikes and halberds. Their armor, *ōyoroi* (great armor), was developed in the late Heian period for archers on horseback. Figure 4.2 gives an idea of what a samurai would have worn during the fourteenth through the early fifteenth century. Typically, leather and iron lames (solid pieces of sheet metal) were bound together to create horizontal tiers. The tiers were covered with lacquer for strength and rigidity and then laced together. Then the sections were joined using fittings made of iron or leather. Armor, helmets, bows and arrows, and swords were made with both function and aesthetics in mind. Colorful designs, varying textures, and the use of silk and gilt copper played a role in broadcasting the wearer's affiliations and power. Producing these items required highly specialized artisans.[9]

Not all warriors were men. Women warriors Tomoe Gozen (said to have been a renowned expert in archery and the sword) and Yamabuki are mentioned in book nine of *The Tale of the Heike*.[10] Whether either was a historical figure, Gozen in particular became a legend, even appearing in movies, video games, and popular books to this day.[11]

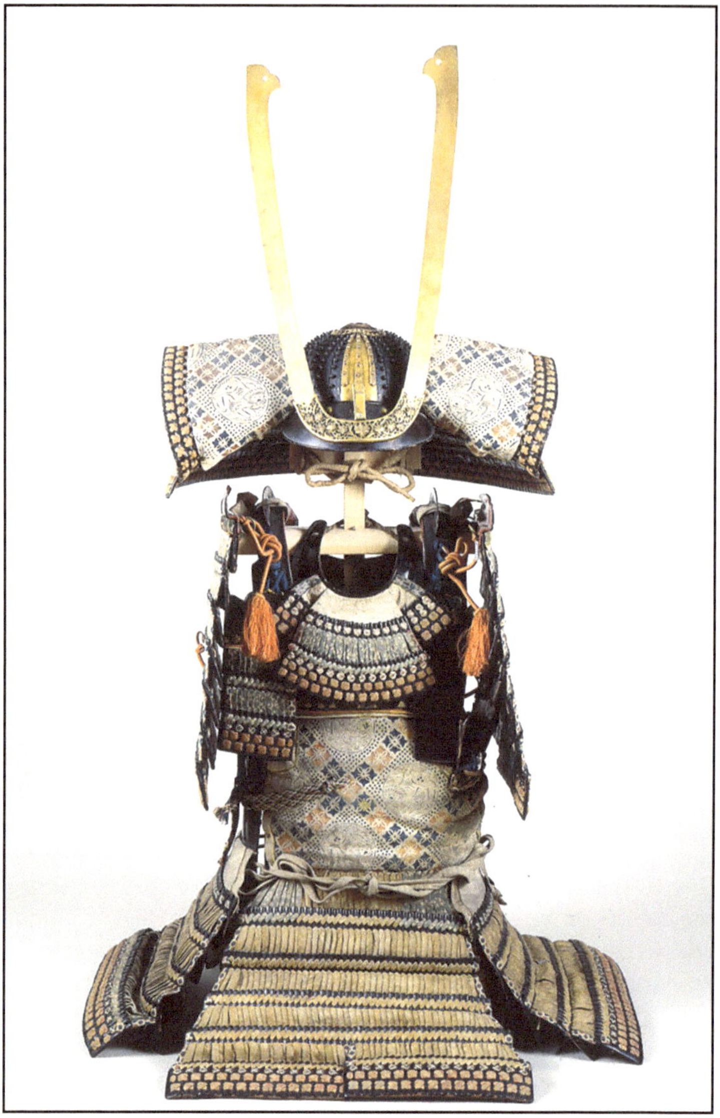

Figure 4.2: Armor (*yoroi*), early fourteenth to early fifteenth century, iron, leather, lacquer, silk, and gilt copper, Metropolitan Museum of Art, New York, Public domain.

Yoritomo and those who followed him promoted virtues such as austere and disciplined living and the cultivation of martial arts. They warned their vassals against indulgence in cultural and literary pursuits. In reality, higher ranked samurai needed to be literate and knowledgeable about the legal system in order to govern, thus a balance was required between *bun* and *bu* (civilian arts and warrior traditions). Consequently, the military became influential patrons of the arts.[12]

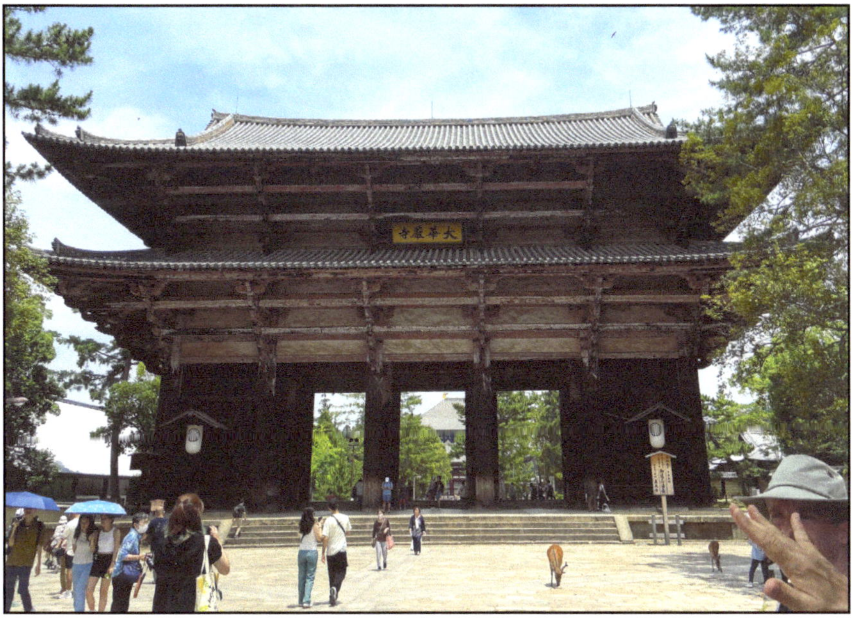

Figure 4.3: Great South Gate of Tōdaiji, Nara, 1199, photo by author.

Much had been destroyed during the Genpei War and other battles. Yoritomo initiated a major reconstruction program beginning with Tōdaiji, authorizing public fundraising for the purpose. The monk Chōgen (1121–1206) traveled around Japan raising funds to build temples and is credited with introducing a new architectural style based on Chinese Song architecture (960–1279). The Great South Gate of Tōdaiji (Figure 4.3), built in 1199, is emblematic of this *daibutsu-yō* style. *Daibutsu-yō* features include long crossbeams that run through pillars, much like modern steel construction, as well as "bracket arms inserted directly into the supporting pillars, a high ceiling and vast interior space, and tiered beams supporting the eaves." These innovations later influenced modern architecture in Japan, including the work of Isozaki Arata (1931–2022).[13]

Temples required sculpture. The Kei studio of sculptors, led by Unkei (d. 1223) and Kaikei (fl. 1185–1223), carved figures using the assembled-wood technique, including the two giant guardian figures for Tōdaiji's South Gate (Figures 4.4a and 4.4b). These Kongō Rikishi (Niō), produced in only sixty-nine days in 1203, required technical skill and a coordinated group effort. They represent the contemporary trend toward more life-like and dramatic expressions. The guardians frown fiercely at the viewer, hips thrust to the side, swirling drapery and flying scarves surrounding them. They appear aggressive and muscular and are huge: each guardian is 8.4 meters in height, weighs four tons, and was constructed with some 3,000 pieces of wood. The eyes are reverse-painted crystal insets, a mid-twelfth century innovation, and glow realistically in candlelight.[14]

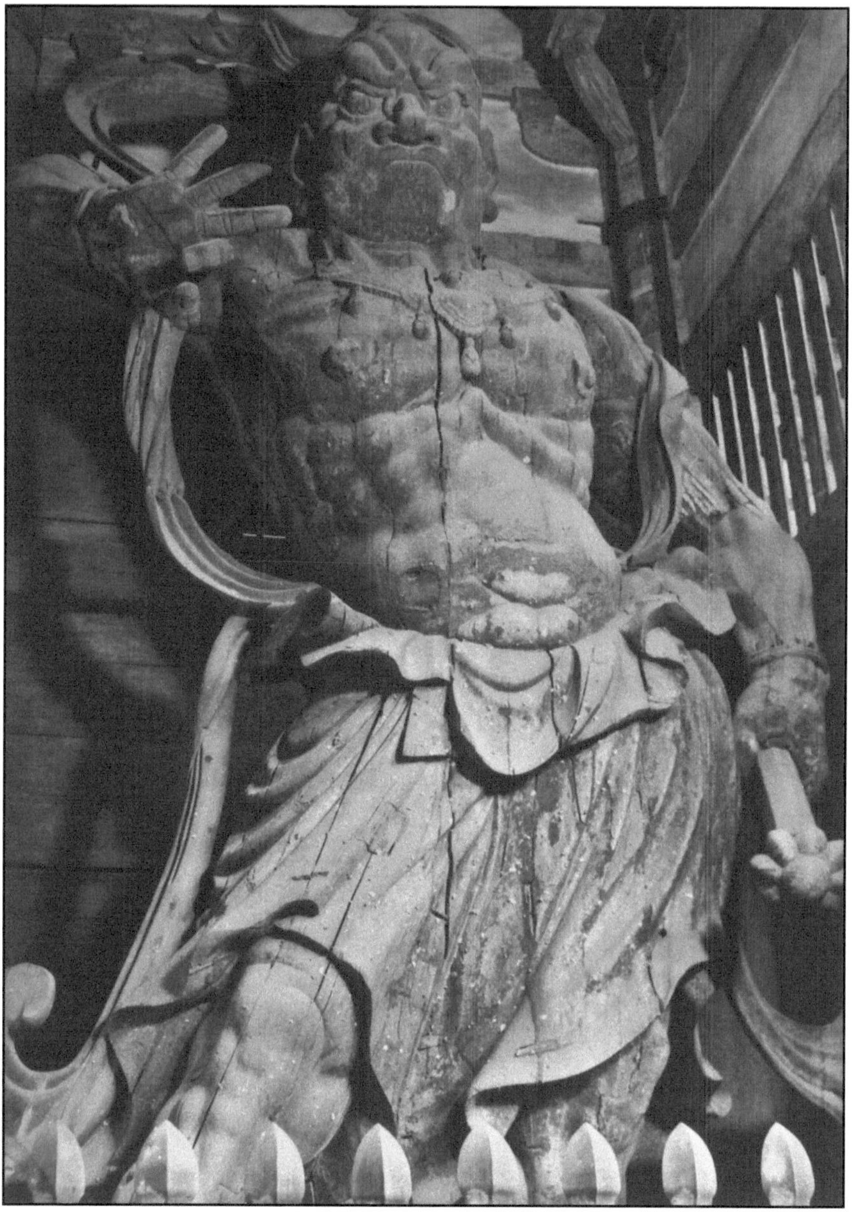

Figure 4.4a: Kongō Rikishi (Ungyō), Unkei, Kaikei, Jōkaku, and Unkei's eldest son, Tankei, 1203, assembled wood with color, Great South Gate, Tōdaiji, Public domain.

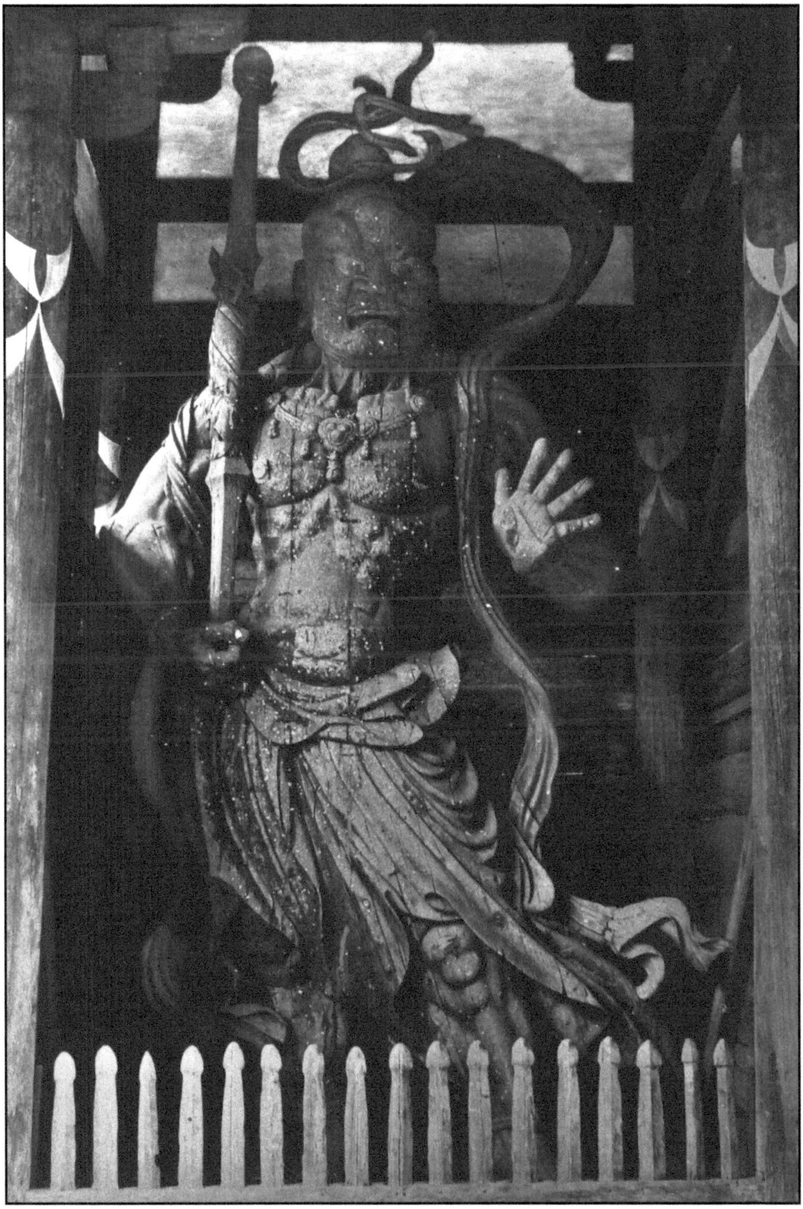

Figure 4.4b: Kongō Rikishi (Agyō), Great South Gate, Tōdaiji, Wikimedia Commons.

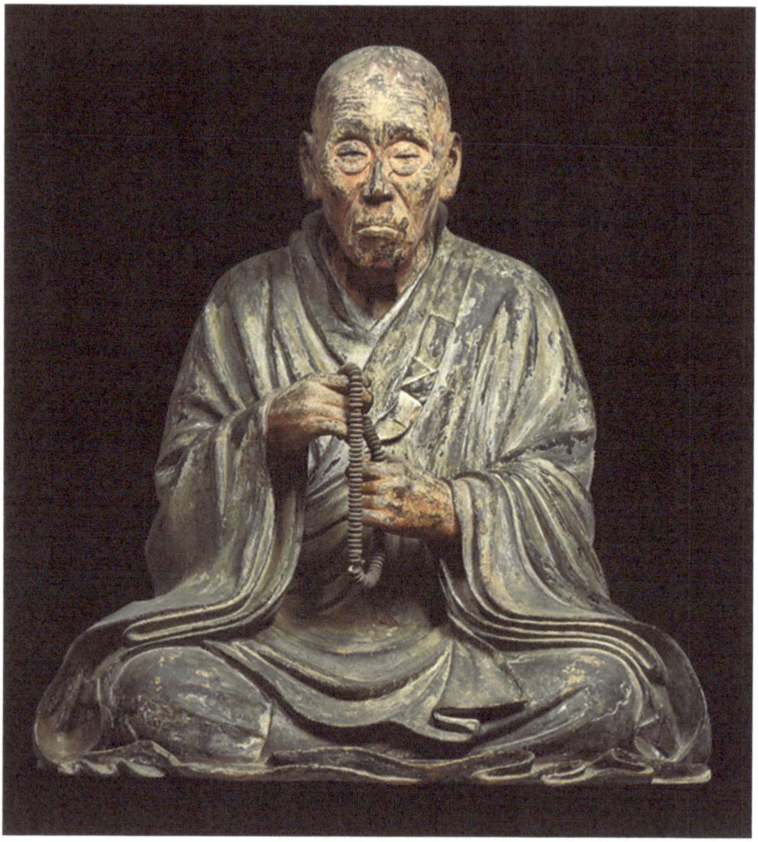

Figure 4.5: Chōgen, attributed to Unkei, first half of thirteenth century, wood with color, Shunjō-dō, Tōdaiji, Public domain.

Unkei was also instrumental in developing a new more realistic portraiture style for sculpture, such as the figure of Chōgen at Tōdaiji, dated to the first half of the thirteenth century and attributed to him (Figure 4.5). Chōgen is depicted reciting the *nenbutsu* and facing Amida's Western Paradise. Attention was paid to realistic details, such as Chōgen's stooped back, the lines in his aged face, his drooping eyelid, and the detailed rosary beads.

Kaikei sculpted Fudō Myō-ō (Sk: Acala, the "Immovable One"), a ferocious-looking deity popular among samurai; as mentioned in Chapter 3, Fudō Myō-ō appears in some of the earliest painted images dating from Heian practices of Esoteric Buddhism (Mikkyō). In Figure 4.6, we see the characteristics that appealed to warriors. Fudō frowns fiercely, holding a sword with a *vajra* handle to fight evil and a rope to rescue humans from purgatory. Fudō also served as a protector of the imperial court and the country as a whole, symbolism that would continue into the late nineteenth century.

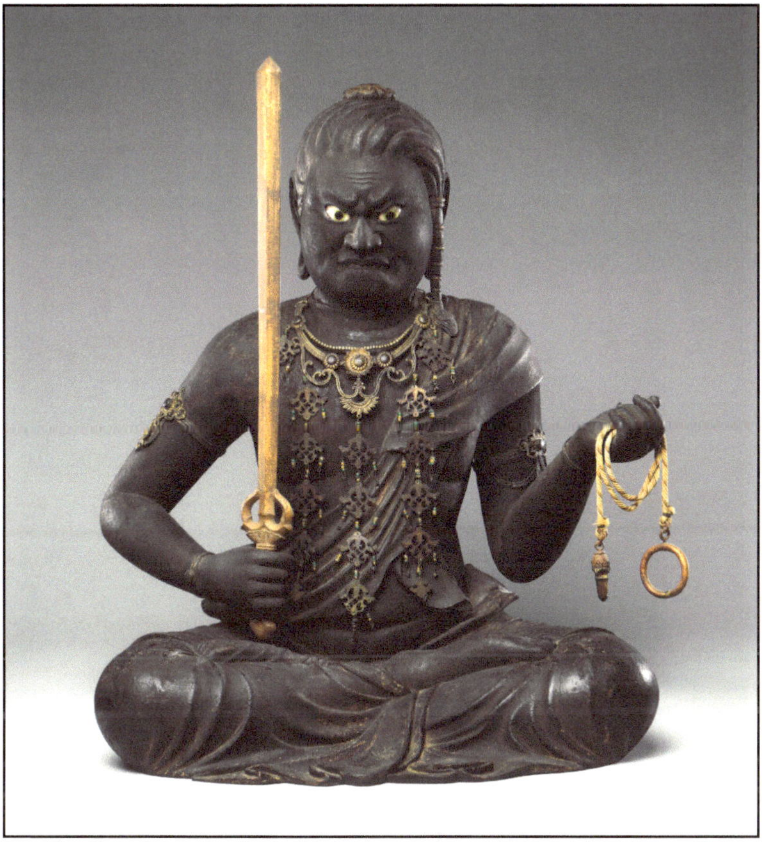

Figure 4.6: Fudō Myōō, Kaikei, early thirteenth century, Japanese cypress with lacquer, color, gold, cut gold leaf (*kirikane*), and inlaid crystal eyes, Metropolitan Museum of Art, New York, Public domain.

Playfulness and humor prevailed during this period, and religious subjects were not exempt. The Tendai priest Kōshū (1276–1350) wrote in his compendium *Keiran shūyōshū* (Leaves gleaned from the mountain streams; 1318) about unconventional paintings of Fudō in which, for example, Fudō suffers from an attack of diarrhea. "He had pulled down his loin cloth and was crouching over a urinal." His two attendants, Kongara Dōji and Seitaka Dōji, hold their noses as Fudō "wipes his bottom with the sacred sword."[15] In this period a tradition of explicit erotic paintings developed, called *osokuzu no-e*; these were known as spring pictures (*shunga*) in the Tokugawa period (1603–1868) or, notably, *warai-e* (laughing pictures).[16]

Zen Buddhism (C: Chan) took hold in Japan during the Kamakura period. Zen emphasizes meditation, self-reliance, restraint, and the idea of Buddhahood in one's lifetime, and the focus on rigorous self-discipline appealed to samurai in

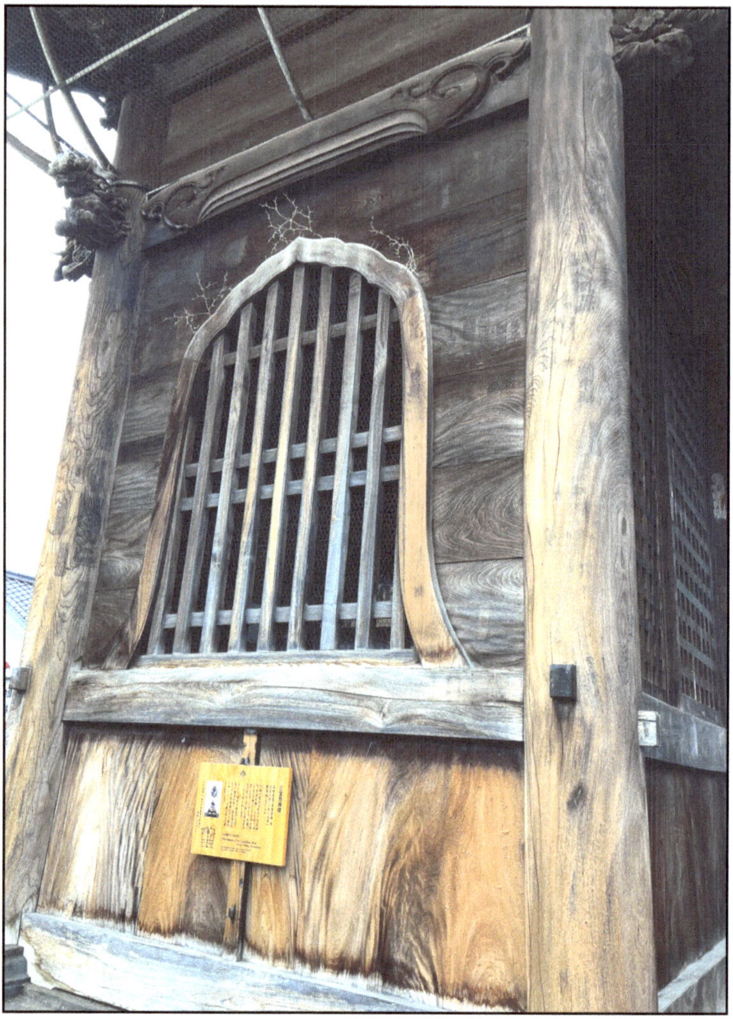

Figure 4.7: Zen-style window, Zenkōji, Nagano City, photo by author.

particular. Japanese monks traveled to China to study with Chan monks, returning years later to spread the teachings. The impact on the arts was profound. Monks and priests produced calligraphy and paintings, promoted tea cultivation and tea drinking, and developed Zen-style architecture and garden design.

The monk Eisai (1141–1215), founder of Rinzai Zen and author of *Kissa yōjōki* (Healthy living through drinking tea; 1211), is credited with having introduced tea seeds to Japan. Tea was used in monasteries as a medication and as a stimulant to assist monks in staying awake during meditation sessions. Eisai's promotion of tea drinking would lay the ground for the broader practice of tea in later centuries.

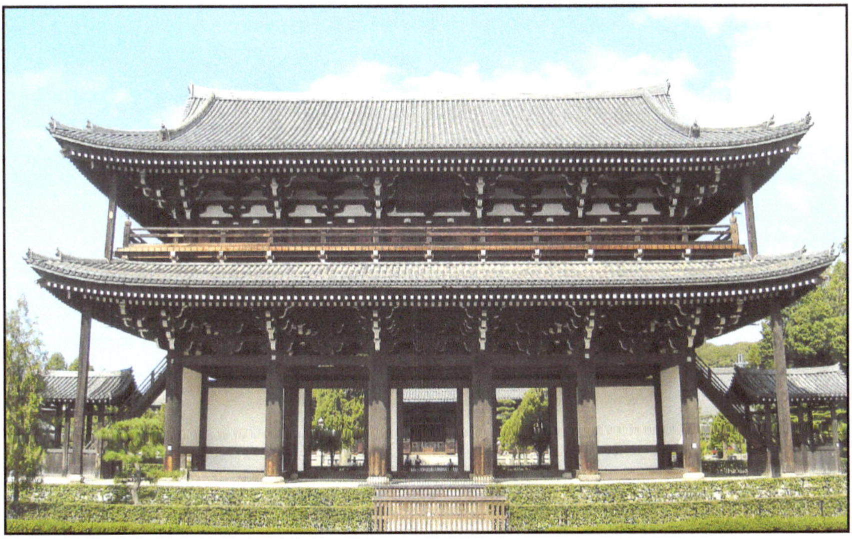

Figure 4.8: Tōfukuji Sanmon, Kyoto, 1425, Zen-style two-story gate with wood frame, Tōfukuji, Kyoto, Wikimedia Commons.

Zen-style (*zenshū-yō*) architecture is characterized by window frames with curved upper sections ending in points (Figure 4.7), steeply angled roofs, *ebi-kōryō* (a type of arched beam), fan rafters, and paneled entrance doors.[17] One technical innovation was the use of an eave support (*kayaoi*), which enabled the roof to curve "both upwards and outwards like an inverted bow."[18] The earliest Zen-style temples still extant date to the fourteenth century; the Tōfukuji Sanmon, the largest Zen temple gate in Japan, was built in 1425 (Figure 4.8). According to a plaque near the gate, the word *sanmon* refers to *sangedatsumon*, meaning "enlightenment gate to Nirvana." The word also means "three gates." Figure 4.9 provides a close-up of the massive pillars, which sit upon stone bases that protect the wood from moisture but also provide a "sliding" effect between the stones and pillars during earthquakes.[19]

Trade with China and fascination with Chinese products (*karamono*) led to creative developments. Handscroll painters drew on Chinese Song-dynasty landscape painting styles to paint with greater attention to background details and a sense of recession into space as seen in a detail from *The Illustrated Miraculous Origins of the Yūzū Nenbutsu School* (*Yūzū nenbutsu engi emaki*; early 1300s, Figure 4.10). This scroll is also representative of the increased number of temple and shrine origin stories. Religious organizations had to secure their own patrons for fundraising purposes; origin narratives were given to prominent donors and used to spread the fame of the shrine or temple illustrated.[20]

Handscrolls that touched on the reality of human suffering, among other themes, were produced in large numbers, serving a wider audience. People

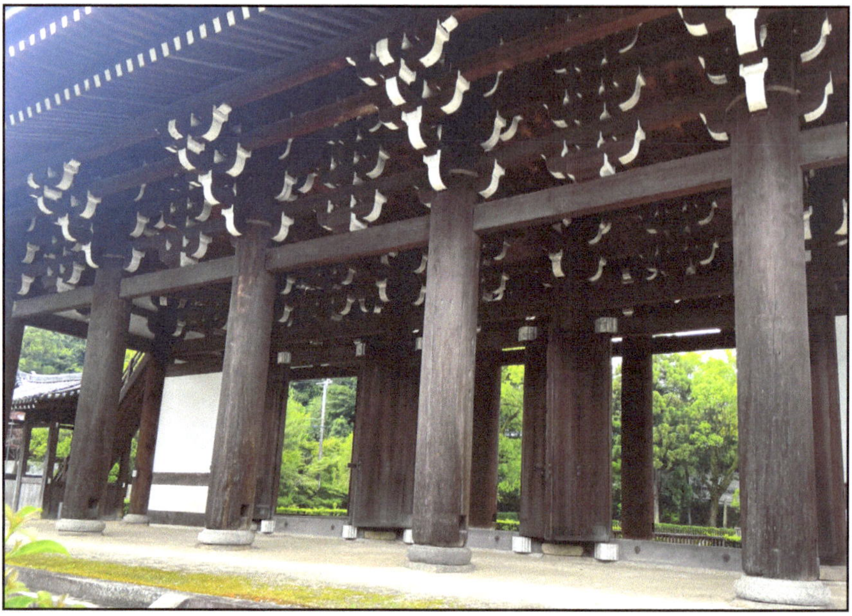

Figure 4.9: Tōfukuji Sanmon (detail), photo by author.

enjoyed genres such as illustrated tales (*monogatari-e*), war tales (*kassen-e*), poetry contests (*uta awase-e*), and popular narratives (*setsuwa-e*). An example of *setsuwa-e* is the *The Tale of Sumiyoshi* (*Sumiyoshi monogatari emaki*; late thirteenth century), based on a tenth-century novel, which tells of a young girl who is abused by her stepmother and her subsequent romance and marriage to a soldier.

The Kamakura period was one of distinctly Japanese cultural developments enhanced and enriched by continental contacts. Kamakura art may be seen as constituting two contrasting cultural currents—the delicate and sensitive courtly art from the Heian period (centered around Kyoto) and a new, more dynamic, muscular, and powerful art that appealed to the samurai, in the east. The reopening of trade with Song China also introduced new architectural styles and cultural practices.

At the same time, there were warnings of unrest to come. Minamoto Yoritomo died in 1199, and his widow, the ruthless "Nun Shogun" Hōjō Masako (1157–1225), rose to power. The Hōjō family controlled the shogunate, but not without the resentment of other powerful lords. Toward the end of the period, the Mongols twice attempted to invade Japan (in 1274 and 1281). They were repulsed by Japanese forces, in battles pictured in the *Illustrated Account of the Mongol Invasion* (*Mōko shūrai ekotoba*; 1293). Samurai were assisted by "divine winds" (*kamikaze*), particularly a typhoon in 1281. (The legend of the *kamikaze* continued through history, culminating in the *kamikaze* pilots in World War II, used by the military as a last desperate strike against U.S. forces in the Pacific.[21])

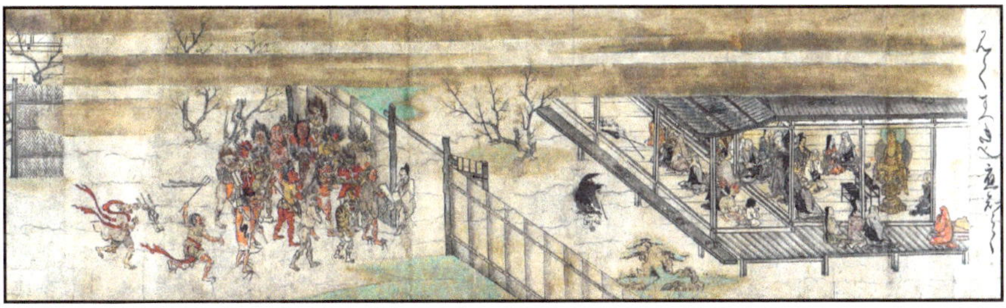

Figure 4.10: *The Illustrated Miraculous Origins of the Yūzū Nenbutsu School* (detail), early fourteenth century, handscroll, ink, color, and gold on paper, Cleveland Museum of Art, Public domain.

Though victorious, the samurai who fought the Mongols were dissatisfied since the defeated Mongols withdrew in their ships, depriving them of the spoils of war. This situation led to further resentment and more battles.

Notes

[1] The Jetavana Temple is Gion Shōja in Japanese. Royall Tyler, trans., *The Tale of the Heike* (New York: Penguin, 2012), 3.

[2] For a full account, see Tyler, *The Tale of the Heike.*

[3] Tyler notes that the "most important reading text" is a 1419–1420 copy of a 1309–1310 manuscript. Tyler, *The Tale of the Heike*, xxii.

[4] The contemporary writer Hideo Furukawa translated *Tale of the Heike* into modern Japanese (published in 2016), and it has since been made into an anime: https://en.wikipedia.org/wiki/The_Heike_Story_(anime).

[5] For full views of the scroll at the Museum of Fine Arts, Boston, see "Heiji Monogatari Emaki (Tale of the Heiji Rebellion)," McGraw Center for Teaching & Learning, Princeton University, http://digital.princeton.edu/heijiscroll/.

[6] Saburo Ienaga, *Painting in the Yamato Style*, trans. John M. Shields, Heibonsha Survey of Japanese Art, vol. 10 (Tokyo: Weatherhill, 1973), 139.

[7] William Coaldrake discusses the *shinden-zukuri* style of the Sanjō Palace in more detail—as well as the building materials being primarily wood, paper, and silk materials, making them particularly vulnerable to fire—in *Architecture and Authority in Japan*, Nissan Institute / Routledge Japanese Studies (London: Routledge, 1996), 85–87 and 92–93.

[8] See Karl Friday, "Once and Future Warriors: The Samurai in Japanese History," *Education About Asia* 10, no. 3 (Winter 2005): 31–38; and Charles Holcombe, *A History of East Asia: From the Origins of Civilization to the Twenty-First Century*, 2nd ed. (Cambridge: Cambridge University Press, 2017), 154–165.

[9] See Yoshiaki Shimizu, ed., *Japan: The Shaping of Daimyo Culture 1185–1868*,

exhibition catalogue (Washington, DC: National Gallery of Art, 1988). For teaching materials, see Ethan Segal, "Can Samurai Teach Critical Thinking? Primary Sources in the Classroom," *Education About Asia* 15, no. 3 (Winter 2010): 5–8.

[10] Tyler, *The Tale of the Heike*, 463–466.

[11] "Tomoe Gozen," in World History Commons, accessed February 15, 2024, https://worldhistorycommons.org/tomoe-gozen.

[12] For a comprehensive survey of military patronage of the arts, see Shimizu, *Japan: The Shaping of Daimyo Culture.*

[13] Nobuo Tsuji, *History of Art in Japan*, trans. Nicole Coolidge Rousmaniere (New York: Columbia University Press, 2019), 190–191.

[14] Tsuji, *History of Art in Japan*, 193–195. See also JAANUS (Japanese Architecture and Art Net Users System), comp. Dr. Mary Neighbour Parent, s.v. "ebikouryou," accessed February 15, 2024, https://www.aisf.or.jp/~jaanus/deta/e/ebikouryou.htm.

[15] Nobuo Tsuji, *Playfulness in Japanese Art*, Franklin D. Murphy Lectures, VII (Lawrence, KS: Spencer Museum of Art, University of Kansas, 1986), 35–36.

[16] Tsuji, *Playfulness in Japanese Art*, 36.

[17] Tsuji, *History of Art in Japan*, 238.

[18] Coaldrake, *Architecture and Authority in Japan*, 100–101. Also, JAANUS, s.v. "kayaoi," accessed February 23, 2024, https://www.aisf.or.jp/~jaanus/deta/k/kayaoi.htm.

[19] For more on earthquake resistance of early Japanese structures, see Koji Nakahara, Toshiharu Hisatoku, Tadashi Nagase, and Yoshinori Takahashi, "Earthquake Response of Five-Story Pagoda Structure of Horyu-ji Temple in Japan," 12WCEE 2000: 12th World Conference on Earthquake Engineering, 2000, https://www.iitk.ac.in/nicee/wcee/article/1229.pdf.

[20] Tsuji, *History of Art in Japan*, 236–237.

[21] Grant Rhode, "Mongol Invasions of Northeast Asia: Korea and Japan," online supplement to *Education About Asia* 25, no. 2 (Fall 2020), 1–5, https://www.asianstudies.org/publications/eaa/archives/china-global-history-and-the-sea-pedagogical-perspectives-and-applications-visual-sidebars-and-recommended-maritime-resources/ accessed May 26, 2024, and https://www.asianstudies.org/publications/eaa/archives/china-global-history-and-the-sea-case-study/, accessed May 26, 2024.

5

Chinese Influences, Japanese Style

The Nanbokuchō and Muromachi Periods

If man were never to fade away . . .
but lingered on forever in the world,
how things would lose their power to move us!

—Yoshida Kenkō, *Essays in Idleness* [1]

Yoshida Kenkō (1283–1350) made this observation in his *Essays in Idleness* (*Tsurezuregusa*; c. 1330–1332), writing in the *zuihitsu* (random jottings) tradition.[2] Kenkō also wrote that beauty is "indissolubly bound to its perishability"—an aesthetic sensibility that was not entirely new but reflected the thought during the next tumultuous centuries.[3]

The Nanbokuchō (1333–1392) and Muromachi periods (1392–1573) were marked by strife and warfare. War broke out when Emperor Go-Daigo (r. 1318–1339) rebelled against the Kamakura shogunate rather than abdicate to another imperial family branch. Vassals of the shogunate defected, and the city of Kamakura was attacked in 1333 and burned; the Hōjō family and their retainers committed suicide. The shogunate collapsed, and sporadic battles between the two imperial courts known as the "Northern and Southern dynasties" continued until 1392.

Japan entered a period of instability as samurai overthrew their lords and daimyo consolidated their power over independent domains. The Ashikaga shoguns ruled from the Muromachi neighborhood in Kyoto, but political turmoil continued into the late fifteenth century with the Ōnin War (1467–1477). Much of Kyoto was destroyed by fire, forcing artisans to flee from the capital to the

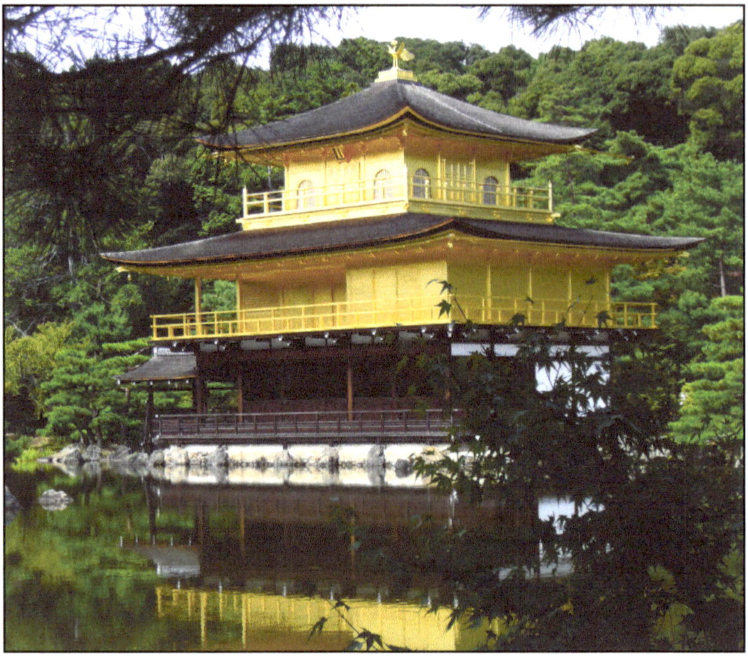

Figure 5.1: Kinkakuji (Golden Pavilion), 1955 reconstruction of 1398 temple, Rokuonji, Kyoto, photo by author.

provinces. During the subsequent Warring States period (*Sengoku jidai*; 1477–1573) there was no effective central government, and provincial governors were unable to control their subordinates. Akira Kurosawa's epic film *Ran* (1985), based in part on Shakespeare's *King Lear*, relates the treachery and horrors of this period as an aging daimyo fails to peacefully transition power to his three sons.

At the same time, the period was also defined by its international flavor, creativity, and innovation, as artists absorbed Chinese influences, selectively incorporating and adapting what came from abroad, and in the process developing a specifically Japanese style. Chinese paintings, calligraphy, and objects of daily use from the Southern Song (1127–1279), Yuan (1271–1368), and Ming (1368–1644) dynasties became popular among Japanese collectors. Historically important Chinese paintings made their way into Japanese collections, with Zen monks acting as brokers.[4] For daimyo and courtiers, it was a statement of power, prestige, and taste to own and display *karamono* (literally, "Chinese things").

The Kitayama era (1392–1467) in particular is considered a "golden age" of shogunate patronage of the arts. One of the most important of these patrons was Ashikaga Yoshimitsu (1358–1408), who built Kinkakuji (Rokuonji) and its surrounding pleasure garden in Kyoto's Kitayama area. The Golden Pavilion within the complex (1398; Figure 5.1) sits on the edge of a lake and was designed in three architectural styles: the first floor in the residential *shinden-zukuri*, the

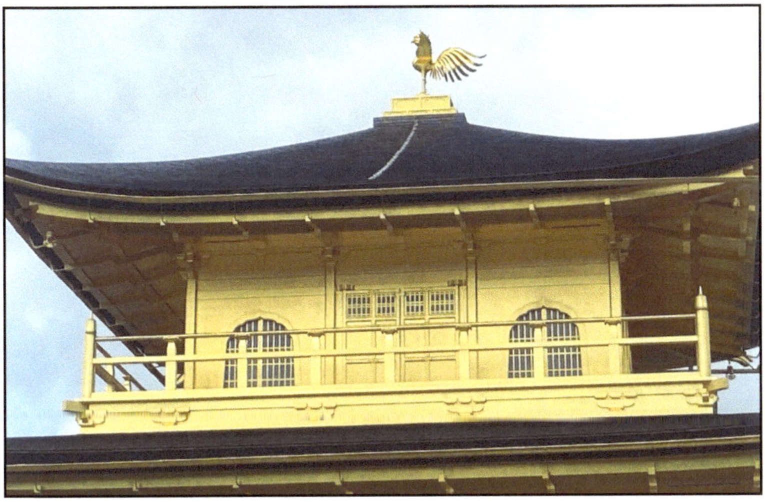

Figure 5.2: Roof detail, Kinkakuji, photo by author.

second floor in combined Japanese and Buddhist hall styles, and the third floor in Zen style.[5] The ground floor, of unpainted wood and white plaster walls, was used for relaxation and also served as a departure point for the small pleasure boats that circled the lake's artificial islands. The Zen-style roof curves upward, shingled with thin *sawara* cypress. Few descriptions of the Golden Pavilion and its original construction survive, but there is some evidence that at least the exterior of the third floor was coated with gold during Yoshimitsu's time. Gold leaf now covers the lacquered outer walls of the upper two stories, and a golden phoenix sits at the roof's apex, above Zen-style windows (Figure 5.2). When the complex was completed in 1408, Yoshimitsu hosted a party in celebration, attended by the emperor.[6]

At such parties, attendees could tour the meeting hall, where Yoshimitsu's Chinese collection was on display. They might also stroll through the surrounding garden or take a boat around the lake, where they enjoyed a microcosm of the macrocosm in carefully planted "natural" profusions of foliage and flowers designed to highlight seasonal changes (Figure 5.3). The concept is reminiscent of the Byōdō-in's Phoenix Hall (Chapter 3), which also had a pond and stroll garden.[7]

Landscape designers also took inspiration from China to create "dry landscape" (*karesansui*) gardens, in which gravel or sand represents water. A well-known example is the dry landscape garden at Daisen-in, a sub-temple within Daitokuji (Figure 5.4).[8] This type of garden is designed to be appreciated from a veranda but never entered. Each element—rocks, gravel, shrubs—is meant to suggest something else, drawing on the viewer's imagination. A flat stone becomes a low bridge; raked white gravel represents water; large rocks are mountains, with cascading waterfalls; small clipped shrubs are trees. This also is a microcosm of the macrocosm, recalling Chinese landscape paintings. A sense of perspective,

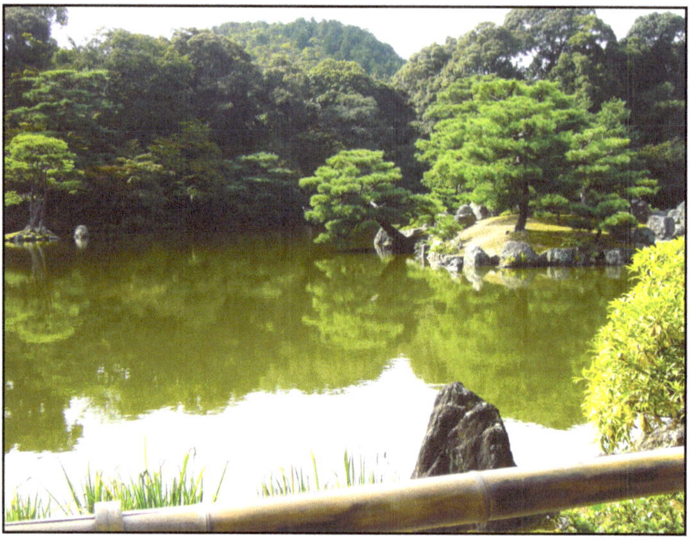

Figure 5.3: Pond and stroll garden, Kinkakuji, photo by author.

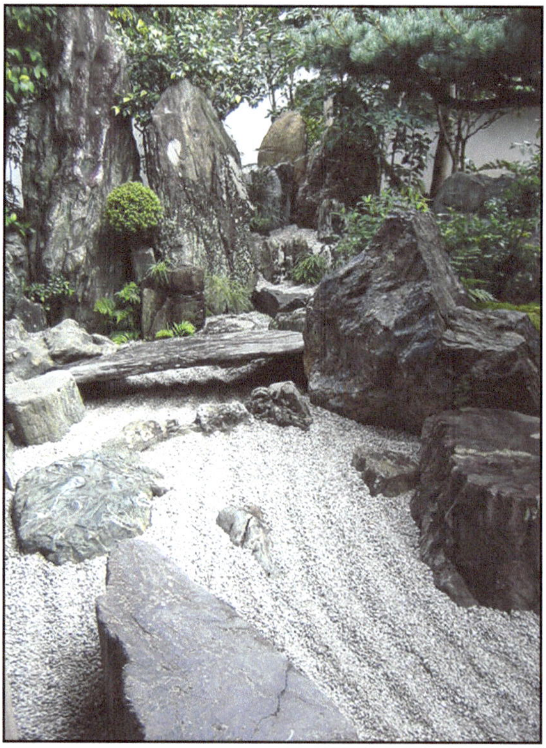

Figure 5.4: Dry landscape garden, late sixteenth century, Daisen-in, a sub-temple of Daitokuji, Kyoto, Wikimedia Commons.

with near, middle, and far distances, is created by the succession of rocks receding toward the garden's back wall, where the texture of the "mountains" suggests the mist and clouds of Song paintings. A large flat rock close to the veranda gives the impression that a viewer is standing at the outer edge of the composition, much like in a Chinese landscape painting.[9] But this type of garden design emphasizes simplicity and an interpretation of characteristically Japanese landscapes. In the twentieth century, Japanese dry landscape gardens would become renowned internationally.[10]

Sub-temples like Daisen-in were developed by Zen priests, whose impact on culture was substantial, as temples became centers for poetry gatherings and tea practice. Zen gardens are typically designed to be viewed from a reading room (*shoin*), part of the *shoin-zukuri* style that became a feature of residential architecture for the wealthy. Sliding partitions (*shōji*) opened on the side facing the garden, bringing room and garden together as one space.[11] Floors were covered with tatami mats made from multiple layers of compressed rice straw covered by tightly woven *igusa* rushes. An alcove (*oshiita*; now called *tokonoma*) served as an elegant focal point and was used to display flower arrangements (*tatebana*; now called ikebana), ceramics, incense burners, or other treasured objects (Figure 5.5). Chief among the items on display would be a hanging scroll (*kakemono*).

A hanging scroll is a painting or calligraphy mounted on a flexible silk or paper backing, often with decorative silk edgings (Figure 5.6). The scroll has a rod at the top and another at the bottom, which enables it to be displayed easily and then rolled up for storage; scrolls were often changed with the season or occasion. Other painting formats were used to divide and partition space. Folding screens

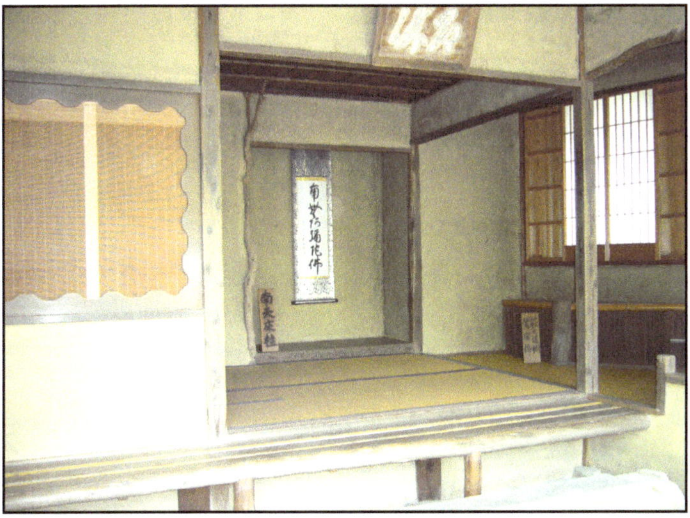

Figure 5.5: Sekka-tei teahouse, Hōrin Jōshō (1593–1668), Kinkakuji, twentieth-century restoration, photo by author.

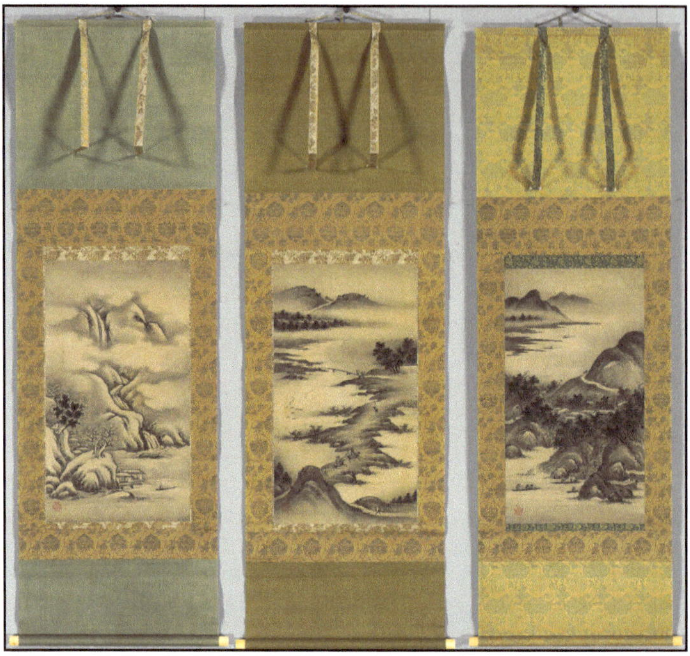

Figure 5.6: *Seasonal Landscapes*, Kano Hideyori, mid- to late sixteenth century, hanging scrolls, ink on paper, Cleveland Museum of Art, Public domain.

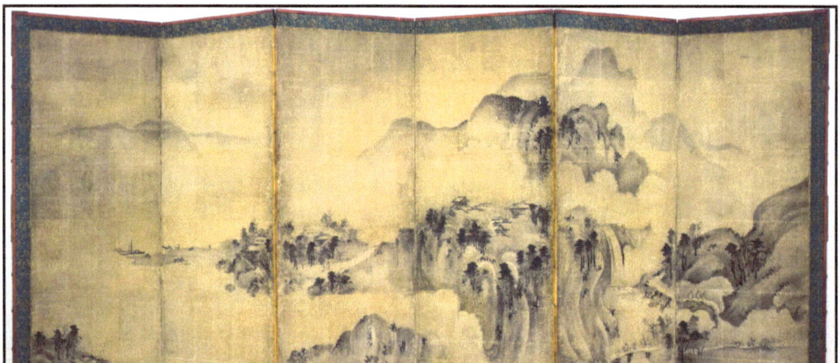

Figure 5.7: *Landscape*, follower of Sesson Shūkei, sixteenth century, six-panel folding screen, ink on paper, Metropolitan Museum of Art, New York, Public domain.

(*byōbu*) were adapted to Japanese architecture: Chinese-style metal hinges used previously were replaced by paper hinges, allowing for a lighter design and more flexibility (Figure 5.7). Paper hinges also led to more panels, resulting in the six-panel format. Painters could now continue a composition over multiple panels, a significant design development. Sliding doors (*fusuma*) were used to divide spaces; when the sliding doors were opened, interior rooms became one large

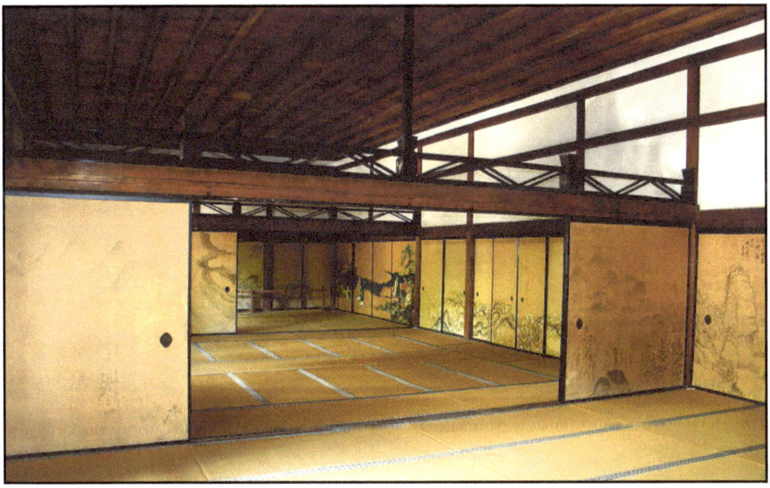

Figure 5.8: Interior of the main building, Ryōanji, Kyoto, late fifteenth century, Wikimedia Commons.

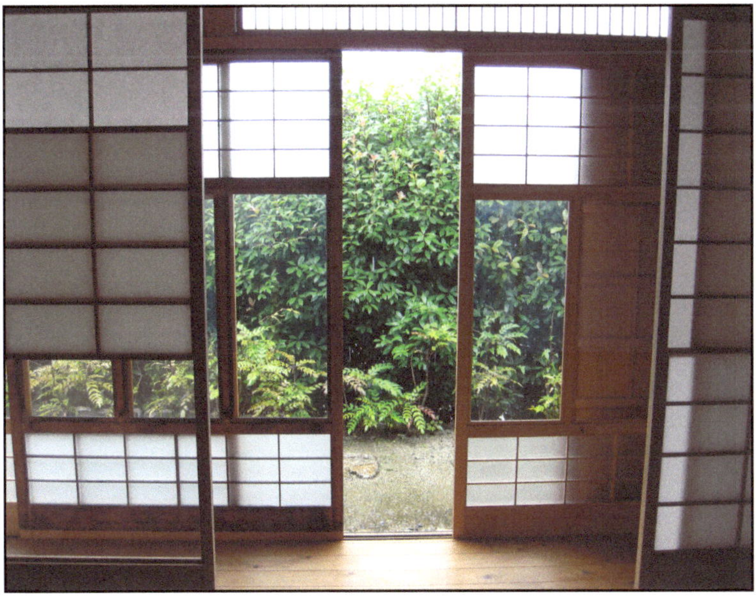

Figure 5.9: Shoji screens and a veranda, 2010, Kobe, photo by author.

room (Figure 5.8). Additionally, the wooden paneled doors on outside walls were supplanted by lighter shoji (*shōji*) partitions made of wood lattice and paper.[12] Shoji closed off a room from a veranda, providing it with a light-infused outer wall (Figure 5.9).[13] Sliding doors and shoji became standard in subsequent building design and are still used today.

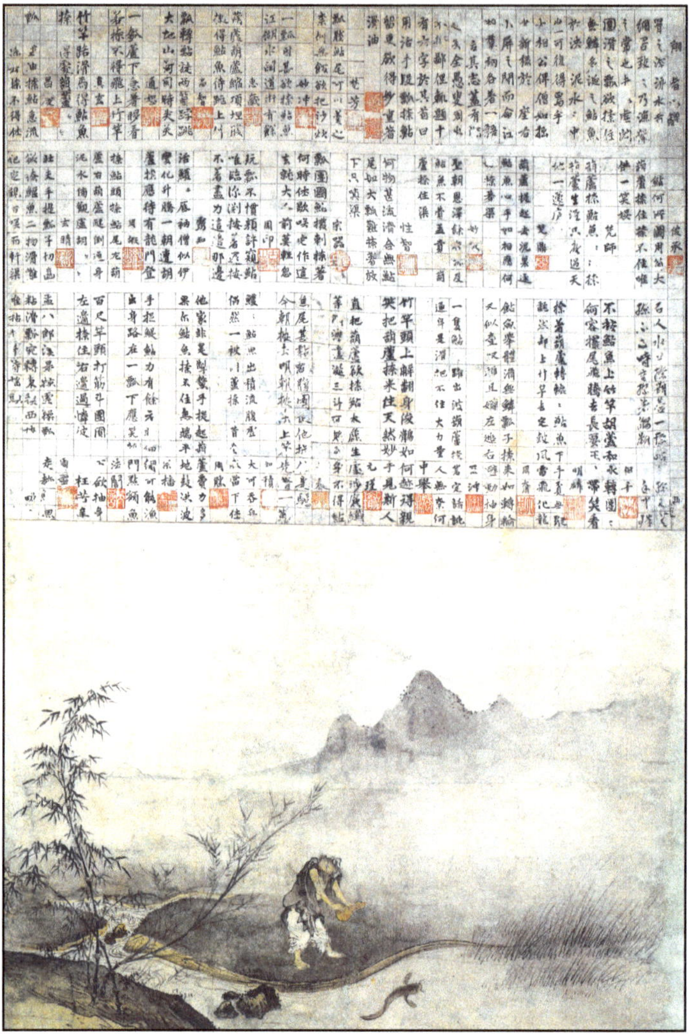

Figure 5.10: *Catching a Catfish with a Gourd*, Josetsu, before 1451, hanging scroll, ink and light color on paper, Taizō-in, Myōshinji, Kyoto, Wikimedia Commons.

Ink paintings (*suibokuga*) were produced in Japan as early as the Kamakura period, but Chinese monks fleeing the Mongol invasions brought new styles of ink painting to Japan. Zen practitioners adapted the Chinese style (ink painting with light colors) for teaching and contemplation. An example is *Catching a Catfish with a Gourd* by the monk painter Josetsu (active c. 1394–c. 1428; Figure 5.10). The subject is a Zen koan (*kōan*), a riddle posed in this case by shogun Yoshimochi (1386–1428). The asymmetrical composition reads from left to right, showing a man attempting to catch a jumping fish with his gourd. The shoreline echoes the

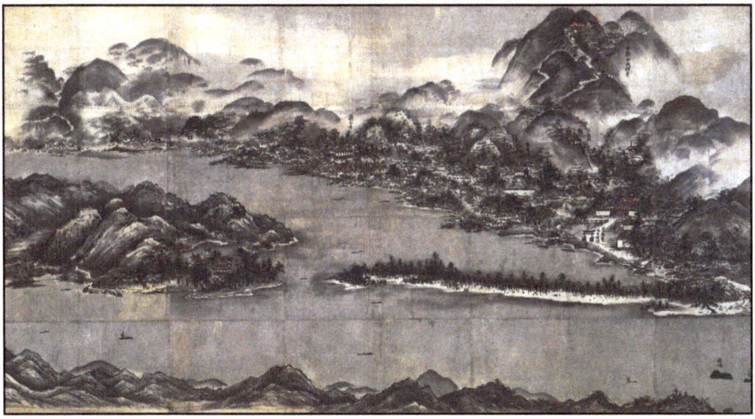

Figure 5.11: *Amanohashidate*, Sesshū Tōyō, c. 1501–1506, hanging scroll, ink and color on paper, Kyoto National Museum, Wikimedia Commons.

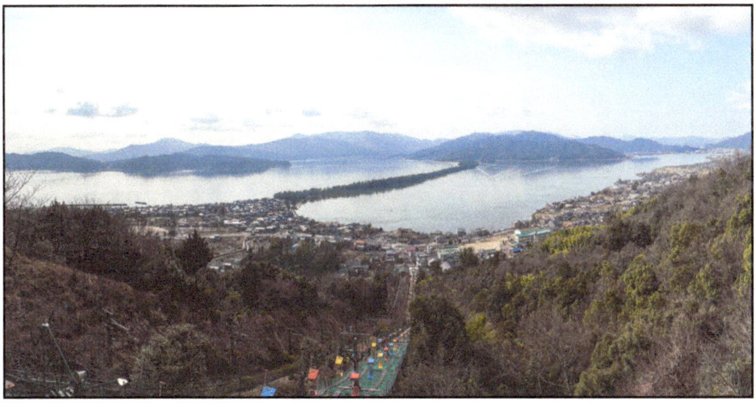

Figure 5.12: Amanohashidate, Kyoto prefecture, Wikimedia Commons.

curves of the catfish's body, while details fade into the mist at the right. At the top thirty-one monks wrote commentary on the meaning of the koan.[14]

There were many ink painters, including those like Shūbun (d. mid-1450s), who were active in the painting academy established by the Ashikaga shoguns. Shūbun's student, the monk painter Sesshū Tōyō (1420–1506?), stands out for his skill, creativity, and innovation: the style he developed was rooted in his study of Chinese paintings yet gradually became more individualistic and more specifically Japanese. For example, he did something rare for the time, which was to sign his work, thus raising the viewer's consciousness of the individual painter's existence. Sesshū worked outside the established academy and was known for wandering the landscape, sketching what he saw. Inspired by his art training in China, Sesshū focused in his later years on famous sites of Japan, including *Amanohashidate* (Heaven's Bridge; c. 1501–1506; Figure 5.11), painted in his early eighties. In his

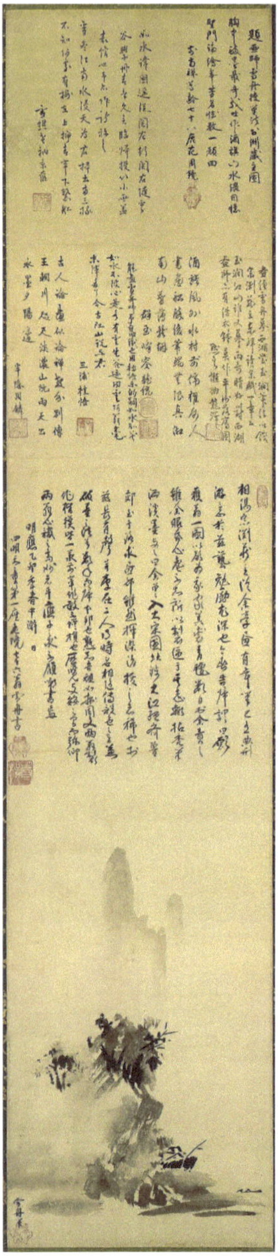

Figure 5.13: *Splashed Ink Landscape*, Sesshū Tōyō, 1495, hanging scroll, ink on paper, Tokyo National Museum, Wikimedia Commons.

response to the Chinese theme of famous sites, he employed typical Chinese landscape elements of mountain, water, and mist to render the natural land bridge in northern Kyoto prefecture. The painting corresponds to the actual site (Figure 5.12).[15]

Another Sesshū painting in the "splashed-ink" style (*hatsuboku*; Figures 5.13 and 5.14) is nearly abstract, forcing the viewer to imagine mist-shrouded mountains in the background. Rocks and foliage are indicated in the foreground with bold, quick brushstrokes. A banner and fence suggest a wine shop or tavern. Derived from Chinese painting, the splashed-ink technique involves spilling, splashing, and pouring ink onto a surface to indicate shapes. Although appearing spontaneous, it in fact consists of a deliberate layering of ink, taking advantage of how layers blend into one another as they dry. Also apparent are dark accents and obvious brushstrokes.[16] Above the landscape is Sesshū's preface, unusual for monk painters in this period, supplemented by poetic writings by leading Zen monks of the time.[17]

Another art form that became prominent in this period is Noh (*nō*), a theatrical form that developed out of a mix of sacred rituals and festival entertainments. The actor Kan'ami (1333–1384) and his son Zeami (1363–1443) are credited with perfecting the form. Zeami was recognized at the age of twelve for his skill and beauty by the young shogun Yoshimitsu who became his patron, but it was Zeami's skill in acting, writing about acting, and producing plays that made Noh the classical theater of Japan.[18] Noh combines vocal and instrumental music, acting and dance, and requires costumes, masks, fans, and stage construction.[19] Costumes are made of silk brocade, embroidery, and gold leaf on silk, and stenciled paste-resist dyeing on hemp. They glowed in the light of torches, particularly in outdoor venues at evening performances (Figure 5.15). The masks (Figures 5.16 and 5.17) are carved from Japanese cypress (*hinoki*) and painted with natural pigments. Actors, then and now, use them to represent different types of characters, such as young women, ghosts, demons, and priests. Treasured

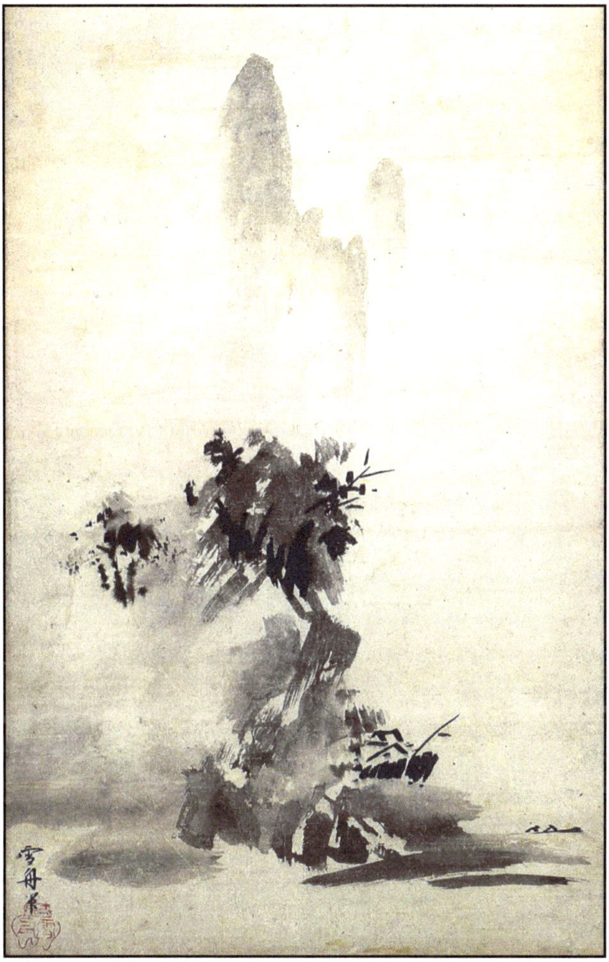

Figure 5.14: *Splashed Ink Landscape* (detail), Tokyo National Museum, Wikimedia Commons.

masks are passed down through generations of actors. Noh was an important cultural and political expression of the *bun-bu* balance mentioned in Chapter 4. Daimyo maintained Noh stages at their mansions and supported troupes of actors and musicians. This in turn drove artisan industries to provide the items needed for performances.

Noh often features ghosts and demons. Also in this vein are paintings of the "Night Parade of One Hundred Demons" (*Hyakki yagyō*; Figure 5.18), illustrating a parade of demons, monsters, Buddhist figures, and implements. Daily-use items come to life and dance or frolic across the composition. This theme would appear repeatedly in the arts even into modern times.[20]

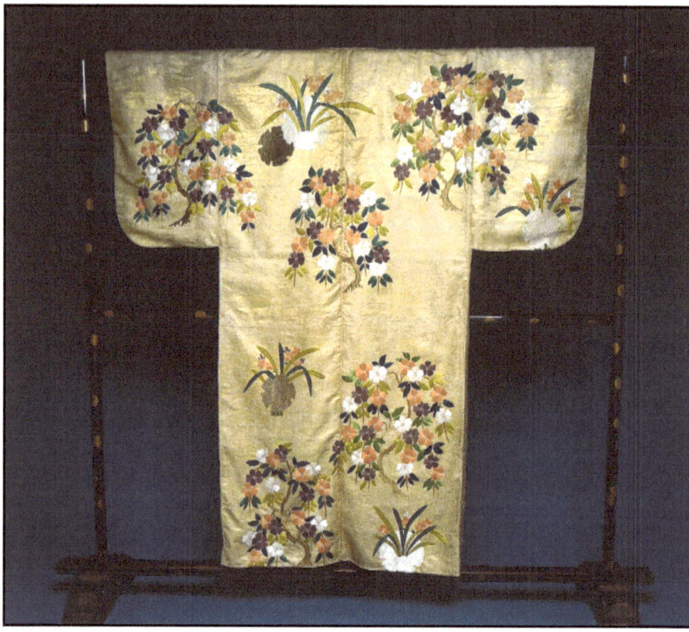

Figure 5.15: Noh costume (*nuihaku*), 1675–1699, silk embroidery and applied gold leaf, Cleveland Museum of Art, Public domain.

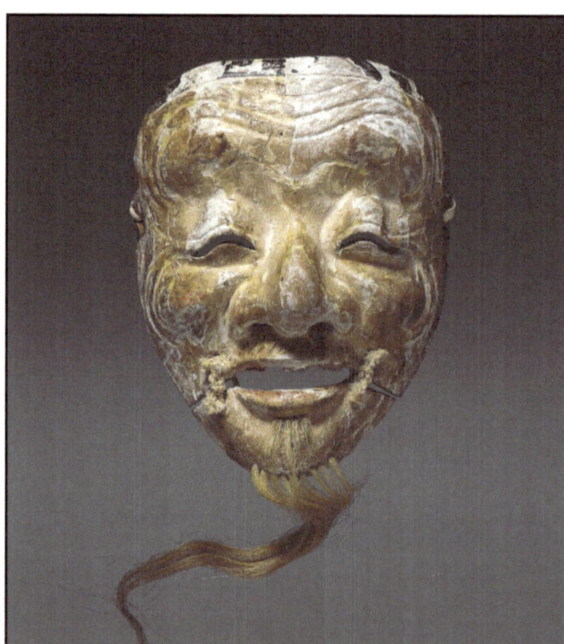

Figure 5.16: Noh mask of Okina, fifteenth century, polychromed wood and hemp, Cleveland Museum of Art, Public domain.

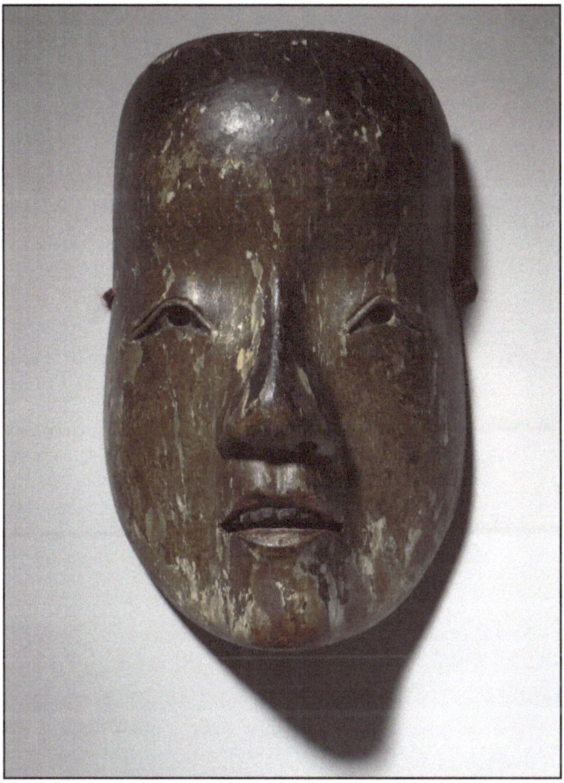

Figure 5.17: Noh mask of Waka-onna (young woman), Muromachi period, polychromed wood, Cleveland Museum of Art, Public domain.

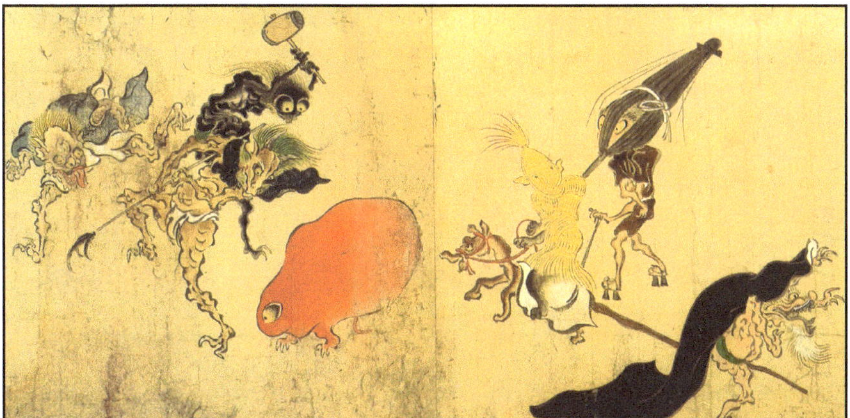

Figure 5.18: *Hyakki yagyō emaki* (*Night Parade of One Hundred Demons*), first half of the sixteenth century, attributed to Tosa Mitsunobu (d. early 1520s), handscroll, ink and color on paper, Daitokuji, Kyoto, Wikimedia Commons.

The official government painting workshops established as early as the Heian period served as models for Muromachi temple and shrine workshops and family-based ateliers. Enterprising painters such as Kano Masanobu (1434–1530) and his son Motonobu (1476–1559) established workshops that came to be known collectively as the Kano school (Figure 5.19). Motonobu's strategic marriage to the daughter of Tosa Mitsunobu (d. early 1520s) brought the *yamato-e* style of the imperial court's Tosa painters into the more Chinese-based style of the Kano school, expanding the Kano repertoire (Figure 5.20).

Kano painters worked for the shogunate as well as for the aristocracy and the rising merchant class. Like other pre-modern guilds, Kano ateliers used an apprenticeship system both to pass their skills and knowledge to the next generation and to control quality and guard the secrets of their craft. An atelier's master painter managed commissions and projects. He sketched in the overall composition, painted crucial details, and made finishing touches. Assistants and young apprentices, depending on their seniority and skills, would prepare the paper, grind ink and pigments, paint backgrounds, and fill in areas of color. This organizational model was profitable and served as a training ground for painters of all types.[21]

The practice of tea drinking (*chadō*, *sadō*, or *chanoyu*) developed further during this period, with the drinking of *matcha* (ground green tea) spreading by the early sixteenth century beyond the military classes. Tea was particularly popular among the merchants of Sakai, an important port city near present-day Osaka.[22] The tea master Murata Jukō (1423–1502) became an advisor to shogun and arts patron Yoshimasa (1434–1490), known for his Kyoto retreat, Ginkakuji (Silver Pavilion; 1489; Figure 5.21). Yoshimasa's philosophy about the aesthetics of architecture and tea reveals a trend toward enhanced simplicity, focusing on the humble, the withered, the spare, and the evocative. Ginkakuji reflects these ideas with Japanese-style living quarters on the first floor, subdued coloring, and a refined simplicity. At the same time, the building and site reference styles that were current, with the second floor in Zen style much like Kinkakuji (Figure 5.1) and a dry landscape garden. Both of these buildings, however, continue a characteristically Muromachi amalgamation of Japanese and Chinese architectural styles, with Zen-style architecture blending with the *daibutsu-yō* (Chapter 4; Figure 4.3), as seen in the Tōfukuji Sanmon (Chapter 4; Figure 4.8).

The culture of tea required tea bowls, water jars, and flower containers; imported Chinese and Korean celadon, porcelain, and stoneware were highly sought after. Japanese stoneware producers in the late Heian period had learned the technique of firing unglazed clay to produce a natural ash glaze. The effect of this type of glaze varied according to where a piece was placed in a kiln, how the ash fell on the piece, and the fluctuation of heat during firing. The kilns at Echizen, Tanba, Shigaraki, and Bizen were producing utilitarian pottery like the large Bizen jar in Figure 5.22, and during the sixteenth century, they began marketing to tea practitioners. Practitioners, for their part, began to incorporate utilitarian vessels

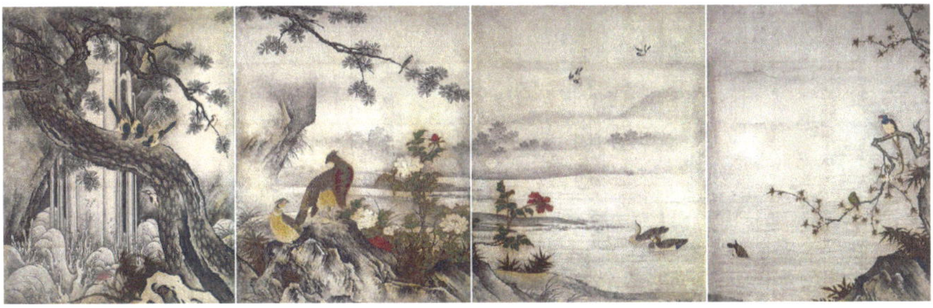

Figure 5.19: *Birds and Flowers of the Four Seasons*, Kano Motonobu, first half of sixteenth century, originally eight *fusuma* panels, hanging scrolls, ink and color on paper, Daisen-in, Daitokuji, Kyoto, Wikimedia Commons.

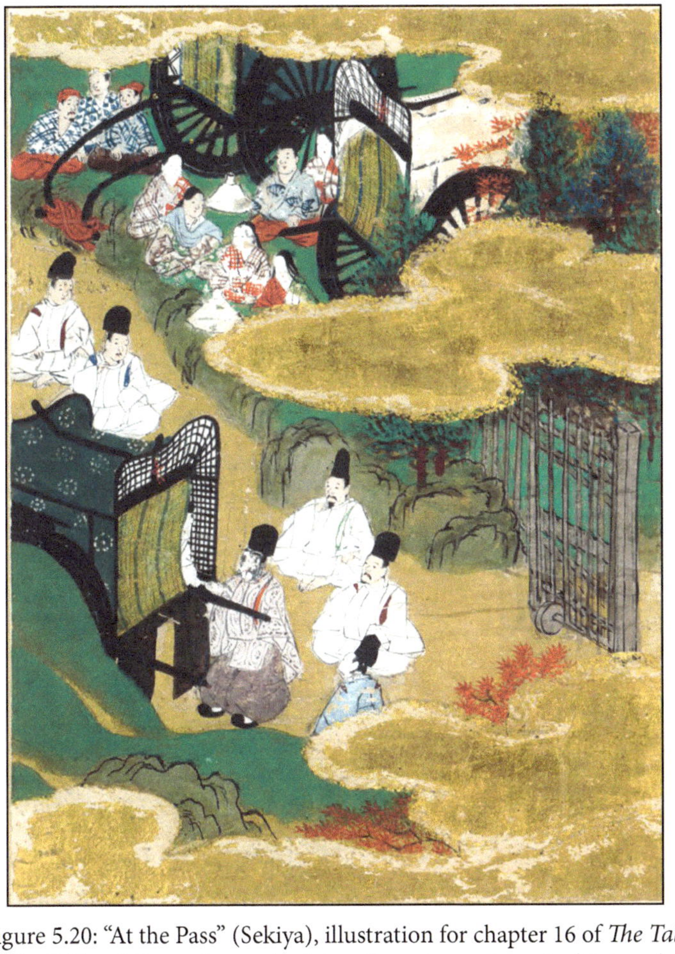

Figure 5.20: "At the Pass" (Sekiya), illustration for chapter 16 of *The Tale of Genji*, Tosa Mitsunobu, early sixteenth century, album leaf, ink, color, and gold on paper, Harvard Art Museums, Public domain.

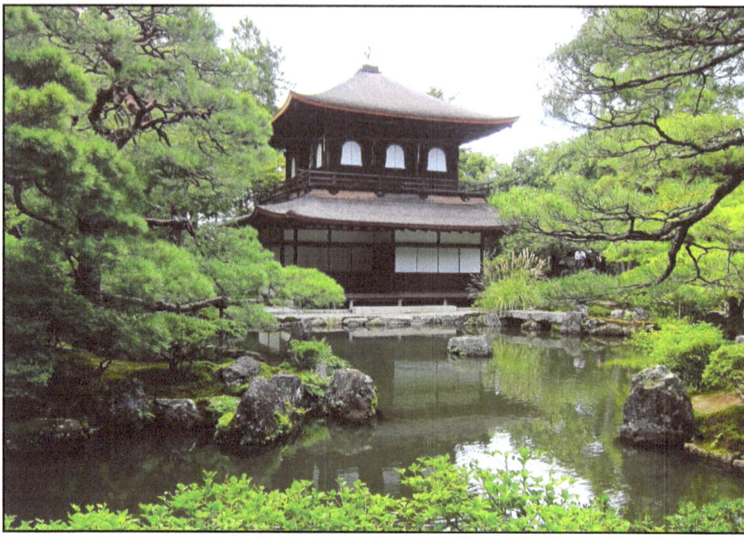

Figure 5.21: Ginkakuji (Silver Pavilion), 1489, two stories with wood frame, Jishō-ji, Kyoto, Wikimedia Commons.

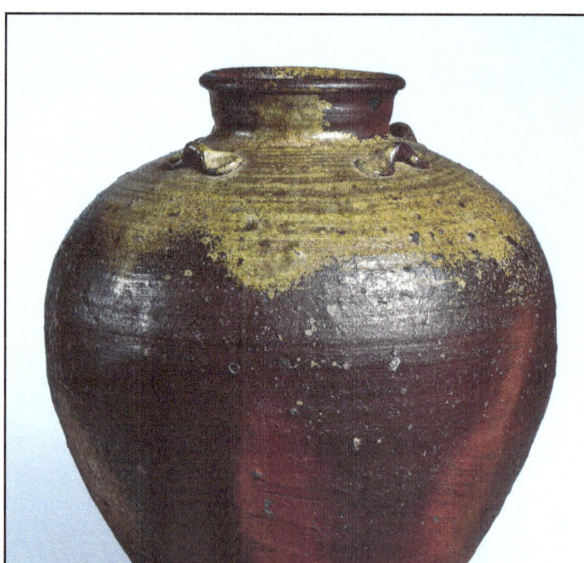

Figure 5.22: Jar with loops, Bizen ware, sixteenth century, stoneware with natural ash glaze, Minneapolis Institute of Art, Public domain.

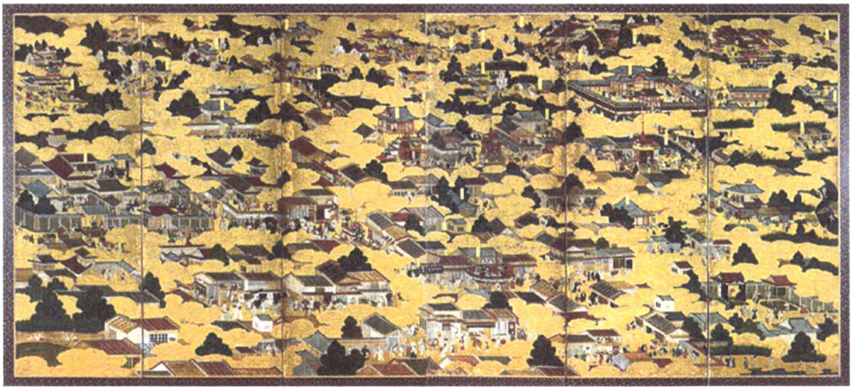

Figure 5.23: Scenes in and around Kyoto, early seventeenth century, folding screen, ink, color and gold on paper, Minneapolis Institute of Art, Public domain.

into their practice, as a taste developed for the rustic. The growing market for the production of tea ceramics was driven by the interaction of marketing, the development of new types of vessels, and practitioners' taste for the look and feel of utilitarian items.[23]

In the sixteenth century, a new subject for screen painting arose, genre scenes (*fūzokuga*) of ordinary people going about their daily lives.[24] One type was scenes in and around the capital (*rakuchū rakugaizu*): aerial views of Kyoto depicting the buildings and lives of everyday people as seen through banks of golden clouds (Figure 5.23).[25] In other arts, high-relief lacquer (*takamaki-e*) was a new technique at this time, metalwork was further refined, and textile designs incorporated imported pieces. Tie-dyeing combined with embroidery and applied designs were introduced to clothing, and women stopped wearing *hakama* (trousers) under their robes in favor of ankle length *kosode*, held together with an obi (sash). This was a major shift in dress, leading to a proliferation of designs and colors in the making of *kosode* for fashionable women.[26]

Notes

[1] Kenkō Yoshida. *Essays in Idleness: The Tsurezuregusa of Kenkō*, trans. Donald Keene. (New York: Columbia University Press, 1998), Section 7, 7.

[2] Marvin Marcus defines *zuihitsu* as "random jottings," adding that this is a style of writing "characterized by personal reflection and musings on the human condition." Sei Shōnagon's *Pillow Book* (*Makura no sōshi*, c. 1010) is an earlier example. For an overview of Japanese literature, see Marvin Marcus, *Japanese Literature from Murasaki to Murakami*, Key Issues in Asian Studies (Ann Arbor: Association for Asian Studies, 2015), 112.

[3] Yoshida, *Essays in Idleness*, xxii.

[4] Nobuo Tsuji lists numerous Chinese paintings that were collected in this period: Nobuo Tsuji, *History of Art in Japan*, trans. Nicole Coolidge Rousmaniere (New York: Columbia University Press, 2019), chap. 7, 244–281.

[5] The Golden Pavilion survived until 1950, when a young mentally unstable monk burned the building to the ground. Yukio Mishima's well-known novel *The Temple of the Golden Pavilion* (1956) blends fiction with fact in recounting the story of the temple's destruction. The temple was rebuilt in 1955.

[6] See Dorinda Neave, Lara C.W. Blanchard, and Marika Sardar, *Asian Art* (Hoboken, NJ: Pearson, 2014), 342, and Kinkakuji, https://www.shokoku-ji.jp/en/kinkakuji/ (accessed April 29, 2024).

[7] See Karen M. Gerhart and Brenda G. Jordan, "A Look at Japanese Gardens," Japan:PITT website, accessed April 19, 2024: https://www.japanpitt.pitt.edu/essays-and-articles/culture/look-japanese-gardens.

[8] The garden dates to the late sixteenth century but is discussed here for its Muromachi-period features. Wybe Kuitert, *Themes in the History of Japanese Garden Art* (Honolulu: University of Hawai'i Press, 2002), 95–98.

[9] Kuitert, *Themes in the History of Japanese Garden Art*, 96.

[10] It is important to remember that Japanese gardens change over time. Rocks are moved, trees and shrubs die and are replanted, caretakers tend the gardens differently, fires and earthquakes take their toll, and new owners dictate their preferences.

[11] Kuitert, *Themes in the History of Japanese Garden Art*, 88.

[12] Conrad Totman argues that this change was the result of deforestation. Conrad Totman, *Japan: An Environmental History* (I. B. Tauris, 2014), 129–130.

[13] The term "shoji" is used today for sliding partitions on a room's outside walls, but it once had a broader meaning. See JAANUS (Japanese Architecture and Art Net Users System), comp. Dr. Mary Neighbour Parent, s.v. "shouji," accessed April 3, 2024, https://www.aisf.or.jp/~jaanus/deta/s/shouji.htm.

[14] Originally, the painting was on one side of a screen, with the commentary on the other side. It has been mounted as a hanging scroll, thus the appearance of a line break between commentary and picture.

[15] With your back to the sand bar and looking at it upside-down, between your legs, the pine trees become legs of a bridge and the land becomes the bridge.

[16] This has also been called the *haboku* style (broken ink), but this is a misunderstanding of both a term Sesshū used in his preface and the difference between *haboku* and *hatsuboku* techniques. See Yukio Lippit, "Of Modes and Manners in Japanese Ink Painting: Sesshū's 'Splashed Ink Landscape' of 1495," *Art Bulletin* 94, no. 1 (March 2012): 55–56.

[17] Lippit provides a detailed analysis of this painting in "Of Modes and Manners in Japanese Ink Painting," 50–77.

[18] See J. Thomas Rimer and Masakazu Yamazaki, trans., *On the Art of the Nō Drama: The Major Treatises of Zeami* (Princeton: Princeton University Press, 1984). Also, Masakazu Yamazaki and Susan Matisoff, "The Aesthetics of Transformation: Zeami's Dramatic Theories," *Journal of Japanese Studies* 7, no. 2 (Summer 1981): 215–257.

[19] For a detailed discussion of Noh, see Kunio Komparu, *The Noh Theater, Principles and Perspectives* (Tokyo: Weatherhill, 1983).

[20] The climactic scene in Isao Takahata's 1994 anime *Pom Poko* from Studio Ghibli is an example of the use of the "Night Parade of One Hundred Demons" theme in contemporary culture.

[21] See Karen M. Gerhart, "Talent, Training, and Power: The Kano Painting Workshop in the Seventeenth Century," in Brenda G. Jordan and Victoria Weston, eds. *Copying the Master and Stealing His Secrets: Talent and Training in Japanese Painting* (Honolulu: University of Hawai'i Press, 2003).

[22] Morgan Pitelka, *Handmade Culture: Raku Potters, Patrons, and Tea Practitioners in Japa*n (Honolulu, University of Hawai'i Press, 2005), 14–15.

[23] Japanese potters had for centuries adapted continental styles and techniques. See Pitelka, *Handmade Culture*, 5–7, and Tsuji, *History of Japanese Art*, 278–280.

[24] This was a development from an earlier type of painting (*keibutsuga*) in which scenes of daily life were combined with the four seasons (winter, spring, summer, fall).

[25] The earliest *rakuchū rakugaizu* (1506) has been attributed to Tosa Mitsunobu. The oldest extant screens date from 1530 and are in the National Museum of Japanese History, Chiba prefecture.

[26] Liza Dalby, *Kimono: Fashioning Culture* (New Haven: Yale University Press, 1993), 36; Tsuji, *History of Japanese Art*, 269–270.

6

Art Is Power

The Azuchi-Momoyama Period

On top of the hill in the middle of the city Nobunaga built his palace and castle, which as regards architecture, strength, wealth, and grandeur may well be compared with the greatest buildings of Europe.

— Luís Fróis, SJ[1]

Toward the middle of the 1500s, Europeans began to arrive in Japan, bringing tobacco, new cooking techniques,[2] new styles of clothing, and a deadly new technology—firearms. Jesuit missionaries such as Francis Xavier (1506–1552) introduced Christianity, which was adopted by as many as 300,000 Japanese in the sixteenth century. For a time, Portuguese dress was considered fashionable, including wearing a cross and rosary.[3] Trade with the outside world increased, spurring development of the port of Nagasaki. Silver and gold mining bolstered trade and created new wealth for daimyo. The late sixteenth century saw continued international engagement, but it was also a time when warlords vied for power and demonstrated their authority and cultural might through monumental castles and cultural pursuits.

During the brief period known as Azuchi-Momoyama (1573–1600), three warlords rose to power: Oda Nobunaga (1534–1582), Toyotomi Hideyoshi (1536–1598), and Tokugawa Ieyasu (1543–1616). Each in turn would gradually but forcefully unify the domains into one military shogunate. Like their contemporaries, these three lords used the arts, including poetry and Noh theater, as expressions of power and authority. They also constructed castles for protection, defense, and as statements of dominance. The era was named after Nobunaga's castle at Azuchi and the flowering peach trees near Hideyoshi's former Fushimi Castle (*momoyama* means "peach mountain").[4]

Japanese castles of this period vastly expanded and improved upon traditional fortifications, drawing on technological and engineering advances. Castles were

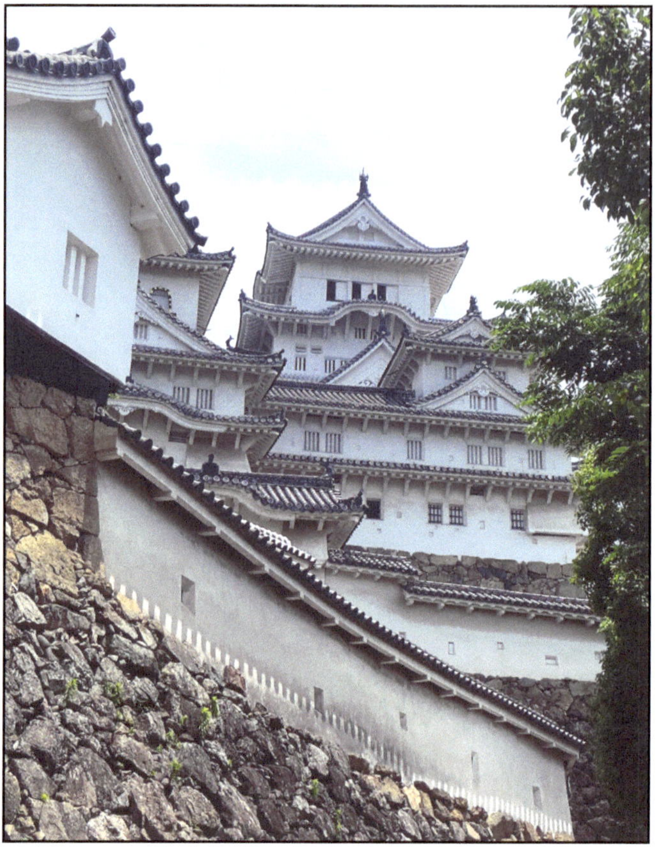

Figure 6.1: Himeji Castle, 1601–1613, Himeji, photo by author.

built quickly, and sited on plains or small hills rather than the earlier practice of building mountain strongholds. Starting with Azuchi, these new types of castles served as more than just military fortifications; they were also administrative centers and residences. From 1596 to 1615, nearly 100 major castles were constructed, many of which rivaled or exceeded the largest castles of medieval Europe.[5]

One of the few extant castles from this period is Himeji (nicknamed White Heron Castle; Figure 6.1), most of which was built in 1601–1613 under the supervision of Ikeda Terumasa (1565–1613).[6] Himeji was one of a number of castles, along with Nobunaga's Azuchi, where the engineering expertise of the Aso family of masons can be seen in the intricately fitted massive stone walls.[7] Thousands of laborers were needed to construct these walls. Within the inner citadel (*honmaru*), one large donjon (*tenshu* or keep) and three additional donjons are connected by parapets and grouped on a square plan. The main donjon is 152 feet (46.3 m) high, and the greater part of the castle covers an area of 2 million square feet (200,000 m^2). A labyrinth of twisting paths on an irregular spiral plan

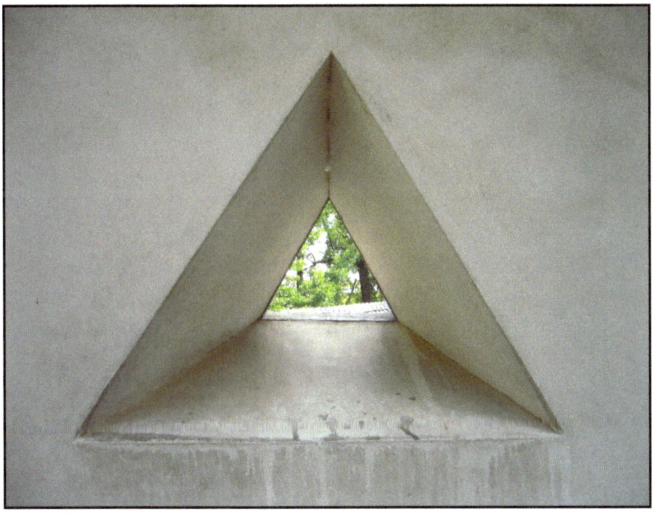

Figure 6.2: Detail of triangular opening in stone wall, Himeji Castle, photo by author.

prevented attackers from easily entering the fortress. Narrow cuts in the walls in the shapes of circles, triangles, and rectangles (Figure 6.2) that widen toward the outside enabled defenders to shoot arrows or fire muskets while making it difficult for attackers to fire back. The main donjon is structured around two colossal pillars, extending from the basement to the upper seventh floor, much like the central pillars of pagodas, which provide stability during earthquakes. The gray tile roofs are embellished with white plaster, and decorative tiles in the shape of *shachi*, creatures with tiger faces and fish bodies, are affixed to the main ridge ends.[8] The architecture thus combines defensive features with expressions of military strength.

Rooms in the castles have distinct functions, and included audience halls and other public spaces. The Kano ateliers were commissioned to produce works for these interiors as well as for temple buildings and the residences of the wealthy—these range from ink paintings that emphasize the expressive nature of line to sliding doors and folding screens painted in heavy mineral pigments on gold leaf. One innovative master of composition and technique was Kano Eitoku (1543–1590), Motonobu's grandson (see Chapter 5). Nobunaga commissioned Eitoku and his studio to produce monumental paintings for Azuchi Castle, with symbols of power such as dragons and tigers, legendary sages, and large trees stretching across sliding doors and screens, surrounded by sweeping areas of gold leaf.

The castle was destroyed in 1582 but a folding screen of Chinese lions (*karashishi*; Figure 6.3) provides an example of Eitoku's work. There is little indication of spatial depth in these paintings; instead, forms fill the foreground, brushwork emphasizes the predominance of line, and gold leaf reflects and enhances light, as seen in Eitoku's *Cypress Trees Screens* (Figure 6.4).[9] Monumental

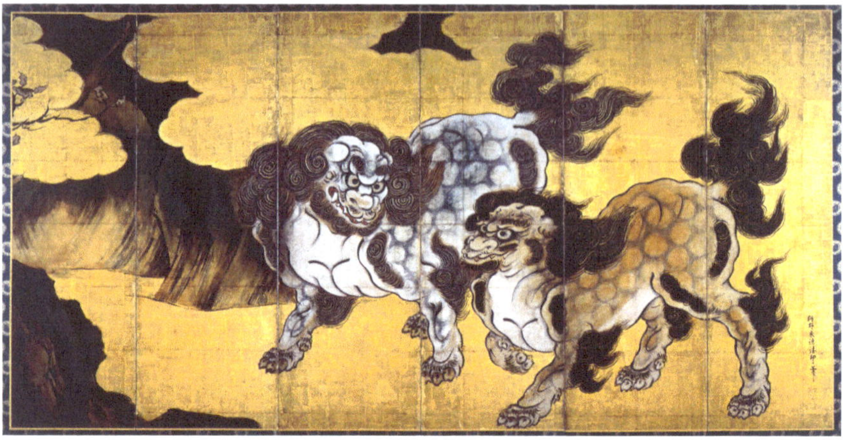

Figure 6.3: Chinese lions (*karashishi*), Kano Eitoku, second half of sixteenth-century, folding screen, color, gold leaf, and ink on paper, Museum of the Imperial Collections, Tokyo, Wikimedia Commons.

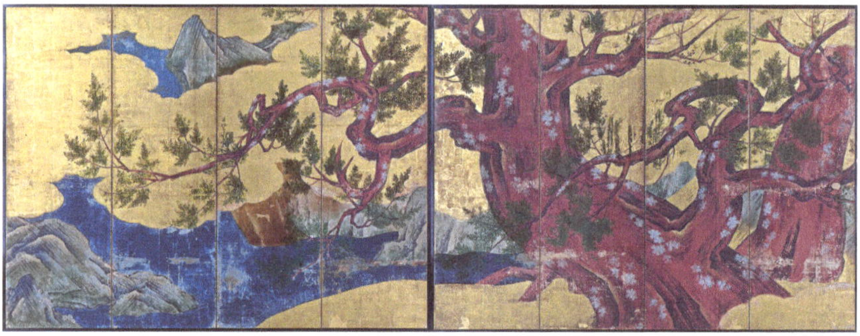

Figure 6.4: *Cypress Trees Screens*, Kano Eitoku, c. 1590, pair of folding screens, color and gold leaf on paper, Tokyo National Museum, Wikimedia Commons.

paintings like these were displayed in public areas such as reception halls, while the art in private rooms tended toward ink-and-color landscapes and more intimate subjects such as birds and flowers. Eitoku's compositional strategies served to demonstrate to visitors Nobunaga's own sense of his power, aesthetic taste, and cultural sophistication.

Eitoku's student Kano Sanraku (1559–1635) carried the monumental style into the next century, but there were also painters who worked outside the Kano ateliers (though many of these were Kano-trained or influenced by Kano painting). Hasegawa Tōhaku (1539–1610) drew on the ink paintings of the Muromachi period as well as the work of Eitoku for his own monumental works, such as the *Pine Forest* pair of folding screens (Figure 6.5). He used ink wash and increasingly darker strokes of ink to suggest a forest in the mist, typical of mountainous areas in Japan. The asymmetrically placed pines and large areas of negative space recall

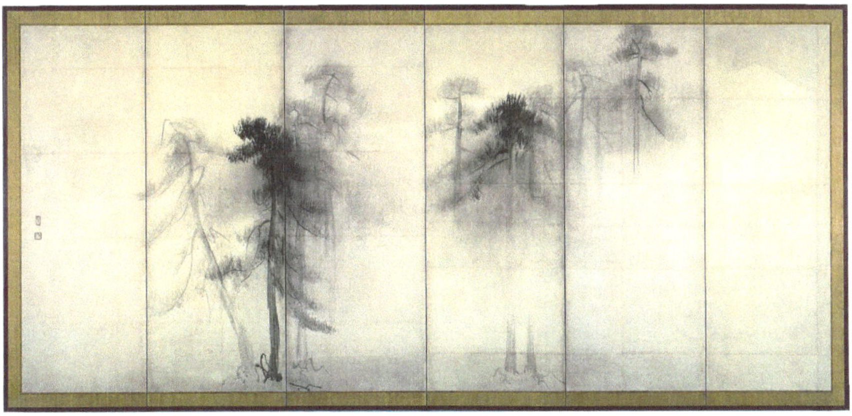

Figure 6.5: *Pine Forest*, Hasegawa Tōhaku, second half of sixteenth century, left half of a pair of folding screens, ink on paper, Tokyo National Museum, Wikimedia Commons.

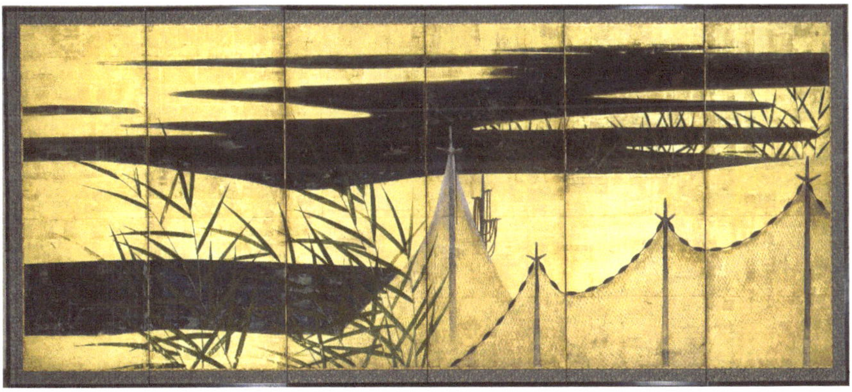

Figure 6.6: *Drying Fishnets in the Four Seasons*, attributed to Kaihō Yūshō, c. 1610, one of a pair of folding screens, ink, color, and gold on paper, Brooklyn Museum, Creative Commons.

Muromachi ink painting, but the large multiple-panel format is characteristically late sixteenth century. Kaihō Yūsho (1533–1615) came from a samurai family, trained as a Zen monk, and was a student of Kano Motonobu (Figure 6.6). In a work attributed to Yūsho, *Drying Fishnets in the Four Seasons*, the painter maintained the flattening of space and lack of depth typical of Momoyama painting but drew upon the Chinese theme of "Fishing Village in Evening Glow," part of the "Eight Views of the Xiao and Xiang Rivers." To this was added a sequence of grasses from early spring's greening to winter's dying, and an asymmetrical placement of forms.[10] This use of asymmetry and flattened space combined with lavish gold and a trend toward mundane subjects continued into the seventeenth century, as seen in the *Crows* folding screens from the early seventeenth century (Figure 6.7).[11]

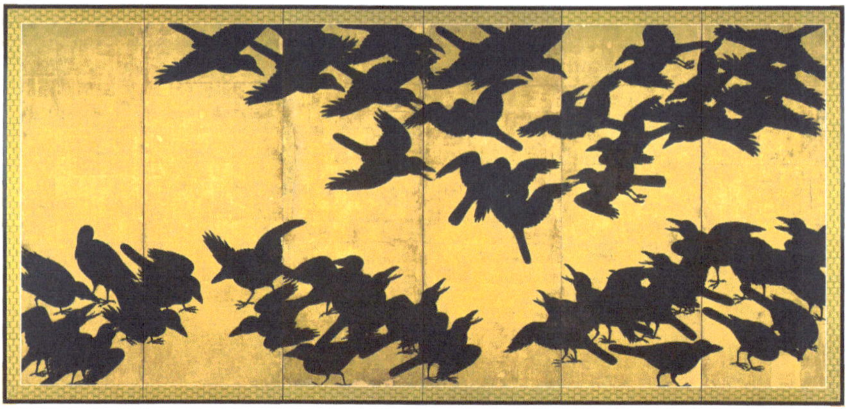

Figure 6.7: *Crows*, artist unknown, early seventeenth century, pair of six-panel screens, ink and gold on paper, Seattle Art Museum.

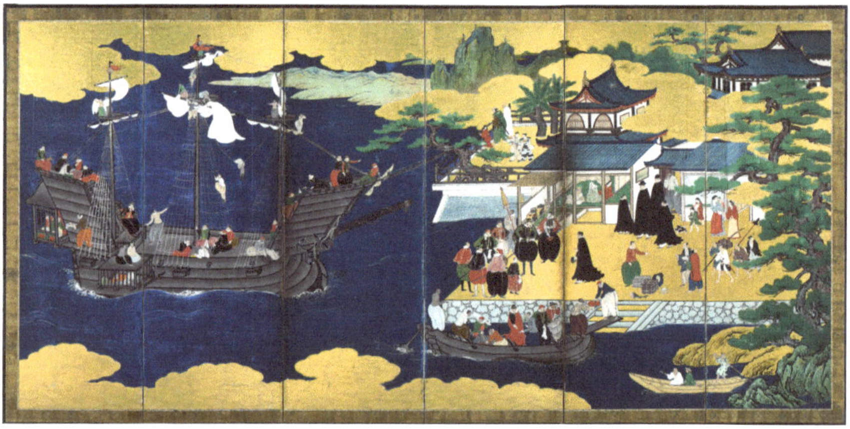

Figure 6.8: Nanban screen, attributed to Kano Sanraku, early seventeenth century, pair of folding screens, ink, gold, and colors on silk, Suntory Museum of Art, Tokyo, Wikimedia Commons.

Genre scenes and scenes in and around the capital of Kyoto (*rakuchū rakugaizu*) were also popular subjects of lavishly created folding screens. Instead of representations of the world of suffering, there was now an interest in scenes of daily life, including foreigners (both Chinese and European) and imports from Europe. Figure 6.8, attributed to Kano Sanraku, shows an aerial view of a Portuguese ship arriving in Japan. Among the figures depicted are Jesuit priests in their black robes, large-nosed Portuguese men wearing voluminous pants and colorful capes, and African men who may have been shipmates, servants, or slaves. Japanese also appear, including a samurai who watches the ship from his veranda. These types of screens attest to the curiosity and interest of Japanese in the new, the different, and the exotic.

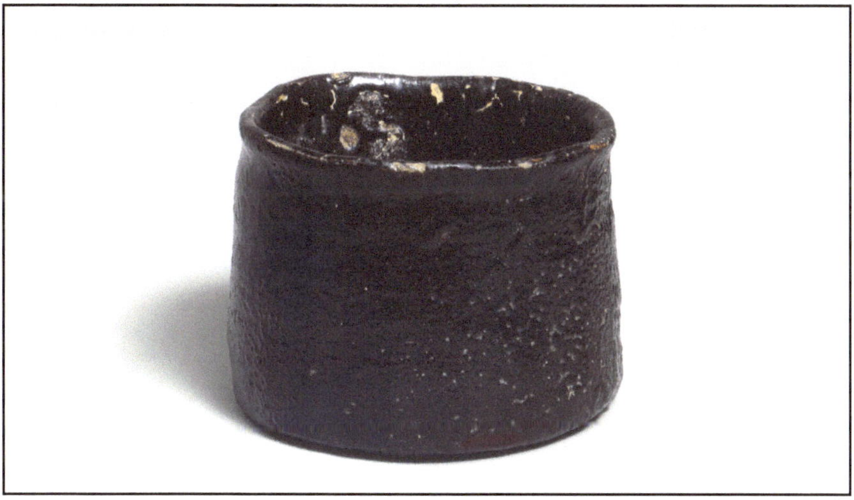

Figure 6.9: Black Seto "Iron Mallet" tea bowl, Mino ware, late sixteenth century, stoneware with black glaze, Metropolitan Museum of Art, New York, Public domain.

The daimyo who built these castles patronized the arts as a demonstration of their cultural competency. Indeed, it was considered de rigueur for leaders to patronize and even participate in Noh, linked verse (*renga*), and the practice of tea. By the sixteenth century, tea drinking had spread to all classes. The way of tea was an expression of wealth and power but also a vehicle of elite interaction, one of the central social rituals of warrior society. At the same time, it also transformed aesthetic tastes and cultural life as the practice of tea had spread to courtiers, merchants, and wealthy farmers through the course of the century.

Following the example of his teacher, Takeno Jōō (1502–1555), Sen no Rikyū (1522–1591) cultivated the aesthetic of the small tea room and modest utensils. Pottery should not be flawless; deliberate imperfections and the patina of age (*sabi*) were valued (Figure 6.9). While the setting was kept simple, it was a refined simplicity (*wabi*), with much attention given to the appearance of spontaneity and naturalness. The teahouse was approached through a garden, where a guest would walk over uneven and irregularly placed paving stones. Moss, ferns, small trees, and shrubs were sited irregularly and shaped to appear natural, although the naturalistic features were controlled by the gardener's choices in pruning and cleaning up (or not) the grounds of leaves and pine needles.

After walking through the tea garden (Figure 6.10), the guest entered the teahouse through a very low door, forcing them to bend over in the process.[12] Swords were left outside. There might be a flower arrangement or a ceramic vase as well as a hanging scroll in the alcove (Chapter 5, Figure 5.5). While the guests admired the choice of items placed there, the host prepared and poured boiling water over powdered green tea (matcha) in a tea bowl and then used a

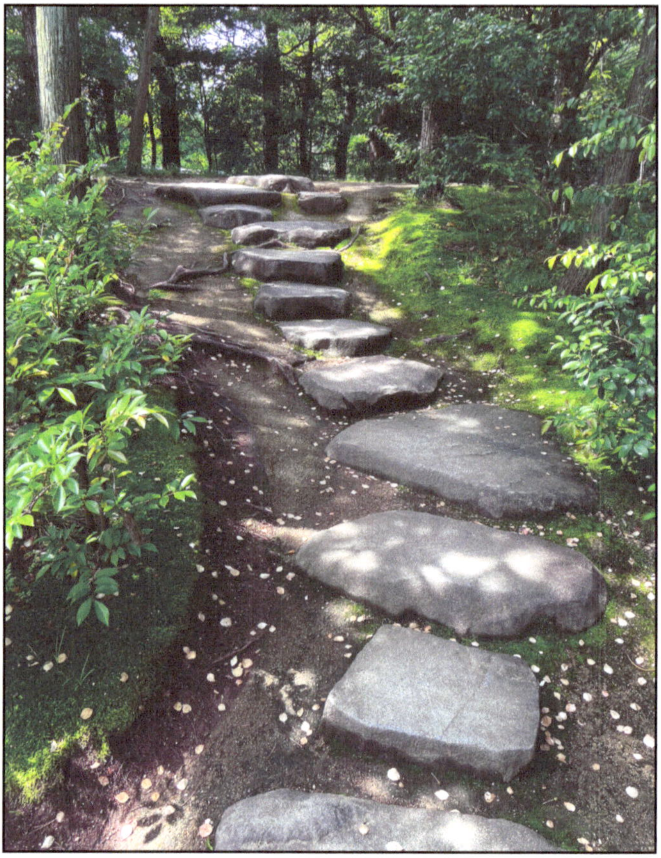

Figure 6.10: Tea garden, Kōkoen, Himeji, photo by author.

bamboo whisk to create a froth. Ideally, the tea ceremony was a quiet and overtly simple experience, not unlike performance art, in which the practice—that is, the experience—is the art. Each ceremony was unique and never to be repeated.[13] As Rikyū wrote, "It is simply to drink tea, knowing that if you just heat the water, your thirst is certain to be quenched. Nothing else is involved."[14]

Consumer demand for tea bowls led to new developments in ceramic production, with potters experimenting with techniques and designs. Imports from abroad also expanded the options for a tea practitioner. Tea practitioners in the late sixteenth century had a variety of choices, including Korean celadons and glazed stoneware, Chinese celadons and porcelain, and pottery from Southeast Asia. During the period of Hideyoshi's failed military invasions of the Korean peninsula in 1592–1598, Korean potters were brought back to Japan, where they developed new kilns.[15]

Bizen and Shigaraki wares, mentioned in Chapter 5, were now produced as tea bowls, flower vessels, and water jars, in addition to their previous use as storage

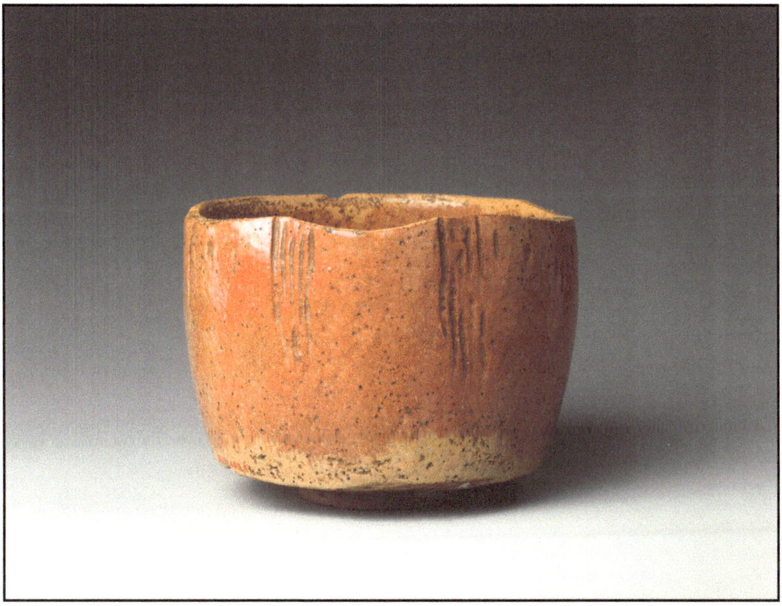

Figure 6.11: Red Raku tea bowl, style of Hon'ami Kōetsu, eighteenth century, earthenware with red slip under clear lead glaze, Metropolitan Museum of Art, New York, Public domain.

jars. These wares were wheel-thrown and unglazed, relying on the kiln's heat to bring out the natural ash glaze. Mino and Seto kilns drew on Chinese ceramic traditions for styles such as Yellow Seto but incorporated other techniques and styles, such as green copper accents and Korean conical shapes for tea bowls. Black Seto, Shino, and Oribe were also popular during this period. Bowls might be wheel-thrown or drape-molded and then glazed. The ware now known as Raku was hand-built from a sandy clay, finished with a lead-based glaze, and fired at low temperatures (Figure 6.11).[16]

As the practice of tea spread, professional tea masters made their living instructing those from the highest ranks of the military to merchants and wealthy farmers. Rikyū was tea master for both Nobunaga and Hideyoshi, and Furuta Oribe (1543–1615) served under Ieyasu. Garden designers, carpenters, potters, metalworkers, bamboo artisans, and papermakers were all in high demand. For participants in a tea ceremony, enjoyment was derived from the participatory nature of the practice, in which some of the more rigid social barriers were temporarily set aside and guests could share in the appreciation of utensils, tea bowls, flower arrangements, hanging scrolls, and other elements of the ceremony.

During this period women began wearing their hair and a corded obi in the Ming Chinese style and began to use cotton and silk for *kosode*, the predecessor of the kimono. New fabrics for both Noh costumes and women's wear included

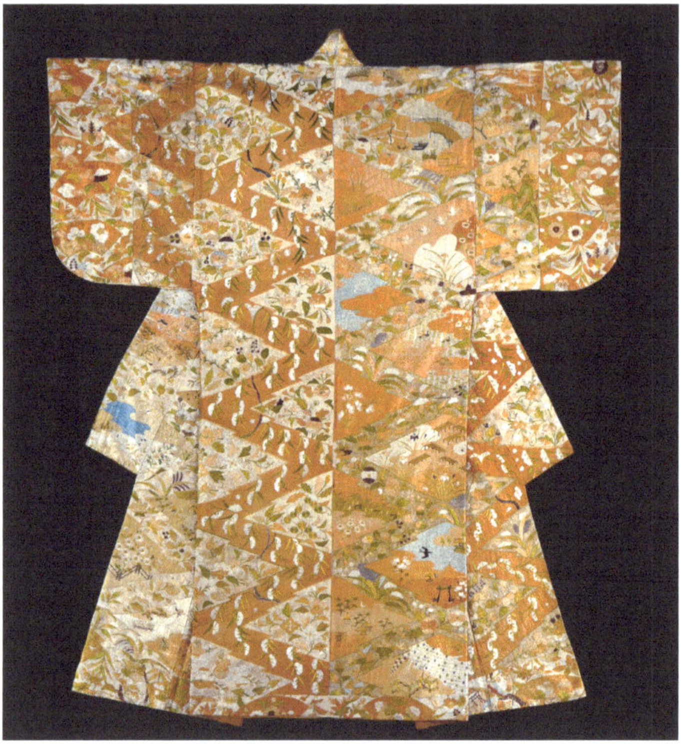

Figure 6.12: Noh costume (*nuihaku*), sixteenth century, silk with resist dyeing, impressed gold leaf, and embroidery, Art Institute of Chicago, Public domain.

techniques such as embroidery; pasted metallic leaf; hand-painted, raised designs; resist dyeing; and tie-dye (Figure 6.12).[17] Among the developments in military clothing was the *tōsei gusoku* armor (literally, "modern equipment"; Figure 6.13), constructed using large sheets of iron or tiers of lames, with "silver leaf, white satin, red woolen cloth . . . white silk lacing. . . and details in *maki-e* lacquer."[18] As seen in the portrait of Honda Tadakatsu (Figure 6.14), helmets also became more flamboyant, with the use of materials such as bear fur and unusual shapes such as antlers.

In 1591, Toyotomi Hideyoshi ordered samurai to move into the castle towns, putting them on stipends and curbing their independence. This led to a consolidation of people into towns, which grew into large urban areas. Hideyoshi died in 1598, but from his deathbed he attempted to secure the succession of his five-year-old son, Hideyori (1593–1615), by appointing a group of five elders to act as guardians. One of these guardians, Tokugawa Ieyasu, challenged and then defeated his opponents at the battle of Sekigahara in 1600. What followed was the domination of the Tokugawa into the nineteenth century and the beginnings of a new age for Japan.

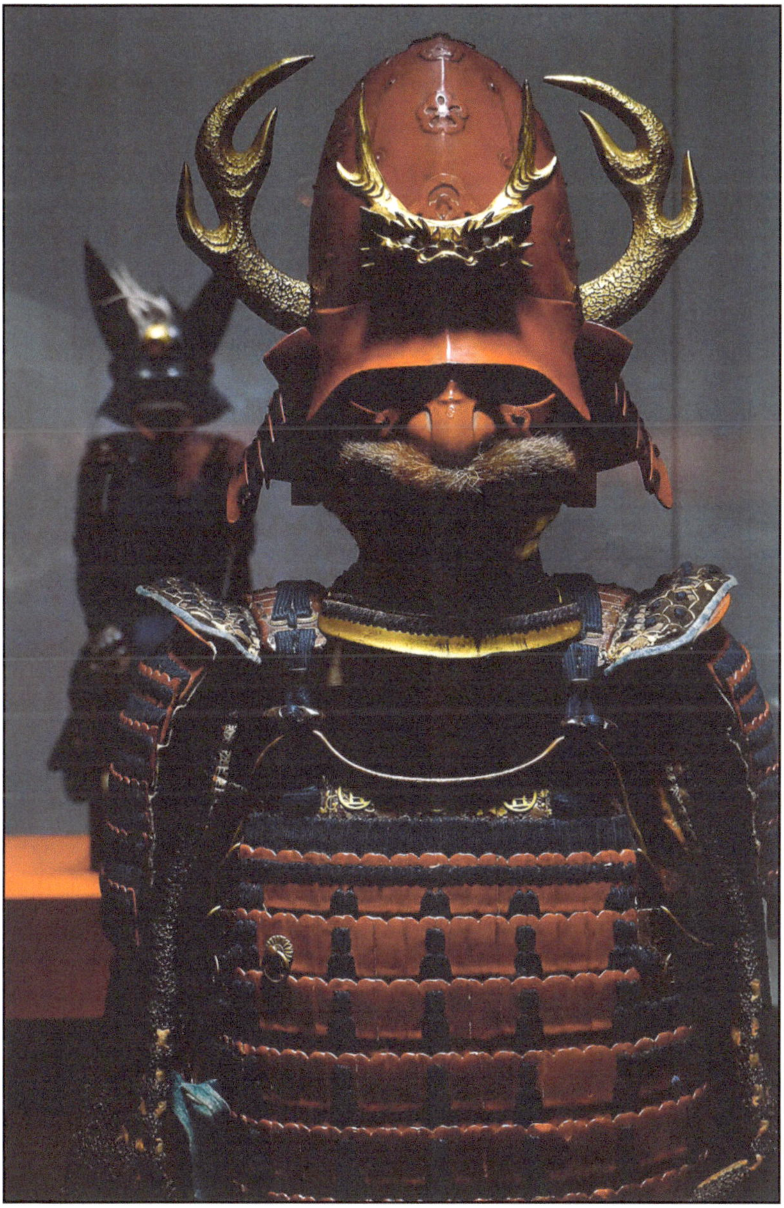

Figure 6.13: *Tōsei gusoku* armor, sixteenth to early seventeenth century, red-lacquered blue-stringed suit, iron, copper, silk, leather, and wool, Suntory Museum of Art, Tokyo, Wikimedia Commons.

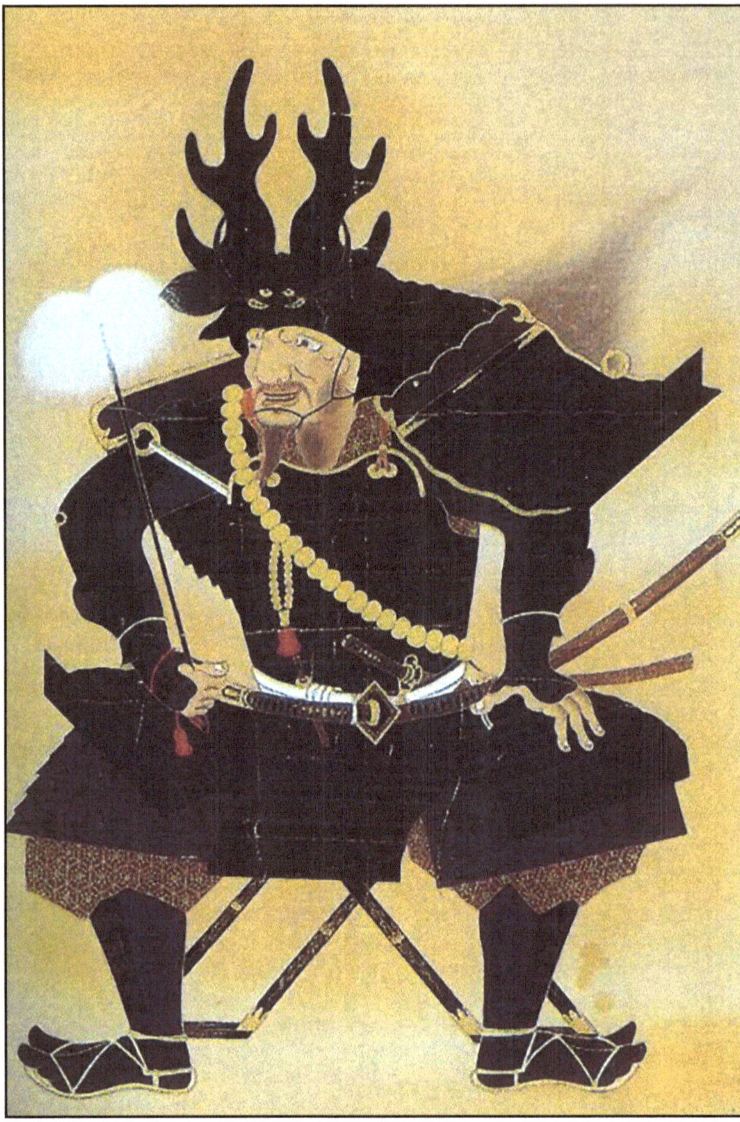

Figure 6.14: Portrait of Honda Tadakatsu (1548–1610), early seventeenth century, hanging scroll, ink and color on silk, Honda Takayuki Collection, Tokyo. Wikimedia Commons.

NOTES

[1] Michael Cooper, *They Came to Japan: An Anthology of European Reports on Japan, 1543–1640* (Berkeley: University of California, 1965), 134.

[2] The European cooking technique of coating food in a flour mixture and deep frying in oil developed into one of Japan's most popular dishes: tempura.

[3] Charles Holcombe, *A History of East Asia: From the Origins of Civilization to the Twenty-First Century*, 2nd ed. (Cambridge: Cambridge University Press, 2017), 187.

[4] The trees were planted on the site after Hideyoshi's death. JAANUS (Japanese Architecture and Art Net Users System), comp. Dr. Mary Neighbour Parent, s.v. "[Momoyama jidai]," accessed March 7, 2025, https://www.aisf.or.jp/~jaanus/.

[5] William H. Coaldrake, *Architecture and Authority in Japan*, Nissan Institute/Routledge Japanese Studies (London: Routledge, 1996), https://doi.org/10.4324/9780203042830, 106–107.

[6] Much of the technical information about the castle comes from Coaldrake, *Architecture and Authority in Japan*, 120–129.

[7] A detailed explanation of how these walls were constructed without mortar can be found in Coaldrake, *Architecture and Authority in Japan*, 115–117.

[8] The plaster is a decorative feature that also serves to secure the tiles in high winds. Coaldrake, *Architecture and Authority in Japan*, 128.

[9] The Cypress Screens painting may originally have been sliding doors, later remounted as folding screens. See "Cypress Trees screen," e-Museum, National Treasures & Important Cultural Properties of National Institutes for Cultural Heritage, Japan, accessed May 11, 2024, https://emuseum.nich.go.jp/detail?langId=en&webView=&content_base_id=100144&content_part_id=0&content_pict_id=0.

[10] See *Drying Fishnets in the Four Seasons*, Brooklyn Museum, accessed May 11, 2024, https://www.brooklynmuseum.org/opencollection/objects/3668.

[11] For details of this work and others from the seventeenth to nineteenth century, see "Investigating Japan's Edo Avant Garde" on the Smithsonian's website: https://investigatingedo.asia.si.edu/art/crows/ (accessed May 11, 2024).

[12] The garden shown here is at Kōkōen, a recreation of an Edo-period daimyo's garden next to Himeji, based on archeological excavations of the site.

[13] Thanks to Matthew Welch, Deputy Director and Chief Curator of the Minneapolis Institute of Art, for this insight during a filmed interview in 2022.

[14] *The One-Page Testament of Rikyū*, quoted in Stephen Addiss, Gerald Groemer, and J. Thomas Rimer, *Traditional Japanese Arts and Culture: An Illustrated Sourcebook* (Honolulu: University of Hawai'i Press, 2006), 134; see also Dennis Hirota, ed., *Wind in the Pines: Classic Writings of the Way of Tea as a Buddhist Path* (Fremont, CA: Asian Humanities Press, 1995), 245.

[15] Morgan Pitelka, *Handmade Culture: Raku Potters, Patrons, and Tea Practitioners in Japan* (Honolulu: University of Hawai'i Press, 2005), 5–7.

[16] Pitelka, *Handmade Culture*, 1–8.

[17] Liza Dalby, *Kimono: Fashioning Culture* (New Haven: Yale University Press, 1993), 38; Tsuji Nobuo, *History of Art in Japan*, trans. Nicole Coolidge Rousmaniere (New York: Columbia University Press, 2019), 288.

[18] Yoshiaki Shimizu, ed., *Japan, The Shaping of Daimyo Culture 1185–1868* (Washington, DC: National Gallery of Washington, 1988), 237–240.

7

A Flourishing of Urban Culture

Early to Mid-Tokugawa Period (1603–1800)

an old pond...
a frog leaps in,
the sound of water
— Bashō[1]

The *haikai* poems of Matsuo Bashō (1644–1694) are emblematic of a new age with fresh approaches to poetry. *Haikai* (popular linked verse) derived from the 5/7/5 poetry form known as *hokku*, which functioned as the first part of a longer poem; *haikai* would later be known as *haiku*. These short poems captured a slice of life and the sensibilities of the moment but could also be humorous, paradoxical, and, above all, fresh and new.[2]

After prevailing at Sekigahara in 1600, Tokugawa Ieyasu was granted the title of shogun in 1603 and established his administrative center (shogunate; *bakufu*) in Edo (present-day Tokyo); this ushered in the Tokugawa or Edo period (1603–1868). The shogunate adopted Neo-Confucianism, focused on maintaining order and peace, and inaugurated a system that divided the populace into status groups: warriors at the apex, followed by farmers, artisans, and merchants.[3] Education spread, with domain schools for samurai and temple schools for commoners. Christianity was deemed a threat to the shogunate, and by 1639 the Spanish and Portuguese were expelled. The Dutch were allowed to remain, confined to the small artificial island of Deshima in Nagasaki harbor. Contacts continued with China, Korea, and the Ryūkyū Islands,[4] but after 1635 Japanese were banned from travel abroad.

The arts flourished in response to urbanization, rising literacy, and consumer demand for the new and different. Popular themes included humor and play, the juxtaposition of the classics with the contemporary, and covert hints of opposition to the ruling order. Chinese styles continued to be integrated into Japanese arts, as the admiration for China remained strong.

From rapid urbanization came the "tripartite metropolis (*santo*)," a metropolis of three cities, which still exists along the Tōkaidō route from Tokyo to Kyoto.[5] The shogunate instituted the *sankin kōtai* (alternate attendance) system, in which daimyo were required to maintain a residence in Edo; they spent alternate years in Edo and in their home domains, moving back and forth between their castle towns and the capital in grand processions. Their families remained in Edo, more or less as hostages, assuring that no daimyo would rise up from the provinces against the Tokugawa. One outcome of this arrangement was that information, technologies, and the arts were transmitted back and forth between cities and provinces, enriching Japanese culture.

Within a century after 1603, Edo was the largest city in the world, with a population of around 1 million people, as high as 1.2 million by 1750. By 1721, Japan had an urban network of more than thirty cities of over 25,000 people. In contrast, London's population by 1760 was around 740,000.[6] These large urban populations required food, clothing, household goods, and a multitude of items for daily living. They also provided a market for entertainment and services. Edo became a city of consumption. Kyoto was a center for luxury goods; Osaka, the city of commerce.

Kabuki theater was born in the seventeenth century.[7] Puppet theater thrived during this period, notably with the plays of Osaka playwright Chikamatsu Monzaemon (1653–1724). Osaka's Ihara Saikaku (1642–1693) wrote witty novels about contemporary life. The pleasure districts such as Yoshiwara in Edo and Shimabara in Kyoto became islands of escapism from the strict regulations of daily life but with their own rules of engagement.[8]

Shoguns employed architecture to both intimidate and impress. Ninomaru Palace within Kyoto's Nijō Castle (1624–1626), demonstrated authority and power in a fortified palatial complex (Figures 7.1 and 7.2) that served as the Tokugawa Kyoto headquarters.[9] The architecture stresses bright colors, ornamentation, images of birds and flowers, and roof tiles with the Tokugawa family crest. The palace was designed in an updated version of *shoin-zukuri* (see Chapter 5). Tatami mats were the unit of measurement for room sizes in the *shoin* style.[10] Earlier features such as bay windows with writing shelves, tokonoma (alcoves), and staggered shelves were also integral to the style.

Shogun Iemitsu (1604–1651) commissioned Kano Tan'yū (1602–1674) and others to paint the sliding doors and walls (called collectively *shōhekiga*) of Ninomaru Palace. The leading Kano painter of his day, Tan'yū designed a theme of large and imposing pine trees stretching across wall surfaces and backed by glittering gold (Figure 7.3). Tan'yū's innovations included the extension of the pines from lower panels into higher ones, to create a more imposing image.[11]

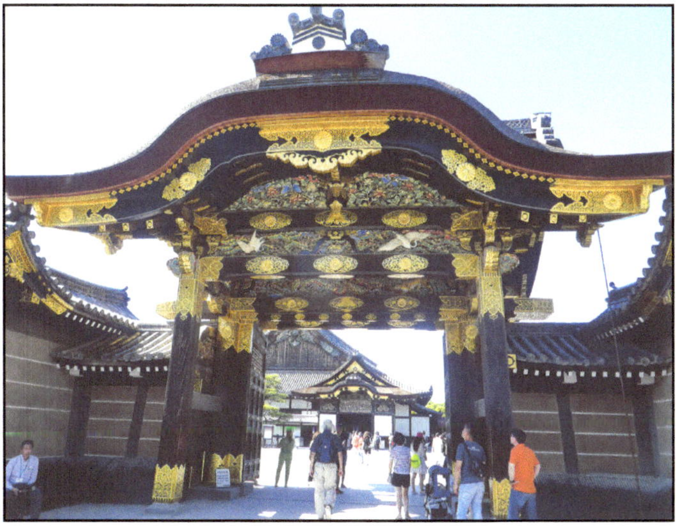

Figure 7.1: Nijō Castle entrance gate, Kyoto, 1624–1626, photo by author.

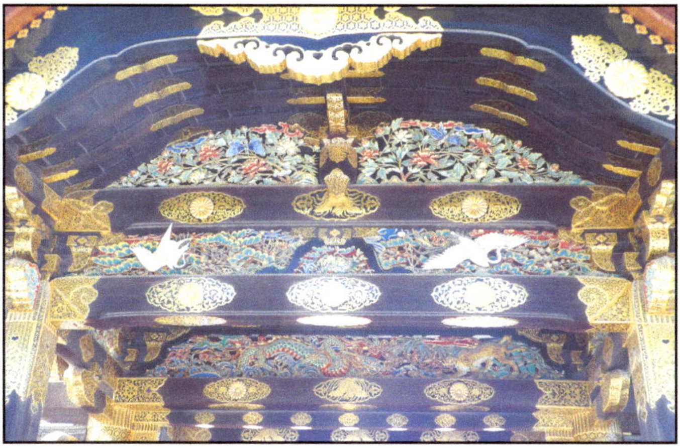

Figure 7.2: Detail of Nijō Castle entrance gate, photo by author.

Ancient pines, gnarled yet alive, convey multilayered meaning, including longevity, immortality, and "uprightness."[12]

Another innovation was to integrate the surrounding garden into the theme. Tan'yū likely worked with the tea master Kobori Enshū (1579–1647) on this design (Figure 7.4). When a room's sliding doors were opened to the garden, the pine trees, rocks, and water outside echoed the paintings inside, knitting all into one thematic whole. This type of garden design became prevalent for daimyo residences.

The daimyo garden contrasts with the dry landscape garden, whose popularity continued as well. Ryōanji in Kyoto is one of the most visited (Figure 7.5); like

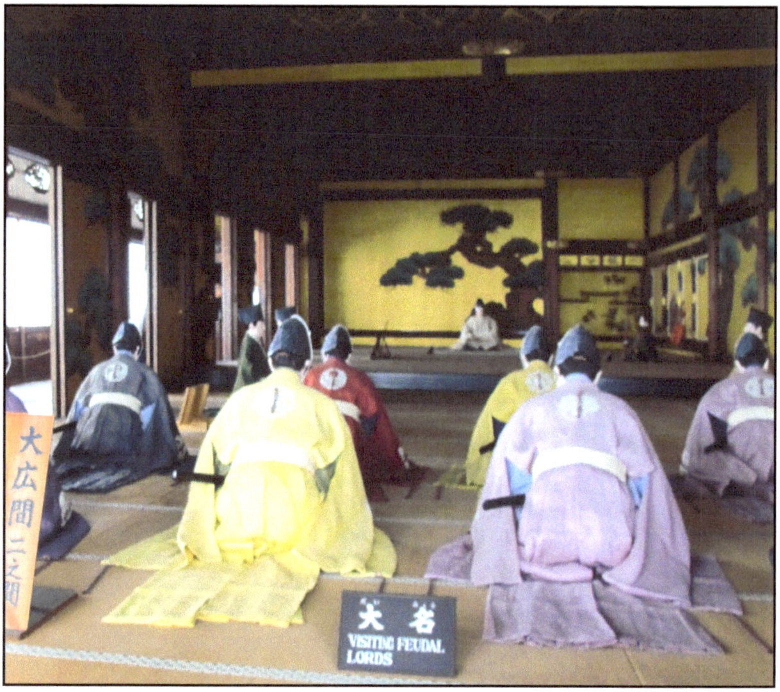

Figure 7.3: Recreation of Ninomaru Palace interior, *shoin-zukuri* style of architecture, Nijō Castle, Kyoto, Wikimedia Commons.

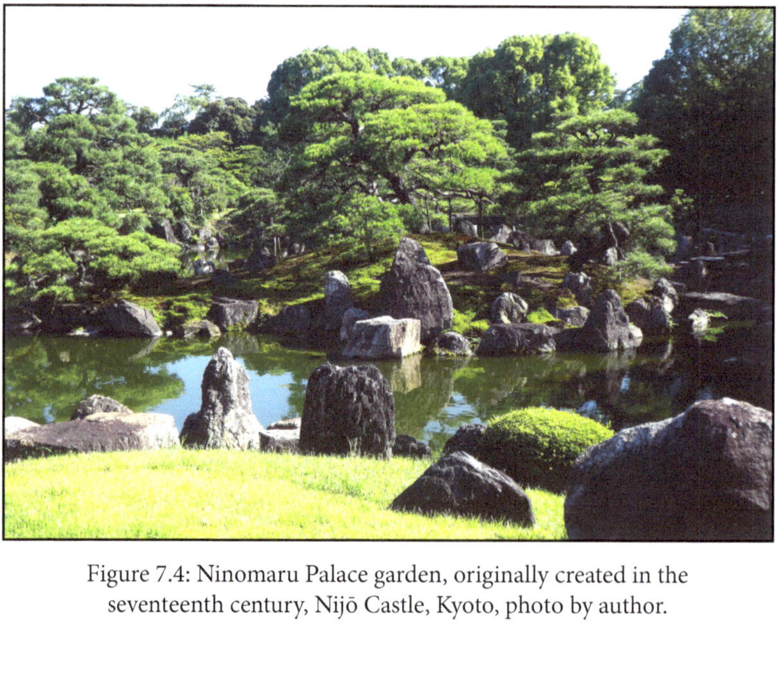

Figure 7.4: Ninomaru Palace garden, originally created in the seventeenth century, Nijō Castle, Kyoto, photo by author.

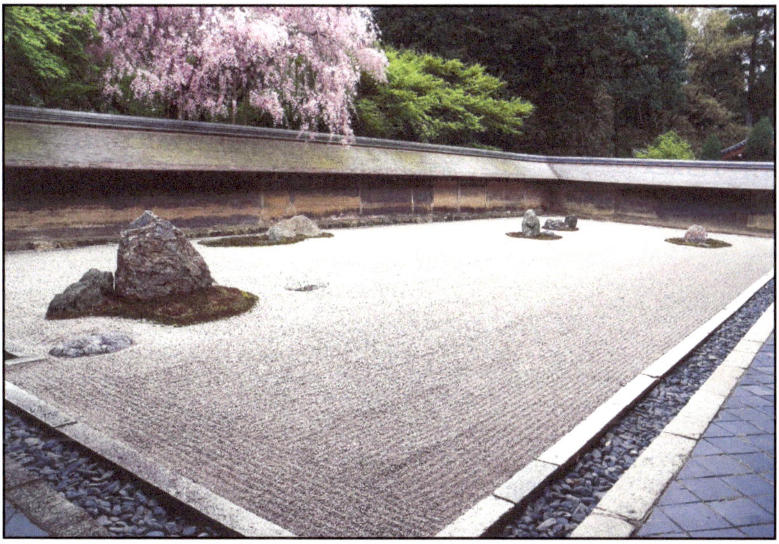

Figure 7.5: Ryōanji dry landscape garden, earliest descriptions date to 1680s, Ryōanji, Kyoto, Wikimedia Commons.

many dry landscape gardens that exist today, it was redesigned over the years.[13] The earliest descriptions of Ryōanji date to the 1680s, when it had nine stones. The present-day garden has fifteen.[14]

The Old Plum Tree (Figure 7.6) by Kano Sansetsu (1590–1651) illustrates early Tokugawa monumental painting. A huge tree in the foreground dominates the composition, anchored by large rocks on either side and a gold-leaf background that reflects candle or lamp light. The ancient plum tree blooming at the start of spring is a symbol of fortitude, endurance, and rejuvenation.[15]

Perhaps the Kano school's most enduring legacy was its impact on the overall field of painting through the training of students. Pupils (*deshi*) learned through observation while doing chores and then through copying using *funpon* (copybooks).[16] Many painters—from *machi eshi* (town painters) to founders of new schools and styles—began their training with Kano teachers. Since painters often knew and influenced each other, there was much cross-fertilization.

Genre painting—images of daily life—became a prevalent theme. The six-fold *Hikone Screen* (Figure 7.7) is a precedent for ukiyo-e (literally, "pictures of the floating world"). The term dates to the late seventeenth century, intersecting the past—the Buddhist sense of a transient world of suffering (*ukiyo*)—with the present. Written with different characters, *ukiyo* at this time meant living for the moment, enjoying the pleasures of life in the here and now. On the screen, the old and the new intermingle: a blind musician and women play shamisen while others are engrossed in a board game against the background of a Chinese landscape; a long tobacco pipe on the floor reflects the custom of smoking tobacco, adopted

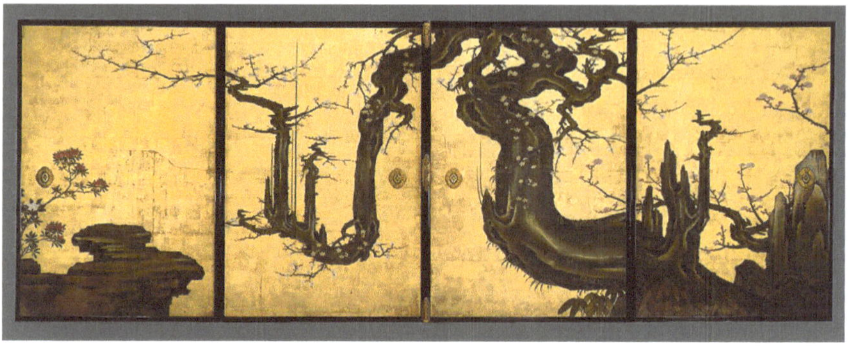

Figure 7.6: *The Old Plum Tree*, Kano Sansetsu, c. 1646, four sliding panels, ink, color, gold, and gold leaf on paper, Metropolitan Museum of Art, New York, Public domain.

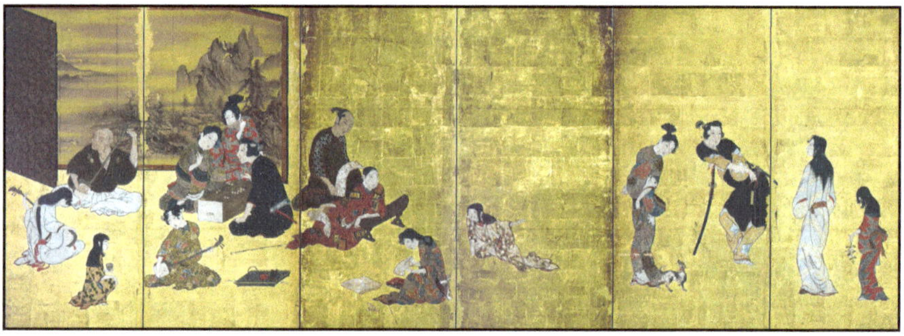

Figure 7.7: *Hikone Screen*, c. 1624–1644, folding screen, ink and color on paper with gold-leaf background, Hikone Castle Museum, Wikimedia Commons.

from the West; a woman on the right walks a small dog (likely imported from Europe). The setting in Kyoto's pleasure quarters juxtaposes the traditional theme of the Chinese Four Accomplishments theme (music, board games, calligraphy, and painting) with contemporary Japanese clothing styles. The *kosode* that had been the undergarment of Heian women (see Chapter 3) is now a fashionable item for both sexes, with a narrow obi (sash or belt) and colorful designs. Over the course of the century, techniques such as *yūzen* (resist dyeing) were developed, and silk became a canvas upon which artistic designs were created with embroidery, brocade, stamped foil, and other techniques.

Woodblock printmaking, a defining art of Tokugawa Japan, was central to a large print industry that included single-sheet prints and books of all types. This was a new phenomenon, and it happened surprisingly quickly—and with significant impact: no longer were printed materials read only by the educated elite. By the end of the 1600s, literacy had spread to nearly all status groups and professions, creating a mass audience for printed material.[17] By 1640 there were more than one hundred publishers in Kyoto, and by 1692 there were over seven thousand publications.[18] Through the distribution of this material, consumers

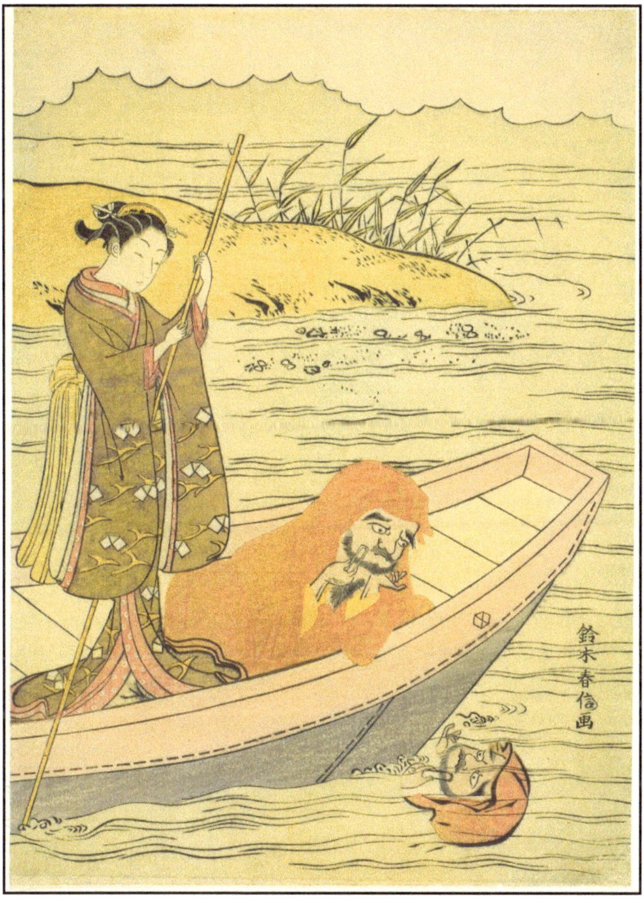

Figure 7.8: *Daruma Looking at His Reflection*, Suzuki Harunobu, c. 1762–1770, color woodblock print, Art Institute of Chicago, Public domain.

developed shared cultural knowledge, in which oblique references and playful twists on both premodern and contemporary culture were enjoyed by all.

An example of this playfulness is the *mitate* (double vision) of *Daruma Looking at His Reflection* (Figure 7.8).[19] Daruma (Bodhidharma) was the Indian monk credited with introducing Buddhism to China. It is said that he meditated for nine years, facing a cave wall in China. An image of Daruma (the sacred) juxtaposed with a courtesan (the profane) can be seen as a reference to the hardship of a courtesan's ten years of service in a brothel exceeding Daruma's nine years of meditation. The interpretation is supported by the word *daruma* being slang for a prostitute, and *darumaya* referring to a brothel.[20]

Printed materials like these were produced collaboratively, with the publisher overseeing the process—choosing the print designer, the carver, the printer, and

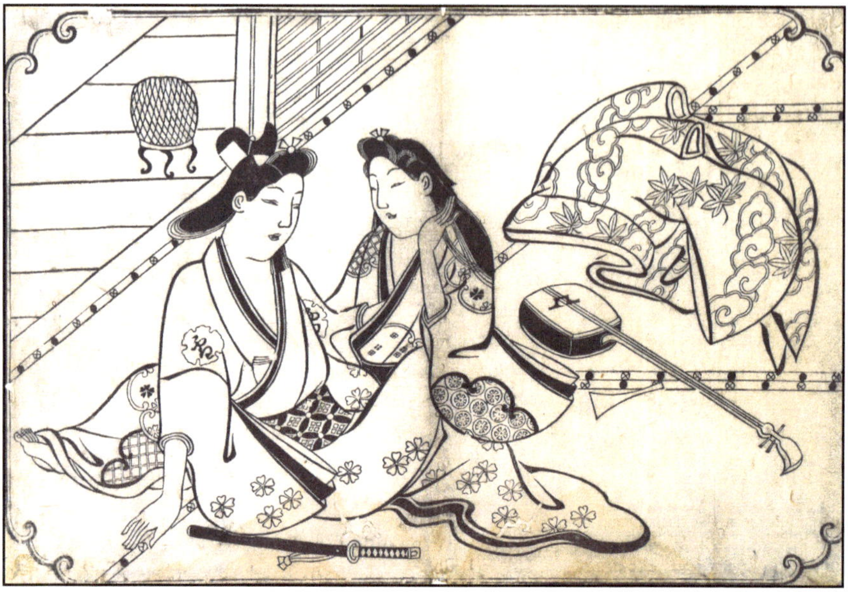

Figure 7.9: *Two Lovers*, Hishikawa Moronobu, c. 1675–1680, woodblock print, leaf from an album of *shunga*, Metropolitan Museum of Art, New York, Public domain.

production details such as paper quality and edition size.[21] They also took into account censorship laws, current fashions in clothing and hairstyles, and which courtesans or Kabuki actors were "in" at the moment. Commissions came from shops, theaters, and teahouses that wanted to advertise, or from private individuals, poetry clubs, or fan clubs for Kabuki actors.

Early prints were black and white illustrations, depicting Kabuki actors and courtesans of the pleasure quarters, notably Yoshiwara in Edo. Hishikawa Moronobu (1618–1694), trained in both Tosa and Kano styles, was perhaps the first print designer to sign his own work. He produced numerous book designs as well as erotic prints (called *shunga*, *warai-e* "laughing pictures," or *makura-e* in this period; Figure 7.9).[22] He was followed by designers of hand-colored prints such as Torii Kiyonobu (1664–1729), who produced prints of Kabuki actors (Figure 7.10) and Kaigetsudō Ando (fl. 1704–1714), known for his paintings and prints of courtesans. Actors and women of the pleasure quarters were fashion trendsetters; Ando's painting (Figure 7.11) shows the wide obi, tied in front, and the colorful designs of the evolving *kosode*.

Inspired by Chinese ceramics, Japanese artists developed overglaze multicolored enamel techniques for porcelain in Hizen province in the seventeenth century, and other similar techniques came from the Arita and Nabeshima kilns, such as underglaze cobalt-blue designs. Imari ware from Arita (Figure 7.12) was popular in Europe. In contrast, Nonomura Ninsei (active mid-seventeenth century) designed multicolored stoneware with designs that drew on *yamato-e*

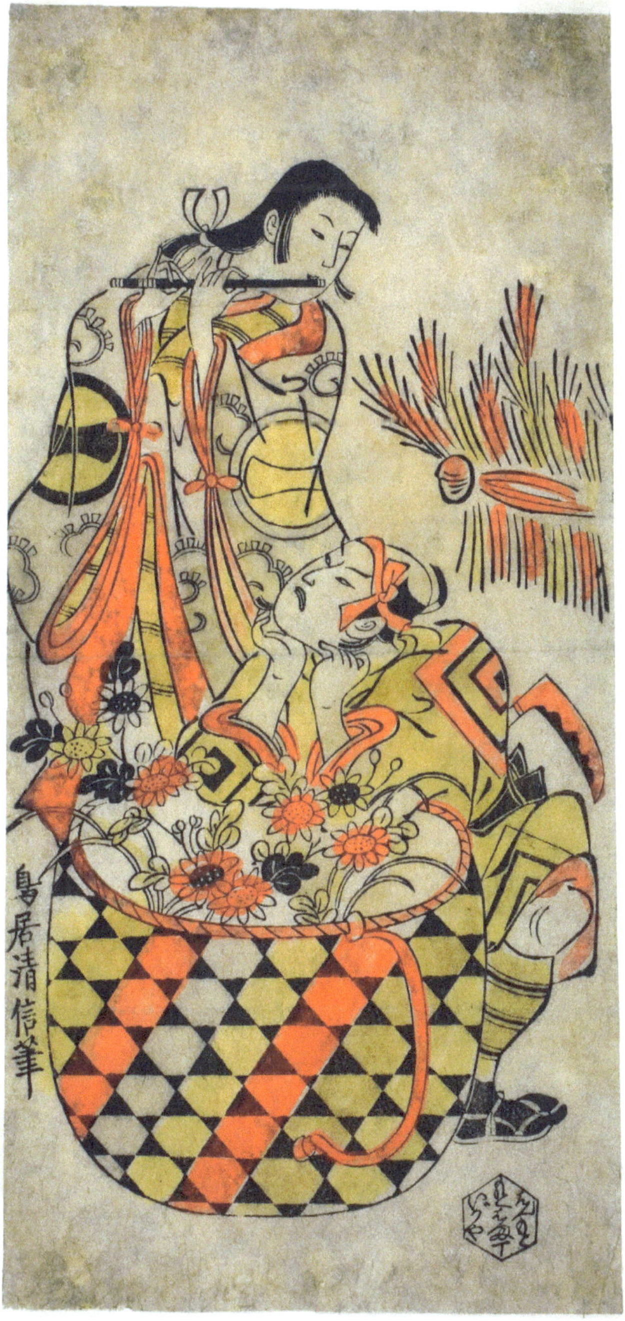

Figure 7.10: *The Actors Ichikawa Danjūrō II and Ichikawa Monnosuke I*, Torii Kiyonobu, 1715–1725, hand-colored woodblock print, Art Institute of Chicago, Public domain.

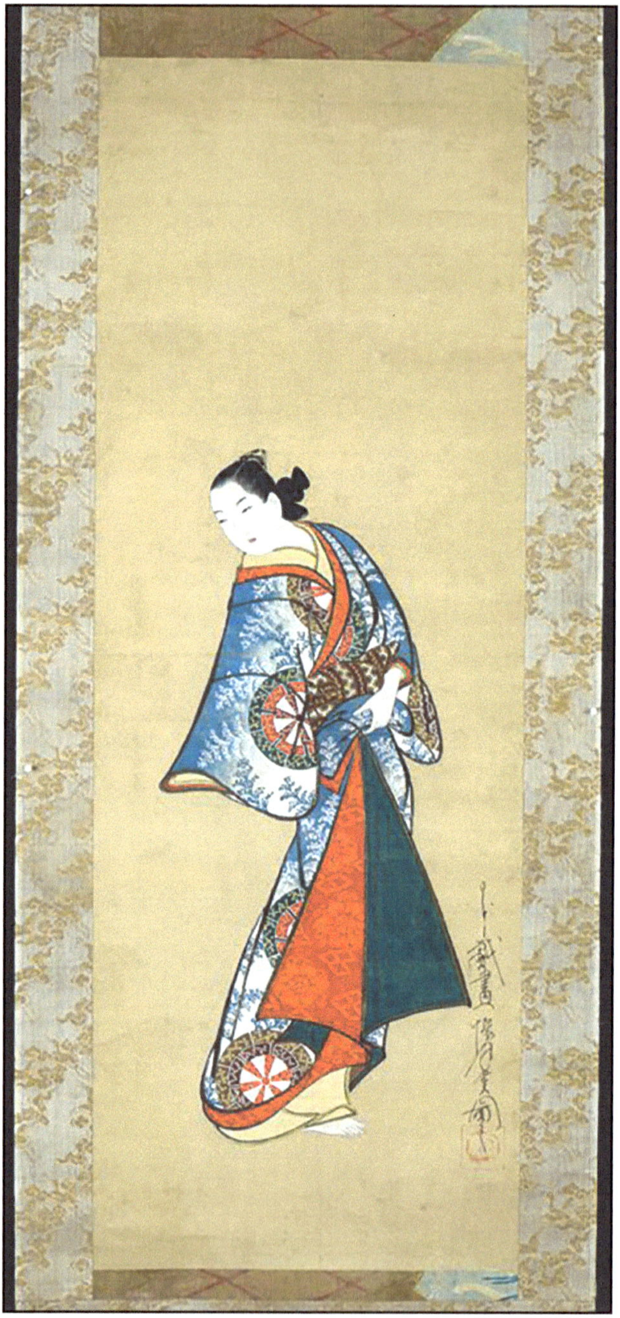

Figure 7.11: *Standing Courtesan in Kimono with Fern and Wheel Pattern*, Kaigetsudō Ando, c. 1710, hanging scroll, ink, color, gold, and shell white on paper, Minneapolis Institute of Art, Public domain.

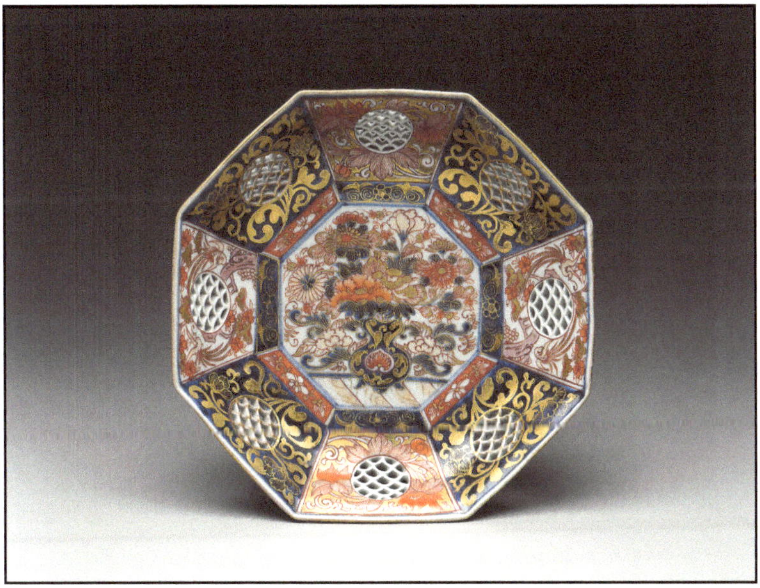

Figure 7.12: Imari plate, Hizen ware, c. 1770, made for the European market, porcelain with colored enamels over transparent glaze and gilded, Metropolitan Museum of Art, New York, Public domain.

themes or with a different twist on a common object, such as the incense box in Figure 7.13. His style was developed further by Ogata Kenzan (see below). Raku ware for the practice of tea also continued to be produced.

Kyoto was known for its fine ceramics, fans, textiles, lacquer, and paintings. There, the classical world of literature and poetry were reinvented by Hon'ami Kōetsu (1558–1637) and Tawaraya Sōtatsu (d. 1643) and their associates, who drew ideas from the Tosa school and Heian-period paintings. They collaborated on publications of prose, poetry, Noh texts, and Chinese literature and history, thus contributing to the shared cultural knowledge that is particular to this period (Figure 7.14). Kōetsu came from a family of sword connoisseurs and used his knowledge of lacquer, metal, and mother-of-pearl for designs and shapes that updated the imagery of Heian arts (Figure 7.15). He was also influential for his ceramics, such as low-temperature, lead-glazed tea bowls (Figure 7.16). He may have practiced tea and possibly was a disciple of Furuta Oribe, who in turn was a disciple of Rikyū.[23]

Sōtatsu began as a fan painter and was known for his use of visual and literary motifs. His *Waves at Matsushima* screens (Figures 7.17 and 7.18), like Sesshū's *Amanohashidate*, depict a *meisho*, a scenic spot with poetic and literary associations. Sōtatsu emphasized design elements, with pine trees, rocks, and sand bars cropped and seen from a high viewpoint, recalling the perspective of handscrolls. The islands are scattered asymmetrically across the picture plane, and

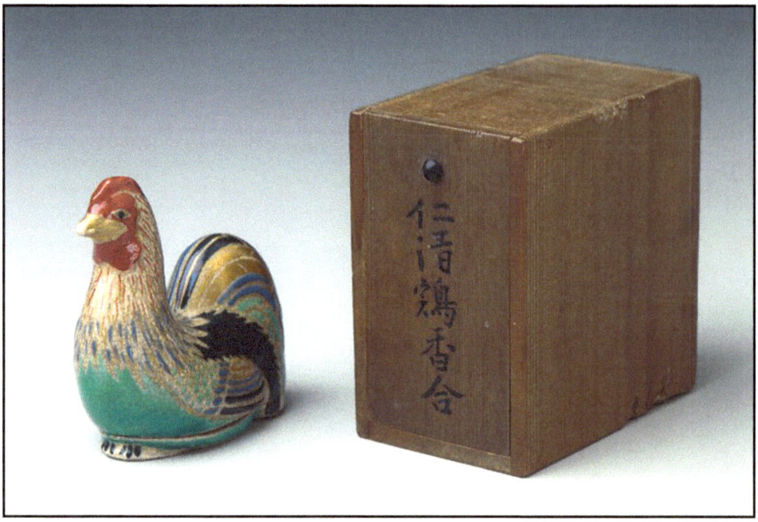

Figure 7.13: Incense box in the shape of a rooster, Nonomura Ninsei, c. 1665, Kyōyaki stoneware with overglaze enamels, Minneapolis Institute of Art, Public domain.

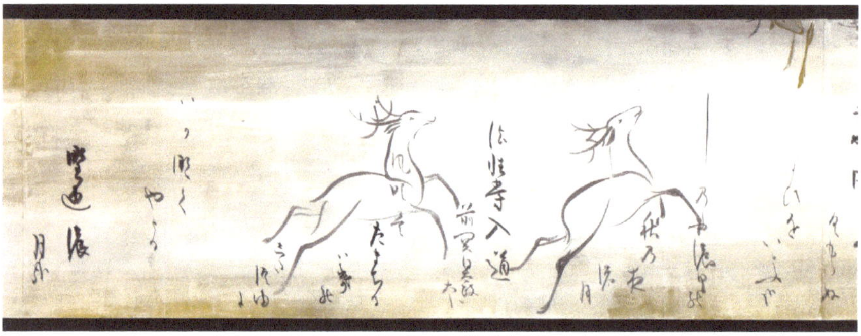

Figure 7.14: *Poem Scroll with Deer* (detail), Tawaraya Sōtatsu, 1610s, handscroll, ink, gold, and silver on paper, Seattle Art Museum.

negative spaces balance the positive shapes of trees and land. Undulating lines of ink alternate with gold to produce the impression of waves.

This artistic style became known as Rinpa (literally, "lineage of Kōrin"), named after Ogata Kōrin (1658–1716) who, along with his brother Kenzan (1663–1743), updated Sōtatsu's and Kōetsu's styles. The Ogata brothers' family owned a Kyoto shop known for luxury textiles. They understood the cultural interests of wealthy merchants, adapting and reinterpreting earlier designs and themes for textiles, ceramics, lacquer, paintings, and calligraphy. Kenzan brought painting and ceramics together with his innovative designs; notably, he signed his pieces, which was not contemporary practice (Figure 7.19).

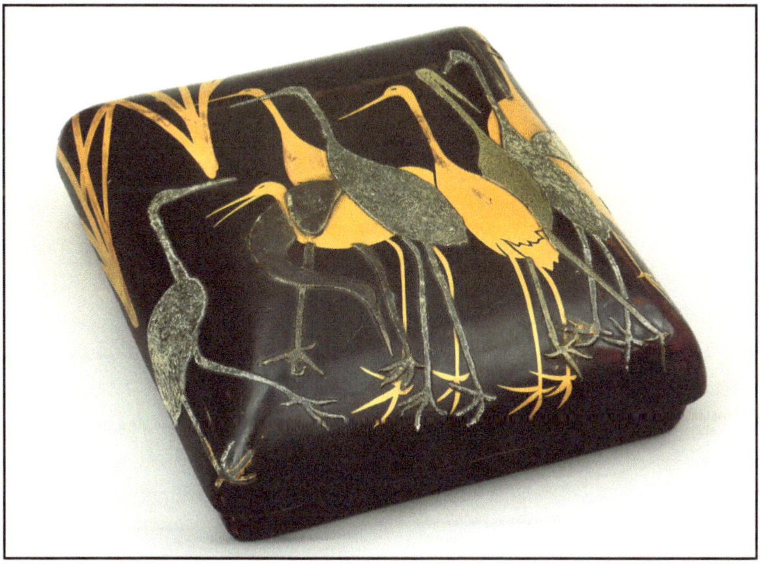

Figure 7.15: Writing box decorated with cranes in reeds, Hon'ami Kōetsu, early seventeenth century, black and gold lacquer on wood, lead and pewter plates, Seattle Art Museum.

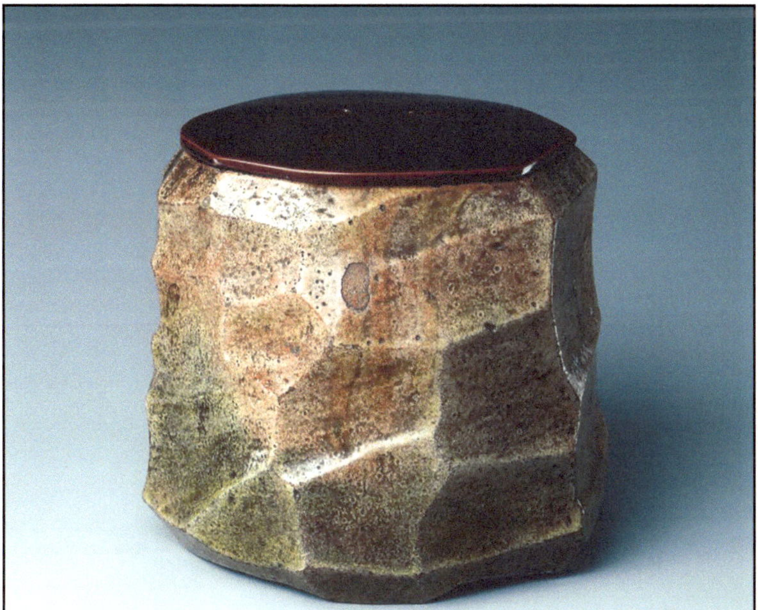

Figure 7.16: Jar, Hon'ami Kōetsu, Kyoto ware, c. 1620, Metropolitan Museum of Art, New York, Public domain.

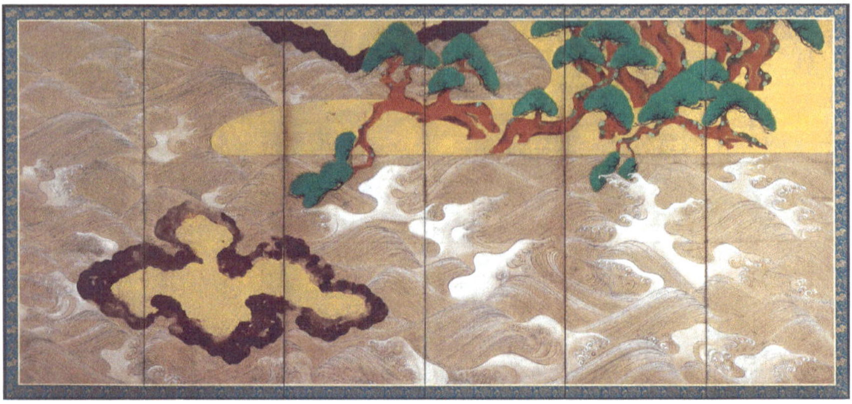

Figure 7.17: *Waves at Matsushima* (left screen), Tawaraya Sōtatsu, early seventeenth century, folding screen, ink, color, gold, and silver on paper, National Museum of Asian Art, Smithsonian Institution, Washington, DC, Creative Commons.

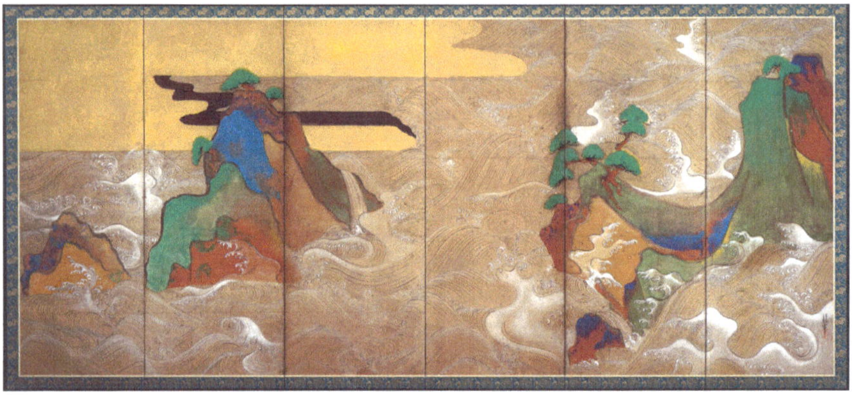

Figure 7.18: *Waves at Matsushima* (right screen), National Museum of Asian Art, Smithsonian Institution, Washington, DC, Creative Commons.

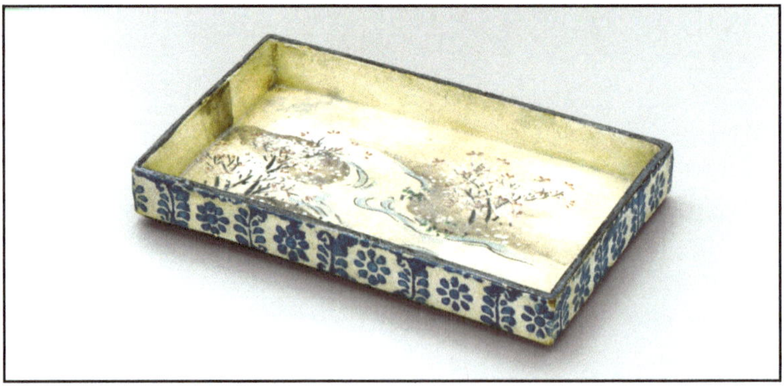

Figure 7.19: Dish with landscape design of blossoming trees, Ogata Kenzan, c. 1699–1712, glazed stoneware, Art Institute of Chicago, Public domain.

Kōrin's *Red and White Plum Blossoms* screens (Figure 7.20) celebrate the appreciation for the early spring blossoming of plum trees on often old and craggy limbs. The trees are cropped, and gold and silver leaf are used to provide a flat background against a stylized river running across both screens. A technique known as *tarashikomi*, in which ink or color is dropped into an already painted area while it is still wet and allowed to spread, provides texture and suggestions of lichen and moss.

After 1720, the government authorized the importation of European scientific publications, primarily through trade with the Netherlands. Confucian philosophy allowed for investigation of the natural world, and thus Dutch Studies (*rangaku*) came into being. Artistic developments during this period include chiaroscuro (contrasts of light and dark), scientific and atmospheric perspectives, and copperplate engraving and oil paint. Hiraga Gennai (1728–1780), Satake Shozan, daimyo of Akita (1748–1785), and his retainer Odano Naotake (1749–1780) were all early adopters of European techniques (Figure 7.21). Gennai was closely associated with Sō Shiseki (see below), who illustrated Gennai's *Materia medica*. Shiba Kōkan (1747–1818) taught himself copperplate engraving and advocated European landscape techniques to render visual reality. He also experimented with oil painting, using "a mixture of oils, wax, egg white, and chalk to emulate the glistening surface" of European works.[24] Kōkan's paintings of Mt. Fuji with their lower horizon line are said to have influenced Hokusai's print designs of Fuji.[25] These new ways of rendering space had broad appeal. Okumura Masanobu (1686–1764) developed the *uki-e* ("floating picture"), in which receding diagonals mimic European perspective techniques to represent interiors of theaters, teahouses, and brothels (Figure 7.22).

Chinese painters visiting Japan brought new ways of rendering nature in a two-dimensional format. Shen Quan (J: Shen Nanpin or Chin Nanpin; c. 1682–1760) introduced Chinese academic painting with his brightly colored and technically accurate depictions of flowers, birds, fish, and insects. The Nagasaki school that resulted popularized this type of *kachōga* (bird-and-flower painting) by Sō Shiseki (1715–1786) and others (Figure 7.23). In this style, stippling builds volume and texture, the *mokkotsu* (boneless) technique creates shape without outlines, and meticulous brushstrokes delineate fine details of feathers and plants. These techniques would influence painters such as Itō Jakuchū (see below).

Japanese also took inspiration from the Chinese scholar-literati traditions and the ideal of the amateur scholar painter. The early Nanga (Southern school painting) or Bunjinga (scholar-literati painting) practitioners included Gion Nankai (1677–1751) and Yanagisawa Kien (1703–1758), both government officials, and Sakaki Hyakusen (1697–1752). Chinese scholarship, poetry, painting, and calligraphy informed these painters' preferences, but they also were practitioners of *haikai* poetry and other Japanese art forms. Although they strived for a life of self-cultivation, individual creativity, and amateur status, many needed to support themselves by selling paintings or teaching. Nanga painters created

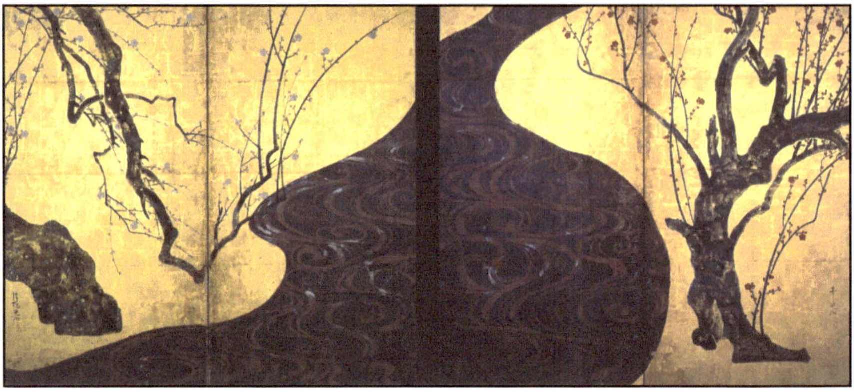

Figure 7.20: *Red and White Plum Blossoms*, Ogata Kōrin, first half of eighteenth century, pair of two-panel folding screens, color and gold leaf on paper, MOA Museum of Art, Atami, Wikimedia Commons.

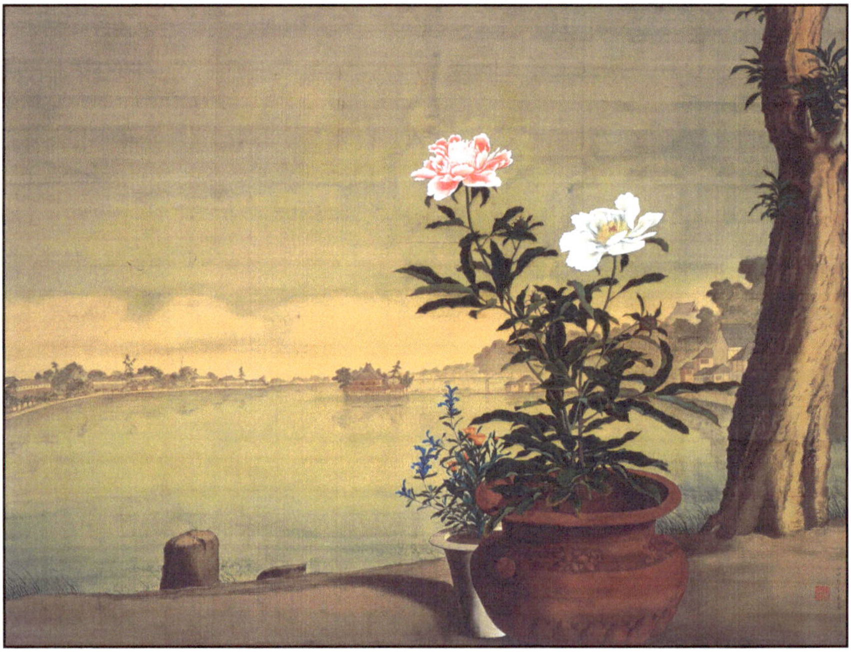

Figure 7.21: *Shinobazu Pond*, Odano Naotake, 1770s, hanging scroll, ink and color on silk, Akita Museum of Modern Art, Wikimedia Commons.

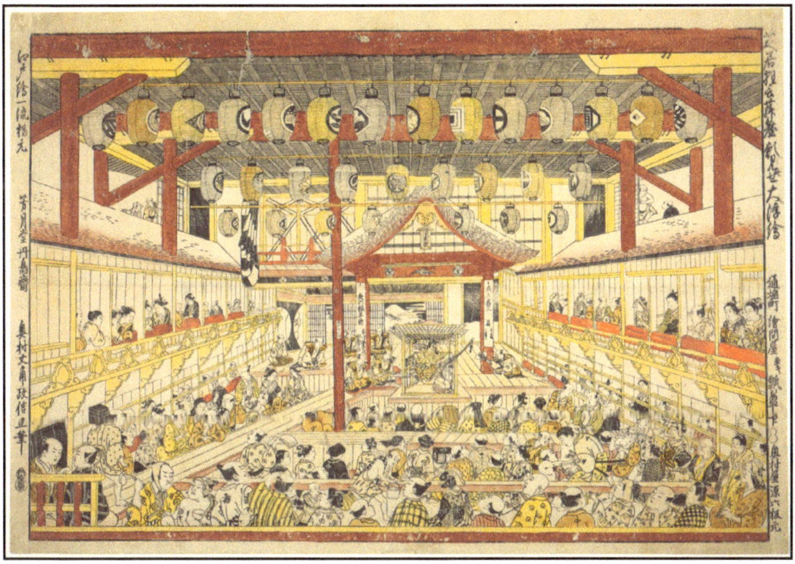

Figure 7.22: *Large Perspective Picture of the Kaomise Performance on the Kabuki Stage*, Okumura Masanobu, c. 1740, hand-colored woodblock print, Art Institute of Chicago, Public domain.

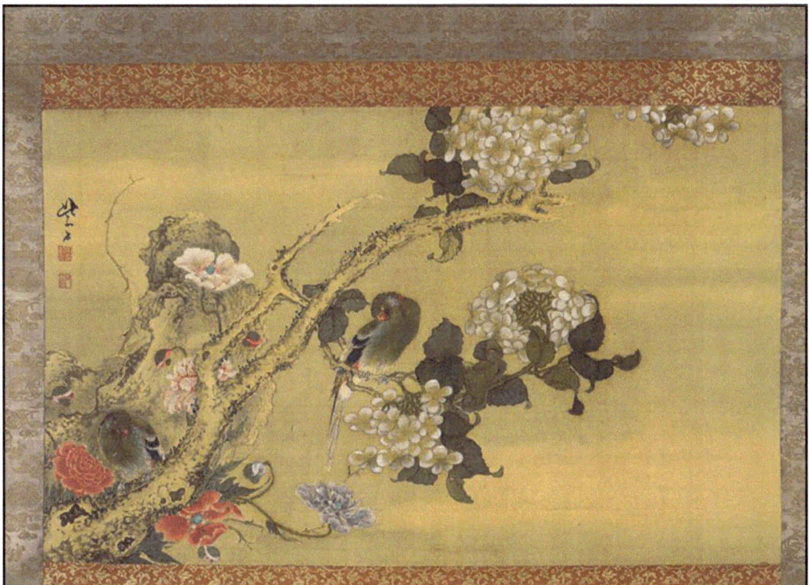

Figure 7.23: *Parakeets Among Hydrangeas and Poppies*, Sō Shiseki, after 1770, hanging scroll, ink and color on silk, Minneapolis Institute of Art, Public domain.

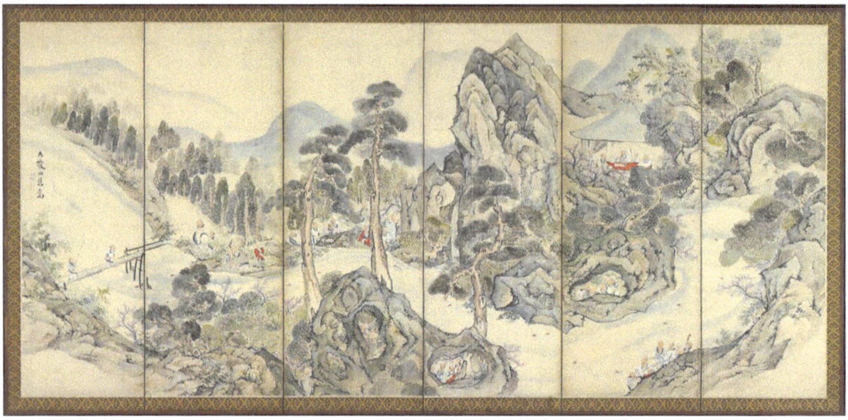

Figure 7.24: *Orchid Pavilion Gathering: Autumn Harvest Festival*, Ike Taiga, c. 1763, one of a pair of folding screens, ink and color on paper, Metropolitan Museum of Art, New York, Public domain.

their own distinct styles, with typically fewer layers of brushstrokes than Chinese counterparts.

Two examples are Ike Taiga (1723–1776) and Yosa Buson (1716–1783). Taiga's style developed from numerous sources: Ming and Qing painting, Rinpa, and the introduction from China of two painting manuals: the *Mustard Seed Garden Painting Manual* (*Kaishien gaden*) and *Painting Manual of Eight Styles* (*Hasshū gafū*). Referencing these sources as well as sketches made during his travels, Taiga painted "true views" (*shinkeizu*) of Fuji and other famous sites (he even climbed Mt. Fuji and other mountains during his travels).[26] This term embodied not only the idea of working from life (*shasei*), but also *shai* ("painting the idea") and *ikkaku* ("the artist's untrammeled personality").[27] His representation of specific sites echoes Sesshū's *Amanohashidate* and Sōtasu's *Pine Islands at Matsushima.*[28] A folding screen of the Orchid Pavilion Gathering, a classic Chinese theme, shows Taiga's typical brush techniques of dots and texture strokes, and richly layered patterns of light colors and ink (Figure 7.24).

Buson was also known for richly layered patterns of color. Born into a farming family, Buson exhibited an affinity for landscape colors and textures and a sense of spontaneity in his *haikai* and *haiga* ("haikai pictures"). His 1769 poem illustrates the play, or "meta-commentary," of the frog imagery by referring to Bashō's most famous *haikai*, while injecting a touch of humor into the traditional imagery of spring:

jumping in
and washing off an old poem—
a frog[29]

Snow Landscape (Figure 7.25) shows Buson's use of gray ink washes to form mountains and a hut by painting negatively—that is, he developed a shape by painting around it. He created the sense of snow on trees by painting branches with texture strokes against the white paper and shaped the "outlines" of the trees with washes of ink. The subject of a man in a hut in the mountains comes from Chinese literati painting, as does the attention to texture, but the flattening and simplifying of the shapes and the move toward abstraction with the use of ink washes is characteristically Nanga style.

During the 1700s, woodblock printmaking developed from hand-colored prints, to one- to three-color printed works, and finally to the full-colored print, an innovation in 1765 seen in the work of Suzuki Harunobu (1725?–1770), whose designs were so popular that they were forged during his lifetime (Figure 7.26).[30] This Harunobu print is a *mitate* (double vision) in the same vein as the *Hikone Screen*. In this design a gameboard and boxes for the playing pieces refer to the Chinese game of *qi* (J: *ki*). An ink painting of bamboo hangs above the gameboard, and calligraphy is displayed in the alcove. Additionally, "the pastime of music is cleverly suggested by the incense" used by the women to scent their robes. "When referring to the act of inhaling incense, the Japanese use the verb 'hear' (*kiku*). Since both music and incense are 'heard,' the fragrance of the incense stands for music in the composition."[31] Thus, we have all Four Accomplishments—music, board games, calligraphy, and painting—represented by contemporary women in fashionable clothing.

A typical full-color print like the Harunobu design required about ten woodblocks; sometimes as many as twenty. An initial run of one thousand prints would test the market, and if it sold well, the publisher would order more to be made.[32] Prints were sold by itinerant street vendors or directly from publishers' shops, and purchasers might paste them on walls or sliding screens in their homes. Prints that were issued in large series were generally kept in boxes or mounted in albums to be enjoyed at leisure.[33]

In Kyoto, Maruyama Ōkyo (1733–1795), who also came from a farming family, took ideas from European one-point perspective and chiaroscuro to bring empiricism to his painting. He sketched from life, including observing the dissections of cadavers, which shaped his approach to figural painting. The *Snow-Covered Pines* screens (Figure 7.27) demonstrate the technique of *mokkotsu* (boneless) painting, discarding the previously linear dominance of Japanese painting. Here, Ōkyo refers to earlier approaches such as the monumental painting of the Momoyama period, while integrating current trends toward scientific objectivity.

Ōkyo's style was adopted by such painters as Matsumura Goshun (1752–1811), who founded the Shijō branch of the Maruyama-Shijō school. Goshun studied under Buson, before drawing on Ōkyo's style for ideas. The painting *Two Crows* (Figure 7.28) reveals not only the boneless technique but also interest in the

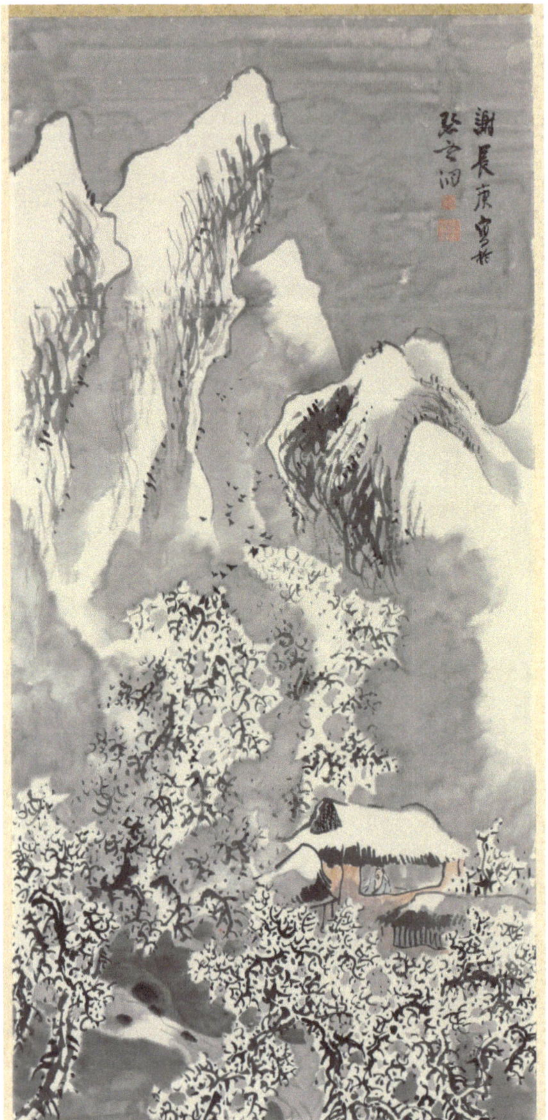

Figure 7.25: *Snow Landscape*, Yosa Buson, c. 1770s, hanging scroll, ink and color on paper, Cleveland Museum of Art, Public domain.

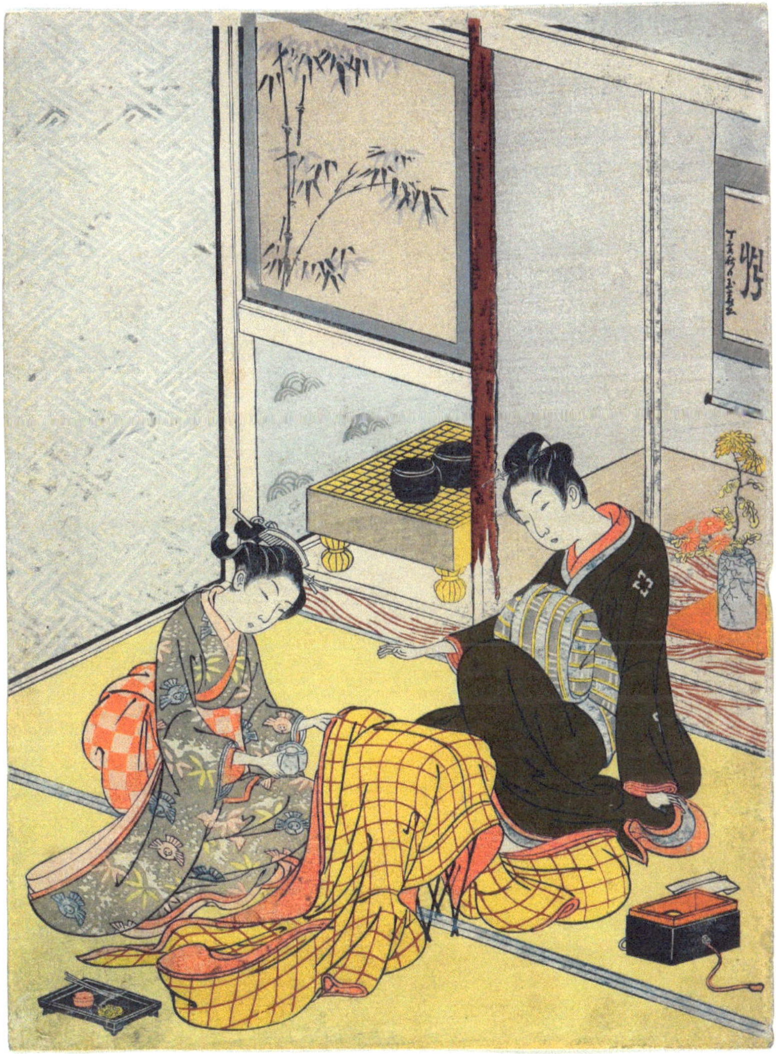

Figure 7.26: *Perfuming a Robe as Visual Parody of the Four Accomplishments, Autumn*, Suzuki Harunobu, 1767, color woodblock print, Minneapolis Institute of Art, Public domain.

mundane and everyday. The Maruyama-Shijō style was hugely popular in Kyoto, influenced the *nihonga* movement of the Meiji period, and still resonates with Japanese painters today.

Maruyama-Shijō painters dominated the successful Higashiyama art exhibitions, begun in Kyoto in 1792, which allowed individualists working outside an established studio the opportunity to exhibit their works.[34] Among these were eccentrics (*kijin*) such as Itō Jakuchū (1716–1800), Soga Shōhaku (1730–1781),

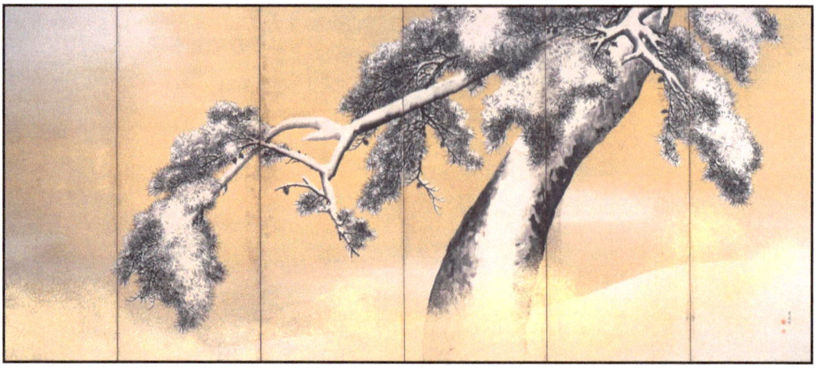

Figure 7.27: *Snow-Covered Pines* (right screen), Maruyama Ōkyo, second half of eighteenth century, pair of six-panel screens, ink and gold on paper, Mitsui Memorial Museum, Tokyo, Wikimedia Commons.

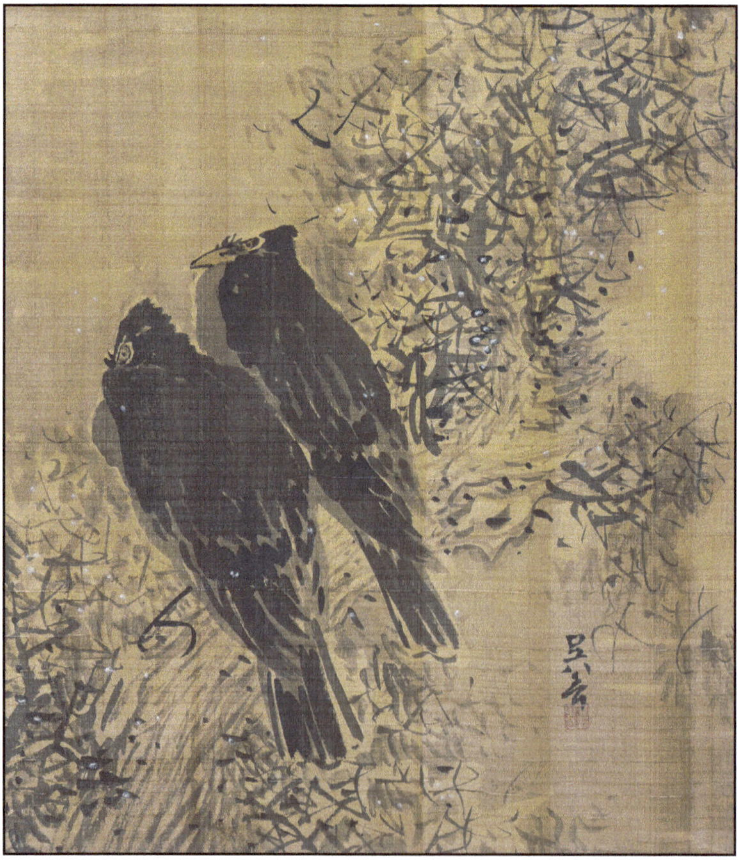

Figure 7.28: *Two Crows*, Matsumura Goshun, late eighteenth to early nineteenth century, hanging scroll, ink and color on silk, Minneapolis Institute of Art, Public domain.

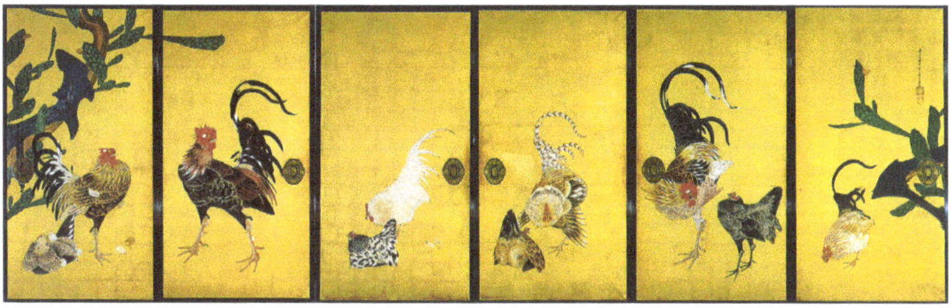

Figure 7.29: *Saboten gunkei-zu fusuma-e* (Cactus and Roosters), Itō Jakuchū, 1789, sliding doors (*fusuma*), ink and color on gold, Saifuku-ji, Osaka, Wikimedia Commons.

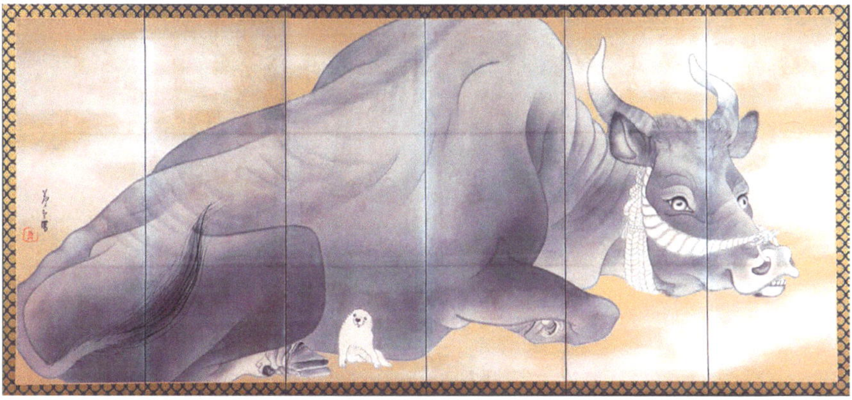

Figure 7.30: *White Elephant and Black Bull*, Nagasawa Rosetsu, c.1789–1801, left screen of a pair of folding screens, ink and gold paint on paper, Wikimedia Commons.

and Nagasawa Rosetsu (1754–1799). The idea of the eccentric originated in both Zen and Daoist thought, but from the late 1700s on, it also suggested a certain resistance to Tokugawa and Confucian authority. Being an eccentric encompassed unconventional behavior and an unworldly artistic ability. To be known as a *kijin* was an attractive characteristic, and individualists created personas that appealed to the buying public.

These painters operated outside the norm. Jakuchū came from a greengrocer family; he took up painting when he was forty. His colorful and detailed paintings of chickens demonstrate his keen observation of nature (he kept chickens in his backyard), and his Buddhist faith permeates many of his works (Figure 7.29).

Rosetsu broke away from Ōkyo's studio, where he had learned the technique of *mokkotsu* as well as scientific perspective. Rosetsu stands out for his sly humor and ability to combine charm, whimsy, and startling juxtapositions in his compositions (Figure 7.30).

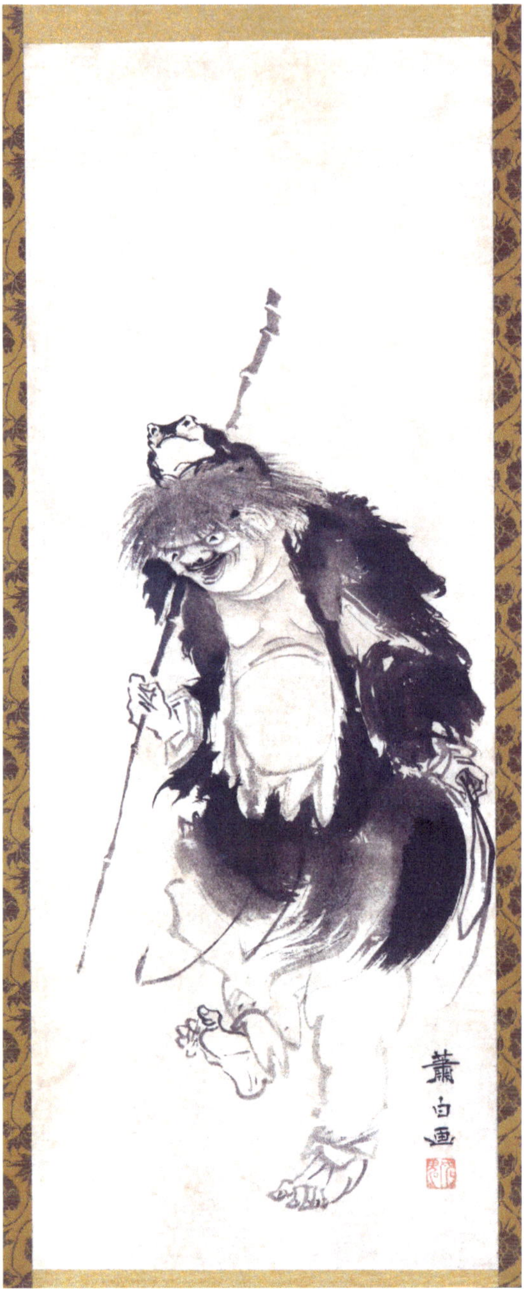

Figure 7.31: *Gama Sennin (Hou Xiansheng) and His Three-Legged Toad*,
Soga Shōhaku, eighteenth century, hanging scroll, ink on paper,
Freer Gallery of Art Collection, Washington, DC, Public domain.

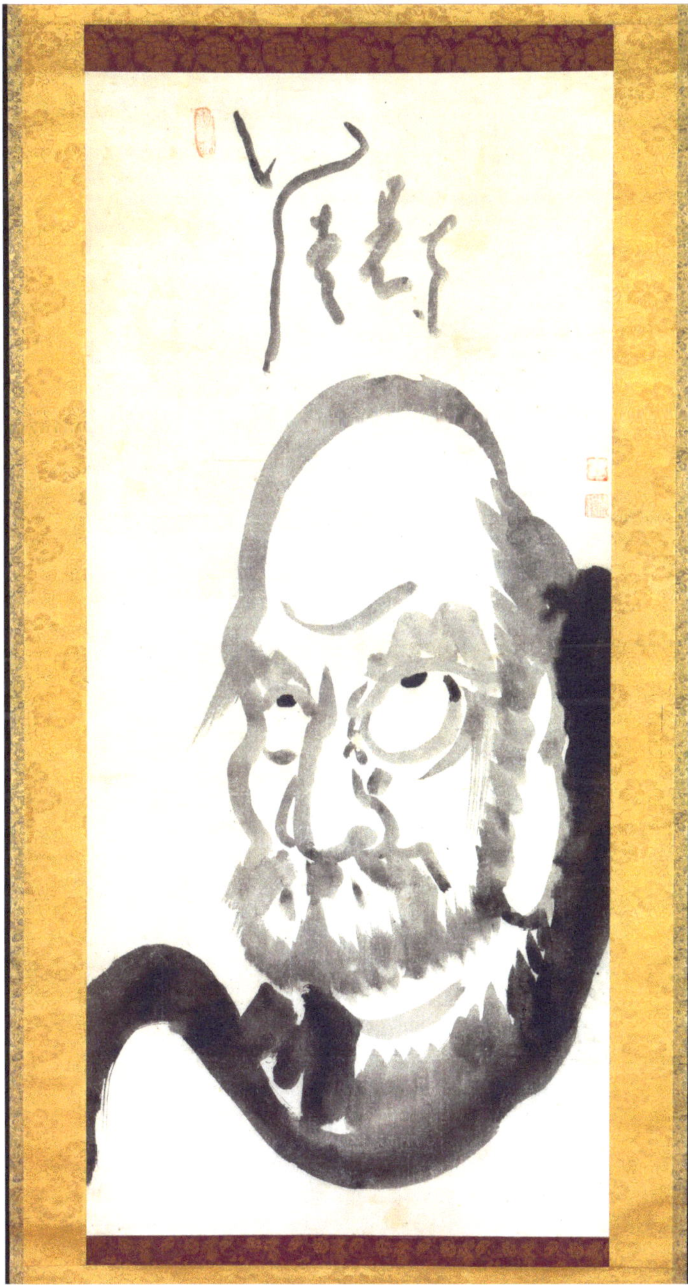

Figure 7.32: *Portrait of Bodhidharma*, Hakuin Ekaku, mid-eighteenth century, hanging scroll, ink on paper, Metropolitan Museum of Art, New York, Public domain.

Soga Shōhaku is believed to have often painted while intoxicated, a practice with Chinese precedents. In *Gama Sennin* (Figure 7.31), the Chinese immortal and his three-legged toad are brushed with rapid strokes of ink, almost sketch-like, contrasting light lines with rough strokes of ink and even messy overlaps of darker ink that are indicative of Shōhaku's style.

Hakuin Ekaku (1685–1768) has been characterized as "the most influential Zen monk of the past five hundred years" owing to the broad impact of his writings and paintings.[35] He produced most of his calligraphy after the age of sixty. Often interjecting humor into his paintings, he took a new approach to traditional Zen subjects. Trickster foxes (*kitsune*) and raccoon-dogs (*tanuki*), blind men crossing a bridge, one-legged beggars, "Night Parade of One Hundred Demons"—these were some of the subjects he used to pose questions, elicit understandings, and assist awakenings.[36] In Figure 7.32 the viewer is challenged by a koan in Hakuin's calligraphy that reads "No matter how one looks at it."[37] This type of brushwork came to be appreciated internationally in the twentieth century and continues to be practiced in Japan today.

Notes

[1] Quoted in Haruo Shirane, *Traces of Dreams: Landscape, Cultural Memory, and the Poetry of Bashō* (Stanford: Stanford University Press, 1998), 13.

[2] For more explanation of the various poetry forms that led to *haikai*, see Shirane, *Traces of Dreams*.

[3] Elizabeth Lillehoj argues for the term "status group" instead of "class" in Lillehoj, ed., *Acquisition: Art and Ownership in Edo-Period Japan* (Warren, CT: Floating World Editions, 2007), 19, note 7.

[4] The Ryūkyū Kingdom (1429–1879) was a vassal state of Japan during the Tokugawa period. The islands were annexed by Japan in the late nineteenth century and renamed Okinawa Prefecture.

[5] Jilly Traganou, *The Tōkaidō Road: Traveling and Representation in Edo and Meiji Japan* (New York and London: RoutledgeCurzon, 2004), 13.

[6] Susan B. Hanley, *Everyday Things in Premodern Japan: The Hidden Legacy of Material Culture* (Berkeley: University of California Press, 1997), 105–106; Jakobina Arch, *Bringing Whales Ashore: Oceans and the Environment of Early Modern Japan* (Seattle: University of Washington Press, 2018), 82; https://www.oldbaileyonline.org/about/population-history-of-london (accessed 17 August, 2024).

[7] Kabuki is believed to have developed from women dancers who performed along the banks of the Kamo River in Kyoto to a series of acrobatic and dance skits, and then to narrative plays with all-male actors, including the *onnagata*, men who specialized in female roles. Satoko Shimazaki provides a detailed history of Kabuki that challenges traditional assumptions, in *Edo Kabuki in Transition: From the Worlds of the Samurai to the Vengeful Female Ghost* (New York: Columbia University Press, 2016).

[8] For more, see Cecilia Segawa Seigle, *Yoshiwara: The Glittering World of the Japanese Courtesan* (Honolulu: University of Hawaiʻi Press, 1993).

[9] William H. Coaldrake, *Architecture and Authority in Japan*, Nissan Institute / Routledge Japanese Studies (London: Routledge, 1996), https://doi.org/10.4324/9780203042830, 138–162; see also Karen M. Gerhart, *The Eyes of Power: Art and Early Tokugawa Authority* (Honolulu: University of Hawaiʻi Press, 1999).

[10] Tatami mat sizes have varied over the centuries. Even now, rooms with tatami floors are described by the number of mats in a room: a six-mat room is a standard size; a four-and-a-half mat room is small; and an eight-mat or ten-mat room is considered large. Sizes also differ by region.

[11] Gerhart, *The Eyes of Power*, 10.

[12] There are also other meanings in this seventeenth-century context. See Gerhart, *The Eyes of Power*, 25–33.

[13] Ryōanji's reputation as a masterpiece of Zen garden design is a product of the twentieth century. See Toshio Watanabe, "A Kyoto garden renewal?: From Meiji to early Showa period," in Pitelka and Tseng, ed., *Kyoto Visual Culture in the Early Edo and Meiji Periods*, 163–181.

[14] Wybe Kuitert, *Themes in the History of Japanese Garden Art* (Honolulu: University of Hawaiʻi Press, 2002), 98–107.

[15] The four-panel sliding doors were designed for the abbot's quarters of a Myōshinji sub-temple. The original composition may not have shown the tree cropped at the top. The painting is attributed to Sansetsu; the entire group of eighteen panels was a joint project of Kano Sanraku and Sansetsu. See, for example, Christine Guth in *Art of Edo Japan: The Artist and the City, 1615–1868* (New Haven: Yale University Press, 2010; reprint 2014), 56–57; and Julia Meech-Pekarik, "Twelve Japanese Screens," *The Metropolitan Museum of Art Bulletin* 37, no. 2 (Autumn 1979), 28–31.

[16] For more on the training of painters in the Tokugawa period, see Brenda G. Jordan and Victoria Weston, eds. *Copying the Master and Stealing His Secrets: Talent and Training in Japanese Painting* (Honolulu: University of Hawaiʻi Press, 2003).

[17] By the late Tokugawa and early Meiji periods in the nineteenth century, estimates of how many children attended school range from 54–79% for boys and 19–25% for girls. These were high percentages for that time, as noted by Susan Hanley in *Everyday Things in Premodern Japan*, 190.

[18] Mary Elizabeth Berry, *Japan in Print: Information and Nation in the Early Modern Period* (Berkeley: University of California Press, 2006), 31.

[19] I've borrowed the term "double vision" from Haruo Shirane (Shirane, *Traces of Dreams*, 73). Technically, the girl pictured in this Harunobu print is not a courtesan; rather, the rendering is typical of Harunobu's representations of the women of Edo. However, this design is usually included in examples of the Daruma and Courtesan theme.

[20] Brenda G. Jordan, *Strange Fancies and Fresh Conceptions: Kyōsai in an Age of Conflict*. (PhD dissertation, University of Kansas, 1993), 307–308.

[21] Margaret M. Kanada provides a useful description of the step-by-step process in *Color Woodblock Printmaking: The Traditional Method of Ukiyo-e* (Tokyo: Shufunotomo, 1989).

[22] Moronobu was born into a Kyoto fabric dyer family and produced *kosode* design books called *hinagata-bon*. For more, see Liza Dalby, *Kimono: Fashioning Culture* (New Haven: Yale University Press, 1993), 270–321.

[23] Morgan Pitelka, *Handmade Culture: Raku Potters, Patrons, and Tea Practitioners in Japa*n (Honolulu, University of Hawai'i Press, 2005), 54–58.

[24] Guth, *Art of Edo Japan*, 146.

[25] Guth, *Art of Edo Japan*, 146.

[26] Melinda Takeuchi provides a detailed discussion of the terms *shinkeizu* and "true views" in *Taiga's True Views: The Language of Landscape Painting in Eighteenth-Century Japan* (Stanford: Stanford University Press, 1992).

[27] Takeuchi, *Taiga's True Views*, 144. For more on *shasei*, see Jordan and Weston, *Copying the Master and Stealing His Secrets*.

[28] Melinda Takeuchi notes that this type of painting, for which she provides the Tōhaku and Sōsetsu examples, was assigned the term *keibutsuga* (scenic view painting) in the modern period (*Taiga's True Views*, 107–108).

[29] Shirane, *Traces of Dreams*, 15.

[30] Shiba Kōkan was one of the artists who forged Harunobu's work.

[31] Matthew Welch and Yuiko Kimura-Tilford, *Worldly Pleasures, Earthly Delights: Japanese Prints from the Minneapolis Institute of Art* (Minneapolis: Minneapolis Institute of Art, 2011), 66.

[32] Chris Uhlenbeck, "Production Constraints in the World of Ukiyo-e: An Introduction to the Commercial Climate of Japanese Printmaking," in *The Commercial and Cultural Climate of Japanese Printmaking*, ed. Amy Reigle Newland (Amsterdam: Hotei Publishing, 2004), 11–12.

[33] Guth, *Art of Edo Japan*, 99.

[34] Guth, *Art of Edo Japan*, 80–81.

[35] Stephen Addiss, *The Art of Zen: Paintings and Calligraphy by Japanese Monks, 1600–1925* (New York: Harry N. Abrams, 1989), 102.

[36] For more about Hakuin, see Addiss, *The Art of Zen*, 102–129.

[37] https://www.metmuseum.org/art/collection/search/78145

8

Rumblings of Discontent

Late Tokugawa Period

The Edokko (child of Edo)

1. He receives his first bath in the water of the city's aqueducts; he grows up in sight of the gargoyles on the roof of Edo castle.
2. He is not attached to money; he is not stingy. His funds do not cover the night's lodging.
3. He is raised in a high-class, protected manner. He is quite unlike either warriors or country bumpkins.
4. He is a man of Nihonbashi [the downtown area of Edo] to the bone.
5. He has *iki* (refinement) and *hari* (strength of character).

— Santō Kyōden (1761–1816)[1]

The Tokugawa shogunate strove for peace and harmony, to be achieved through the hard work, frugal living, and upright morals of its citizens, within a predominantly agricultural economy and strict status groups. This ideology, however, conflicted with the developing money economy and city dwellers' desire for entertainment. Throughout the eighteenth century and into the nineteenth, a tension existed between the government's view of an ideal society and the realities of day-to-day life, intensified by rising living standards and increasing numbers of merchants and artisans (*chōnin*), including those outside the status system who provided entertainment. The Edokko *chōnin* described in the opening quote exemplifies the bravado of the Edo-born populace.

As early as the 1600s, the shogunate was issuing injunctions that ranged from limiting the size of houses to restricting the use of expensive textiles such as silk, or types of shoes and household articles. Luxury was condemned in favor of frugal living; entertainments such as Kabuki and puppet theater were targeted for

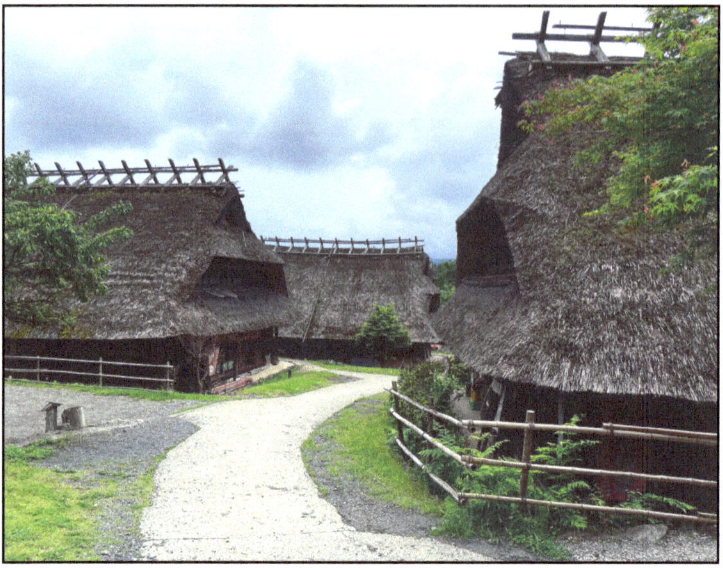

Figure 8.1: *Minka* houses, Saiko Iyashi no Sato Nenba, open air museum (reconstruction of a former farming village), near Mt. Fuji, photo by author.

regulation.[2] Yet by the end of the 1700s, such efforts had clearly failed, evidenced by the proliferation of sumptuary laws and the increasing criticism of the government and its unwillingness to adapt to a rapidly changing society.[3]

The rising standard of living is reflected in residential architecture.[4] Before the Tokugawa period, housing for commoners (farmers, merchants, artisans) was constructed from local materials, using wood, thatch, and bamboo, and was often destroyed by earthquakes, fires, and the damp climate. But as economic development spread and building techniques improved, wealthy farmers and townspeople built more permanent dwellings.[5] The term *minka* refers to these houses, which developed from commoner dwellings of the fifteenth and sixteenth centuries and varied in style depending on their location. They often had thickly thatched gabled roofs and interior elements in the *shoin* style, such as tokonoma (alcoves), *genkan* (a formal entry), tatami mats, sliding wall partitions, and shoji screens. The images in Figures 8.1 and 8.2 from the reconstructed village of Saiko Iyashi no Sato Nenba near Mt. Fuji demonstrate these features. Affluent homeowners circumvented regulations designed to enforce simplicity and frugality by, for example, adhering to the size limitations but using the eaves and steep roofs to create whole rooms or more than one story inside.

From the 1700s on, homeowners began to use more bedding as cotton came into widespread use. Bedding and other material items required storage, so *tansu* (chests) and *oshiire* (built-in storage for bedding) were designed to meet these

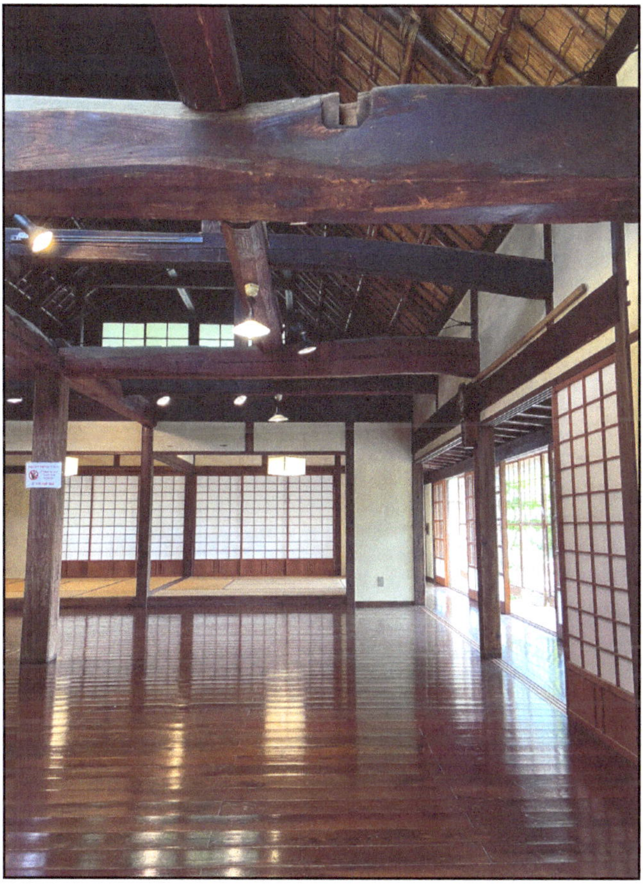

Figure 8.2: Interior of *minka* house, Saiko Iyashi no Sato Nenba, photo by author.

needs. Storehouses (*kura*) also became quite common. By 1877, when Edward S. Morse began to study *minka*, structures with these features were widespread for middle-class and wealthy commoners.[6]

Clothing was changing as well. By the nineteenth century, the *kosode* was becoming the modern kimono, as seen in a print by Utagawa Kunisada (1786–1864; Figure 8.3; the term kimono only came into broad use toward the end of the century).[7] From Hishikawa Moronobu on, books illustrating the latest patterns kept consumers up to date on current fashions. The fabric, motifs, and colors used for *kosode* were often seasonal or auspicious images such as iris (summer) or pines (winter). In addition to the techniques mentioned in Chapter 7, tie-dye, paste resist, and *sashiko* (stitched decoration) were used.

The Ryūkyū Kingdom (now Okinawa Prefecture) had become a vassal state of Japan in 1609, and the shogunate supported the kingdom's continued trade

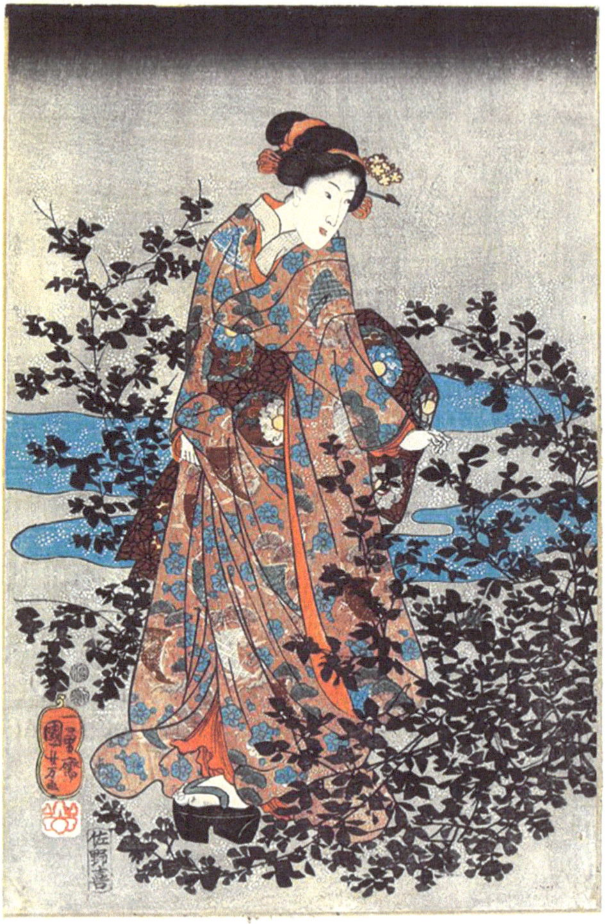

Figure 8.3: *The Jewel River of Bush Clover in Ōmi Province*, Utagawa Kunisada, 1847–1852, color woodblock print triptych, left sheet, Minneapolis Institute of Art, Public domain.

with both China and Japan. Textiles such as ikat (*kasuri*) made their way to Japan through such trade and as tribute to the shogun. Ikat is a form of dyeing where threads are bound and dyed in such a way that, when woven, they form patterns (Figure 8.4). Colorful and creative designs and dyeing techniques influenced the *kosode* and expanded the range of artistic possibilities for other textiles as well. Ryūkyūans also developed the *bashōfu* textile, made from the fibers of the *bashō* plant, sometimes referred to as the Japanese banana plant. In addition, Ryūkyūans imported cotton and silk for royalty, woven and dyed with techniques such as *bingata* (a type of multicolored dyeing using stencils with resist paste). The unlined robe in Figure 8.5 is made from ramie and *bingata* and was likely a summer garment for a wealthy Ryūkyūan woman.[8] Motifs in this robe include pine and plum trees, rocks and water, and flying cranes.[9]

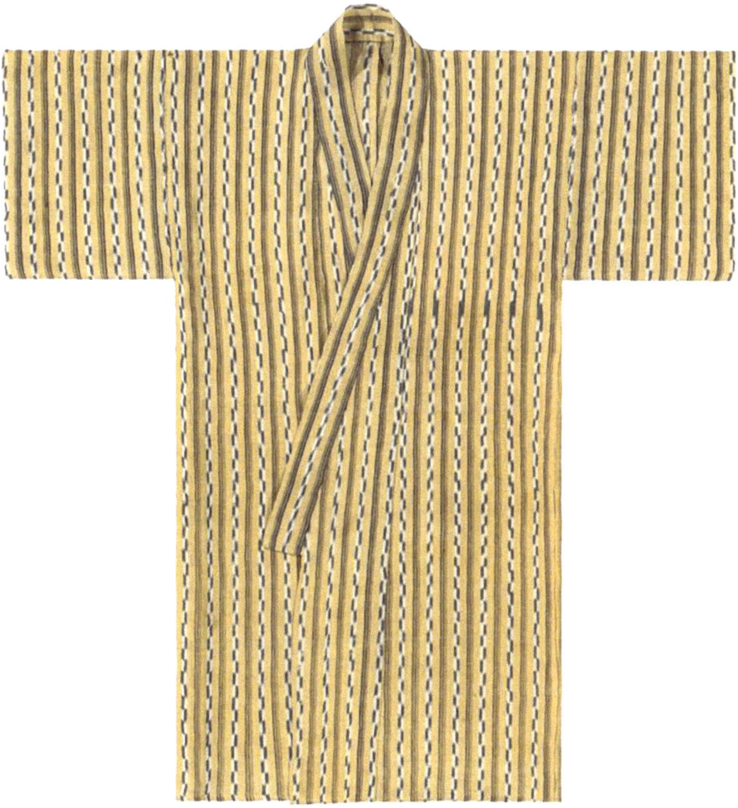

Figure 8.4: Ryūkyūan robe with ikat stripes, early twentieth century, banana fiber and cotton, Minneapolis Institute of Art, Public domain.

As with residential architecture, clothing was subject to numerous edicts that forbade displays of fine materials and designs. Fashion-minded consumers subverted these regulations by adhering to the rules on outer layers of robes while wearing fashionable inner layers. Examples include lining a *kosode* with fine fabric dyed in beautiful colors and patterns or commissioning an artist to paint the lining.

In fashion, the arts, and popular literature such as *kibyōshi* (satirical illustrated books) and *ninjōbon* (romance novels), new terms came into use to express refinement and discriminating taste, including *share* (witty and refined), *kinkin* (fashionable), *hade* (flashy), *hasuha* (stylish), *shibumi* (understated), and *iki* ("urbane, plucky stylishness"[10])—the manifestation of the Edo preference for lightness and suggestion.[11] There was also a certain playfulness to the aesthetic. Those who embodied *iki* did so with a disregard for money and an ability to convey their taste with nonchalance—through the fine quality of an undergarment, for example. A print entitled "Fancy-free Type" by Kitagawa Utamaro (c. 1753–1806) expresses a number of these sensibilities (Figure 8.6).

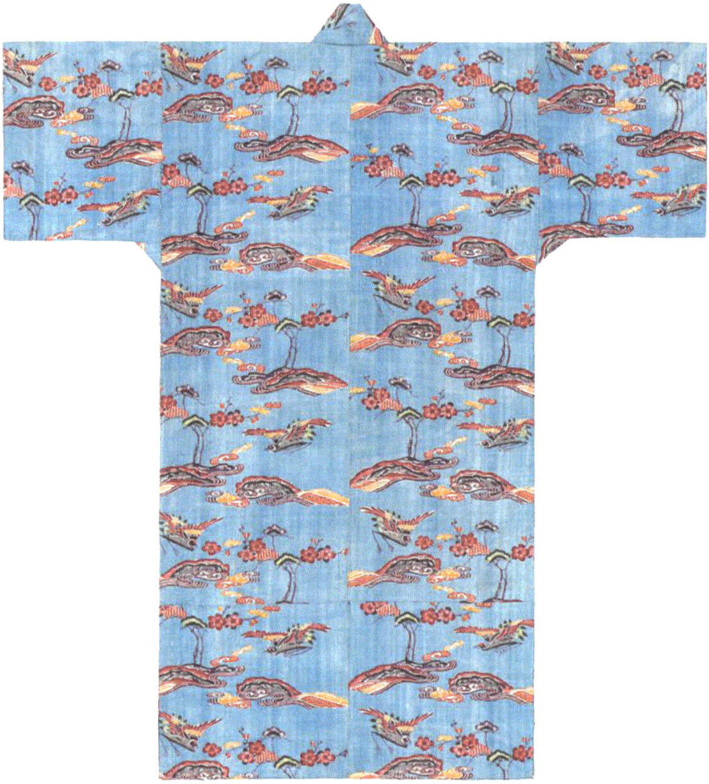

Figure 8.5: Ryūkyūan robe with *bingata* (stencil resist with applied pigments), nineteenth century, ramie, Minneapolis Institute of Art, Public domain.

One underappreciated characteristic of Tokugawa arts was the extensive cross-fertilization among artists, intellectuals, and art lovers. Interactions crossed status lines as samurai, merchants, and artists mingled in the same circles, meeting in restaurants and private residences for discussions and sharing of ideas. There are many examples of these cultural salons. In Osaka, sake merchant Kimura Kenkadō (1736–1802) was at the center of a circle that received visits by Shiba Kōkan and Tani Bunchō (1763–1841) and promoted Ike Taiga's work in Osaka and Kyoto.[12]

The Sakai family of Himeji Castle welcomed a variety of individuals to their main Edo residence, where a young Sakai Hōitsu (1761–1828) was exposed to *haikai* poets, painters, scholars, and others. Among the participants in these salons were Kano painters, Sō Shiseki of the Nagasaki School, and Ōta Nanpo (1749–1823), a shogunal official and influential *kyōka* ("mad poetry") poet.[13] Hōitsu, who associated with both Tani Bunchō and Confucian scholar and poet Kameda Bōsai (1752–1826), revitalized the Rinpa style of Kōrin with refined and skillful painting and a touch of humor.[14] In the screen of cherry and willow trees (from the pair *Cherry and Maple Trees*; Figure 8.7), Hōitsu depicted numerous

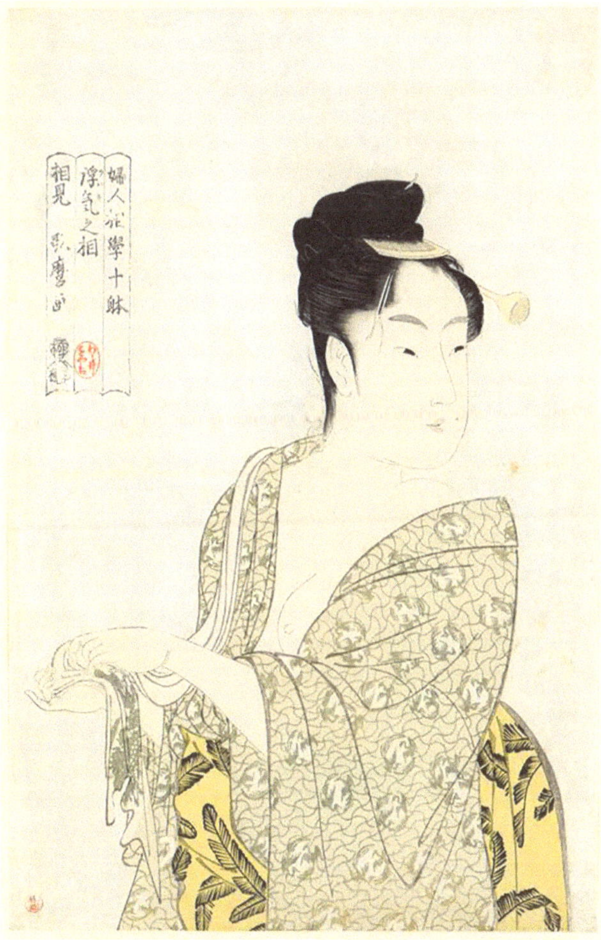

Figure 8.6: "Fancy-Free Type" from the series *Ten Types in the Physiognomic Study of Women*, Kitagawa Utamaro, 1792–1793, color woodblock print with mica, Minneapolis Institute of Art, Public domain.

signs of spring, including primroses, fiddleheads, dandelions, cherry blossoms, and the early leaves of a willow, all rendered with Kōrin's characteristic *mokkotsu* and *tarashikomi* techniques (see Chapter 7).

Tani Bunchō, a samurai attached to the powerful Tokugawa advisor Matsudaira Sadanobu (1759–1829), led a cultural salon in Edo and is thought to have popularized the painting and calligraphy gatherings (*shogakai*) that brought painters of different styles together to demonstrate their skills before paying audiences.[15] In addition to being a skilled painter, Bunchō was hugely influential as a teacher, instructing in numerous styles, including Nanga and European painting styles.[16]

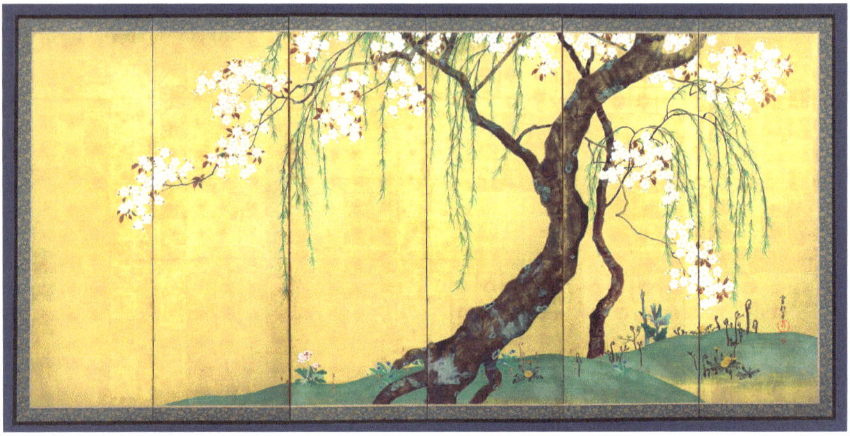

Figure 8.7: *Cherry and Maple Trees*, Sakai Hōitsu, early 1820s, one of a pair of six-panel screens, ink, color, and gold leaf, on paper. Metropolitan Museum of Art, New York, Public domain.

Bunchō's associate and student Watanabe Kazan (1793–1841), chief retainer of the Tahara estate, also hosted painting and calligraphy gatherings, and his work demonstrates the blending of different styles and the influence of Dutch studies. In his unfinished portrait of the giant Ōzora Buzaemon (Figure 8.8), Kazan used a camera obscura to project an image onto the surface to make a preliminary drawing before delineating the robes with ink. The twenty-five-year-old Buzaemon was over seven feet tall, and his handprints (seen in the lower left) were popular with the public.[17] In the painting, Kazan used shading in the face and robes and a three-quarter view of Buzaemon's face, elements likely drawn from his study of European works. The viewer's eye is drawn to Buzaemon's downward glance, which captures the young man's reported shyness and discomfort with his celebrity. There is a long history of portraiture painting and paintings of physical maladies (see *Scroll of Afflictions*, Chapter 3), but Kazan's innovation is to render the reality of Buzaemon's size and emotional affect with no trace of voyeurism.[18]

The camera obscura is only one of the European devices that fascinated the Japanese and was increasingly used by artists in late Tokugawa to aid in two-dimensional renderings of images. Nagasawa Rosetsu is said to have used a microscope to view a flea before painting it on a screen.[19] This magnification of insects in particular was used to create frightening images in books and prints; Utagawa Kunisada illustrated enlarged insects for *The Plum, Pine, and Bamboo-Cutter's Tale* (*Matsu to ume taketori monogatari*; 1809), a novel by Santō Kyōden (1761–1816).[20] Other scientific imports caught the attention of the Japanese, among them magnifying glasses, telescopes, and spectacles; the latter had been introduced as early as the 1600s but were now imported in the tens of thousands. These lensed instruments were collectively known as *megane*, and made their way into book illustrations and woodblock prints.[21]

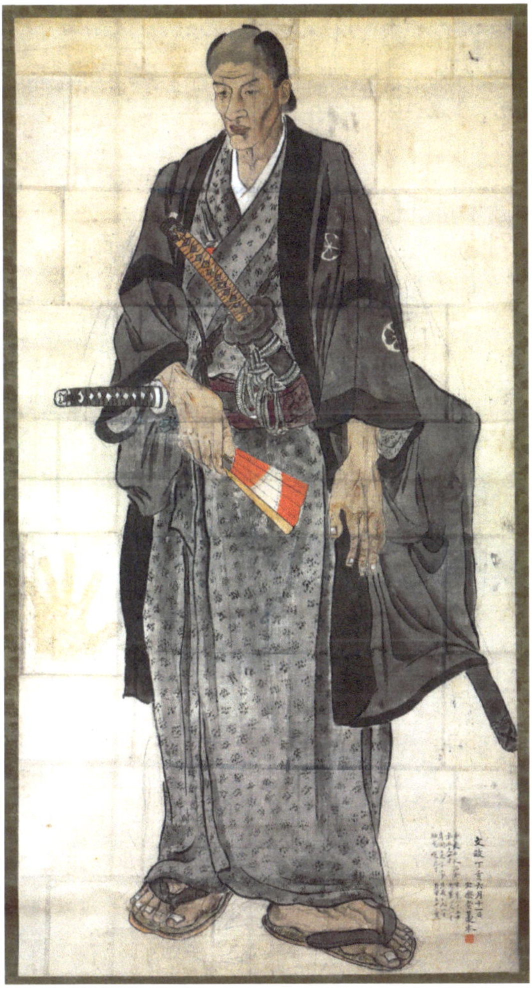

Figure 8.8: *Portrait of Ōzora Buzaemon*, Watanabe Kazan, 1827, hanging scroll, ink and color on paper, Cleveland Museum of Art, Public domain.

Publishers and print designers were continually looking for ways to keep up with current trends and consumer demands, and the influx of these European devices influenced their work. For a brief period, popular actors with loyal followings were represented in "big head" prints, as seen in the unorthodox portrayals of Tōshūsai Sharaku (active 1794–1795) (Figure 8.9) and Katsukawa Shunshō (1726–1792). These prints were banned in 1800 as "conspicuous" (*medatsu*), though their popularity may have been the reason.[22]

In addition to the numerous regulations that dictated lifestyles, certain topics and subjects were censored for the publishing industry. These included current

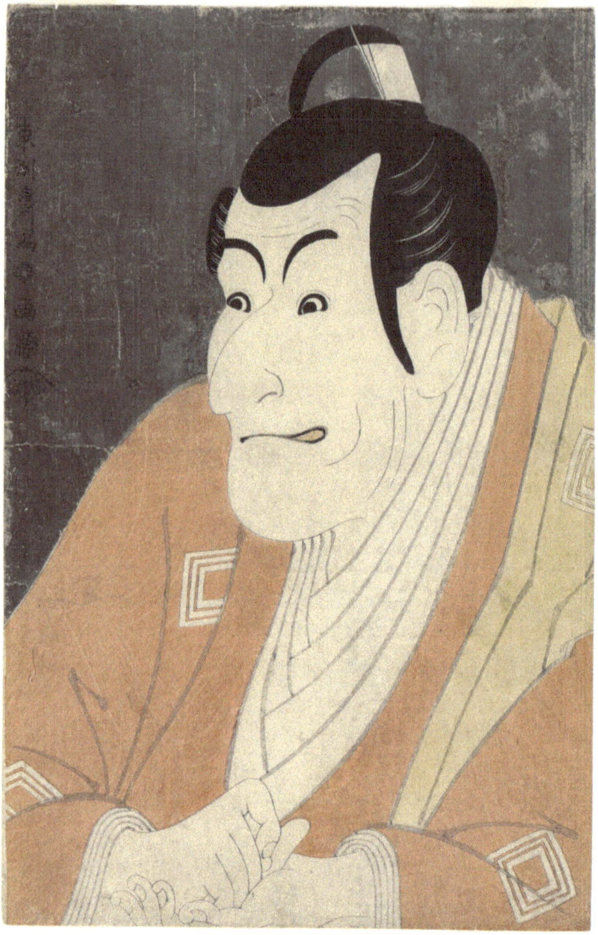

Figure 8.9: *Ichikawa Ebizo IV as Takemura Sadanoshin*, Tōshūsai Sharaku, 1794, color woodblock print, Cleveland Museum of Art, Public domain.

events, direct criticism of the shogunate, luxury, erotica, and political subversion. Cases of shogunate censorship and punishment include those of Watanabe Kazan, whose criticism of the shogunate led to his imprisonment and suicide; Kitagawa Utamaro, sentenced in 1805 to three days in jail and fifty days in handcuffs for producing prints deemed offensive; and popular author Santō Kyōden and his publisher Tsutaya Jūzaburō (1750–1797), punished for the publication of three *sharebon* (witty novelettes) in 1791.[23]

The woodblock print tripytch *The Earth Spider Generates Monsters at the Mansion of Lord Minamoto Yorimitsu* by Utagawa Kuniyoshi (1797–1861) is a particularly well-known example of censorship (Figure 8.10). Minamoto Yorimitsu (948–1021) is shown sleeping while being enchanted by the Earth Spider and

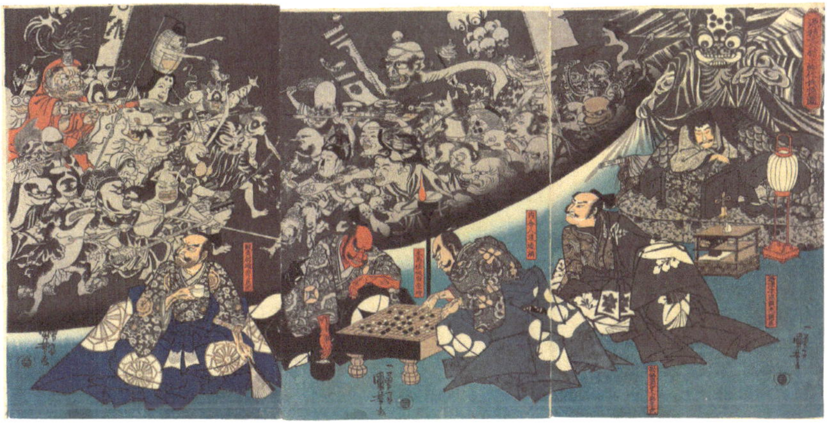

Figure 8.10: *The Earth Spider Generates Monsters at the Mansion of Lord Minamoto Yorimitsu*, Utagawa Kuniyoshi, 1843, color woodblock print triptych, National Museum of Asian Art, Smithsonian Institution, Washington, DC.

dreaming of a horde of *bakemono* (literally, "changing thing," or shapeshifter).[24] His retainers sit to the left, some playing the board game *go*, oblivious to the disturbance in the air. The *bakemono* figures include characters from the "Night Parade of One Hundred Demons," Buddhist imagery such as the red-robed Daruma in the upper left, Chinese Lucky Gods, Tokugawa images such as the lantern demon (to the right of Daruma), and the huge Earth Spider in the upper right, resembling a spider viewed under a microscope.

Whether or not Kuniyoshi and his publisher intended this triptych as satire or subversion, consumers were convinced that it was a criticism of the current regime. The print was released in 1843 during the Tempō Reforms, which were a response to natural disasters, widespread crop failure, rural uprisings, and increasing awareness of economic disparities. The public believed that this hugely popular triptych was filled with hidden references criticizing shogun Ieyoshi (1793–1853) and his senior advisor, Mizuno Tadakuni (1794–1851). The *bakemono* were thought to represent the oppressed public. Demand for the prints exceeded supply, and government officials were not amused. The publisher and Kuniyoshi were let off lightly since there was no proof that they intended the print to be an attack on the shogunate. Nevertheless, knockoff versions continued to be published, and those responsible were punished.[25]

Despite government censorship, publishing flourished. Large print runs became common in the 1800s. A limited edition might be 500 prints, but prints were routinely issued in much higher numbers, up to 6,000 or more.[26] It is thought that over 20,000 prints of each design were made for the *Hōeidō Tōkaidō* series (c. 1832–1833) by Utagawa Hiroshige (1797–1858) and published by Takenouchi Magohachi (Hōeidō) from the original blocks (Figure 8.11).[27] *Stories of the True*

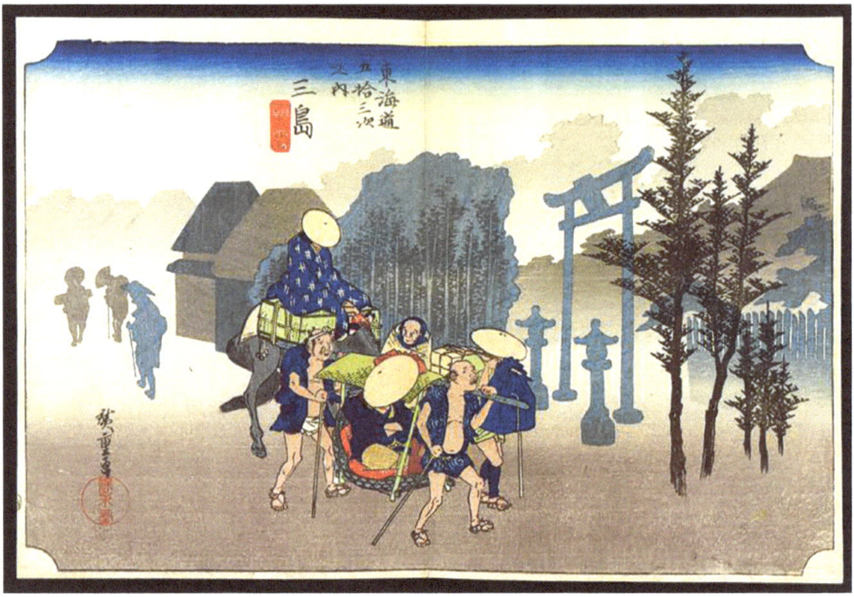

Figure 8.11: "Mishima, Morning Mist" from *Tōkaidō Hōeidō* series, Utagawa Hiroshige, c. 1832–1833, color woodblock print, Minneapolis Institute of Art, Public domain.

Loyalties of the Faithful Samurai, a series by Utagawa Kuniyoshi, brought sales of 408,000 prints.[28]

Although images of Kabuki actors and *bijin* (beautiful women) continued to sell, landscapes, bird-and-flower images, and stories from Chinese and Japanese history became more prevalent. Landscape prints gained in market share as people traveled more, for both pleasure and business. Travel was undertaken for official government business, by pilgrims visiting temples and shrines or famous sites, for the required daimyo processions to and from Edo, and by foreign embassies doing the same. Consequently, a travel industry developed, with travel guides and maps published as early as 1659.[29]

The travel industry promoted the idea of *omiyage*, souvenirs that travelers brought back to family and friends or kept as mementos. Prints became popular souvenirs; according to the travel guide *Tōkaidō meisho zue* (*Famous Views Along the Tōkaidō*), the prints were the "best gifts to bring home."[30]

Publishers went on to seek the tourist trade by relocating their shops or opening new branches along the major roads on the outskirts of Edo.[31] Tapping into the rich tradition of famous places, they published print series on Edo, Kyoto, and other sites, including landmarks in the countryside. During this period, these series expanded from thirty-six to more than a hundred prints in a set, and include some of the most well known nineteenth-century prints.

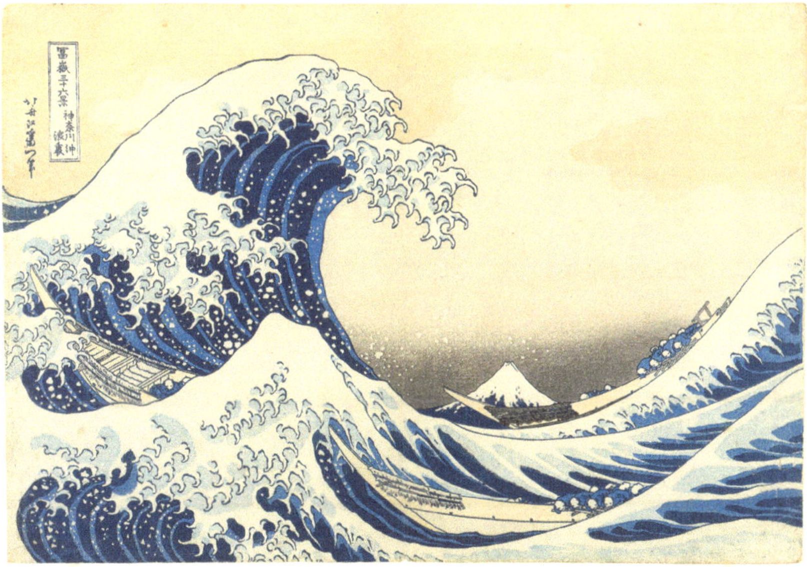

Figure 8.12: "Under the Wave off Kanagawa" from *Thirty-Six Views of Mount Fuji*, Katsushika Hokusai, 1830–1833, color woodblock print, Minneapolis Institute of Art, Public domain.

Among these are Katsushika Hokusai's *Thirty-Six Views of Mt. Fuji* (1830–1833), of which "Under the Wave off Kanagawa" is the most iconic example (Figure 8.12). Fuji is a symbol of Japan with multiple associations and is often represented in art.[32] Hokusai designed the series incorporating the European techniques of lowered horizon lines, atmospheric perspective, scientific perspective, and diminishing perspective (objects in the distance are smaller than those in the foreground). A huge wave is about to swamp a boat filled with men, while its curvilinear shape draws the viewer's eye to Mt. Fuji, centered in the background.

The color used in this print is significant: Berlin Blue (aka Prussian Blue) had been introduced to Japan earlier, but in the 1830s it was used frequently in prints.[33] Later in the 1800s and early 1900s, this blue was mistaken as a traditional Japanese pigment similar to indigo, despite it being a chemical manufactured in Europe.[34] Prints like "Under the Wave off Kanagawa" were exported to Europe and the United States in the late 1800s and were visually understood by artists and popular with consumers owing in part to the use of these European visual techniques and colors. Woodblock prints were among the most sought-after Japanese *objets d'art* by collectors, artists, and consumers in Europe and the U.S., and had a significant influence on painting and prints of the late nineteenth century, particularly in the Japonisme movement.

Printing techniques and materials became even more sophisticated. Hiroshige portrayed scenes along the Tōkaidō, the main road between Edo and Kyoto, that

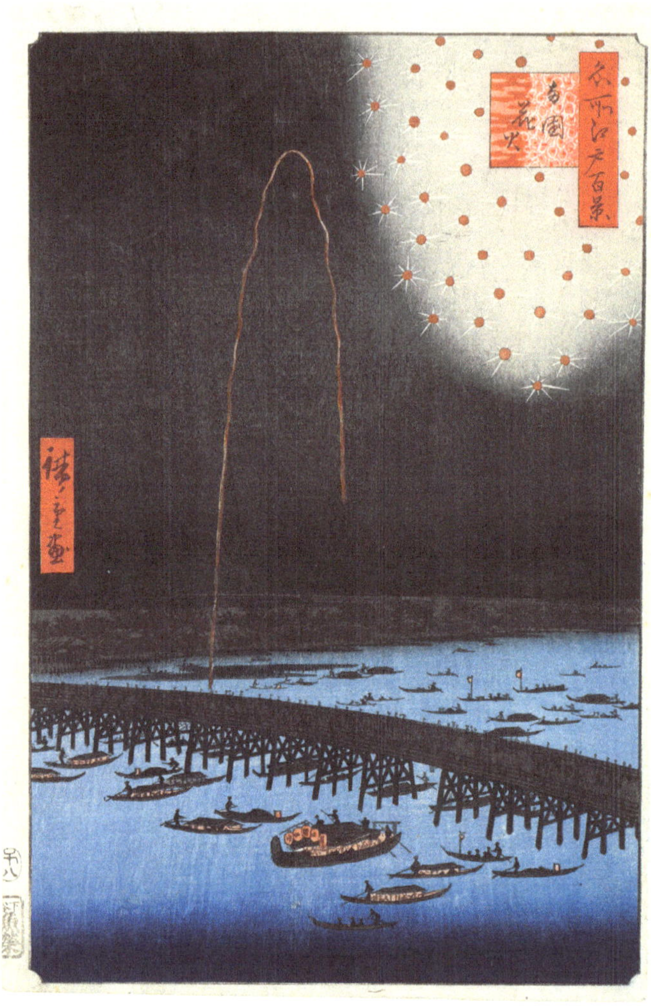

Figure 8.13: "Fireworks at Ryōgoku" from *One Hundred Famous Views of Edo*, Utagawa Hiroshige, 1858, color woodblock print, Minneapolis Institute of Art, Public domain.

were appreciated both in Japan and abroad. He is also known for *One Hundred Famous Views of Edo*, of which "Fireworks at Ryōgoku" (1858; Figure 8.13) demonstrates enhanced techniques: the printer's careful rubbing of the background reveals the grain of the woodblock; various colors are used for the cartouche in the upper right; there are variations in the red stream of fireworks hovering over the bridge; and depth is created by shading in the dark sky and in the light-to-dark printing of the water.[35] These kinds of technical skills and innovations continued throughout the nineteenth century.[36]

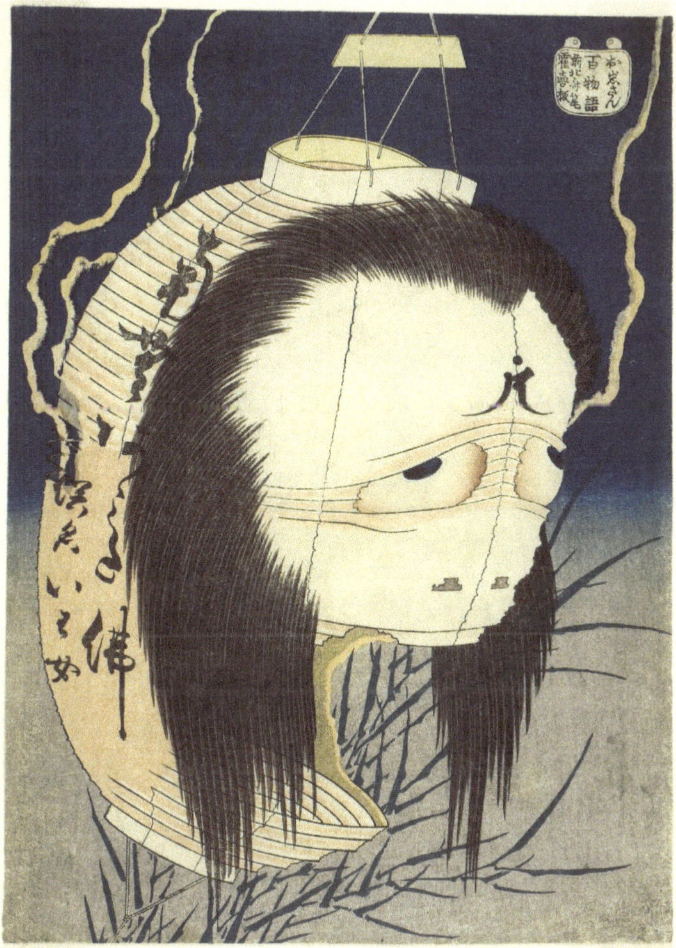

Figure 8.14: "Oiwa" from the series *One Hundred Ghost Tale*s, Katsushika Hokusai, 1831–1832, color woodblock print, Art Institute of Chicago, Public domain.

So many different types of prints were published during the 1800s that enumerating them all is difficult. Kunisada was known for his depictions of women but also designed prints of firefighters with their elaborate full-body tattoos. Kuniyoshi kept cats in his studio, advocated working from life, and was known for his warrior prints, humor, and circumventions of regulations (such as when he avoided the prohibition to represent Kabuki actors by disguising their faces on Noh masks or turtleshells). The long tradition of the strange and mysterious in Japan became even more prevalent in the nineteenth century, as human ghosts (*yūrei*) and *bakemono* were featured in Kabuki theater, prints, and paintings. Hokusai's design of the ghost Oiwa from his series *One Hundred Ghost Tales* (Figure 8.14; 1831–1832) brings to life the abused and terrorized woman

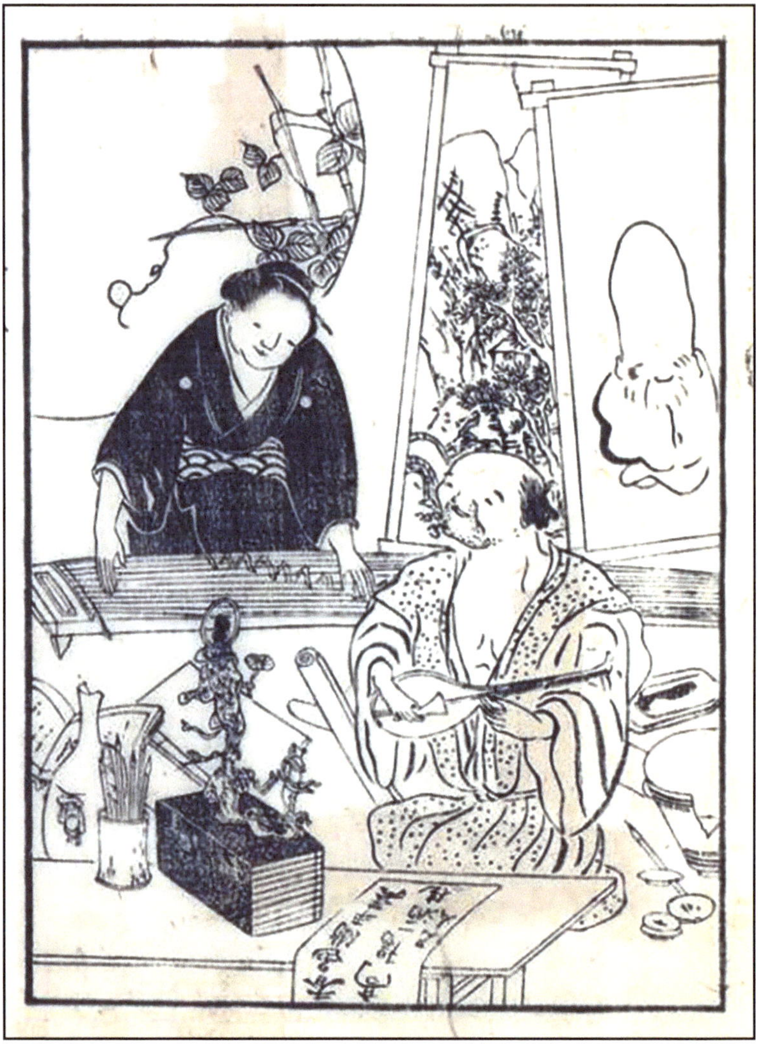

Figure 8.15: Gyokuran and Taiga, from the *Kinsei kijin den*, Mikuma Katen, 1790, woodblock printed book, New York Public Library Digital Collections, Public domain.

ghost Oiwa from one of the most famous Kabuki plays of that period, *Yotsuya Kaidan*. In this print we also see the use of Berlin Blue, and the popular theme of the paper lantern transforming into a frightening visage.

Alongside the world of prints, Kano academic painters continued to serve constituents with traditional works, the Tosa school continued to be patronized by the imperial court, and Maruyama-Shijō paintings were the style of choice for many consumers. Nanga painters also had a wide following, participated in painting and calligraphy gatherings, and were involved in the cultural salons.

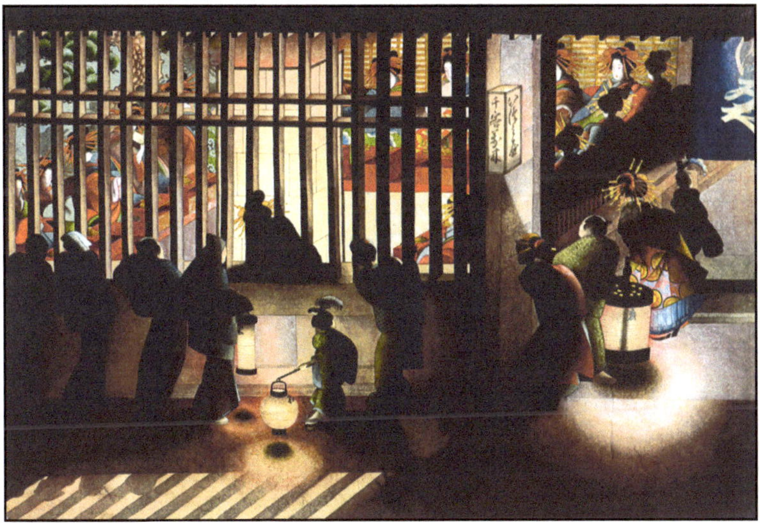

Figure 8.16: *Night Scene in Yoshiwara*, Katsushika Ōi (active 1818–1854), hanging scroll, ink and color on paper, Ōta Memorial Museum of Art, Tokyo, Wikimedia Commons.

Zen painters maintained the characteristics of their forerunners, but with more individualistic approaches. A leading master, Sengai Gibon (1750–1837), turned to painting in his later years and, like Hakuin, created new subjects and displayed considerable humor and wit, making him extremely popular in his day. He was so in demand that he composed this poem:

To my dismay
I wonder if my small hut
is just a toilet—
since everyone who comes here
seems to bring me more paper![37]

The number of women in the arts increased, owing to wider access to education and to their being more accepted by merchant, artisan, and wealthy farmer families, and by Nanga and ukiyo-e circles. Most of these women were poets and writers as well as painters.[38] The following are just a few examples: Kiyohara Yukinobu (1643–1682) was a successful Kano painter whose great-uncle was Tan'yū and father was painter Kusumi Morikage (c. 1620–1690).[39] Yamazaki Ryūjo (active 1716–1735) created ukiyo-e works of beautiful women (*bijin*). Ike Gyokuran (1727/1728–1784) joined her husband Ike Taiga in composing poetry, brushing paintings, and making music (Figure 8.15). Katsushika Ōi (active 1818–1854), Hokusai's daughter, lived with her father after a divorce, and like him, cared little for money or possessions.[40] Ōi's painting *Night Scene in Yoshiwara* (Figure 8.16) uses chiaroscuro to dramatically represent the after-dark entertainment world in one of Edo's prominent pleasure districts. Lanterns illuminate the inside of a courtesan's room, with backlit figures gathered outside. The wood lattice is also backlit on the right, but it has highlights and shadows, creating a three-dimensional appearance. Outside the room, shadows play against glimpses of color caught in the lantern light.

Through the mid-century and into the 1860s, there were rumblings of discontent among the people. The shogunate found itself increasingly under pressure as its ideology and governance fell out of step with economic and cultural developments, inflation, crop failures, social unrest, and pressure from foreign powers for contact and trade. In 1853, Commodore Matthew Perry (1794–1858) and his "black ships" entered Edo Bay, threatening military action. On Perry's return in 1854, the shogunate signed the Convention of Kanagawa, opening up the first two ports to wider trade with foreign nations. In 1858, the United States and the Tokugawa shogunate signed the Treaty of Amity and Commerce, which was followed by similar treaties with France, Great Britain, Russia, and the Netherlands.

Dissatisfaction with these concessions spread among some members of the imperial court and the southwestern daimyo. In response, honorary chief councilor Ii Naosuke (1815–1860) conducted the Ansei Purge in 1858. Naosuke was subsequently assassinated outside of Edo Castle in 1860 by Mito and Satsuma domain samurai. Throughout the 1850s and 1860s, the southwestern domains of Satsuma and Chōshū opposed the shogunate's capitulation to foreigners with the slogan "Revere the emperor, expel the barbarians." Foreigners were killed by samurai venting their anger. In 1863, the emperor delivered the "Imperial Order to Expel Barbarians," and the Satsuma and Chōshū domains attacked U.S. ships in the Shimonoseki Straits.

The alternate attendance rule for daimyo was relaxed in 1862, and Edo lost half its population. This period of unrest and economic instability led to the downfall of the Tokugawa shogunate and the dawn of a new era. An 1864 woodblock print triptych by Kawanabe Kyōsai (1831–1889) draws on the long history of using frogs, snakes, and other animals in satire, capturing the sense of instability plaguing the shogunate. It is thought to be a commentary on the Shimonoseki Straits battles, with two armies facing off in the water (Figure 8.17). Frog warriors use cattail stalks as spears and lotus leaves for boats and clothing. Images of severed heads and blood are scattered throughout the design.

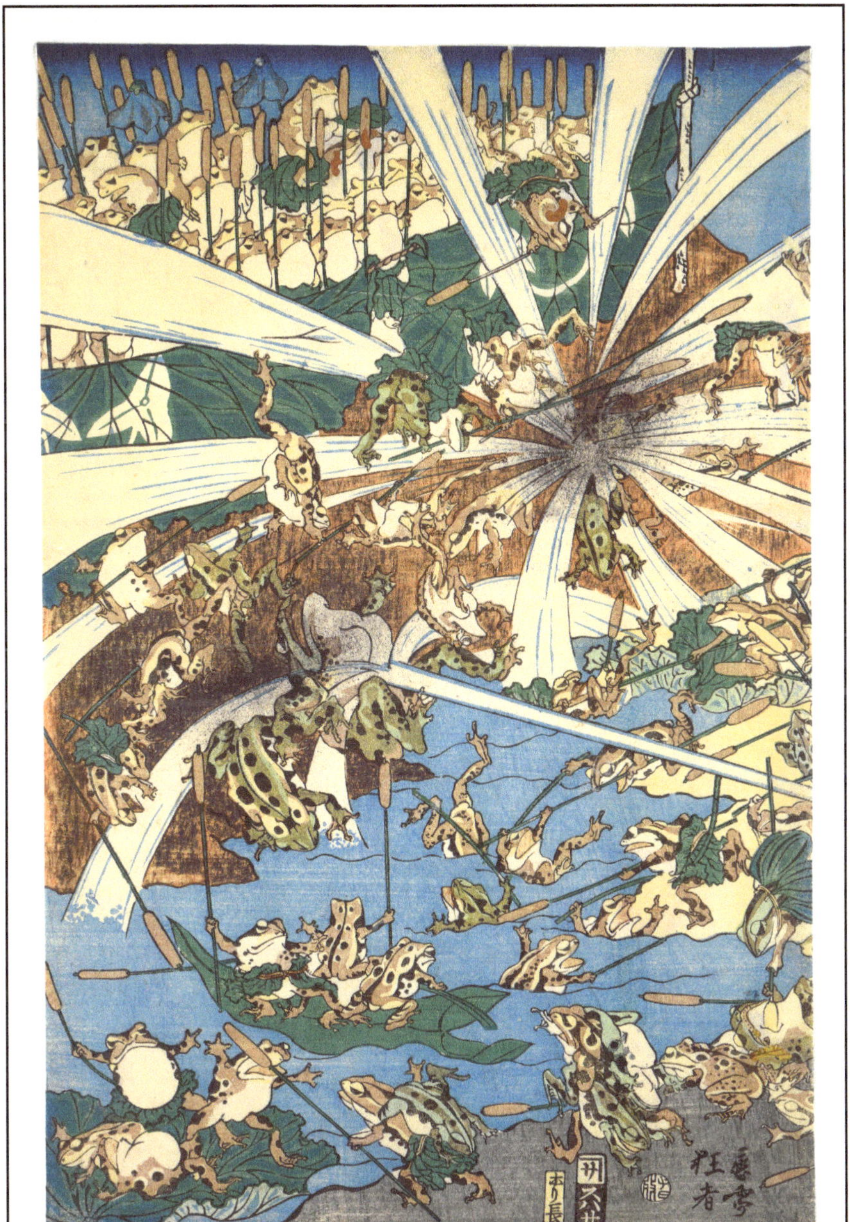

Figure 8.17: *Fūryū: The Great Battle of the Frogs*, Kawanabe Kyōsai, 1864, color woodblock print triptych, New York Public Library Digital Collections, Public domain.

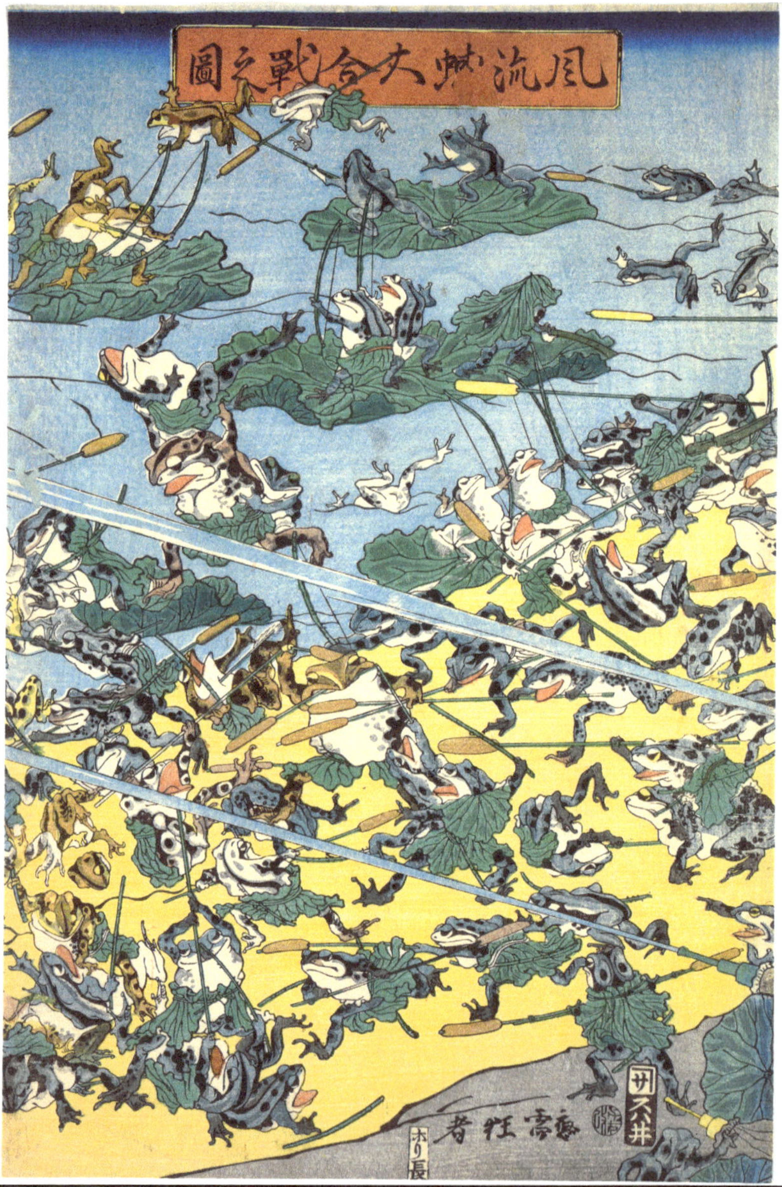
風流蛙大合戰之圖

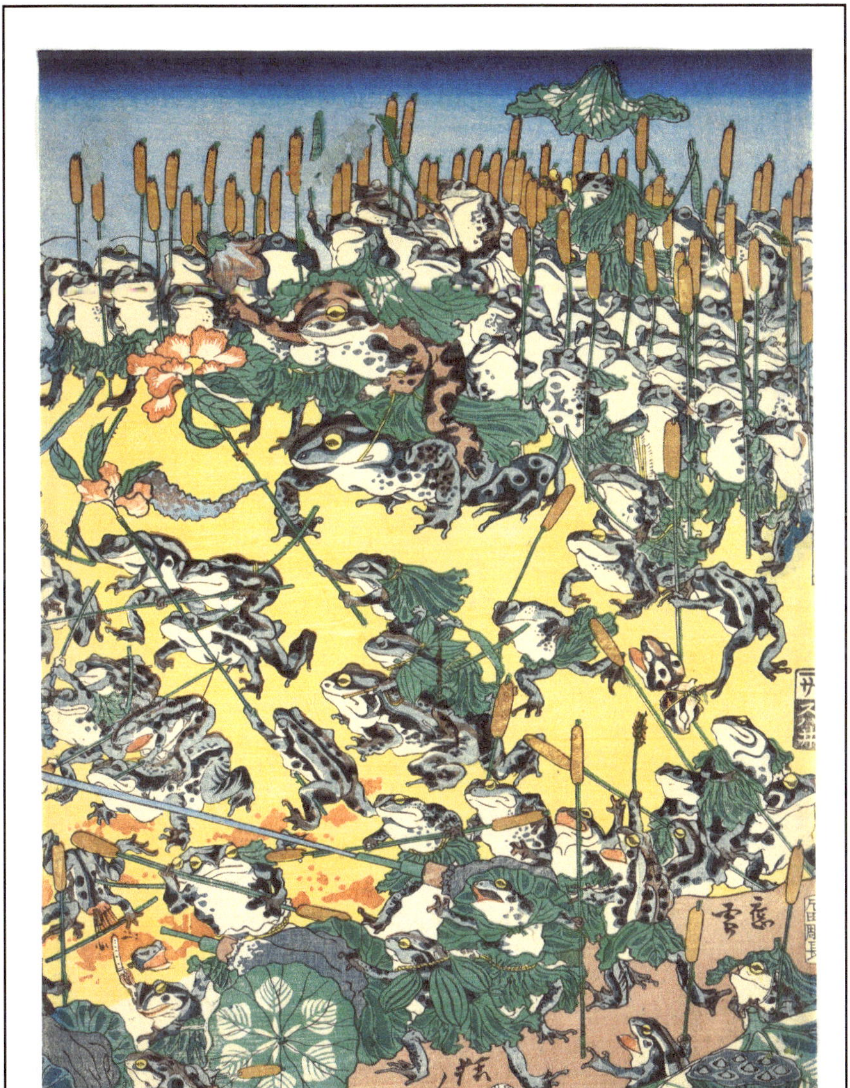

Notes

[1] Matsunosuke Nishiyama, *Edo Culture: Daily Life and Diversions in Urban Japan, 1600–1868* (Honolulu: University of Hawai'i Press, 1997), 42.

[2] Tokugawa officials were by no means the only rulers to enact numerous sumptuary laws. Ancient China, Greece, and Rome had sumptuary laws, as well as nations and city states in Europe during the fifteenth and sixteenth centuries. Regulations were meant to keep the classes clearly separated, and to discourage luxury and regulate lifestyles. As in Tokugawa Japan, they were difficult to enforce. Donald H. Shively, "Sumptuary Regulation and Status in Early Tokugawa Japan," *Harvard Journal of Asiatic Studies* 25 (1964–1965): 135–136.

[3] Much has been written about the Tokugawa shogunate's inability to maintain social control. Regarding how the arts were affected, see, for example, Katsuya Hirano, *The Politics of Dialogic Imagination: Power and Popular Culture in Early Modern Japan* (Chicago: University of Chicago Press, 2014); and Sarah E. Thompson and H.D. Harootunian, *Undercurrents in the Floating World: Censorship and Japanese Prints* (New York: Asia Society Galleries, 1991).

[4] Takeshi Nakagawa provides a detailed study of Tokugawa domestic architecture in *The Japanese House: In Space, Memory, and Language*, trans. Geraldine Harcourt (Tokyo: International House of Japan, 2005).

[5] Susan B. Hanley, "Housing and Furnishings," in *Everyday Things in Premodern Japan: The Hidden Legacy of Material Culture* (Berkeley: University of California Press, 1997), chapter 2.

[6] For more, see Edward S. Morse, *Japanese Homes and Their Surroundings* (Boston: Ticknor, 1886; Rutland, VT: Tuttle, 1986).

[7] Liza Dalby, *Kimono: Fashioning Culture* (New Haven: Yale University Press, 1993), 60–63.

[8] Thomas Murray and Virginia Soenksen, *Textiles of Japan: The Thomas Murray Collection at the Minneapolis Institute of Art* (Munich: Prestel, 2018), 384–385, 446.

[9] For an overview of Japan's textiles, see Keith Reimink, "Dressed by Nature: Japanese Clothing Through Time," video interview with Andreas Marks, Mary Griggs Burke Curator of Japanese and Korean Art and Director of the Clark Center for Japanese Art, Minneapolis Institute of Art, National Consortium for Teaching About Asia, 2023, https://vimeo.com/1058777910/f075c16e48.

[10] Hiroshi Nara, *The Structure of Detachment: The Aesthetic Vision of Kuki Shūzō* (Honolulu: University of Hawai'i Press, 2004), 1, 109.

[11] Nara, *The Structure of Detachment*, 2.

[12] Christine Guth, *Art of Edo Japan: The Artist and the City, 1615–1868* (New York: Abrams, 1996; New Haven: Yale University Press, 2014), 130–131.

[13] Satoko Tamamushi, "Sakai Hōitsu and Art Ownership," in *Acquisition: Art and*

Ownership in Edo-Period Japan, ed. Elizabeth Lillehoj (Warren, CT: Floating World Editions, 2007), 130.

[14] Guth, *Art of Edo Japan*, 120–123.

[15] Guth, *Art of Edo Japan*, 124; see also Alexander Hofmann, *Performing / Painting in Tokugawa Japan* (Berlin: Dietrich Reimer Verlag, 2011).

[16] Frank Chance, "In the Studio of Painting Study: Transmission Practices of Tani Bunchō," in *Copying the Master and Stealing His Secrets: Talent and Training in Japanese Painting*, ed. Brenda G. Jordan and Victoria Weston (Honolulu: University of Hawai'i Press, 2003), 60–85; Guth, *Art of Edo Japan*, 124.

[17] Watanabe Kazan, *Portrait of Ōzora Buzaemon* (1827), Cleveland Museum of Art, https://www.clevelandart.org/art/1980.177.

[18] For more, see James T. Ulak, "Kazan's Portrait of a Giant: Ozorabuzaemon," *Bulletin of the Cleveland Museum of Art* 70, no. 3 (March 1983): 99–111.

[19] Timon Screech, *The Lens Within the Heart: The Western Scientific Gaze and Popular Imagery in Later Edo Japan* (Honolulu: University of Hawai'i Press, 2002), 54–56. See also Sumie Jones, ed., with Kenji Watanabe, *An Edo Anthology: Literature from Japan's Mega-City, 1750–1850* (Honolulu: University of Hawai'i Press, 2013), 479–480.

[20] Screech, *The Lens Within the Heart*, 198–200.

[21] Screech, *The Lens Within the Heart*, 181–183.

[22] Thompson and Harootunian, *Undercurrents in the Floating World*, 70.

[23] The books were superficially historical and claimed to be didactic, but these tactics to avoid censorship failed. Thompson and H.D. Harootunian, *Undercurrents in the Floating World*, 62.

[24] The word *bakemono* appears in a variety of contexts from the Tokugawa period, and referred to shapeshifters, things that are strangely formed or frightening, and even monsters. Michael Dylan Foster, *The Book of Yōkai: Mysterious Creatures of Japanese Folklore* (Berkeley: University of California Press, 2015), 17–19.

[25] Melinda Takeuchi, "'Minamoto Raiko' and 'The Earth Spider': Demons and Protest in Late Tokugawa Japan," *Ars Orientalis* 17 (1987): 5–38; Thompson and Harootunian, *Undercurrents in the Floating World,* 82; Foster, *The Book of Yōkai*, 42, 129–130. See also Katsuya Hirano, "Social Networks and Production of Public Discourse in Edo Popular Culture," in Lillehoj, *Acquisition*, 111–125.

[26] Matthi Forrer, "The Relationship Between Publishers and Print Formats in the Edo Period," in *The Commercial and Cultural Climate of Japanese Printmaking*, ed. Amy Reigle Newland (Amsterdam: Hotei, 2004), 178, 183.

[27] Chris Uhlenbeck, "Production Constraints in the World of Ukiyo-e: An Introduction to the Commercial Climate of Japanese Printmaking," in Newland, *The Commercial and Cultural Climate of Japanese Printmaking*, 12.

[28] Uhlenbeck, "Production Constraints in the World of Ukiyo-e," 12.

[29] For more, see Mary Elizabeth Berry, *Japan in Print: Information and Nation in the Early Modern Period* (Berkeley: University of California Press, 2006).

[30] Uhlenbeck, "Production Constraints in the World of Ukiyo-e," 15.

[31] Forrer, "The Relationship Between Publishers and Print Formats in the Edo Period," 185–186.

[32] Fuji is a famous place (*meisho*), linked to Shinto and Buddhism practices, a centuries-old pilgrimage site, and serves as a symbol of the nation of Japan. See, for example, "Fujisan, Sacred Place and Source of Artistic Inspiration," UNESCO World Heritage Convention, 2013, https://whc.unesco.org/en/list/1418/.

[33] See Henry D. Smith, "Hokusai and the Blue Revolution in Edo Prints," in *Hokusai and His Age*, ed. John T. Carpenter (Amsterdam: Hotei, 2005), 235–269.

[34] Smith, "Hokusai and the Blue Revolution in Edo Prints," 235–236.

[35] James McNeill Whistler's *Nocturne in Black and Gold: The Falling Rocket* (1875) is one of numerous paintings of fireworks or bridges that reflect his exposure to prints like this.

[36] Twenty-first century research has debunked many assumptions about Japanese prints. One outdated theory held that the golden age of prints was over by the 1800s, when, in fact, innovations in composition, printing quality and techniques, and new materials all contributed to continuing creative advances. The second assumption was that the Japanese themselves did not value prints. Because prints were generally mass-produced for commercial purposes, they were considered well into the twentieth century to be "low art." It is true that some prints were used as packing material for ceramics sent to Europe in the nineteenth century, but high-quality prints were not treated in this way. It is also true that prints were inexpensive; a single-sheet print could be purchased for around the cost of a bowl of noodles. These cheaper prints, however, were produced with lower quality paper, fewer colors, and less skilled printing. Finally, there was also the assumption that the woodblocks wore out easily, so only the first few hundred prints might be made from them. This is also false, as evidenced by many examples of thousands of prints generated from the original blocks.

[37] Stephen Addiss, *The Art of Zen: Paintings and Calligraphy by Japanese Monks, 1600–1925* (New York: Abrams, 1989), 179.

[38] Patricia Fister, *Japanese Women Artists, 1600–1900* (Lawrence, KS: Spencer Museum of Art, 1988), 13–14.

[39] For more, see Fister, *Japanese Women Artists, 1600–1900.*

[40] Both Gyokuran and Ōi were independent spirits. Gyokuran didn't shave her eyebrows and was somewhat oblivious to clothing and makeup. Ōi bought prepared food rather than cook and did little in the way of housekeeping. She and Hokusai moved whenever their dwelling became too dirty and cluttered to endure. Fister, *Japanese Women Artists, 1600–1900*, 74–76 and 128–130.

9

Civilization and Enlightenment

Early Meiji Period

If you tap a head with the modern haircut, you will hear the sound of civilization and enlightenment.

— A popular saying that refers to an 1871 edict allowing samurai to cut off their topknots

In 1867, the Tokugawa shogunate fell and a new government was established, centered on Emperor Meiji (1852–1912). From 1868 to 1889, the Meiji government launched an all-out effort to industrialize and modernize the country, with remarkable strides made in just twenty years. Edo was renamed Tokyo, and became the capital of Japan. The early years of the Meiji period (1868–1912) became known as an era of *bunmei kaika* (civilization and enlightenment).

New developments included newspapers, railroads, factories processing tea and silk for export, delegations to Europe and the United States, technological advances, and participation in international and domestic expositions to showcase science, technology, and domestic industries. The arts were called upon to boost the national economy while, at the same time, being drawn into a debate over the purpose of art in a modern nation-state. The pursuit of a modern painting style caused friction between advocates of Western-style painting and those promoting a Japanese style, which used traditional formats and materials.

Japan was positioned for rapid change, with Tokugawa-era infrastructure in place, high literacy rates, and a centuries-old practice of assimilating and adapting foreign influences.[1] To bring Japan into the company of the world's advanced nations, government leaders studied Western industries, technologies, military systems, and political frameworks. They also wanted to renegotiate the unequal treaties forced upon Japan in the 1850s. To this end, Japanese delegations traveled abroad, and foreign specialists (*oyatoi*) were brought in to teach and consult. These

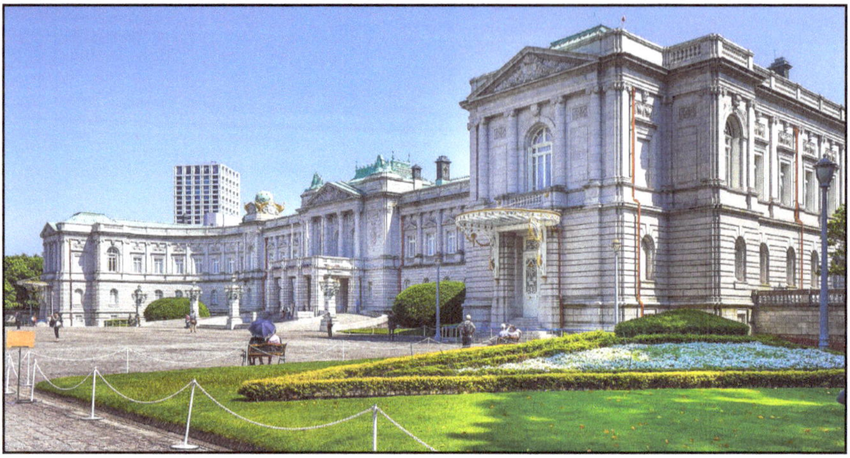

Figure 9.1: Akasaka Palace, Katayama Tōkuma, 1909, steel-reinforced masonry, Wikimedia Commons.

oyatoi were often young, many in their twenties when they accepted positions at Tokyo University and in government offices. Among them was a young British architect who accepted government commissions for modern architecture.

Josiah Conder (1852–1920) arrived in 1877 and taught the first generation of architects at Tokyo University. His pupils became the future of Meiji architecture: Tatsuno Kingo (1854–1919), who designed the Bank of Japan (1890–1896) and Tokyo Station (1914); Katayama Tōkuma (1852–1917), architect for the Akasaka Palace (1909); Tsumaki Yorinaka (1859–1916), designer of the Yokohama Specie Bank (1904); and Sone Tatsuzō (1852–1937), designer of the Old Keio University Library (1912).[2] Katayama's Neo-Baroque Akasaka Palace marked a technological breakthrough: the main structure was constructed in stone reinforced with steel imported from the Carnegie Works in Pittsburgh, with the assistance of American engineers, an earthquake-resistant design (Figure 9.1).[3]

Conder presented his students with a new concept: architecture is art, and counts among a nation's highest achievements. Architects, therefore, should be recognized as both artists and intellectuals.[4] His own designs included the 1881 Ueno Museum, as seen in a woodblock print of the 1881 Domestic Industrial Exposition (Figure 9.2); the Holy Resurrection Cathedral (Nikorai-dō; 1891), and the private residence of industrialist Iwasaki Hisaya (1865–1955; built in 1896). One of his most iconic buildings was the Rokumeikan (Deer Cry Pavilion; 1883; Figure 9.3), commissioned by the government for Western-style entertaining. Although Foreign Minister Inoue Kaoru (1836–1915) had requested a completely Western design, Conder employed what he called a "Renaissance villa" style, incorporating "Saracenic" elements such as "vaguely Moorish" second-floor arches supported by "dark, bulbous pillars with palm-frond capitals" and metal filigree work.[5] The Rokumeikan was a venue for parties and balls, meetings, dinners, and receptions at which Japanese men and women in Western clothing mixed with

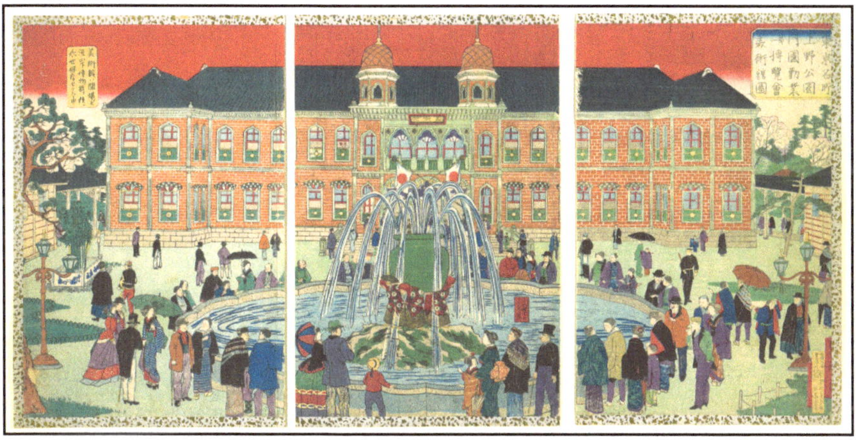

Figure 9.2: Illustration of the Museum at the Second National Domestic Industrial Exhibition in Ueno from the series *Famous Places in Tokyo*, Utagawa Hiroshige III, 1881, color woodblock print triptych, Metropolitan Museum of Art, New York, Public domain.

foreigners. Official guests were also housed there in grand fashion, since Tokyo did not have a Western-style hotel at the time. The Rokumeikan had a significant role in "civilization and enlightenment," serving as the center of Western-style social life, with parties attracting as many as a thousand guests.[6]

Meiji architecture benefited from master carpenters, who used traditional tools and methods to construct Western-style buildings such as the Mitsui House, designed by Shimizu Kisuke II (1815–1881), and the former Kaichi School in Matsumoto, by Tateishi Seijū (1829–1894; Figure 9.4), one of the first public elementary schools in Japan.[7] Master carpenters and professional architects played a crucial role in providing Japan with office buildings, hotels, and other structures that bolstered Japan's self-image as a modern, progressive nation.[8]

New concepts called for new terminology. In keeping with Western definitions of "art," the Japanese created terms to describe previously nonexistent categories, such as *kenchiku* (architecture). *Bijutsu* (fine art) was first used at the Vienna International Exposition in 1873. Other new terms included *kaiga* (painting), *chōkoku* (sculpture), and *kōgei* (craft). Before, words referring to a picture or a painting included *shoga* (painting and calligraphy), *ga*, *e*, or *zu*. The new term *yōga* referred to painting (*ga*) using Western (*yō*) styles and techniques; *nihonga* referred to Japanese-style painting. Such terms reflected new ways of thinking about what constituted "art" for a modernizing country.[9]

Japan had been incorporating knowledge from Europe since the 1500s. In the 1860s, shogunal and domain delegations traveled abroad for study and fact-finding. The port city of Yokohama had opened to foreigners in 1859, and artists responded to the public's curiosity by producing woodblock prints called

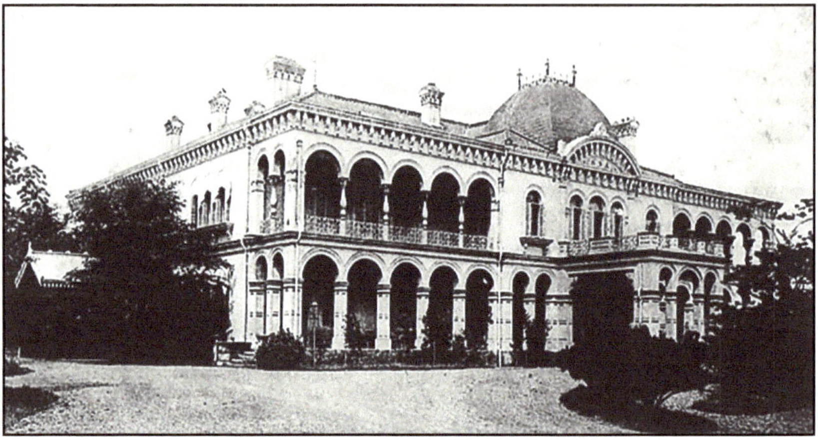

Figure 9.3: Rokumeikan, Josiah Conder, 1883, "Renaissance villa" style of architecture, Wikimedia Commons.

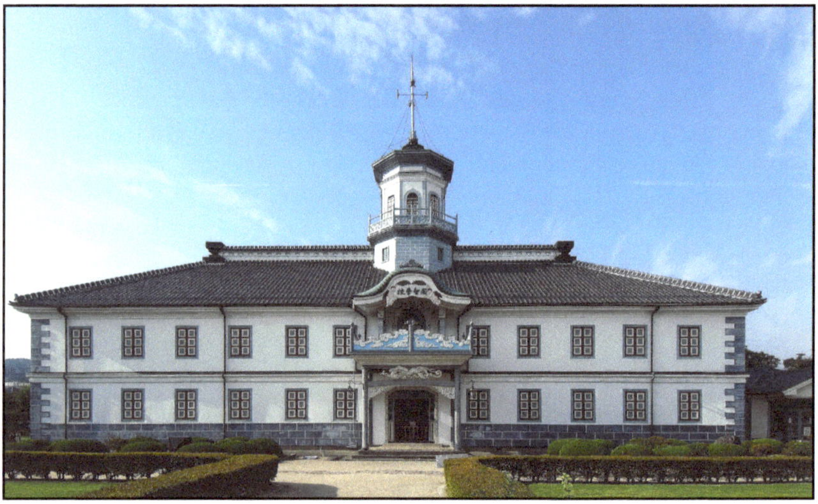

Figure 9.4: Kaichi School, Tateishi Seijū, 1876, two stories with step tower, wood frame, Matsumoto, Wikimedia Commons.

Yokohama-e, depicting people living in the foreign enclave near the capital. The shogunate established the Institute for Dutch Studies in 1856, where Takahashi Yuichi (1828–1894) was admitted to the Painting Bureau. After learning painting techniques from Kawakami Tōgai (1827–1881), Yuichi studied oil painting with English artist Charles Wirgman (1832–1891) in Yokohama in 1866. Oil painting was not yet established in Japan, but Yuichi became an early proponent of the theories and techniques of this newly introduced medium, advocating for verisimilitude and noting the merits of oil paint in conveying a subject's character (Figure 9.5).[10]

Over time, art schools opened and art associations formed. The Technical Art School was founded in 1876 and staffed with Italian instructors, including the Barbizon-school painter Antonio Fontanesi (1818–1882), who trained *yōga* painters such as Yamamoto Hōsui (1850–1906), Goseda Yoshimatsu (1855–1915), Asai Chū (1856–1907; Figure 9.6), and Yamashita Rin (1857–1939). Yamashita Rin was accepted to the school when women were still not admitted to comparable schools in France.[11] Asai Chū later profoundly influenced the next generation of oil painters in Kyoto, such as Umehara Ryūzaburō (1888–1986). Yamamoto, Goseda, and Asai traveled to Europe to study, particularly to France; Yamashita Rin studied Christian icons in Russia, returning to paint icons for churches in Japan.

Kyoto was in some respects ahead of Tokyo in its response to the new artistic trends: the Kyoto Exhibition was launched in 1871, plans to create a Kyoto Museum were announced in 1875, the Kyoto Prefectural School of Painting opened in 1880, and the Kyoto Art Association was founded in 1890.[12] Elsewhere, particularly in Tokyo, public art exhibitions proliferated with government support. Japan also participated in European expositions, beginning with the 1851 Great Exhibition at the Crystal Palace in London, followed by the 1867 Paris International Exposition and the 1873 Vienna International Exposition. The government promoted the production of high-quality arts and

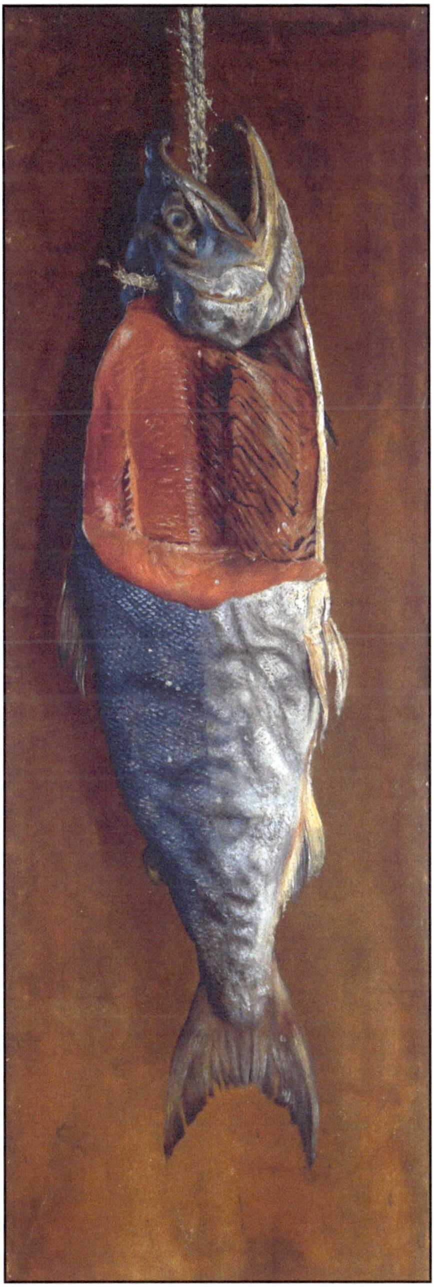

Figure 9.5: *Salmon*, Takahashi Yuichi, 1877, oil on paper, University Art Museum, Tokyo University of the Arts, Wikimedia Commons.

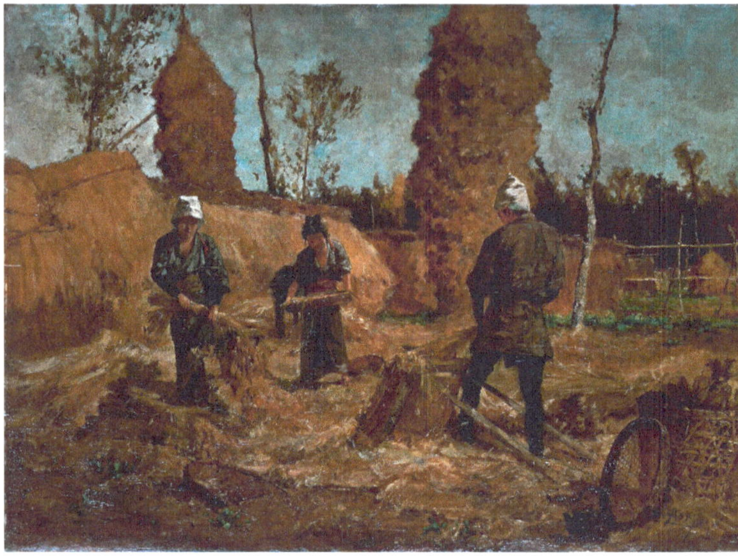

Figure 9.6: *Harvest*, Asai Chū, 1890, oil on canvas, University Art Museum, Tokyo University of the Arts, Wikimedia Commons.

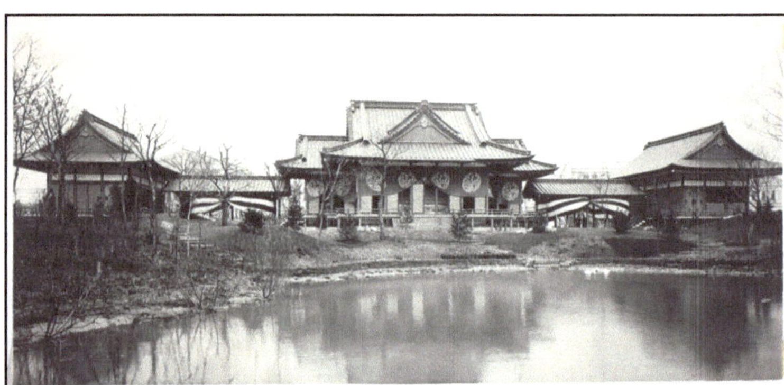

Figure 9.7: Japanese Pavilion at the World's Columbian Exposition, Kuru Masamichi, 1893, Wikimedia Commons.

artisan wares for export. This was the period of the Japonisme movement in the West, followed by the Arts and Crafts Movement and Art Nouveau; anything Japanese—from umbrellas and fans to tea, silk, lacquer, ceramics, woodblock prints, metalwork, and cloisonné, to name a few—was the rage in Western countries.

After Japan's success at the 1876 Centennial Exhibition in Philadelphia, the government began to hold domestic industrial expositions, starting with the 1877 First Domestic Industrial Exposition in Ueno Park, Tokyo, where thousands of works were displayed.[13] Subsequent domestic exhibitions were held in 1881

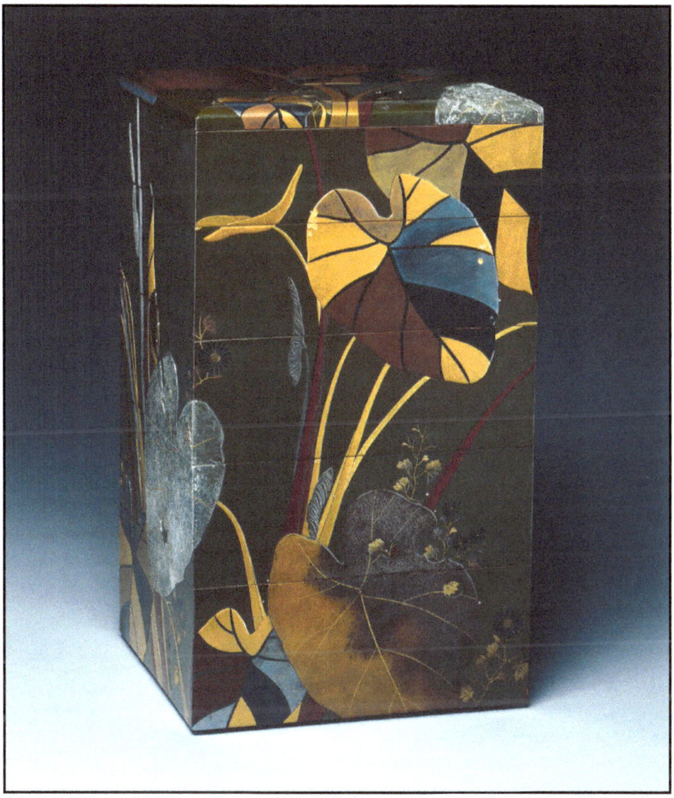

Figure 9.8: Stacked food container (*jūbako*) with design of taro plants and chrysanthemums, mid-nineteenth century, Shibata Zeshin, lacquered wood, gold and silver *hiramaki-e*, *takamaki-e*, and colored *togidashimaki-e*, Metropolitan Museum of Art, New York, Public domain.

(Figure 9.2), 1890, 1895, and 1903. Meanwhile, Japan continued to participate in international expositions, including the 1893 World's Columbian Exposition in Chicago, for which Conder's pupil Kuru Masamichi (1858–1914) designed the Japan pavilion based on the early eleventh-century Phoenix Hall (Figure 9.7; see Chapter 3).

Artisans were encouraged to produce high-quality work for sale abroad, with specialists such as Gottfried Wagener (1831–1892) hired to perfect the process of ceramics production and increase exports. Wagener arrived in 1868 and oversaw the exhibits at the Vienna International Exposition. Companies such as the newly formed Kiryū Kōshō Kaisha and Eishinsha commissioned works from artisans for export and exhibitions. Kiryū Kōshō Kaisha established a branch in New York in 1877 and another in Paris the following year. These companies, as well as the studios of master craftsmen, produced and sold works that catered to Western

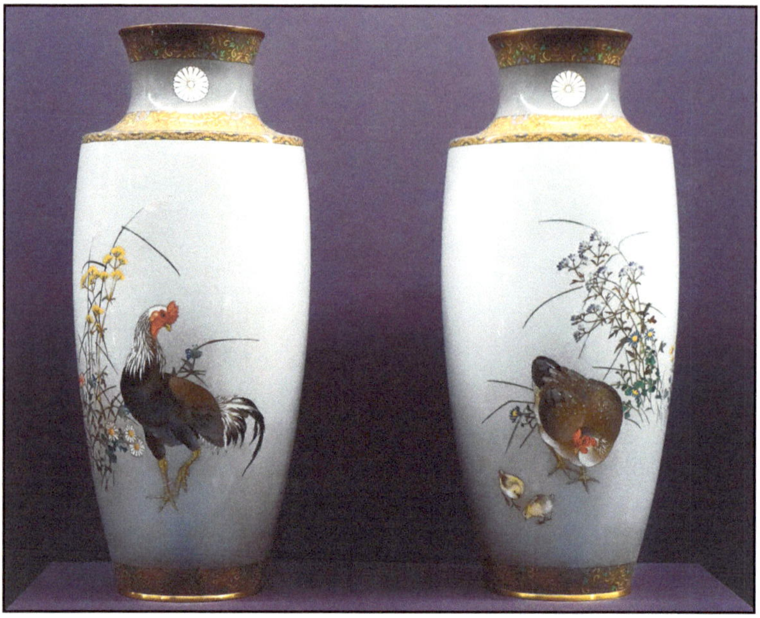

Figure 9. 9: Vases with Hen and Rooster, Namikawa Sōsuke, c. 1890–1900, *musen* and cloisonné enamels worked in gold and silver wire, gilt copper rims and feet, Khalili Collection of Japanese Art, Wikimedia Commons.

tastes, often incorporating new techniques and creative designs into established forms. Visitors to international and domestic exhibitions marveled at the skill and aesthetic qualities of Japanese arts such as ceramics, metalworking, cloisonné, and lacquer.

Lacquer was one of the main export items at this time. Painter and lacquerware designer Shibata Zeshin (1807–1891) developed a technique that involved adding clay or egg white to thicken the lacquer, resulting in a surface that "retains its grooves even after it has dried."[14] Creating a stacked food container (Figure 9.8), Zeshin combined gold and silver low relief and high-relief lacquer techniques with multicolored painting in lacquer, reflecting his training in the Maruyama-Shijō school as well as Rinpa influence in the natural motif of taro leaves.

Groundbreaking as well was the cloisonné wireless enamel technique of Namikawa Sōsuke (1847–1910), who developed a painterly style with gradations of color and wash-like effects, drawing on designs by Zeshin and Watanabe Seitei (1852–1918; Figure 9.9).[15] Nature themes and lifelike figures of insects, birds, and other creatures (including dragons) impressed visitors to international expositions with the quality of the craftsmanship. An important example is *Twelve Falcons* (Figure 9.10) by Suzuki Chōkichi (1848–1919), commissioned by the art dealer Hayashi Tadamasa (1856–1906), and displayed at the World's Columbian Exposition. Hawks and eagles are centuries-old subjects in Japanese art, symbols

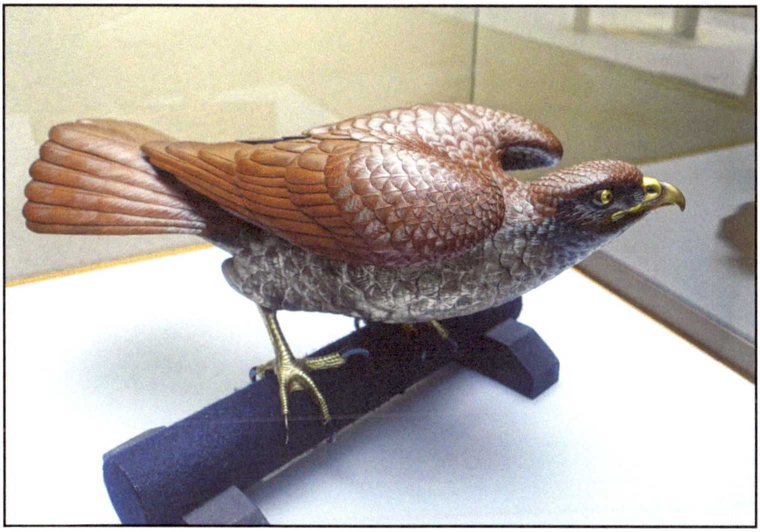

Figure 9.10: *Twelve Falcons*, Suzuki Chōkichi, 1893, cast bronze, lacquer, casting, gilding, and inlay, National Museum of Modern Art, Tokyo, Wikimedia Commons.

of military might. The life-sized birds took a team of twenty-four craftsmen four years to make under Chōkichi's direction, and each demonstrates a different metalworking technique. Metal casting, inlay, and patination—the process of covering the metal with a shiny layer—combine to create works that blur the boundaries between sculpture and craft.[16]

Kyoto dominated Japanese textile production. There, businesses sought to reinterpret the Maruyama-Shijō painting style (Chapter 7) as a naturalistic modernism, and painters often provided the designs for textile productions, large and small, particularly at the Nishijin works. Nishijin production capitalized on French Jacquard loom weaving techniques to produce wall hangings and other highly prized work, revitalizing Kyoto's economy. Western arts were moving toward naturalism as well, and thus the finely woven, almost painterly textiles became popular abroad. A silk embroidered hanging with the Hō-ō bird (Figure 9.11) is an example of the type of large textile produced for export to Europe.[17]

During the 1880s, as Japanese re-evaluated the influx of all things Western and its impact on native culture, oil painting's stature with the government fell. The government found an advocate for revitalizing traditional arts in Ernest Fenollosa (1853–1908), a recent Harvard graduate who had arrived in 1878 to take up an appointment at Tokyo University, teaching political philosophy and aesthetics.

In 1882 Fenollosa delivered a speech entitled *Bijutsu shinsetsu* ("The True Theory of Art) to the semi-governmental art association Ryūchikai (Dragon Pond Society). In this seminal talk, Fenollosa proposed "a new set of art concepts and terms that encouraged art-related discussion in Japan."[18] Speaking to a receptive

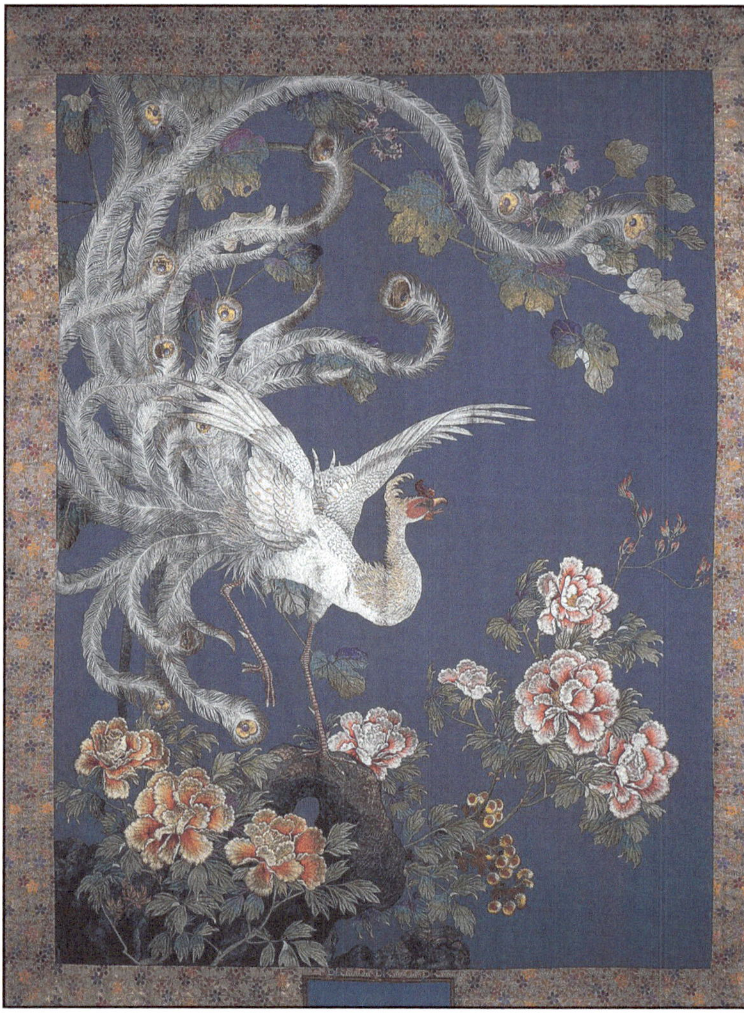

Figure 9.11: Textile hanging with Hō-ō Bird, c. 1895–1910, silk embroidery with woven silk border, Khalili Collection of Japanese Art, Wikimedia Commons.

audience, he advocated for revitalizing premodern Japanese painting, which he argued would contribute to the nation's development and the emerging sense of cultural nationalism that Ryūchikai supported.[19] Fenollosa's impact on subsequent artistic developments was mixed. His stature as a respected intellectual made him a prominent spokesperson for the preservation of premodern arts and the importance of art education. At the same time, Fenollosa's championing of *nihonga* as a national painting style created conflict between advocates of *yōga* and those of *nihonga* during a time when the mixing of styles and creative developments were occurring on their own.[20]

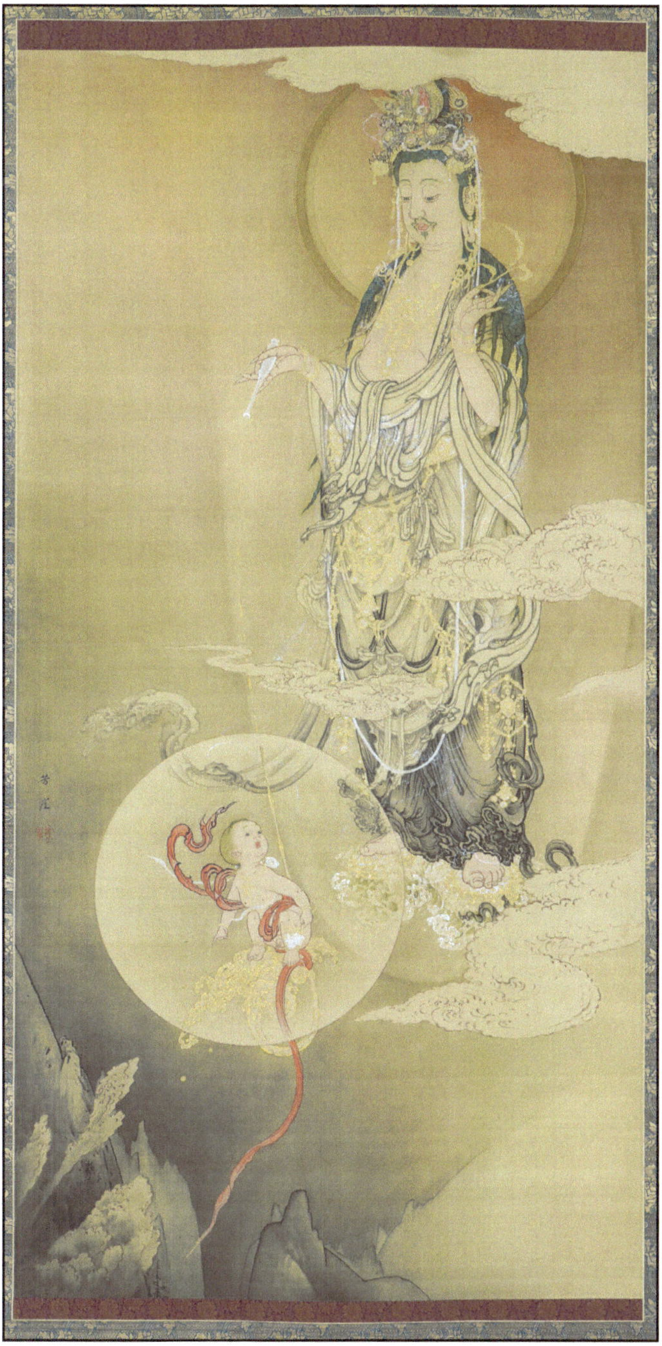

Figure 9.12: *Merciful Mother Kannon*, Kano Hōgai, 1883, hanging scroll, ink, color, and gold on silk, National Museum of Asian Art, Smithsonian Institution, Washington, DC.

The government had separated Buddhism and Shintō in 1868, resulting in the destruction of many temples. The re-evaluation of traditional arts in the 1880s led to the documentation and preservation of Buddhist temples as cultural heritage and "art." Fenollosa and his former student Okakura Kakuzō (Tenshin; 1863–1913), who had himself become a leading intellectual, were involved in this movement. In 1884, he and Okakura traveled with a group to Nara, where the eighth-century Guze Kannon at Hōryūji (Chapter 2) was unveiled for the first time in centuries. This event became one of the catalysts for the protection of Buddhist arts. At the end of the century, the first systematic laws designed to preserve and restore important art and architecture were enacted, eventually resulting in Japan's designations of National Treasures and Important Cultural Properties.

Fenollosa also had an impact on the careers of two painters who were key figures in the development of *nihonga*. Kano Hōgai (1828–1888) and Hashimoto Gahō (1835–1908) had trained in the high-ranking Kano Kobikichō atelier but fell on hard times after the loss of their military patronage. Both went through the Kano apprenticeship, honing their skills by assiduously copying from painting manuals and paintings. After the Meiji Restoration, Hōgai studied Western painting, including copperplate engraving; he painted a Western-style landscape on Japanese paper using calligraphy ink, and even used ink on Whatman watercolor paper for landscape paintings.[21] Thus, when Fenollosa recruited him in 1883 to produce paintings, Hōgai was receptive to Fenollosa's introduction to the techniques, materials, and themes of Western art.

A well-known Hōgai work is the 1883 *Hibo Kannon* (*Merciful Mother Kannon*; Figure 9.12), a large painting that draws on Hōgai's extensive experience with Chinese and Japanese precedents, the practice of devotion to Kannon (Avalokiteshvara bodhisattva) in Japan, and the *komochi kannon* tradition of Kannon and child.[22] Hōgai's approach includes dramatic compositions, brighter pigments, and Western shading and foreshortening. The androgynous mustached Kannon holds a willow twig in her left hand and a vase in her right, from which streams liquid that creates a bubble enclosing a baby who looks up at her. The effect is striking, and the painting was well received at the Second Exposition of Japanese Art in Paris in 1884. Both it and later works by Hōgai became part of the canon of *nihonga* in Japan.

After Fenollosa's 1882 speech, in which he disparaged Nanga, the government no longer promoted the style.[23] However, Nanga continued to be popular with the public. Okuhara Seiko (1837–1913) was a well-educated and skilled woman painter and calligrapher who trained some three hundred students, including Okakura Kakuzō. A successful artist, poet, and teacher, she counted political figures such as Kido Takayoshi (1833–1877) among her friends and demonstrated that a dynamic personality and artistic skill could propel a woman to fame in a man's world (Figure 9.13).[24]

A woman colleague of Seiko's was the Nanga painter Noguchi Shōhin (1847–1917); they had mutual acquaintances, such as Kido Takayoshi, and moved in the

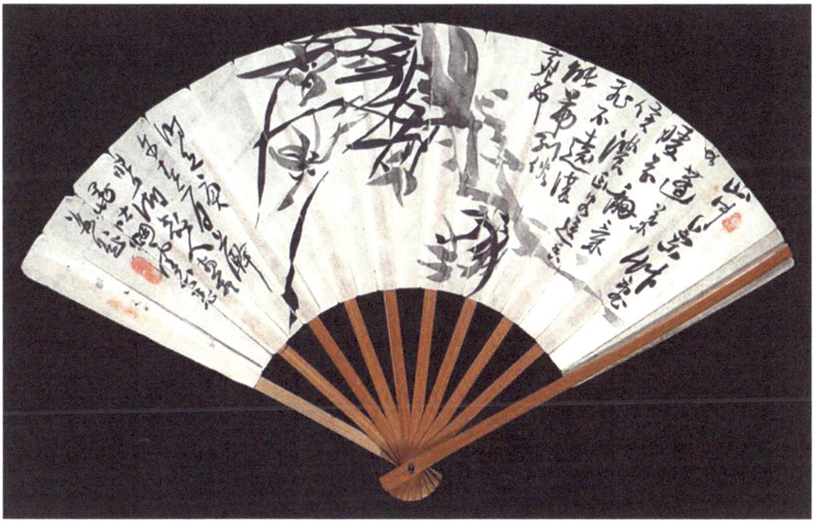

Figure 9.13: *Orchids*, Okuhara Seiko, 1870, fan, ink on mica paper, Minneapolis Institute of Art, Public domain.

same social circles. Shōhin became a prominent figure in the Tokyo art world. She won exhibition prizes, including at the 1893 Chicago World Exposition, and served as a judge for national exhibitions.[25]

Bringing together the premodern with the new and crossing stylistic boundaries were hallmarks of mid to late nineteenth-century art. After 1854, print designers had a rich variety of subjects and materials to work with, including images of foreigners in places like Yokohama. Techniques and colors continued to evolve. Meiji prints often featured bright reds and purples that were new and exciting—much like the newness of gas streetlamps, railroads, and topcoats and hats. The print series *Twenty-Four Things We Like About Civilization* (Figure 9.14; 1877) by Toyoharu Kunichika (1835–1900) exemplifies the public's fascination with the new era. In the first of this series, the subject is beef, illustrated by a Kabuki actor carrying a slaughtered bull on his shoulder. Contemporary life is also seen in the print *Concert of European Music* (Figure 9.15; 1889) by Hashimoto Chikanobu (1838–1912).[26] The printing quality shows in the burnished black of the men's suits; the dresses of the two women violinists are in the French style featured in *La mode illustrée* a few years earlier.[27]

Painter and print designer Kawanabe Kyōsai (1831–1889) embodied the syncretism of the period, connecting him with the late Tokugawa eccentric individualists (see Chapter 8). He welcomed foreigners to his studio and counted among his friends Josiah Conder and Captain Frank Brinkley (1841–1912), owner and editor of the *Japan Weekly Mail*. Kyōsai often satirized contemporary developments in his prints, of which *Fudō Myō-ō Kaika* (The Enlightenment of Fudō Myō-ō, 1874; Figure 9.16) is a prime example. The design is a play on

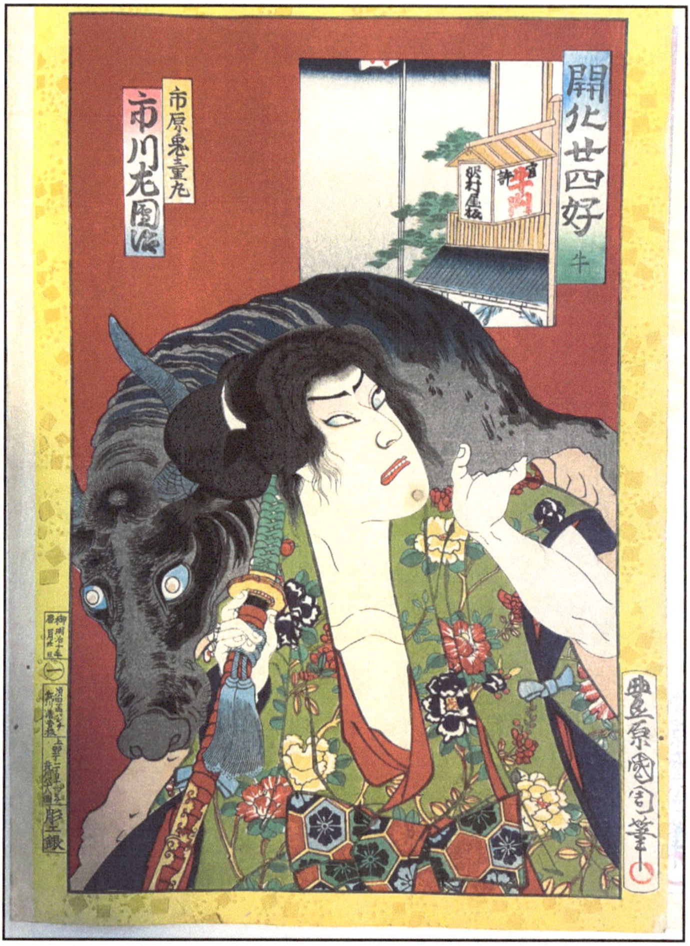

Figure 9.14: *Twenty-Four Things We Like About Civilization, No. 1 Beef*, Toyoharu Kunichika, 1877, color woodblock print, collection of the author.

the traditional image of this Buddhist deity. Fudō Myō-ō's role was to battle the enemies of Buddhism with his sword and bring humans into the fold with his rope. An important deity for the samurai, by the 1870s Fudō was seen as a protector of the nation.

In this satirical print, Fudō is reading a contemporary newspaper. His acolytes prepare deer meat for him—one cooks it in the flames surrounding Fudō, the other carves it on a plate. Eating red meat had been a practice in rural areas, but now meat consumption was encouraged for the health of the population at large. This is Fudō's "civilization and enlightenment," with a wordplay on *kaika* (enlightenment), meaning both enlightenment in the Buddhist sense and a new kind of enlightenment: modernization.[28]

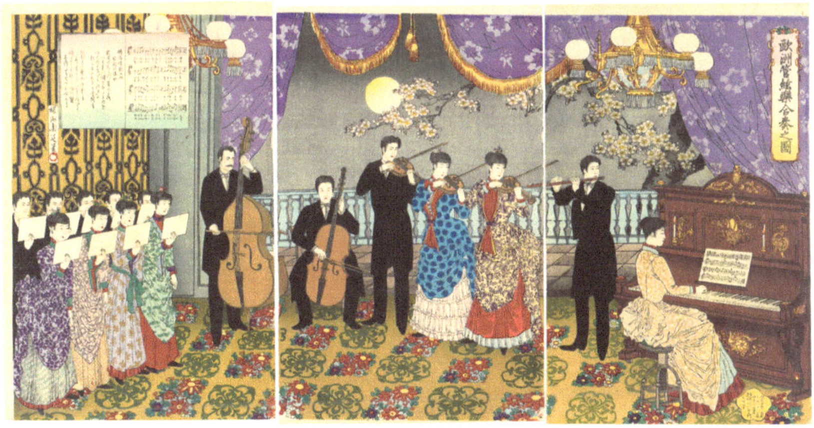

Figure 9.15: *Concert of European Music*, Hashimoto Chikanobu, 1889, color woodblock print triptych, Metropolitan Museum of Art, New York, Public domain.

Satirical images continued a centuries-old tradition of caricatures (*giga*) and became widely available to the public through magazine and newspaper publications. The modern manga as a mass-produced medium began with magazines like Charles Wirgman's *Japan Punch* (1862–1887); Kanagaki Robun (1829–1894) and Kyōsai's *Eshinbun Nipponchi* (*Illustrated Newspaper Japan*, 1874; Figure 9.17), thought to be the first manga magazine; and Nomura Fumio's (b. 1836) satirical *Marumaru Chinbun*, which began publishing in 1877 and ran for thirty years, with illustrations by Honda Kinkichirō (1850–1921).

Tsukioka Yoshitoshi (1839–1892) was another prominent print designer whose work integrates the contemporary with traditional culture, as seen in his 1883 *Fujiwara no Yasumasa Playing the Flute* (Figure 9.18). The print depicts a Heian-period courtier subduing a would-be robber with his music, bringing an ancient tale to a contemporary audience. Yoshitoshi employed Western techniques such as a lowered horizon line, foreshortening, and shading with newer elements such as wisps of clouds obscuring the moon and dark reeds fading away in the background. Bold outlines and strong diagonals that flatten the space are juxtaposed with depth created by atmospheric perspective. Like Kyōsai, Yoshitoshi also produced prints of ghosts and *bakemono* (see Chapter 8), responding to the Japanese public's continued interest in depictions of the strange and mysterious.

Contemporary Japan also featured in designs by Kobayashi Kiyochika (1847–1915). Kiyochika learned to paint in Western styles in Yokohama, becoming an expert at rendering natural and artificial light, which he then employed in his woodblock prints. One of the iconic images of Japan at this time was the steam locomotive. Kiyochika designed *View of Takanawa Ushimachi under a Shrouded Moon* (Figure 9.19) during a period when gas streetlamps were being installed in

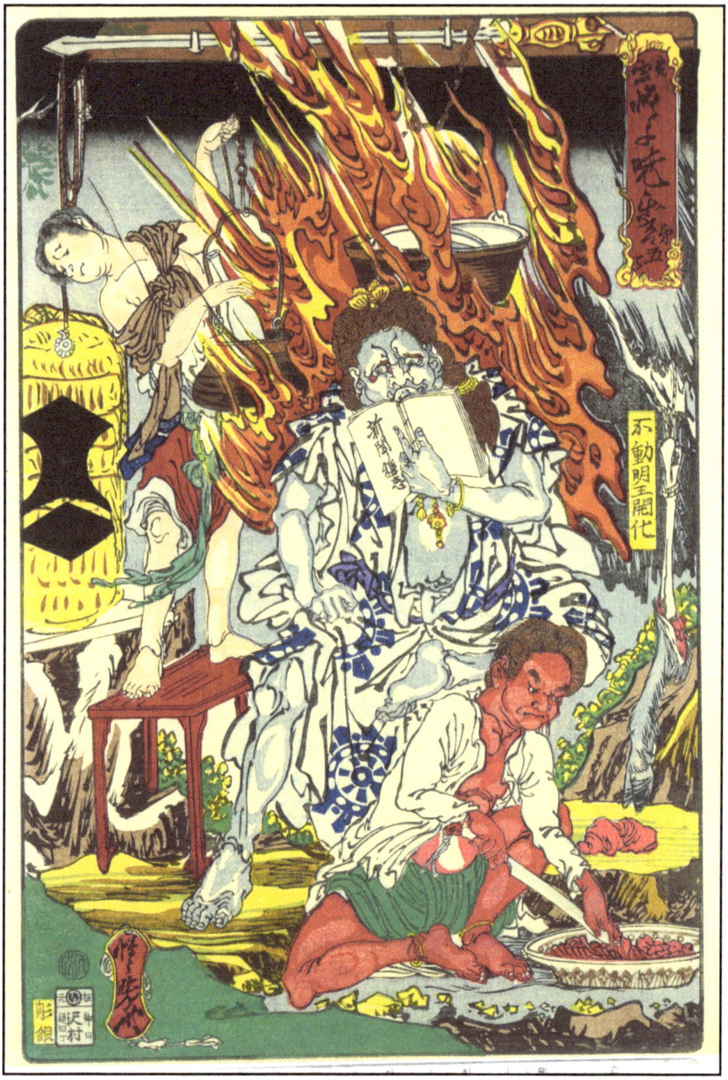

Figure 9.16: *The Enlightenment of Fudō Myō-ō*, no. 5 from the series *Kyōsai rakuga*, Kawanabe Kyōsai, 1874, color woodblock print, Israel Goldman Collection, London.

places such as Ginza, giving Tokyo after dark an entirely new appearance. The red and pink light shining from the engine is superimposed on the darkening sky in the background. Shadows under the train assume a light source from the right, and the warm glow from inside the train is reflected in the water below.[29]

Woodblock prints were used as newspaper inserts, to illustrate current events and for satire and critiques of the rapid changes to the country in early Meiji. They were also used to promote Japan's military prowess during the Sino-Japanese

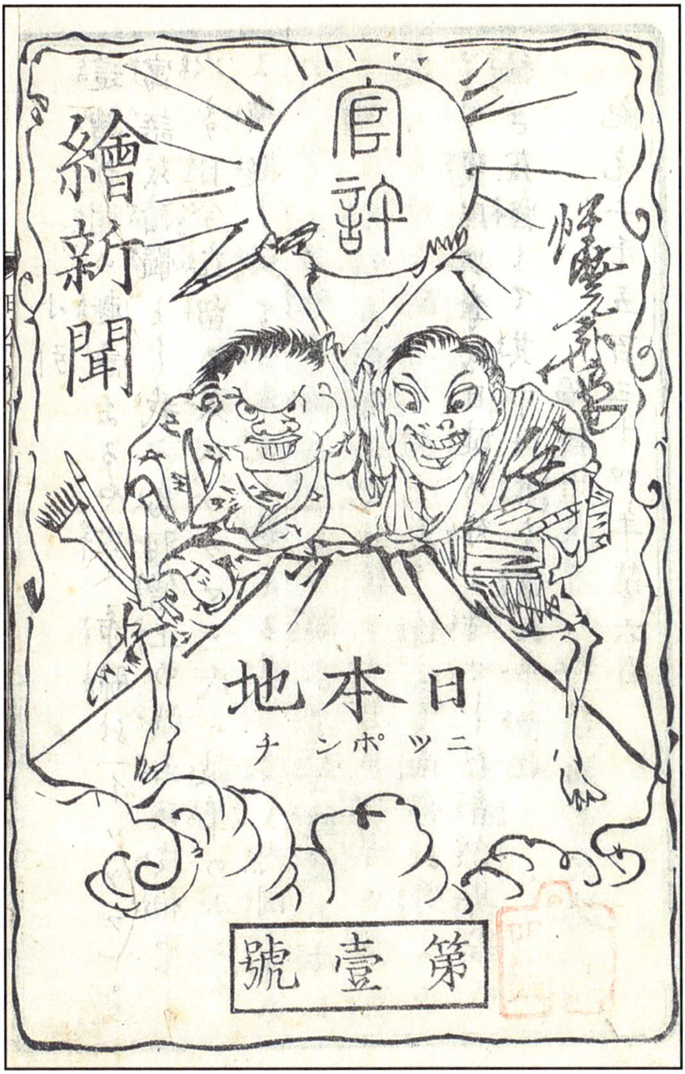

Figure 9.17: *Eshinbun Nipponchi, No. 1*, Kawanabe Kyōsai and Kanagaki Robun, 1874, satirical magazine cover, Wikimedia Commons.

War (1894–1895), when both print designers and to a lesser extent photographers were called upon to document the war in progress. Kiyochika employed the effects of light to heighten the drama in his war prints while also celebrating military technology such as electricity in *Use of Electricity During the Siege of Pyongyang* (Figure 9.20), in which Japanese troops shine lights on Chinese targets during a battle in northern Korea.

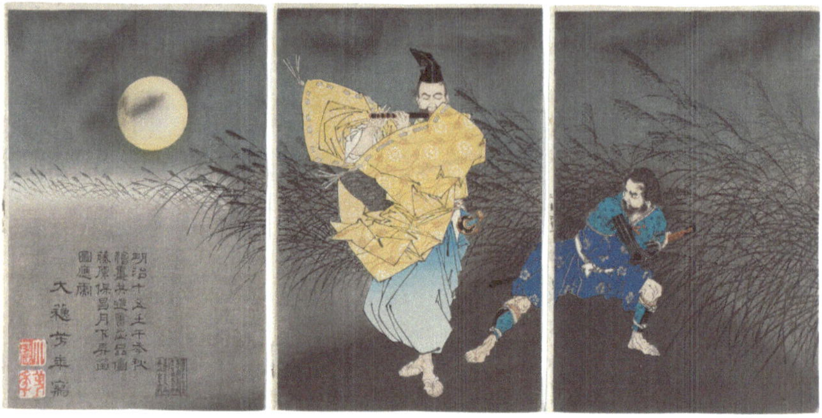

Figure 9.18: *Fujiwara Yasumasa Playing the Flute by Moonlight*, Tsukioka Yoshitoshi, 1883, color woodblock print triptych, Minneapolis Institute of Art, Public domain.

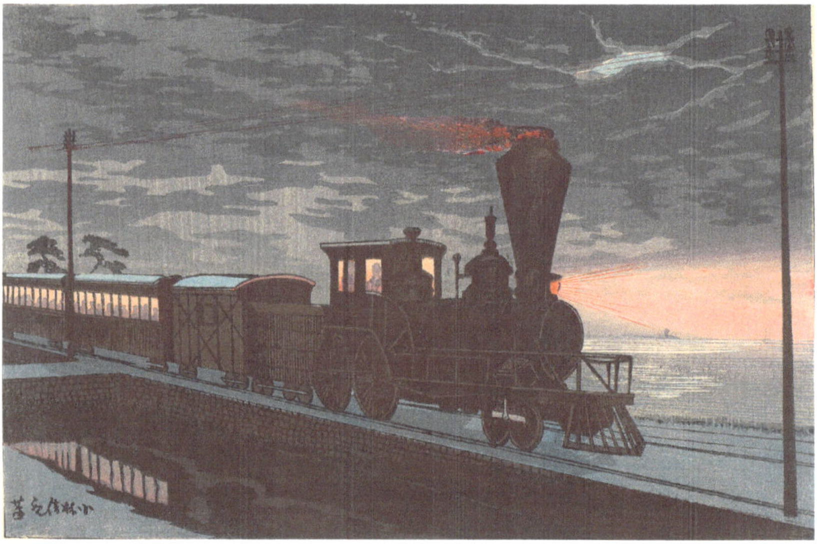

Figure 9.19: *View of Takanawa Ushimachi Under a Shrouded Moon*, Kobayashi Kiyochika, 1879, color woodblock print, National Museum of Asian Art, Smithsonian Institution, Washington, DC.

The term for modern sculpture (*chōkoku*) was introduced at the Technical Art School, where the Italian sculptor Vincenzo Ragusa (1841–1927) taught modeling and bronze casting. European sculpture, including the concept of public statuary, quickly took hold in Japan. The bronze statue of Kusunoki Masashige (1294–1336) by Takamura Kōun (1852–1934) was the first equestrian statue in Japan (1893–1900; Figure 9.21); he also produced a bronze statue honoring the leader of the Satsuma Rebellion, Saigō Takamori (1828–1877), completed in 1898.[30] Saigō is a tragic hero, not a typical subject in Western public statuary.

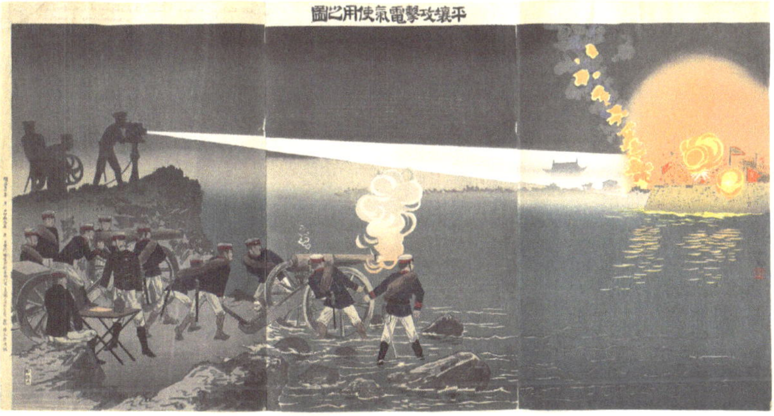

Figure 9.20: *Use of Electricity During the Siege of Pyongyang*, Kobayashi Kiyochika, 1894, color woodblock print triptych, Metropolitan Museum of Art, New York, Public domain.

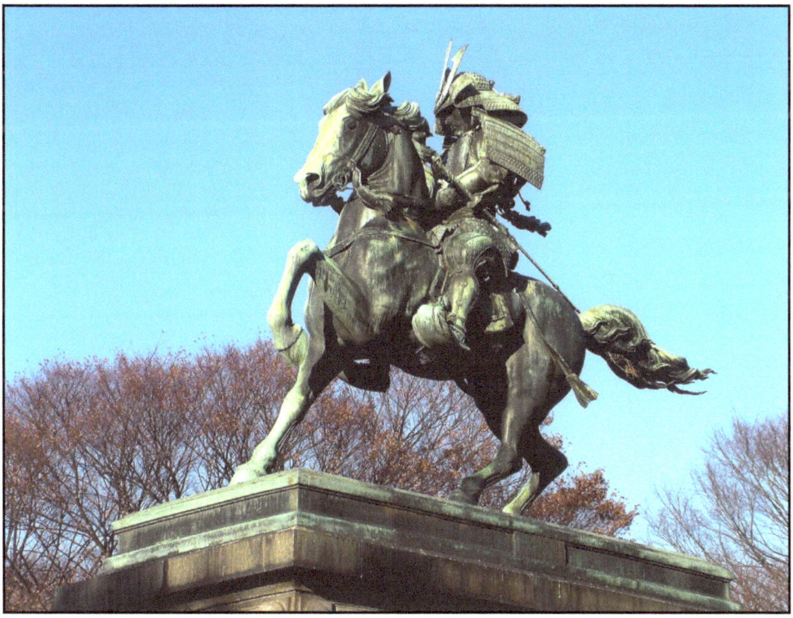

Figure 9.21: *Kusunoki Masashige*, Takamura Kōun and others, 1893–1900, bronze, Imperial Palace, Tokyo, Wikimedia Commons.

In the 1880s and 1890s, artists were increasingly aware of European artistic trends and were responding in turn. Japan's first *yōga* association, the Meiji Art Society, was founded by Asai Chū and others in 1889. Kuroda Seiki (1866–1924) studied in France under academic painter Raphaël Collin (1850–1916), learning the Impressionist methods of rendering light. Along with his colleague Kume

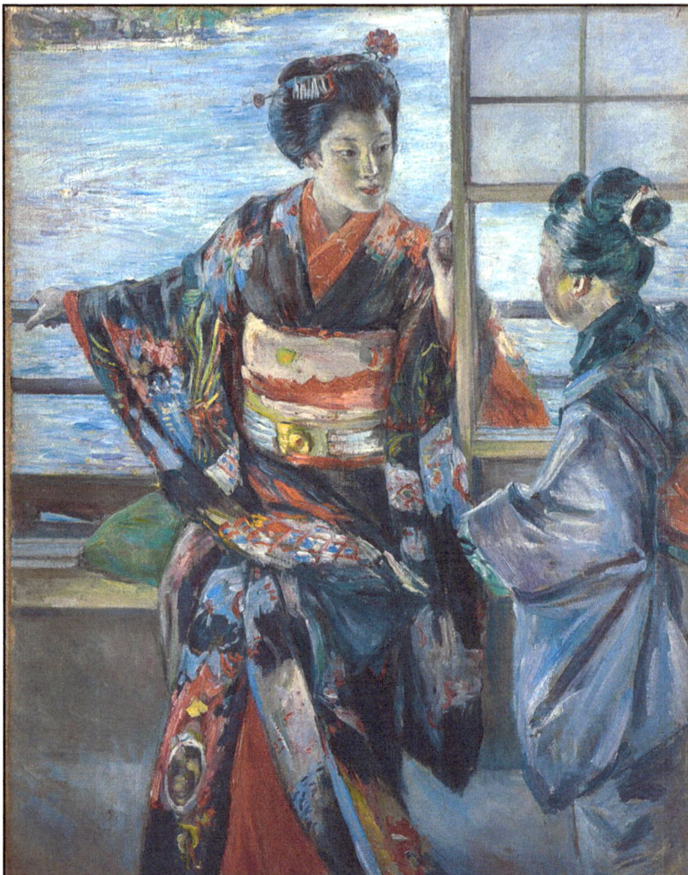

Figure 9.22: *Maiko*, Kuroda Seiki, 1893, oil on canvas, Tokyo National Museum, Wikimedia Commons.

Keiichirō (1866–1934), he introduced brighter and softer colors to Japanese oil painting, a style known as Shinpa (new painting) or Murasaki-ha (purple school) (Figure 9.22). Kuroda and Kume were instrumental in founding the White Horse Society for *yōga* painters in 1896, and Kuroda is regarded as the "father of modern *yōga*" in Japan, particularly for his training of the next generation of oil painters. His paintings of nudes, such as *Morning Toilette* (1893) and the triptych *Wisdom, Impression, Sentiment* (1899), created controversy in Japan. Although an established subject in Europe, nude paintings, publicly displayed in an exhibition, were not well received by critics.[31]

In Kyoto, the Kyoto Prefectural School of Painting[32] offered both *yōga* and *nihonga* courses, with Maruyama-Shijō painter Kōno Bairei (1844–1895) and Nanga painter Tanomura Chokunyū (1814–1907) among the professors. Nanga evolved in Kyoto with Tomioka Tessai (1836–1924), who painted well into his eighties (Figure 9.23; dated to 1924).

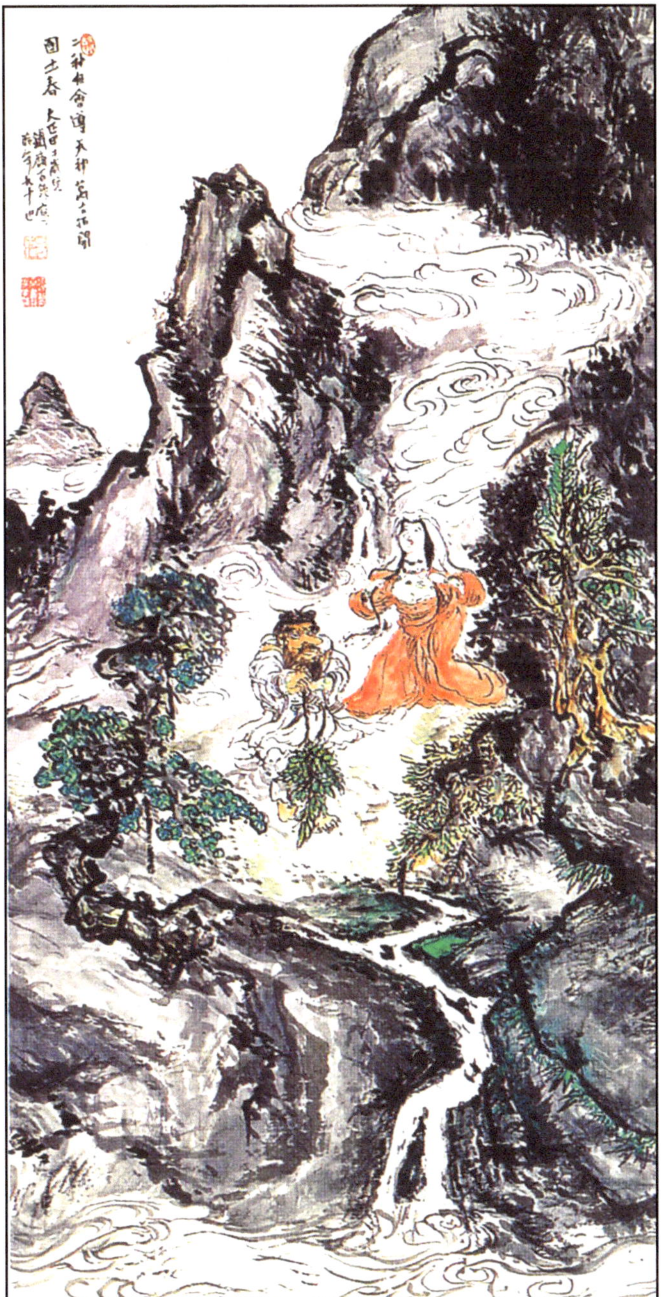

Figure 9.23: *Two Divinities Dancing*, Tomioka Tessai, 1924, hanging scroll, ink and color on silk, Tokyo National Museum, Wikimedia Commons.

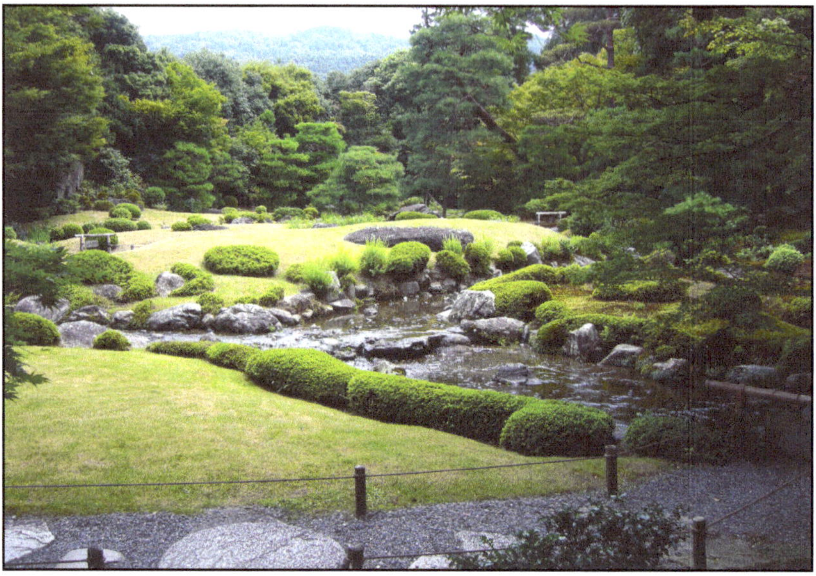

Figure 9.24: Murin-an Garden, Kyoto, Ogawa Jihei VII (Ueji), 1894–1902, Wikimedia Commons.

Also in Kyoto, the politician Yamagata Aritomo (1838–1922) commissioned landscape designer Ogawa Jihei VII (Ueji; 1860–1933) to create a new type of garden, a "natural" landscape, for his villa. Created in "a non-symbolic naturalistic style" the garden featured multiple streams, expanses of lawn, and fir trees (Figure 9.24).[33]

Fenollosa and Okakura had promoted the idea of an art school for some years, and the Ministry of Education approved the plan in 1887. The Tokyo School of Fine Arts enrolled the first students in 1889, the same year the Meiji Constitution was promulgated.[34] Fenollosa and Okakura were both appointed to high-ranking positions. Hashimoto Gahō became the leading professor of painting. Okakura was the first principal and over time expanded the curriculum to include *yōga*, with Kuroda Seiki becoming professor in 1896. Many artists who would later play a role in twentieth-century art studied at this school. Also in 1889, Okakura and Takahashi Kenzō (1855–1898) founded the art journal *Kokka*, still published today.

Differences of opinion about curriculum at the Tokyo School of Fine Arts were apparent from the beginning. Issues about salary and Fenollosa's usefulness as an instructor led to the elimination of his position in the 1889–1890 academic year. In 1898, Okakura was also forced out of the school; he subsequently founded the Japan Art Institute with former students and colleagues such as Yokoyama Taikan (1868–1958), Hishida Shunsō (1874–1911), Hashimoto Gahō, and Shimomura Kanzan (1873–1930). Okakura encouraged these *nihonga* artists to paint on the same grand scale as the *yōga* painters. The group's first endeavor was the Inten, an exhibition that promoted *nihonga*. Inten exhibitions would run until 1903 and later be revived by Taikan in 1914.

From the 1890s on, an increasing number of artists, writers, and intellectuals traveled abroad, particularly to France. Direct exposure to European art, especially contemporary painting, galvanized these artists to join the call for freedom of expression. On their return to Japan, they introduced their students to current trends in the West and experimented in their own art. They and their fellow artists and writers who were unable to travel abroad spread knowledge about Western art through magazines, newspapers, and essays. Even without the cultural and historical background of European artistic traditions, Japanese artists embraced the different contemporary artistic movements and art as self-expression, strived to learn the latest techniques, and went on to develop their own styles. Some even made their reputations in Europe. The tensions between different schools of thought and practice in Japan persisted, however, and the new century saw a flurry of art groups and affiliations rise and fall.

Notes

[1] See, for example, Susan B. Hanley, *Everyday Things in Premodern Japan: The Hidden Legacy of Material Culture* (Berkeley: University of California Press, 1997); and Ellen P. Conant, ed., *Challenging Past and Present: The Metamorphosis of Nineteenth-Century Japanese Art* (Honolulu: University of Hawai‘i Press, 2006).

[2] Architecture as authority during the Meiji period is discussed in William H. Coaldrake, *Architecture and Authority in Japan*, Nissan Institute / Routledge Japanese Studies (London: Routledge, 1996), chapter 9, “Building the Meiji State,” 208–250.

[3] Coaldrake, *Architecture and Authority in Japan*, 218–221.

[4] For more, see Toshio Watanabe, “Japanese Imperial Architecture: From Thomas Roger Smith to Itō Chūta,” in Conant, *Challenging Past and Present*, 240–253.

[5] Dallas Finn, “Reassessing the Rokumeikan,” in Conant, *Challenging Past and Present*, 228. For more on this subject, see Finn, 227–239; and Toshio Watanabe, “Josiah Conder’s Rokumeikan: Architecture and National Representation in Meiji Japan,” Japan 1868–1945: Art, Architecture, and National Identity, *Art Journal* 55, no. 3 (Fall 1996): 21–27.

[6] Finn, “Reassessing the Rokumeikan,” 227–239. The building was used as a club and hotel after 1897 and was eventually torn down, in 1941.

[7] See “Former Kaichi School (National Treasure),” Japan Tourism Agency, accessed November 28, 2024, https://matsu-haku.com/kaichi/about. For more on master carpenters, see Cherie Wendelken, “The Tectonics of Japanese Style: Architect and Carpenter in the Late Meiji Period,” in Japan 1868–1945: Art, Architecture, and National Identity, *Art Journal* 55, no. 3 (Fall 1996): 28–37. See also Nobuo Tsuji, *History of Art in Japan*, trans. Nicole Coolidge Rousmaniere (New York: Columbia University Press, 2019), 391–393.

[8] For more, see Jonathan M. Reynolds, "Japan's Imperial Diet Building: Debate over Construction of a National Identity," in Japan 1868–1945: Art, Architecture, and National Identity, *Art Journal* 55, no. 3 (Fall 1996): 38–47; and Tsuji, *History of Art in Japan*, 393–395.

[9] Dōshin Satō published an important study of Meiji arts: *Modern Japanese Art and the Meiji State: The Politics of Beauty*, trans. Hiroshi Nara (Los Angeles: Getty Research Institute, 2011).

[10] Rosina Buckland, *The Splendor of Modernity: Japanese Arts of the Meiji Era* (London: Reaktion Books, 2024), 76–81; Tsuji, *History of Art in Japan*, 375–376.

[11] Tsuji, *History of Art in Japan*, 379–380.

[12] For more on Kyoto arts during this period, see Morgan Pitelka and Alice Y. Tseng, eds. *Kyoto Visual Culture in the Early Edo and Meiji Periods: The Arts of Reinvention*, Routledge Studies in the Modern History of Asia (New York: Routledge, 2016).

[13] Tsuji, *History of Art in Japan*, 378; Buckland, *The Splendor of Modernity*, 102–103.

[14] Chelsea Foxwell and Bradley M. Bailey, *Meiji Modern: Fifty Years of New Japan* (New Haven: Yale University Press, 2023), 209.

[15] Foxwell and Bailey, *Meiji Modern*, 34–35.

[16] Buckland, *The Splendor of Modernity*, 190–191; Tsuji, *History of Art in Japan*, 396–397.

[17] See Julia Sapin, "Naturalism Fusing Past and Present: The Reconfiguration of the Kyoto School of Painting and the Revival of the Textile Industry," in Pitelka and Tseng, *Kyoto Visual Culture*, 138–160; Buckland, *The Splendor of Modernity*; Joe Earle, *Splendors of Meiji, Treasures of Imperial Japan: Masterpieces from the Khalili Collection* (St. Petersburg, FL: Broughton International Publications, 1999), 324.

[18] Hiroshi Nara, *Fenollosa's Legacy in Late Nineteenth-Century Japan: An American Scholar's Role in Resurrecting the Art of Japan* (Lanham, MD: Lexington Books, 2024), 138.

[19] See Nara, *Fenollosa's Legacy*, 133–139.

[20] For a full translation of *Bijutsu shinsetsu* and detailed analysis of Fenollosa's involvement in the arts, see Nara, *Fenollosa's Legacy in Late Nineteenth-Century Japan.*

[21] Satō, *Modern Japanese Art*, 313.

[22] See Martin Collcutt, "The Image of Kannon as Compassionate Mother in Meiji Art and Culture," in Conant, *Challenging Past and Present*, 197–224.

[23] Nara, *Fenollosa's Legacy*, 71–72.

[24] For more on Seiko, see Patricia Fister, *Japanese Women Artists, 1600–1900* (Lawrence, KS: Spencer Museum of Art, 1988), 161–165; and Martha J. McClintock

and Victoria Weston, "Okuhara Seiko: A Case of *Funpon* Training in Late Edo Literati Painting," in Brenda G. Jordan and Victoria Weston, eds. *Copying the Master and Stealing His Secrets: Talent and Training in Japanese Painting* (Honolulu: University of Hawai'i Press, 2003), 116–146.

[25] For more on Shōhin, see Fister, *Japanese Women Artists*, 165–168; Buckland, *The Splendor of Modernity*, 272–273; and various entries in Ellen P. Conant et al., *Nihonga, Transcending the Past: Japanese-Style Painting, 1868–1968* (Saint Louis: The Saint Louis Art Museum, 1995).

[26] See Bruce A. Coats, *Chikanobu: Modernity and Nostalgia in Japanese Prints* (Leiden: Hotei, 2006).

[27] Julia Meech-Pekarik, *The World of the Meiji Print: Impressions of a New Civilization* (New York: Weatherhill, 1987), 163. Some of the performers have been identified. Meech-Pekarik, 163–165.

[28] For more on Kyōsai, see Jordan and Weston, *Copying the Master*; Brenda G. Jordan, "Strange Fancies and Fresh Conceptions: Kyōsai in an Age of Conflict" (doctoral dissertation, University of Kansas, 1993); and Koto Sadamura, *Kyōsai: The Israel Goldman Collection* (London: Royal Academy of Arts, 2022).

[29] The appearance of shadows dates to the Tokugawa period, but the play of light here is more extensive than would have been seen earlier. For more, see James T. Ulak, "Kiyochika's Tokyo I: Master of Modern Melancholy (1876–1881), MIT Visualizing Cultures, https://visualizingcultures.mit.edu/kiyochika_tokyo/ki_essay01.html

[30] Kōun is usually credited as the designer of the Kusunoki Masashige statue, but his contribution was the primary modeling of the figure, with collaborators assisting with this and the design of the horse. Okazaki Sessei cast the figure later. For more see Buckland, *The Splendor of Modernity*, 177–180.

[31] See, for example, the Kuroda Memorial Hall website: https://www.tobunken.go.jp/kuroda/index.html#main, in particular https://www.tobunken.go.jp/kuroda/gallery/english/tikanjo01.html.

[32] The Kyoto Prefectural School of Painting opened in 1880; in 1889, it was renamed the Kyoto City Technical School of Painting and, later, the Kyoto City Technical School of Art. Since 1950, it has been known as the Kyoto City University of Arts.

[33] See Toshio Watanabe, "A Kyoto Garden Renewal? From Meiji to the Early Showa Period," in Pitelka and Tseng, *Kyoto Visual Culture*, 163–181.

[34] See Nara, *Fenollosa's Legacy*, 114–121; and Victoria Weston, "Institutionalizing Talent and the Kano Legacy at the Tokyo School of Fine Arts, 1889–1893," in Jordan and Weston, *Copying the Master,* 147–177.

10

Striving Toward Freedom of Expression

The Twentieth Century

> I seek absolute *Freiheit* [freedom] in the art world. Therefore, I want to recognize an infinite authority in the artist's *Persoenlichkeit* [personality]. . . . Even if someone paints a "green sun," I will not say it is wrong. . . . I'd like to savor the tone of the green sun as part of the work.
>
> —Takamura Kōtarō, "A Green Sun"[1]

"A Green Sun," an essay by Takamura Kōtarō (1883–1956), was published in 1910 in the literary magazine *Subaru*, the same year that the literature and arts journal *Shirakaba* (White Birch) was founded. *Shirakaba* published images of modern European art to a new generation in Japan. Japanese artists were now embracing the concept of artistic self-expression, and the late Meiji and Taisho (1912–1926) periods saw a flurry of artistic movements, influences, and developments. The role of art in the public sphere continued to be debated, particularly the tension between art as personal expression and art serving the nation-state. What did it mean to be Japanese artists, surrounded as they were by both European influences and Japanese traditions?

Japan's efforts to rise in the world order culminated in an 1889 treaty with Great Britain that ended many of the inequalities of the treaty port system. In 1895, Japan had defeated China in the Sino-Japanese War and annexed Taiwan. Japan then prevailed over Russia in the 1904–1905 Russo-Japanese War and annexed Korea in 1910, following the example of other major colonizers such as Great Britain and France. Japan now claimed a place among the world's powers, and the arts were drawn into the discourse around Japanese nationalism and self-esteem.

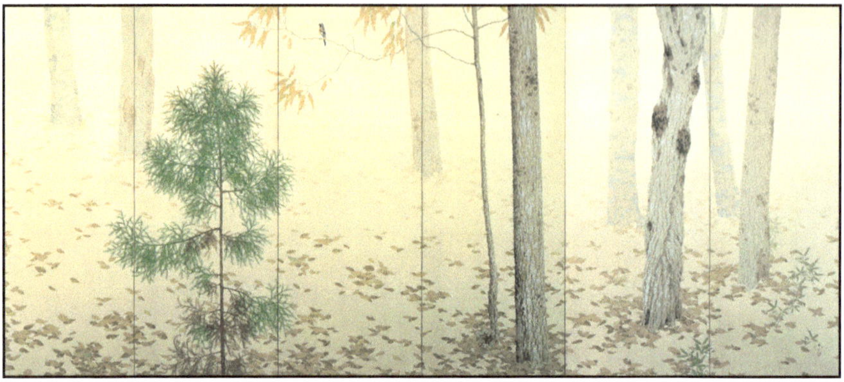

Figure 10.1: *Fallen Leaves* (right screen), Hishida Shunsō, 1909, pair of six-panel screens, ink and color on paper, Eisei-Bunko Museum, Tokyo, Wikimedia Commons.

Within this discourse, some drew a connection between Greece and Japan dating back to antiquity. In the late 1800s, Christopher Dresser (1834–1904), Ernest Fenollosa, and Okakura Kakuzō associated ancient Greece with Japan, seeing Japan as the terminus of the Silk Roads across Eurasia. Fenollosa drew a connection between Greco-Indian Buddhist art that traveled from Gandhara, India, to China and Japan, citing the Hōryūji wall paintings (Chapter 2) as an example. Architect Itō Chūta (discussed below) claimed a connection with Greek architecture, citing the entasis in the pillars of Hōryūji's Second Gate as direct evidence of Greek influence.

Japanese scholars now question these ideas, but during the late Meiji period, evidence was less important than the idea that Greece "helped produce a historical narrative of Japanese cultural identity that was beneficial to the country when it was needed most, during Japan's modernizing effort." This way of thinking continued with the writings of Watsuji Tetsurō (1889–1960) and Kuki Shūzō (1888–1941), which led to the rise of postwar Nihonjinron, treatises claiming a unique Japanese identity.[2] Even *The Tale of Genji* (Chapter 3) was cited in support of Japan's cultural superiority and national identity.[3]

Japan's connections to Europe sparked controversy between advocates of *yōga* and those of *nihonga*, and between the more progressive and conservative elements within each group. In 1907, the Ministry of Education inaugurated a yearly exhibition known as the Bunten that would become embroiled in these divisions. The Bunten was widely advertised, heavily attended, and hugely influential, becoming the primary public venue for painters. The Bunten introduced landmarks of *nihonga* like Hishida Shunsō's *Fallen Leaves* (1909, Figure 10.1), a pair of folding screens that continue the traditional seasonal theme and format, but with meticulously detailed bark and leaves, and a photography-like cropping of trunks as if the viewer were looking through a window.

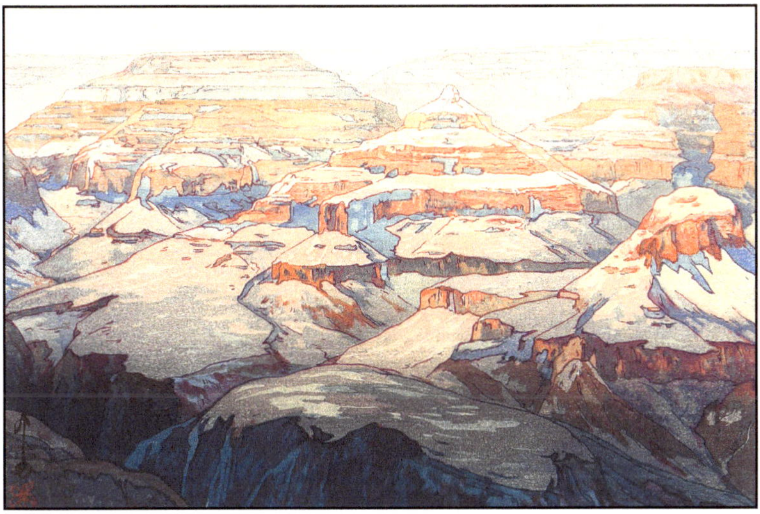

Figure 10.2: *Grand Canyon*, Yoshida Hiroshi, 1925,
color woodblock print, Wikimedia Commons.

Despite its importance, the Bunten was criticized by progressive artists. Artists were becoming familiar with contemporary movements like Post-Impressionism, German Expressionism, Fauvism, Cubism, and Futurism, and many began to push back, promoting artistic self-expression.[4] In 1912, the novelist Natsume Sōseki (1867–1916) called for a *salon des refusés*.[5] Meanwhile, artists and writers founded journals that exposed readers to contemporary European arts, including *Shirakaba* (1910–1923) and other influential publications such as *Mizue* (Watercolor), *Chūō bijutsu* (Central Review of Art), and *Bijutsu shinpō* (Art News). Newspapers and department store exhibitions also contributed to the spread of knowledge about contemporary art, both Japanese and Western.

Independent groups formed, such as the Pacific Painting Society (1902), which elevated the medium of watercolor painting practiced by Asai Chū and Goseda Yoshimatsu. A founding member, Yoshida Hiroshi (1876–1950) became well known abroad for his printing technique and landscape designs that echoed the tradition of *meisho-e* (famous places) but with subjects such as the Grand Canyon (Figure 10.2). Fujishima Takeji (1867–1943) joined the Tokyo School of Fine Arts as an instructor in 1896, worked in a Romantic style (Figure 10.3), and produced Art Nouveau–style illustrations for the literary magazine *Myōjō*. Yorozu Tetsugorō (1885–1927) broke with the academism of the Tokyo School of Fine Arts with his graduation painting *Nude Beauty* (1912; Figure 10.4). In the same year, Takamura Kōtarō, Kishida Ryūsei (1891–1929), and others formed the Fuzankai, a charcoal sketching society that promoted Expressionism.

Independent exhibitions countering the Bunten followed these developments, including the Nikakai in 1914. In 1919, responding to continued criticism, the

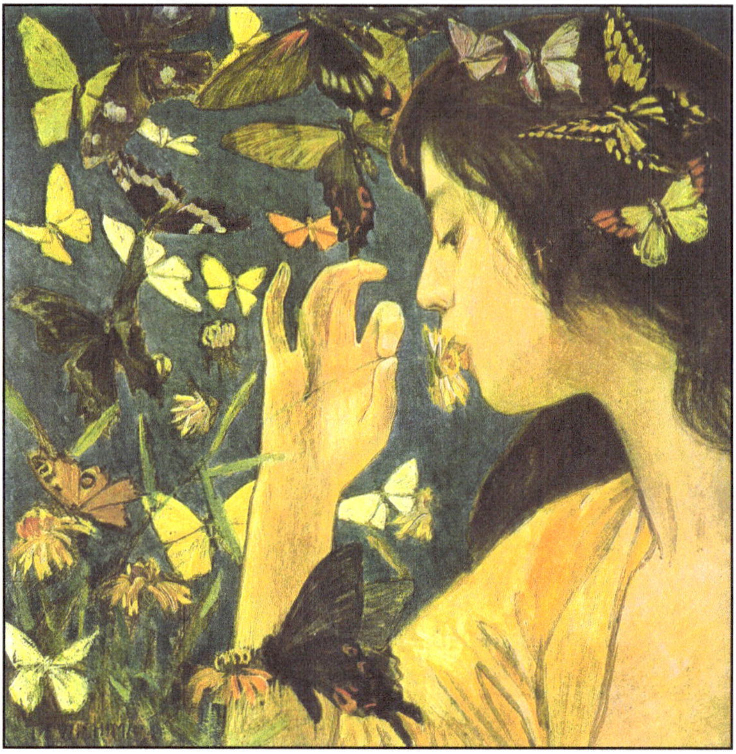

Figure 10.3: *Butterflies*, Fujima Takeji, 1904, oil on canvas, private collection, Wikimedia Commons.

Bunten became the Teiten (and continues today as the Nitten). Still, conflicts in the art world continued, and art circles continued to form and then dissolve over the decades.

For some painters, the realistic landscape style of Takahashi Yuichi (Chapter 9) inspired new interpretative possibilities. Kishida became a leader in this development, drawing upon his study of Northern European Renaissance works to delineate a different type of Japanese landscape in meticulous detail.[6] *A Road Cut Through a Hill* (Figure 10.5) is not a traditional *meisho* but an anonymous road rising up and away from the viewer, with strong contrasts and heightened color using the blue sky against an orange ground.

Many painters were drawn to France for inspiration and study, among them Sakamoto Hanjirō (1882–1969), Yasui Sōtarō (Figure 10.6; 1888–1955), and Umehara Ryūzaburō (1888–1986). Umehara was a leader in *yōga* during the interwar and postwar periods. Having studied with Asai Chū, he then continued his studies in France (1908–1913), where he sought out Pierre-Auguste Renoir (1841–1919) and was greatly influenced by him. Umehara also encountered ancient Greek and Roman art and met Pablo Picasso (1881–1973).

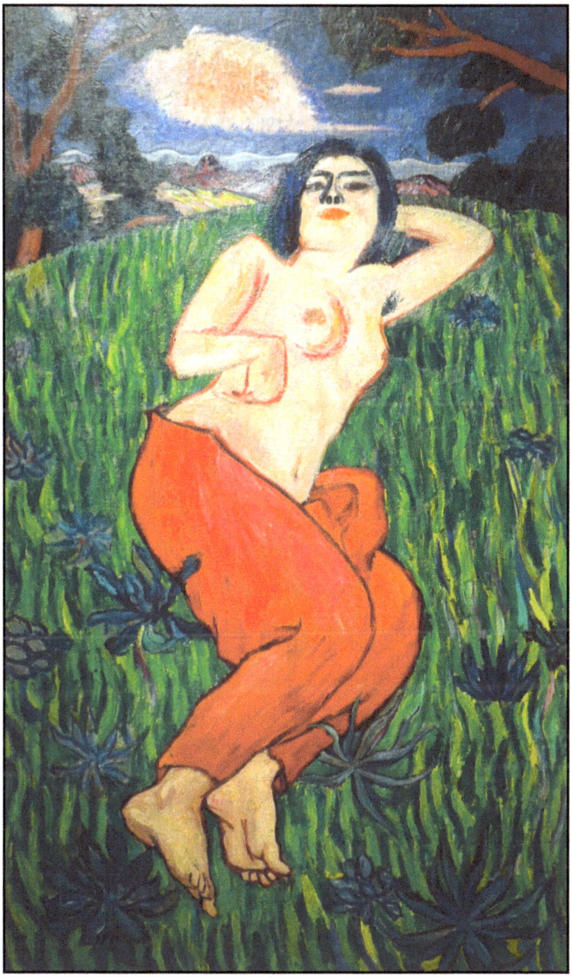

Figure 10.4: *Nude Beauty*, Yorozu Tetsugorō, 1912, oil on canvas, National Museum of Modern Art, Tokyo, Wikimedia Commons.

Meanwhile in Kyoto, Takeuchi Seihō (1864–1942) invigorated *nihonga* after a European trip by incorporating the visual realism and expressive quality of European painting into his work (Figure 10.7; 1903). In his teaching, Seihō emphasized the importance of working from life as well as the ability to use different modes of expression.[7] His female student Uemura Shōen (1875–1949) became widely recognized for her technically skilled images of women, including the Maruyama-Shijō mother and child theme that also appears in Kitagawa Utamaro's prints (Chapter 8). Shōen focused on the humanizing aspect of women in a style that was often criticized as old-fashioned. Her painting of a mother and child (Figure 10.8; 1934) is demonstratively modern, with a contemporary color palette, meticulous rendering of the textile design in the background screen, and a

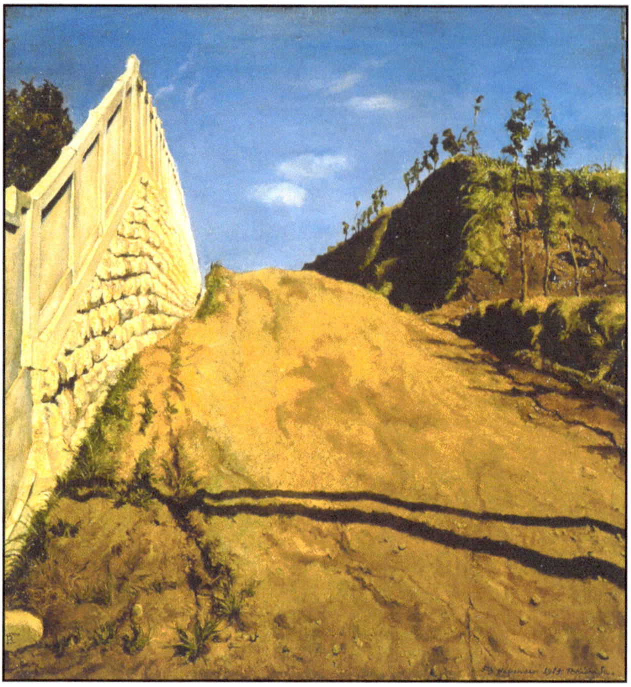

Figure 10.5: *A Road Cut Through a Hill*, Kishida Ryūsei, 1915, oil on canvas, National Museum of Modern Art, Tokyo, Wikimedia Commons.

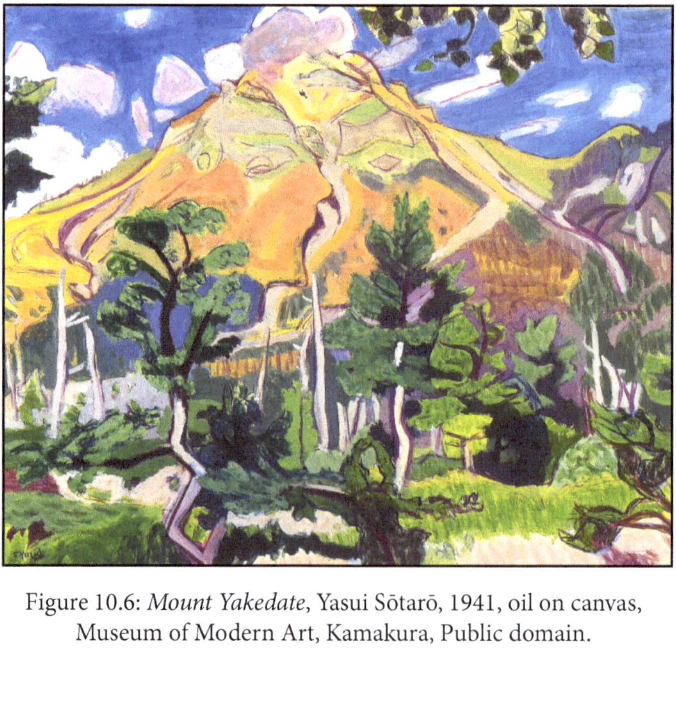

Figure 10.6: *Mount Yakedate*, Yasui Sōtarō, 1941, oil on canvas, Museum of Modern Art, Kamakura, Public domain.

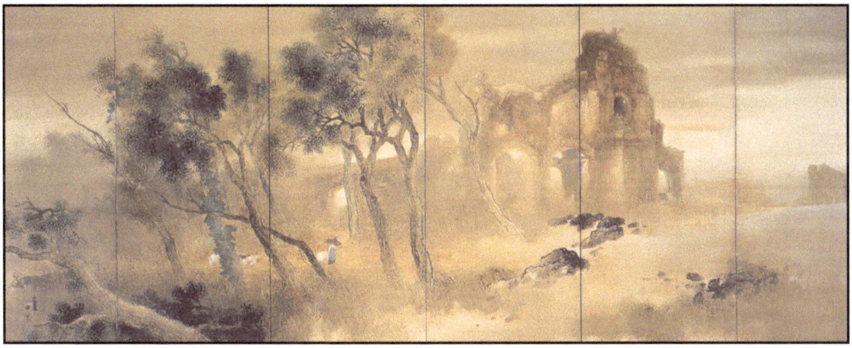

Figure 10.7: *Historic Spot of Rome* (left screen), Takeuchi Seihō, 1903, pair of six-panel screens, ink and color on silk, Umi-Mori Art Museum, Hiroshima prefecture, Wikimedia Commons.

spareness in the overall composition. Along with Noguchi Shōhin (Chapter 9), she was appointed an Imperial Household Artist, a rarity for women painters.[8]

Nihonga was also modernized by Yokoyama Taikan in Tokyo, who had become a leader of the movement. He revived the Inten in 1914, in part to counter Bunten standards as well as to honor Okakura Kakuzō, who had died the previous year. Taikan's *Spring Dawn over the Holy Mountain of Chichibu* (1928; Figure 10.9) captures floating clouds of mist against richly dark mountains in ink, recalling the tradition of famous sites (for example, Sesshū's *Amanohashidate*; Chapter 5).

Woodblock printmaking underwent dramatic changes as well. In the new century, the cost of print production could not compete with technologies such as lithograph and photogravure. A new niche was needed for the woodblock method. In 1907, the publisher Watanabe Shōzaburō (1885–1962) began to work with both Japanese and foreign artists to produce high-quality, limited edition prints for the foreign market; these were called *shin hanga* (literally, "new prints"). Watanabe sought traditional subjects (landscapes, beautiful women, and actors) but with a focus on contemporary Japan and presented in a fresh way. Painters and designers who worked with Watanabe include Hashiguchi Goyō (1880–1921), Itō Shinsui (1898–1972; Figure 10.10), Yamamura Kōka (1886–1942; Figure 10.11), and Kawase Hasui (1883–1957; Figure 10.12). A number of these collaborators had studied painting at the Tokyo School of Fine Arts or had been students of the painter Kaburaki Kiyokata (1878–1972).[9]

Another print movement began in the early 1900s with a painting student at the Tokyo School of Fine Arts, Yamamoto Kanae (1882–1946), who is credited with producing the earliest print in which the artist handles all the steps in the production process, from design to engraving the wood to printing. Inspired by Expressionist woodblock prints and Symbolist copperplate etchings as seen in journals such as *Shirakaba* and *Bijutsu Shinpō*, Yamamoto and others started producing "creative prints" (*sōsaku hanga*). Takehisa Yumeji (1884–1934) and

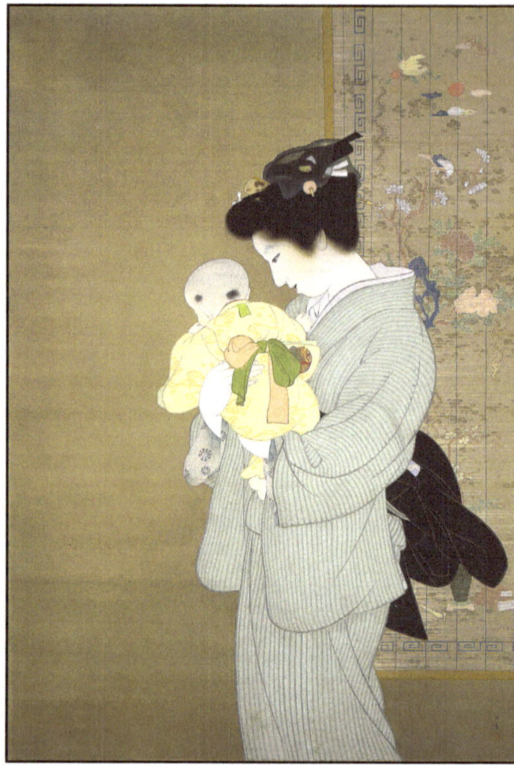

Figure 10.8: *Mother and Child*, Uemura Shōen, 1934, color on silk, framed, National Museum of Modern Art, Tokyo, Wikimedia Commons.

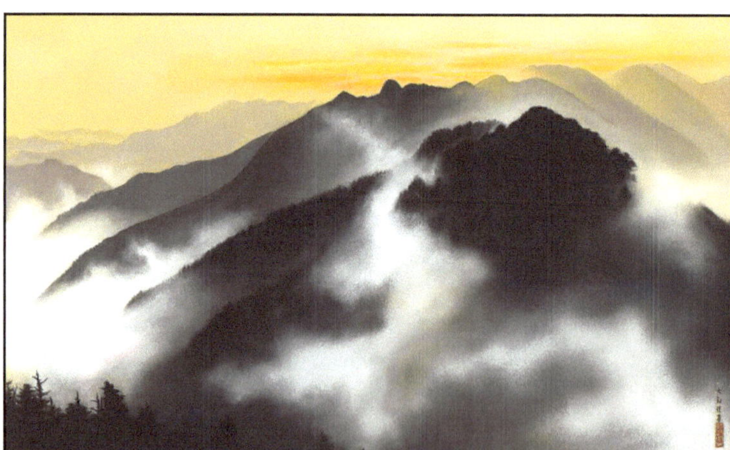

Figure 10.9: *Spring Dawn over the Holy Mountain of Chichibu*, Yokoyama Taikan, 1928, hanging scroll, ink and gold wash on silk, Household of Princess Chichibu, Wikimedia Commons.

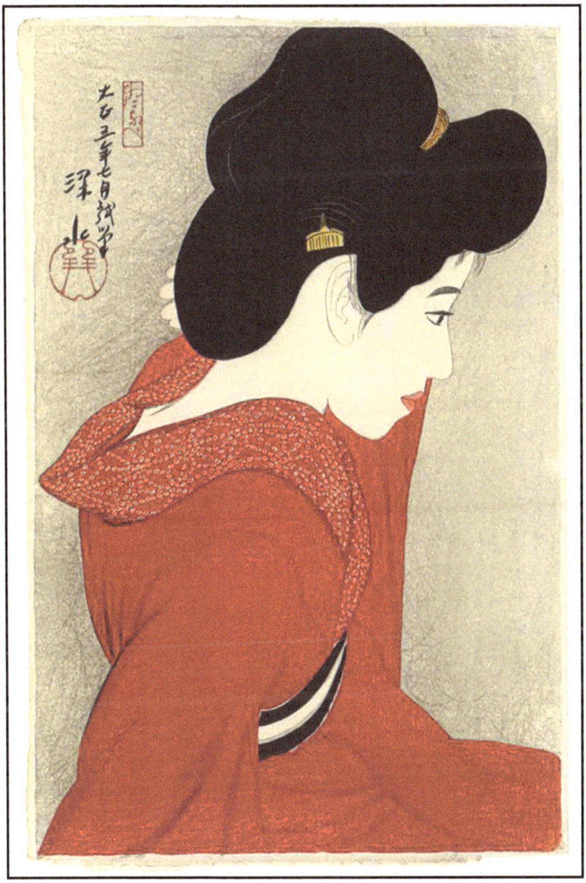

Figure 10.10: *Woman Looking at a Mirror*, Itō Shinsui, 1916, color woodblock print, Minneapolis Institute of Art, Public domain.

Onchi Kōshirō (1891–1955) were early practitioners, with Onchi becoming the leader of the movement. Onchi used found objects in his blocks, such as wax paper and string, and he carved multiple blocks to produce multicolored prints. In his portrait of the author Hagiwara Sakutarō (1886–1942), one of only seven portraits that he created, he used "transparent layers of color" to render the facial expression of the poet who was the first to write colloquial free verse poetry in Japanese (Figure 10.13; 1943).[10] Produced during a period of war, Onchi's print captures the sense of anguish Hagiwara is said to have felt over Japan's militarism, as well as traces of his depression and alcoholism.[11]

During much of the twentieth century, visual arts such as *shin hanga*, *sōsaku hanga*, and graphic arts were not considered fine art on the same level as painting. Yet, print designers, painters, and graphic artists began in the early 1900s to produce sophisticated designs for magazine illustrations and postcards that played

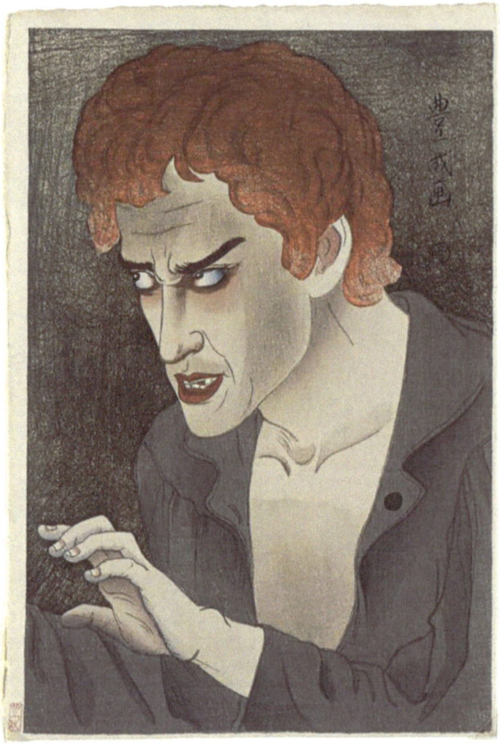

Figure 10.11: *The Actor Morita Kan'ya XIII as Jean Valjean*, Yamamura Kōka, 1921, color woodblock print, based on *Les Misérables* at the Yūraku Theater, December 1920, Minneapolis Institute of Art, Public domain.

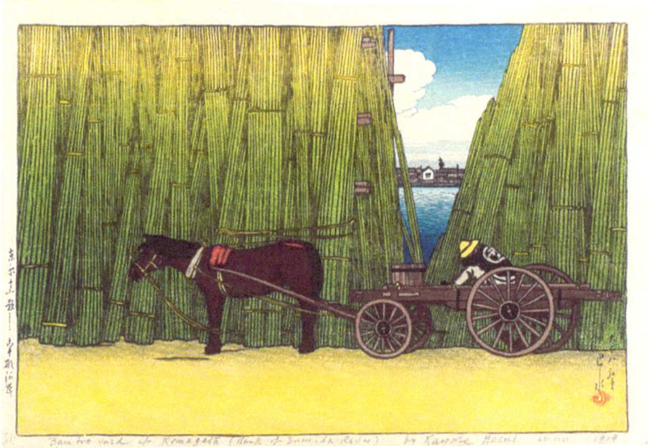

Figure 10.12: *Komagata Embankment* from the series *Twelve Scenes of Tokyo*, Kawase Hasui, 1919, color woodblock print, Minneapolis Institute of Art, Public domain.

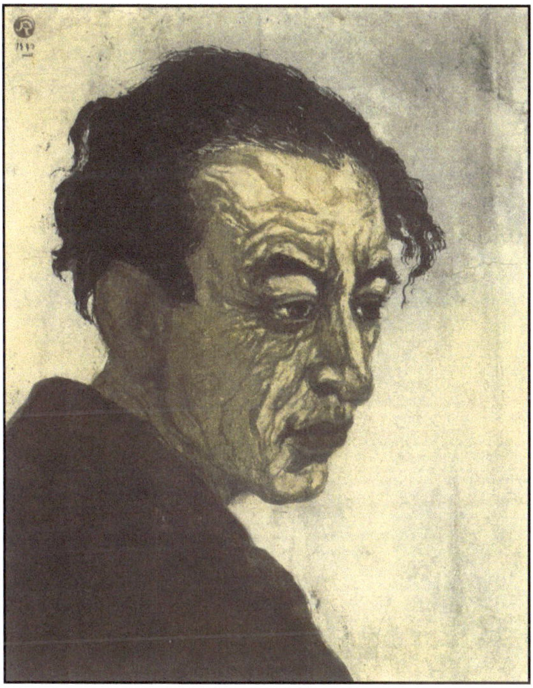

Figure 10.13: *Portrait of Hagiwara Sakutarō*, Onchi Kōshirō, 1943, color woodblock print, National Museum of Modern Art, Tokyo, Public domain.

a part in the growing commercial sector. Mass-produced postcards were not unlike the woodblock prints of earlier centuries in that they responded to consumer taste, served as travel souvenirs, were used in advertising, and reflected contemporary life. Text and image blended, a long tradition in Japanese art, as purchasers wrote messages directly on the image side and used the reverse for the recipient's address. Designers drew on Art Nouveau, Art Deco, Rinpa, Shijō, and other styles to create a variety of designs, like the 1906 image by Ichijō Narumi (1877–1910; Figure 10.14). Notably, companies such as Mitsukoshi not only connected Japanese consumers with art through their exhibitions but also issued artistically designed postcards and posters and journals such as Mitsukoshi's monthly *Jikō*.[12]

In architecture, Tatsuno Kingo's grand Tokyo Station (Figure 10.15; completed 1914) was an homage to the power of engineering with its red-brick facade and steel framing, as well as serving as the emperor's station.[13] It was built around the same time as other iconic train stations, such as New York's Grand Central (1913). Steel and concrete were also used to repair the Daibutsu hall at Tōdaiji (Chapter 2), which was in danger of structural failure. The project was managed by Tsumaki Yorinaka, Itō Chūta (1867–1954), and Sekino Tadashi (1868–1935), three University of Tokyo engineering graduates who drew upon their training in Western architecture and engineering to rebuild the damaged hall.[14]

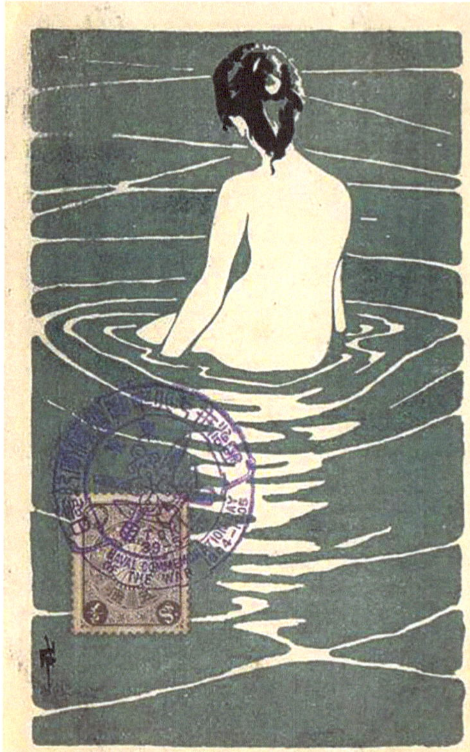

Figure 10.14: *Female Nude Seated in Water*, Ichijō Narumi, 1906, color lithograph, ink on card stock, published by the Japanese Postcard Club, Museum of Fine Arts, Boston, Wikimedia Commons.

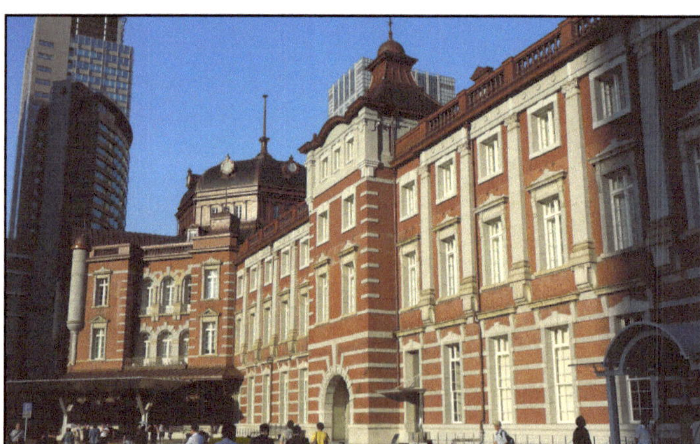

Figure 10.15: Tokyo Station, Tatsuno Kingo, 1914, steel framing with red-brick facade, Wikimedia Commons.

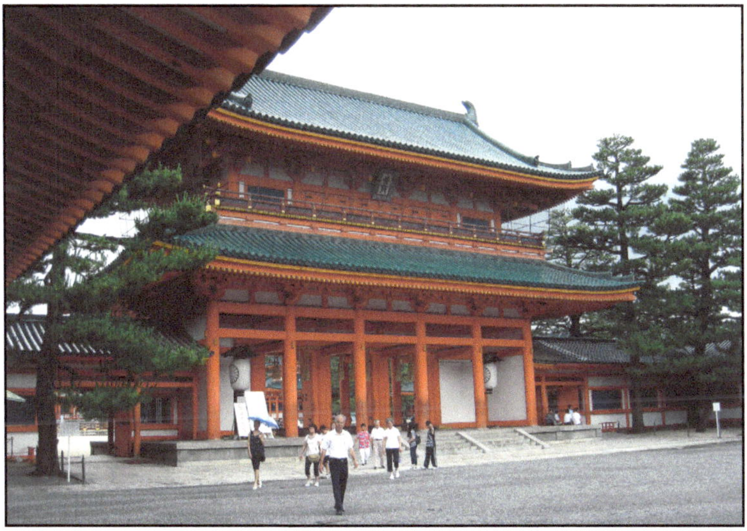

Figure 10.16: Heian Jingū, Kyoto, Itō Chūta, 1895, cypress wood with red lacquer, photo by author.

Itō Chūta had been a student of Tatsuno Kingo and likely attended Josiah Conder's lectures (Chapter 9). For his graduation project, he wrote the "first fully argued modern theory of architecture produced by a Japanese," followed by his doctoral dissertation, "A Treatise on the Architecture of Hōryūji," which has been described as the "first scholarly work of modern art history in Japan."[15] He played an important part in the formulation of the laws for the preservation and protection of national treasures mentioned in Chapter 9 and is known for his Shintō shrine architecture, including Heian Jingū in Kyoto (Figure 10.16; 1895), and Meiji Jingū (1920) and Yasukuni Jinja (1924) in Tokyo. He aimed to identify the roots of Japanese architecture in early prototypes such as the Shōsō-in or Ise Shrine (Chapter 2) and thus contribute to Japan's national identity.[16]

Others sought the essence of Japanese art in a more modest sphere. During the 1920s, philosopher and art critic Yanagi Sōetsu (1889–1961) coined the word *mingei* (folk art) as part of an effort to redefine and elevate handmade artisan works such as ceramics, lacquerware, and metalwork. He was joined by ceramicists Tomimoto Kenkichi (1886–1963), Kawai Kanjirō (1890–1966), and Bernard Leach (1887–1979) in promoting wares that were practical, handmade, usually crafted by unknown artists, had regional characteristics, and were affordable. The ceramicist Hamada Shōji (1894–1978) founded the Mingei Association of Japan with Leach and Kawai, as well as the Japan Folk Crafts Museum in Tokyo (founded 1936). Designated a Living National Treasure by the Japanese government in 1955, Hamada produced ceramic pieces using a variety of glazing techniques such as *tenmoku* (iron), *nuka* (ash glaze), salt glaze, and *kaki* (persimmon glaze) (Figure 10.17).[17]

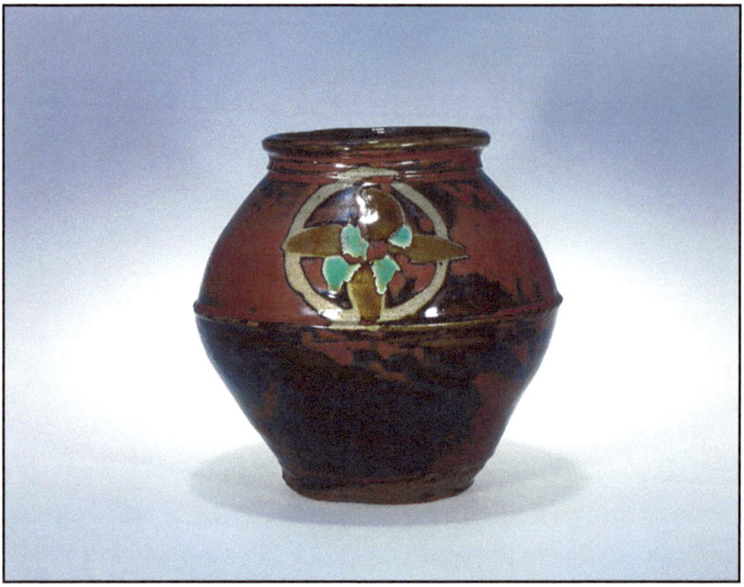

Figure 10.17: Vase, Hamada Shōji, twentieth century, glazed stoneware, Minneapolis Institute of Art, Public domain.

Also in the 1920s, the avant-garde art collective MAVO formed, led by Murayama Tomoyoshi (1901–1977). Expressing their interpretation of individualism, the group became more active after the 1923 Great Kantō Earthquake. Murayama had been influenced by Dadaism and Russian Constructivism during his studies in Germany. The group he led did not adhere to a unified ideology, although most had some involvement with the Japanese Futurist movement. MAVO engaged in activities such as theatrical and dance performances, poster design, art criticism, architectural projects, the writing of a manifesto, book illustrations, and publication of an art magazine (Figure 10.18). Their primary focus was individual expression and social revolution, breaking down the barriers between daily life and art. MAVO was short-lived, but it influenced commercial art in Japan as well as aspects of visual and political culture.[18]

Advocacy of artistic individual expression increasingly came under attack as the political environment in Japan moved toward authoritarianism. This trend began after the Great Kantō Earthquake and continued through the global economic depression beginning in 1929 and Japan's 1931 military conquest of Manchuria. Leftist artists and writers were suppressed and pressured to change their ideologies; some were arrested and jailed. Both ultranationalists and leftists argued for the sociopolitical function of art but from opposing viewpoints. In January 1941 the art magazine *Mizue* published an article detailing the views of the Information Section of the Imperial Army that included an explicit attack on the idea of self-expression and artistic freedom. In April, painter Matsumoto

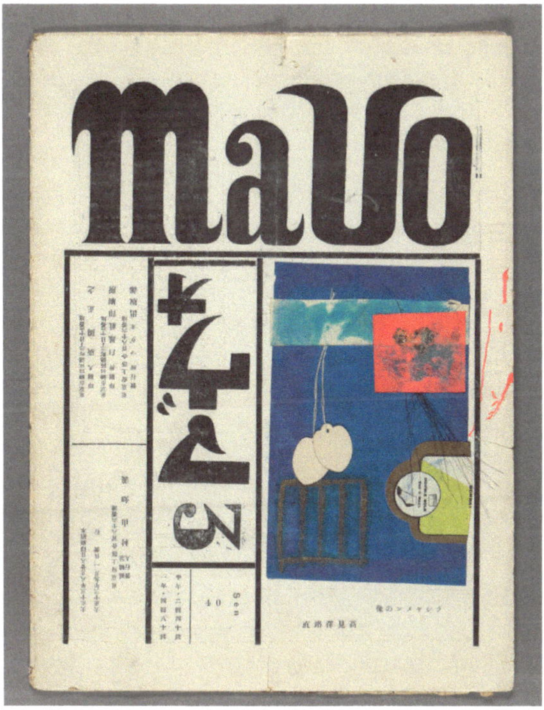

Figure 10.18: Front cover of the avant-garde art magazine *MAVO*, no. 3 (September 1924), New York Public Library Digital Collections, Public domain.

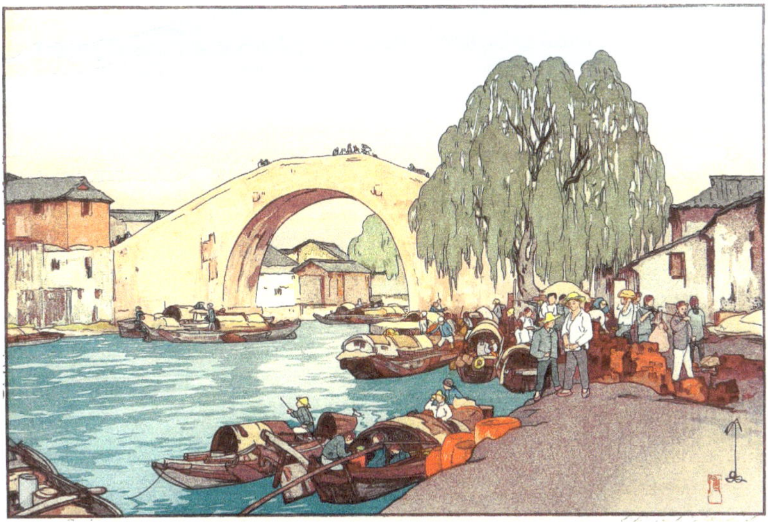

Figure 10.19: *Suzhou, China*, Yoshida Hiroshi, 1940, color woodblock print, Wikimedia Commons.

Shunsuke (1912–1948) countered with the essay "The Living Artist," also published in *Mizue*. Matsumoto challenged the authoritarian view of art, arguing for the importance of freedom of expression and subjectivity: "We do not stop painting even in the most difficult environment because, for us, the act of creating means our step-by-step, gradual growth as human beings."[19]

Ultimately, Matsumoto's essay drew few supporters. Many artists complied with the military propaganda directives and supported the war effort with their work. The military particularly favored *yōga* painters for their realistic detail and ability to reach the populace with information about the war efforts and inspire support for them.[20] Print designer Munakata Shikō (1903–1975) donated prints of Fudō Myō-ō, the Buddhist protector of the nation, to the imperial navy. Watanabe Shōzaburō commissioned Kawase Hasui to design four prints of Japanese soldiers in China in 1937. Hundreds of artists traveled to China as military-service painters, including Yoshida Hiroshi, Onchi Kōshirō, and Itō Shinsui. Both Yoshida and Shinsui's sketches were turned into postcards; Onchi's photographs of China and Yoshida's Chinese scenes were exhibited in Tokyo department stores (Figure 10.19).[21]

Although many artists were patriotic, even those who cooperated with the military continued to believe that they could retain their creative autonomy, as demonstrated by Onchi's portrait of Hagiwara Sakutarō mentioned above. Nevertheless, the government would continue to exercise control over art as World War II raged, rationing art supplies, silencing the art press, ending independent exhibitions, and shutting down private painting societies.[22]

Notes

[1] Kōtarō Takamura, *A Brief History of Imbecility: Poetry and Prose of Takamura Kōtarō*, trans. Hiroaki Sato (Honolulu: University of Hawai'i Press, 1992), 180–186.

[2] Hiroshi Nara, "An Adoring Gaze: The Idea of Greece in Modern Japan," in Almut-Barbara Renger and Xin Fan, eds., *Receptions of Greek and Roman Antiquity in East Asia* (Leiden: Brill, 2019), 197–198; for more, see Nara, "An Adoring Gaze," 175–201.

[3] Nara, "An Adoring Gaze," 198, n. 66.

[4] See, for example, Shūji Takashina, J. Thomas Rimer, and Gerald D. Boas, *Paris in Japan: The Japanese Encounter with European Painting* (St. Louis: Washington University, 1987).

[5] J. Thomas Rimer, "Tokyo in Paris/Paris in Tokyo," in Takashina et al., *Paris in Japan*, 69.

[6] Nobuo Tsuji, *History of Art in Japan*, trans. Nicole Coolidge Rousmaniere (New York: Columbia University Press, 2019), 416–418.

[7] Ellen P. Conant et al., *Nihonga, Transcending the Past: Japanese-Style Painting, 1868–1968* (St. Louis: Saint Louis Art Museum, 1995), 104–105; 322–323.

[8] For more, see Conant et al., *Nihonga, Transcending the Past.*

[9] For an excellent overview of *shin hanga*, see Andreas Marks et al., *Seven Masters: 20th-Century Japanese Woodblock Prints from the Wells Collection* (Minneapolis: Minneapolis Institute of Art, 2015). See also publications by Kendall H. Brown, such as *Kawase Hasui: The Complete Woodblock Prints* (Amsterdam: Hotei, 2004; 2nd ed. 2008).

[10] Tsuji, *History of Art in Japan*, 420.

[11] Kendall H. Brown, "Out of the Dark Valley: Japanese Woodblock Prints and War, 1937–1945," *Impressions* 23 (2001): 66.

[12] For a full study of this topic, see Anne Nishimura Morse, J. Thomas Rimer, and Kendall H. Brown, *Art of the Japanese Postcard: The Leonard A. Lauder Collection at the Museum of Fine Arts, Boston* (Boston: MFA Publications, 2004).

[13] William H. Coaldrake, *Architecture and Authority in Japan*, Nissan Institute / Routledge Japanese Studies (London: Routledge, 1996), 222–239.

[14] Coaldrake, *Architecture and Authority in Japan*, 244–249.

[15] Toshio Watanabe, "Japanese Imperial Architecture from Thomas Roger Smith to Itō Chūta," in Ellen P. Conant, ed., *Challenging Past and Present: The Metamorphosis of Nineteenth-Century Japanese Art* (Honolulu: University of Hawai'i Press, 2006), 241.

[16] For more, see Watanabe, "Japanese Imperial Architecture," 240–253.

[17] The Japan Folk Crafts Museum website: https://mingeikan.or.jp/?lang=en.

[18] For more, see Gennifer Weisenfeld, "Mavo's Conscious Constructivism: Art, Individualism, and Daily Life in Interwar Japan, *Art Journal* 33, no. 3 (Fall 1996): 64–73; and Gennifer Weisenfeld, *MAVO: Japanese Artists and the Avant-Garde, 1905–1931* (Berkeley: University of California Press, 2002).

[19] Quoted in Mark Sandler, "The Living Artist: Matsumoto Shunsuke's Reply to the State," *Art Journal* 33, no. 3 (Fall 1996): 81.

[20] Mayu Tsuruya, "The Ascent of *Yōga* in Modern Japan and the Pacific War, in Hiroshi Nara, ed. *Inexorable Modernity: Japan's Grappling with Modernity in the Arts* (Lanham, MD: Lexington Books, 2007), 69–100.

[21] Brown, "Out of the Dark Valley," 67–69; see also Nishimura Morse et al., *Art of the Japanese Postcard,* 2004.

[22] Sandler, "The Living Artist," 74–82.

11

Creativity and Innovation on the International Stage

Postwar to 2000

Even amidst the hatred and carnage, life is still worth living. It is possible for wonderful encounters and beautiful things to exist.

— Miyazaki Hayao, Studio Ghibli

The atomic bombing of Hiroshima and Nagasaki brought the war in the Pacific to an end. The aftermath of World War II was a turning point in the arts, with the challenges of rebuilding devastated cities and recovering from the war. The military occupation by the Allied Forces redefined state authority and pushed Japan toward democracy. The occupation was followed by the Korean War in the 1950s; the "economic miracle" of the 1960s, which also saw extensive urban growth and environmental pollution; the oil shocks of the 1970s; the economic success of the 1980s; and the recession of the 1990s, a decade that includes the devastating 1995 Kobe earthquake.

Doing justice to the arts of postwar Japan, when many Japanese artists and architects became world renowned, would require an entire book. The printmaker Munakata Shikō achieved international success in 1951, winning first prize at the São Paulo International Biennale, followed by the Grand Prix at the Venice Biennale in 1956 for his large monochrome set *Two Bodhisattvas and Sakyamuni's Ten Great Disciples* (Figure 11.1).[1] Other printmakers such as Saitō Kiyoshi (1907–1997) also became known outside of Japan.

Kusama Yayoi (1929–2026), an internationally recognized contemporary Japanese artist, uses painting, performance, sculpture, Pop art, installations, and Minimalism in her work. She was a central figure in the New York avant-garde world during the 1960s, exhibiting alongside the likes of Andy Warhol (1928–

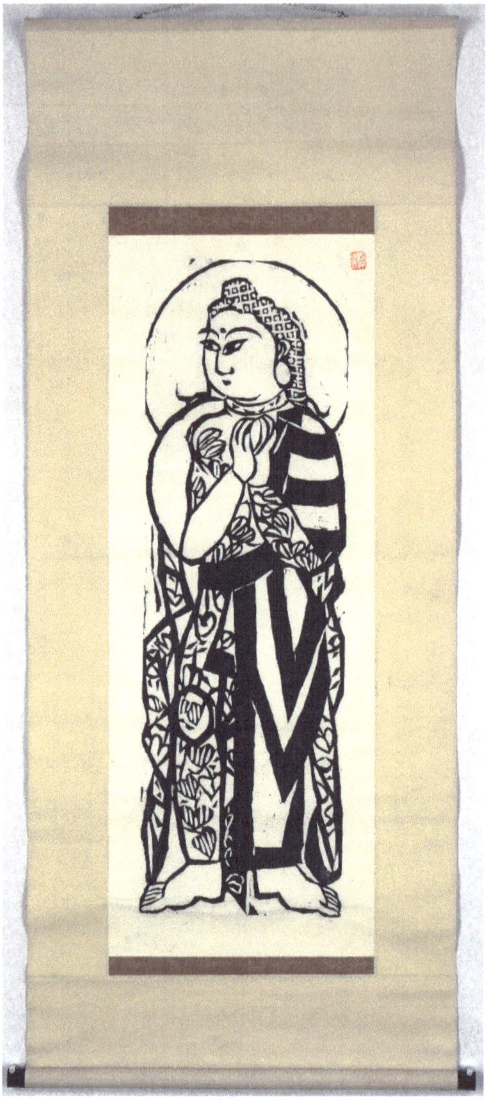

Figure 11.1: Manjusri from *Two Bodhisattvas and Sakyamuni's Ten Great Disciples*, Munakata Shikō, 1939, scroll-mounted woodcut, Carnegie Museum of Art, Pittsburgh.

1987) and Claes Oldenburg (1929–2022), and has had a significant impact on the international art scene for decades (Figure 11.2).

In the Kansai region, which includes Kyoto, contemporary art developed independently of direct outside influence. In 1954, Nikakai artist Yoshihara Jirō (1905–1972) and his colleagues established the avant-garde Gutai Art Association,

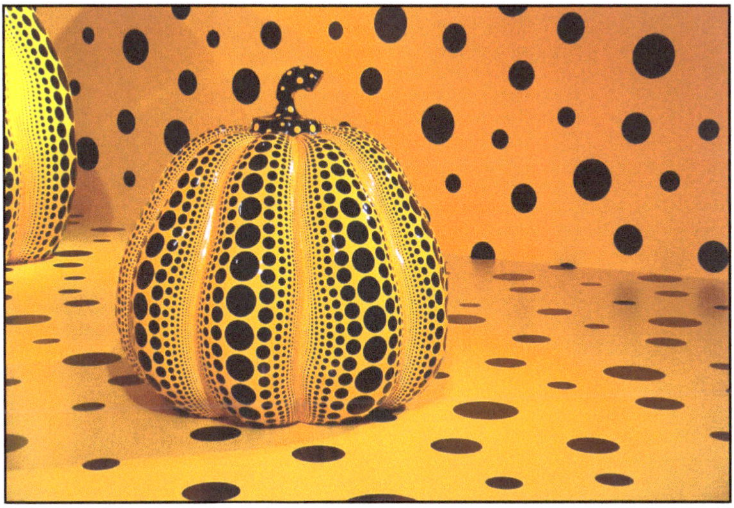

Figure 11.2: *Plastic Pumpkin*, Kusama Yayoi, 2016, fiberglass-reinforced plastic, Public domain.

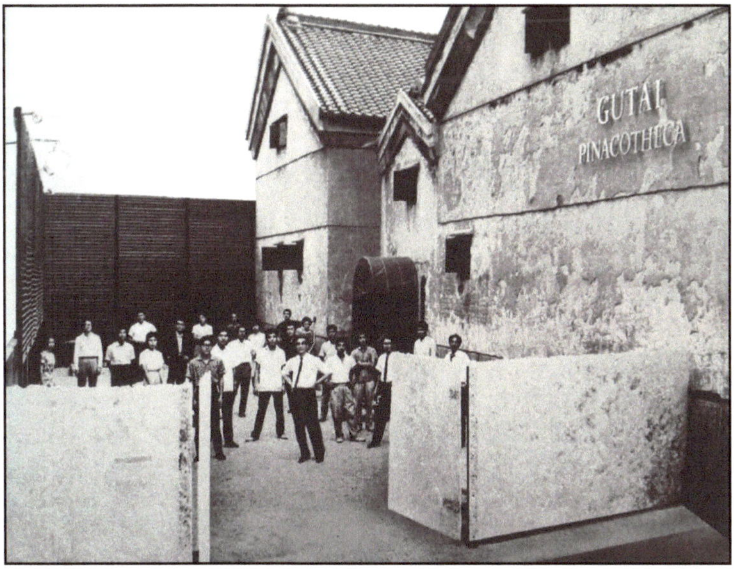

Figure 11.3: Gutai Pinacotheca, 1962, Wikimedia Commons.

for artists working in a range of traditional and contemporary arts, from calligraphy and artisan crafts to performance art and installations (Figure 11.3). For these artists, the making of art itself through performance or a "happening" *was* the art, and painting with objects other than paint brushes was a means to a new expression. Performances included the 1955 *Challenge to the Mud* in which

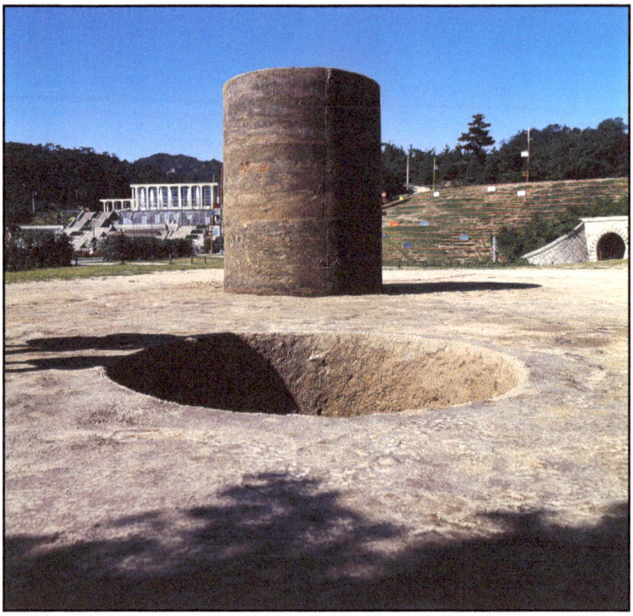

Figure 11.4: *Phase—Mother Earth*, Sekine Nobuo, 1968, earth, Wikimedia Commons.

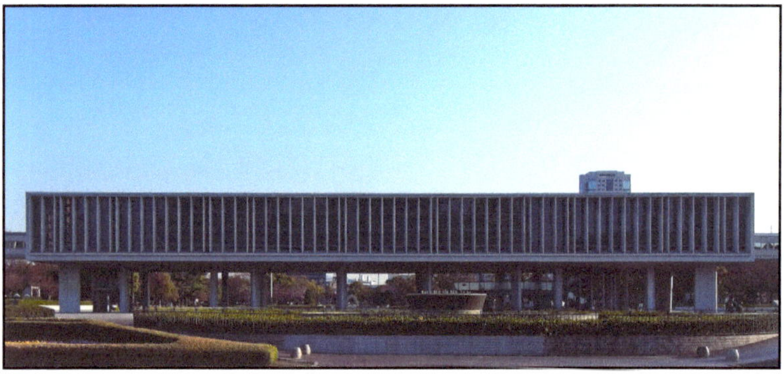

Figure 11.5: Hiroshima Peace Memorial Museum, Tange Kenzō, 1955, steel-framed reinforced concrete and glass, Wikimedia Commons.

Shiraga Kazuo (1924–2008) rolled in mud, and the 1955 *Laceration of Paper* in which Murakami Saburō (1925–1996) ran through a paper screen. Internationally known, particularly among American artists, Gutai artists are credited with anticipating the performance and conceptual art of the following decades.

A new word came into Japanese terminology—*aato* (art), referencing the evolving world of computer technology and the dissolving lines between the visual arts and multimedia encompassing painting, manga, film, anime, photography, design, and performance art. An example of early *aato* collectives was the Hi

Red Center, founded in 1963 by Takamatsu Jirō (1936–1998), Akasegawa Genpei (1937–2014), and Nakanishi Natsuyuki (1935–2016). The collective aimed to blend art with social commentary and performance art. Akasegawa used copies of thousand-yen notes to wrap a variety of everyday objects, which resulted in a censorship case that went to Japan's Supreme Court. He was tried and convicted for money imitation.[2]

Artists were also involved in the Anpo protests of the 1960s, against the renewal of the United States–Japan Security Treaty that allowed the United States to continue to maintain military bases on Japanese soil. Painters, photographers, and filmmakers chronicled the protests and reacted to them with their own work. Many of the artists' experiences became the basis for Linda Hoaglund's documentary film *ANPO: Art X War*.[3] The 1960s also saw the emergence of the Mono-ha movement, in which artists engaged with materials and their properties, such as earth. The sculptor Sekine Nobuo (1942–2019) created the seminal work *Phase—Mother Earth* (Figure 11.4), a hole in the ground accompanied by a corresponding cylinder of compressed earth removed from the hole.

In architecture, the postwar period was one of major advances in technology and a flurry of construction and building. Tange Kenzō (1913–2005) achieved international recognition with his blend of premodern Japanese architectural styles with the International Style. His significant designs include the Yoyogi National Gymnasium for the 1964 Tokyo Olympics. When completed in 1964, the two buildings were the largest tensile structures in the world, using suspension-roof structuring and invoking the monumentality of Buddhist temples such as Tōdaiji (Chapter 2).[4] Tange's earlier Hiroshima Peace Memorial Museum is a steel-framed reinforced concrete and glass building that echoes Le Corbusier (Charles-Édouard Jeanneret, 1887–1965) in its use of *pilotis* (columns), which elevate the structure off the ground, and ribbon windows (Figure 11.5; 1955). This Minimalist style echoes the post-and-lintel construction and raised floors of premodern Japanese architecture such as the Ise Shrine (Chapter 2).[5]

Isozaki Arata (1931–2022), who worked for Tange, is recognized for his versatility and use of geometric forms, as seen in Mito Art Tower (Figure 11.6), constructed of twenty-eight titanium pyramids.[6] His overseas commissions include the Museum of Contemporary Art, Los Angeles (1986) and the Team Disney building in Florida (Figure 11.7). Andō Tadao (b. 1941) is a self-taught architect who focuses on simplicity and concrete as a primary material; his works include the Hyōgo Prefectural Museum of Art (Figure 11.8; 2002), the Pulitzer Arts Foundation in St. Louis, Missouri (2001), and the Modern Art Museum of Fort Worth, Texas (2002). All three architects have won the Pritzker Architecture Prize. Japanese landscape and garden design has also had a deep and lasting impact around the world, introducing asymmetry and minimalism, and specific natural elements such as water features and rock formations.[7] A prominent example in the U.S. is the Portland Japanese Garden in Oregon.

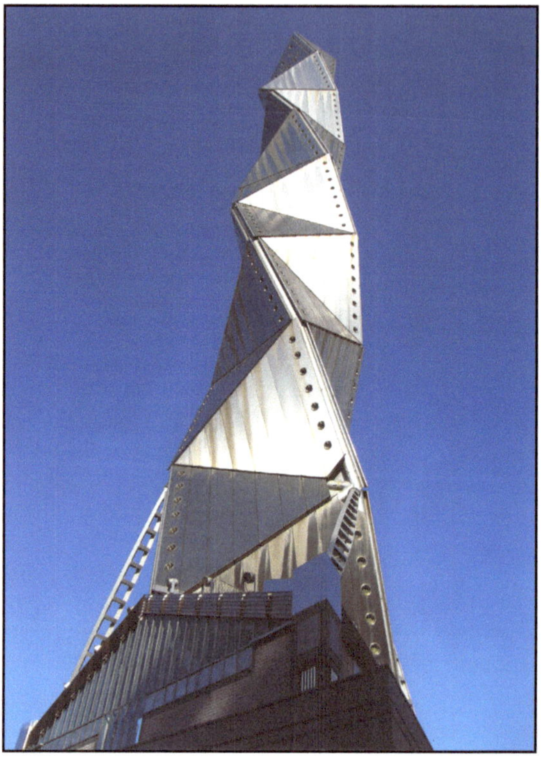

Figure 11.6: Mito Art Tower, Isozaki Arata, 1990, Wikimedia Commons.

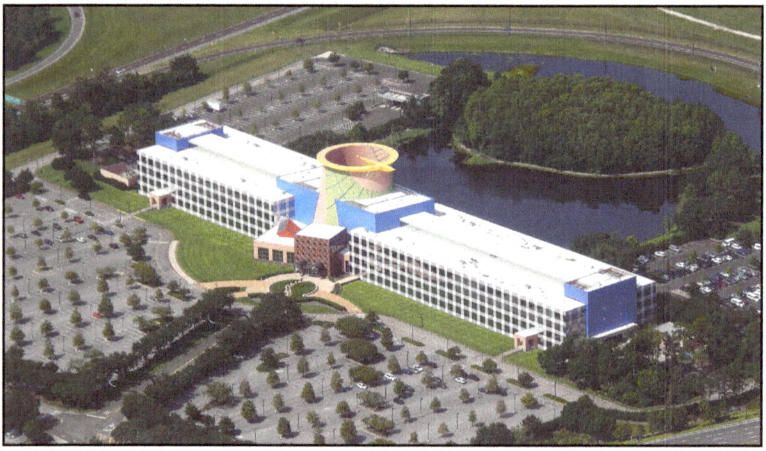

Figure 11.7: Team Disney Orlando, Izosaki Arata, 1991, postmodern, Lake Buena Vista, Florida, Wikimedia Commons.

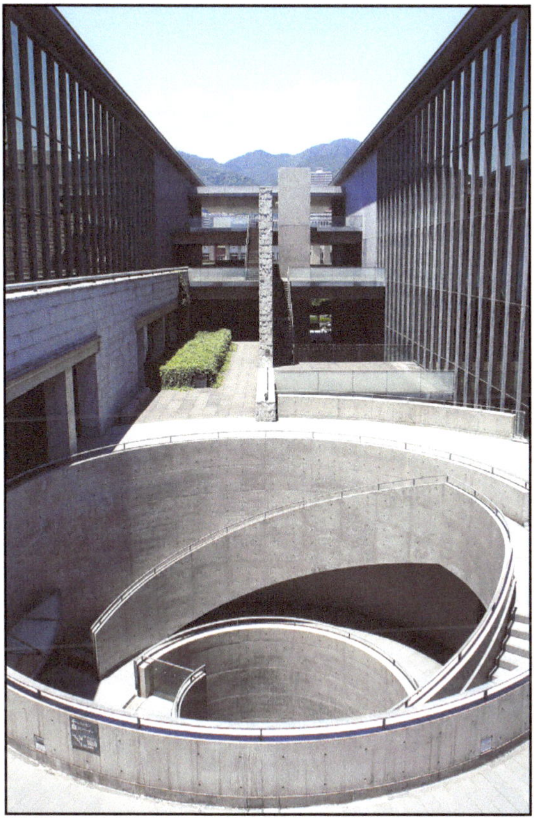

Figure 11.8: Hyogo Prefectural Museum of Art, Andō Tadao, 2002, Kobe, Wikimedia Commons.

Anime (film animation) and manga became international sensations as Japanese artists and film directors looked to both history and contemporary culture to create art that appealed to younger audiences. Japan has a long history of caricature and satire, dating as far back as the graffiti found inside Nara-period Buddhist statues (Chapter 2). Playfulness, humor, ghosts, demons, and *bakemono* (shapeshifters) were integrated into the developing arts of manga, anime, and videogames.[8] The centuries-old integration of text and image and the rise in literacy during the Tokugawa period created a culture of reading books and magazines that catered to specific audiences, with illustrations and text appearing in the same frames. Satire and political critique abound in Japanese pop culture but have been neutralized in places like the United States where Japanese pop culture rapidly rose in popularity.[9] Western-style caricature introduced in the Meiji period and American-style comic strips also contributed to the development of manga, and Disney Studio animation influenced anime. Japanese pop culture, however, has its own distinct characteristics, including prevalent themes like *yōkai* (mysterious things; monsters), *kawaii* (cute), and a fascination with technology.[10]

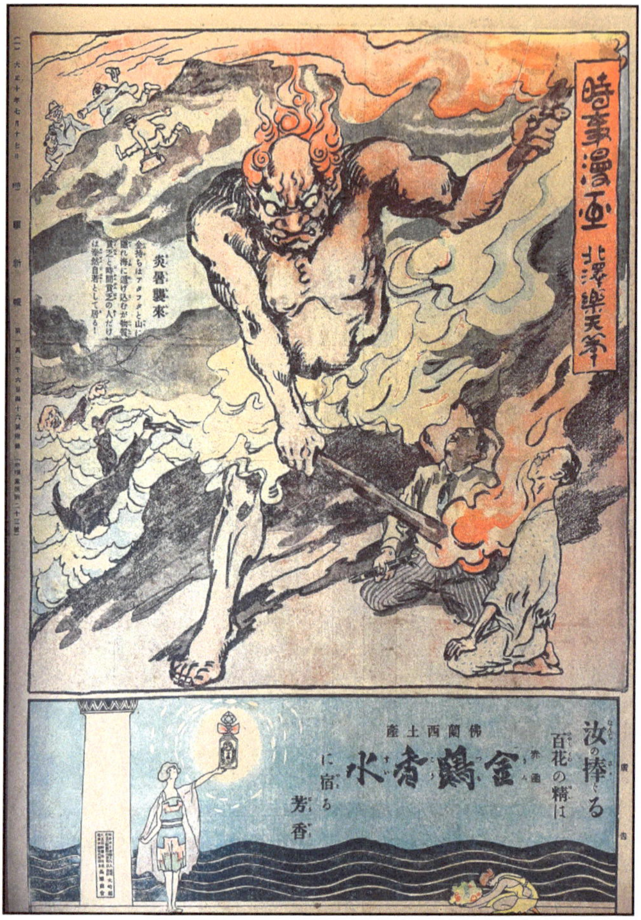

Figure 11.9: "Calamity's Intense Heat" from *Jiji manga*, Kitazawa Rakuten, July 17, 1921, manga tear sheets, full-color Sunday supplement, *Jiji shinpō* newspaper, courtesy of The Ohio State University's Billy Ireland Cartoon Library and Museum.

Manga in the early twentieth century continued with Kitazawa Rakuten (1876–1955), who published *Jiji manga* from 1902 to 1932 in the Sunday edition of the newspaper *Jiji shinpō*. His July 17, 1921 image "Calamity's Intense Heat" (Figure 11.9) features an angry demon torturing two men as others run away into the sea. The caption reads "The wealthy run helter-skelter to take refuge in the sea but only the people who are materialistically poor and short of time are calm and collected." Okamoto Ippei (1886–1948) introduced cinematic effects to manga, and Tagawa Suihō (1899–1989) created *Norakuro*, a popular series about an orphan dog in military service, published by Kodansha in the boys' magazine *Shōnen kurabu* (1914–1962).[11] Tezuka Osamu (1928–1989) was the leading master of postwar manga. He had studied Disney studio animation and produced

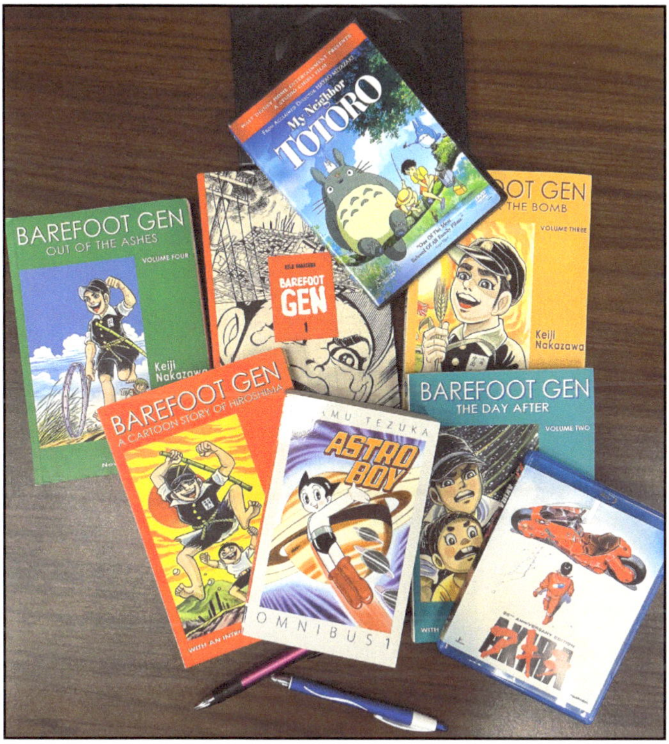

Figure 11.10: Collection of Japanese anime and manga, private collection, photo by author.

numerous classics such as *Astro Boy* (*Tetsuwan Atomu*, 1952–1968) and *Metropolis* (1949). His unfinished *Phoenix* (*Hi no Tori*) is considered a classic. Like *The Tale of Genji* it is a massive tome, some 3,000 pages of stories involving the search for immortality, taking place in different historical settings and into the far future.

Other manga artists include Shirato Sanpei (Okamoto Noboru; 1932–2021), who created historically based stories that focus on social oppression and injustice during the Tokugawa period (for example, *Legend of Kamui*, 1964–1971); Tsuge Yoshiharu (1937–2026), who built surrealist worlds (*Screw System*, 1968); and Chiba Tetsuya (b. 1939), known for his sports stories such as *Tomorrow's Joe*, with text by Takamori Asao (Takamori Asaki; 1936–1987). Nakazawa Keiji (1939–2012) is known for his *Barefoot Gen* series, based on his experiences as a survivor of the Hiroshima atomic bomb (Figure 11.10).[12]

Commercially produced anime in Japan likely began in 1917 with *Kid Deko's New Picture Book: The Story of Imosuke's Boar Hunt*, created by Shimokawa Hekoten (1892–1973). Masaoka Kenzō (1898–1988) created Japan's first full-cel animated film, the acclaimed short *Spider and Tulip* (1943). Anime was also used for propaganda purposes during World War II, with films like Seo Mitsuyo's

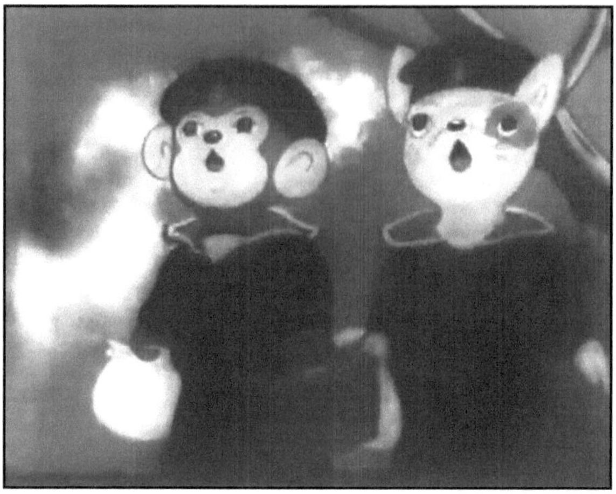

Figure 11.11: *Momotarō's Divine Sea Warriors*, directed by Seo Mitsuyo, 1945, still from the anime propaganda film, Public domain.

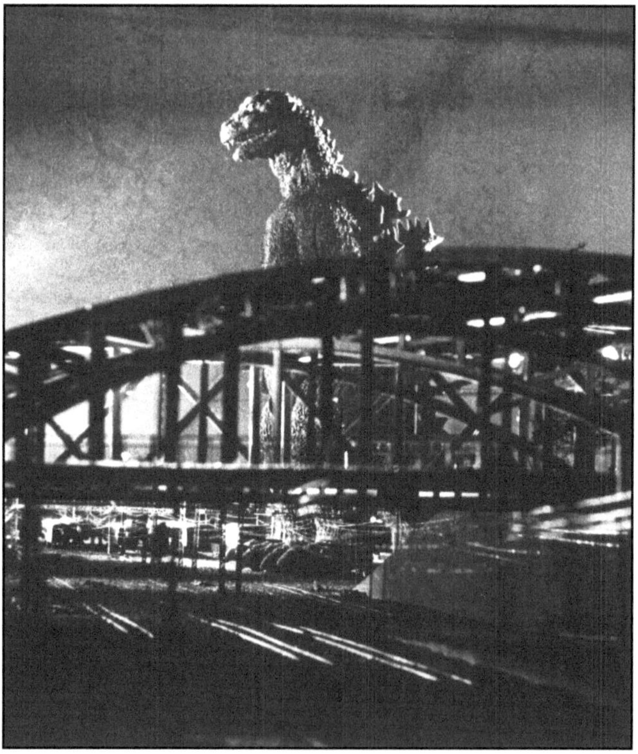

Figure 11.12: On the set of the film *Gojira* (*Godzilla*), 1954, crew members operating the Godzilla suit, Tōhō Studio, Tokyo, Public domain.

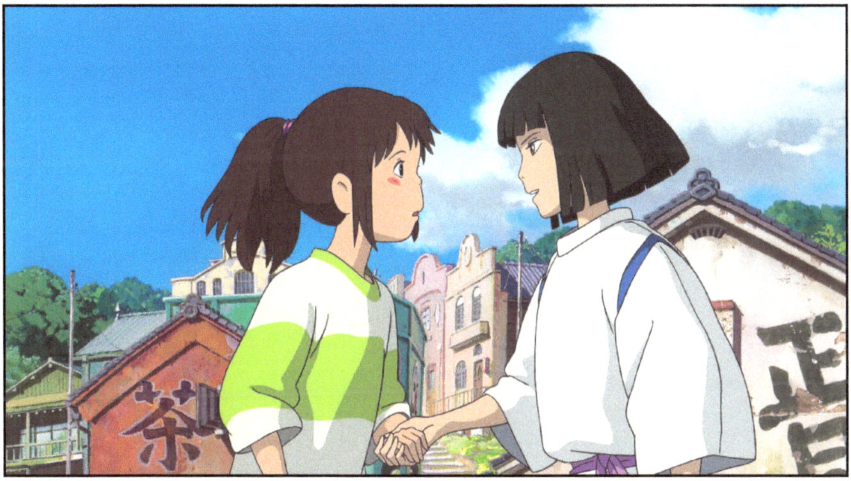

Figure 11.13: Scene from *Spirited Away*, Miyazaki Hayao, 2001, anime, Studio Ghibli, Public domain.

(1911–2010) *Momotarō's Divine Sea Warriors* (Figure 11.11; 1945). The Tōei Motion Picture Company produced full-length anime in the postwar period, such as *The Tale of the White Serpent* (1958).

Japan found international audiences with its monster movies, starting with the 1954 release of Tōhō Studio's *Gojira*, an anti-nuclear and anti-American film inspired by Hollywood's *King Kong*, heavily edited for its U.S. debut in 1956 as *Godzilla, King of the Monsters* (Figure 11.12).[13] The original *Gojira* reflects the Japanese fascination with ultimate destruction, as seen in films such as the post-apocalyptic *Akira* (1988), a highly influential anime based on the 1982 manga by Ōtomo Katsuhiro (b. 1954) in which a Neo-Tokyo is destroyed. *Grave of the Fireflies* (1988), an unusually realistic anime by Studio Ghibli, directed by Takahata Isao (1935–2018), is set in the final days of World War II in Japan. The script is based on a 1967 short story by Nosaka Akiyuki (1930–2015). Japan's trauma during and in the aftermath of World War II has had a lasting impact on postwar arts in general.

Studio Ghibli, founded by Miyazaki Hayao (b. 1941) and Takahata Isao, has turned out full-length anime films, many of which became highly successful internationally. *My Neighbor Totoro* (1988) combines elements of nature spirits, *kawaii*, and the beauty of nature in colorful and watercolor-like imagery. Other films such as *Princess Mononoke* (1977) and *Pom Poko* (1994) challenge the human relationship to nature and the destruction of habitats. Many of the Studio Ghibli films also draw upon the tradition of *bakemono*, *yōkai*, and nature spirits, as in *Spirited Away* (Figure 11.13; 2001).

The film *Gojira* and the subsequent Godzilla series is an example of cross-fertilization between Japan and the United States. The films of director Kurosawa Akira (1910–1998) were copied and adapted by Hollywood. For example, *Yojimbo*

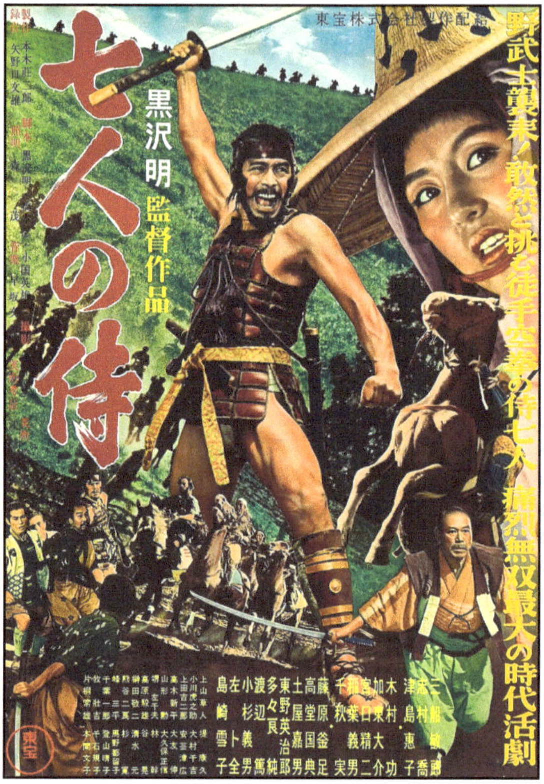

Figure 11.14: Tōhō movie poster *Seven Samurai*, directed by Kurosawa Akira, 1954, feature-length film, Wikimedia Commons.

(1961) was remade as *A Fistful of Dollars* (1964)—nearly scene for scene—and the influential *Seven Samurai* (Figure 11.14; 1954) became *The Magnificent Seven* in the United States (1960).

Japanese photographers and designers have also contributed to the contemporary art scene in Japan. Domon Ken (1909–1990) was known for his use of black-and-white photography (Figure 11.15), with subjects ranging from Buddhist icons such as the Yakushi Nyorai (Chapter 3) to photorealism, as in the series *The Children of Chikuhō*, which documented the harsh life of coalminers in northern Kyushu and was published as a book in 1960.

Nihonga and *yōga* continue to be popular with the Japanese public; both styles have come to incorporate elements of the other, a trend that dates back to the Meiji period. By the latter half of the twentieth century, painters in these styles were merging into international currents as well as looking to premodern Japanese art for inspiration. *Nihonga* painter Yoyama Misao (1920–1973) ventured into abstraction while using the traditional theme of "Eight Views of the Xiao and

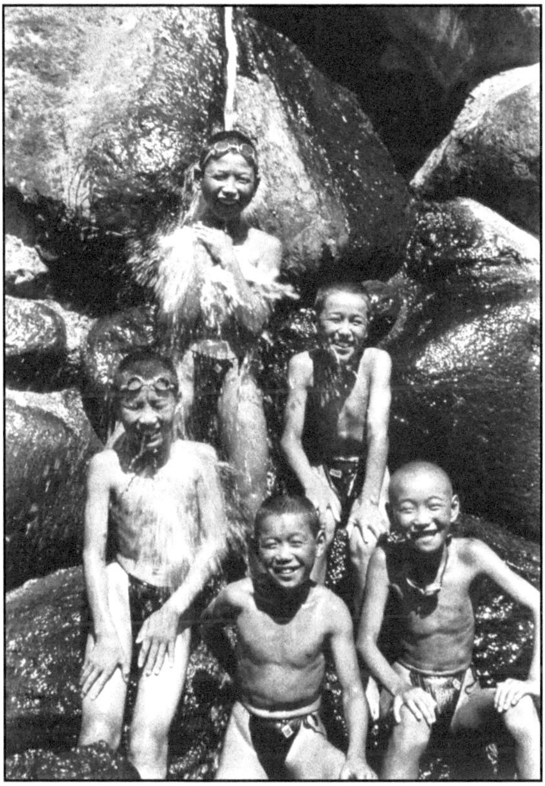

Figure 11.15: *Bathing* - Shizu'ura, 1936, Public domain.

Xiang Rivers," while *yōga* artist Yoshihara Jirō (1905–1972) looked to Hakuin's circles to create a series called *White Circle*.[14] The contemporary visual artist Murakami Takashi (b. 1962) coined the word "Superflat" in 2000 to describe the two-dimensional character of Japanese visual arts.

These are just a few of the many international artists and art forms originating in Japan. However, Japanese art has long had a global impact, beginning with the export of items such as ceramics, woodblock prints, and Japanese silk textiles, followed by a surge of everyday items (umbrellas, fans, furniture) and artisan crafts that flooded Europe and the United States in the nineteenth century.

Throughout Japanese history, there have been some distinctive cultural threads and trends that continue even today. In this short survey, we have chronicled a culture that consistently seeks to learn from abroad yet transforms what is introduced to suit Japanese tastes and needs. Even the most traditional artistic styles and schools changed over time; nothing has been entirely stagnant. At their best, the Japanese have put much effort into high-quality production, with skills honed over decades of learning and practice. Whether we are looking at a particularly superb example of cloisonné from the Meiji period or the refined style of a Japanese consumer appliance today, quality and style are paramount to the process of creation in Japan. Japanese aesthetic sensibilities like simplicity, refinement, and sensitivity to nature pervade visual and material culture from the earliest poetry to contemporary TV commercials. Popular culture reveals the long history of humor, satire, and parody, a fascination with the strange and mysterious, and an eagerness to engage with the new.

There are numerous examples of contemporary artists deliberately drawing upon traditional ideas, materials, and styles. Avant-garde artist Okamoto Tarō (1911–1996) was influential in arguing for the aesthetic value of Jōmon pottery rather than regarding those ceramics only as ancient artifacts. Fashion designer Mori Hanae (1926–2022) fused Kabuki and Noh costumes with her creativity for clothing designs. Many artists have drawn on the seasonal focus (four distinct seasons and seventy-two shorter micro-seasons) that has dominated much of Japanese art over the centuries. Other characteristics that continue to the present are minimalism, the use of negative space, the concept of *ma* (space or pause), image and text blends, calligraphy, emphasizing two-dimensionality, drawing on the long tradition of *giga*, the fascination with the strange and mysterious, the love of the "cute," and so on. The blending of the premodern with the contemporary to create something new is characteristic of much of twentieth-century Japanese art. This dynamic has driven (and still drives) the innovation and creativity in the arts of Japan and has led artists worldwide to engage with Japanese art, and Japanese artists, in turn, to engage with the world.

Notes

[1] This image is part of a set purchased by the Carnegie Museum of Art in Pittsburgh in 1957. The mounted print was produced in 1939, and it is likely that Munakata's success at the Biennale inspired the CMOA to purchase the set. Correspondence with curator Akemi May, May 12, 2025.

[2] William A. Marotti, "Simulacra and Subversion in the Everyday: Akasegawa Genpei's 1000-yen Copy, Critical Art, and the State, *Postcolonial Studies* 4, no. 2 (2001): 211–239.

[3] Examples of these artists' works can be found in the film (https://anpomovie.com/) as well as in an article by Linda Hoaglund, "The Lost Art of Resistance," accessed December 30, 2024, http://lhoaglund.com/the-lost-art-of-resistance.

[4] William H. Coaldrake, *Architecture and Authority in Japan*, Nissan Institute / Routledge Japanese Studies (London: Routledge, 1996), 256–266.

[5] See "Kenzō Tange Hiroshima Peace Memorial Museum 1949–1955 (Showa period)," Daiwa Anglo-Japanese Foundation, Art History in Schools, accessed February 9, 2025, https://www.arthistoryinschools.org.uk/alevelresources.

[6] See Naser Nader Ibrahim, "Art Tower Mito in Japan by Arata Isozaki," *Amazing Architecture*, accessed April 3, 2025, https://amazingarchitecture.com/skyscrapers/art-tower-mito-in-japan-by-arata-isozaki.

[7] See, for example, publications by Kendall H. Brown, *Visionary Landscapes: Japanese Garden Design in North America; The Work of Five Contemporary Masters* (Singapore: Periplus, 2017); and *Quiet Beauty: The Japanese Gardens of North America* (Rutland, VT: Tuttle, 2013).

[8] For videogames, see Rachael Hutchinson, *Japanese Culture Through Videogames* (London: Routledge, 2019).

[9] For an excellent overview of postwar Japanese pop culture, see William M. Tsutsui, *Japanese Popular Culture and Globalization: Key Issues in Asian Studies* (Ann Arbor: Association for Asian Studies, 2010). I am using Tsutsui's definition of popular culture in this chapter as that which is "commercial culture, mass produced, and mass consumed." Tsutsui, 4.

[10] Tsutsui, *Japanese Popular Culture*, 20–21. For more on *yōkai*, see Kazuhiko Komatsu, *An Introduction to Yōkai Culture: Monsters, Ghosts, and Outsiders in Japanese History*, trans. Hiroko Yoda and Matt Alt (Tokyo: Japan Publishing Industry Foundation for Culture, 2017); and Michael Dylan Foster, *Pandemonium and Parade: Japanese Monsters and the Culture of Yōkai* (Berkeley: University of California Press, 2009).

[11] Nobuo Tsuji, *History of Art in Japan*, trans. Nicole Coolidge Rousmaniere (New York: Columbia University Press, 2019), 467.

[12] For more on Japanese popular culture, see Timothy J. Craig, ed., *Japan Pop! Inside the World of Japanese Popular Culture* (New York: M.E. Sharpe, 2000).

[13] For a history of the Godzilla films, see William Tsutsui, *Godzilla on My Mind: Fifty Years of the King of Monsters* (New York: St. Martin's Griffin, 2004).

[14] Ellen P. Conant, et al. *Nihonga, Transcending the Past: Japanese-Style Painting, 1868–1968* (The Saint Louis Art Museum, 1995), 284–285; Tsuji, *History of Art in Japan*, 475.

Image Credits

Chapter 1

Fig. 1.1: Deep vessel with handles, c. 3500–2500 BCE, earthenware with carved and incised decoration. H. 33 cm x W. 31.8 cm. The Harry G. C. Packard Collection of Asian Art, Gift of Harry G. C. Packard, and Purchase, Fletcher, Rogers, Harris Brisbane Dick, and Louis V. Bell Funds, Joseph Pulitzer Bequest, and The Annenberg Fund Inc. Gift, 1975, 1975.268.183. Metropolitan Museum of Art, New York, Public domain.

Fig. 1.2: "Flame pot" (*kaen doki*), Jōmon period (c. 13,500 BCE–300 BCE), earthenware. H. 53.1 cm. Mary Griggs Burke Collection, Gift of the Mary and Jackson Burke Foundation, 2015, 2015.300.258. Metropolitan Museum of Art, New York, Public domain.

Fig. 1.3: "Jōmon Venus" from the Tanabatake archeological site, Middle Jōmon period, earthenware. H. 27 cm. Togari-ishi Archeological Museum, Nagano prefecture. Photo © Takuma-sa, Wikimedia Commons.

Fig. 1.4: *Dogū* figurine, 1000–800 BCE, earthenware with traces of color. H. 19.37 cm. The John R. Van Derlip Fund, 2016.46. Minneapolis Institute of Art, Public domain.

Fig. 1.5: Yayoi jar, c. 100–300 CE, earthenware with incised decoration. H. 25.4 cm x D. 22.9 cm. The Harry G. C. Packard Collection of Asian Art, Gift of Harry G. C. Packard, and Purchase, Fletcher, Rogers, Harris Brisbane Dick, and Louis V. Bell Funds, Joseph Pulitzer Bequest, and The Annenberg Fund Inc. Gift, 1975, 1975.268.378. Metropolitan Museum of Art, New York, Public domain.

Fig. 1.6: Bronze bell (*dōtaku*), first century BCE–first century CE, bronze. H. 20.32 cm x W. 25.4 cm. The William Hood Dunwoody Fund, 64.1. Minneapolis Institute of Art, Public domain.

Fig. 1.7: Tomb of Emperor Nintoku, fifth century. L. 842 m x W. 659 m x H. 40 m. Sakai, Osaka. © National Land Image Information (Color Aerial Photographs), Ministry of Land, Infrastructure, Transport and Tourism.

Fig. 1.8: *Haniwa* horse, fifth–sixth century, earthenware with traces of pigment. H. 59.7 cm x W. 66 cm. The Norweb Collection, 1957.27. Cleveland Museum of Art, Public domain.

Chapter 2

Fig. 2.1: Fushimi Inari Taisha *torii*, Kyoto, wood gate with vermillion paint. Photo by author, 2023.

Fig. 2.2: Ise Grand Shrine, Inner Shrine, Japanese cypress (*hinoki*) structure with thatched *kaya* roof. Mie prefecture. Photo © N yotarou, Wikimedia Commons.

Fig. 2.3: *Haniwa* house, early fifth century. H. 54 cm, terracotta, excavated from Chausuyama tomb, Akabori village, Sawa county, Gunma prefecture. Tokyo National Museum. Photo © Saigen Jiro, Public domain.

Fig. 2.4: Hōryūji main hall and pagoda, Nara, post-and-lintel wooden structure (mostly Japanese cypress) with tile roofs, late seventh century. Photo by author, 2023.

Fig. 2.5: Yumedono Hall, Hōryūji, Nara, octagonal wooden structure with tile roof, original hall: 739, reconstructed in 1230. Photo by author, 2023.

Fig. 2.6: Shaka Triad, Hōryūji main hall, Nara, attributed to Tori Busshi. 623 CE, gilt-bronze, center image: H. 87.5 cm, Wikimedia Commons.

Fig. 2.7: Guze Kannon, Yumedono Hall, Hōryūji, Nara, first half of the seventh century, wood with gold leaf. H. 180 cm. *Horyuji Okagami* [The Great Art of Horyuji Temple], vol. 51, 1918, Tokyo Bijutsu Gakko, Public domain.

Fig. 2.8: Two dancing *haniwa*, sixth century, terracotta, excavated from Nohara Tumulus, Kumagaya-shi, Saitama. Tokyo National Museum, Wikimedia Commons.

Fig. 2.9: Amida Paradise from the *Pure Land Paradises of Four Buddhas,* late seventh to early eighth century, color on kaolin-covered plaster wall. Hōryūji, Nara, Wikimedia Commons.

Fig. 2.10: Main hall (*kondō*) of Tōdaiji, Nara, reconstruction: 1688–1707, timber-frame structure. Photo by author, 2007.

Fig. 2.11: Daibutsu, original statue dates to 755; damaged and restored over the centuries, bronze. H. 15 m. Tōdaiji, Nara. Photo by author, 2023.

Fig. 2.12: Kichijōten, eighth century, ink, color, and gold on hemp. H. 53 cm x W. 32 cm, Yakushiji, Nara, Wikimedia Commons.

Chapter 3

Fig. 3.1: Sai-in Mandala (Womb World Mandala), second half of the ninth century, hanging scroll, color on silk. H. 185.1 cm x W. 164.3 cm. Tōji, Kyoto, Wikimedia Commons.

Fig. 3.2: Taima Mandala, fourteenth century, hanging scroll, ink, color, and gold on silk, image: H. 91.8 x W. 72.7 cm. Rogers Fund 1957, 57.156.6. Metropolitan Museum of Art, New York, Public domain.

Fig. 3.3: Yakushi Nyorai, early ninth century, wood. H. 170.6 cm. Jingoji, Nara. Photo © Domon Ken, Wikimedia Commons.

Fig. 3.4: *The Descent of Amida*, twelfth century, triptych of hanging scrolls, ink and color on silk, center scroll: 210.4 x 210.5 cm. Yūshi Hachimankō Jūhachi Ka-in, Mt. Koya, Wikimedia Commons.

Fig. 3.5: Phoenix Hall, Byōdō-in, 1053, timber-frame building with tile roof, Uji, Kyoto prefecture. Photo © Martin Falbisoner, Wikimedia Commons.

Fig. 3.6: Amida Nyorai at Phoenix Hall, Jōchō, 1053. Japanese cypress with gold leaf. H. 278.8 cm. Byōdō-in, Uji. Photo © Domon Ken, Public domain.

Fig. 3.7: *Shinden-zukuri* architectural style, miniature model of the Higashi Sanjō-dono in Kyoto, Wikimedia Commons.

Fig. 3.8: Page from *Tsurayuki Anthology*, vol. 2, known as *Ishiyama-gire*, attributed to Fujiwara Sadanobu (1088–1156), 1112, ink on assembled dyed paper decorated with silver and gold, image: H. 20.16 cm x W. 16.03 cm. Provenance: Nishi Honganji, Kyoto. Mary Griggs Burke Collection, Gift of the Mary and Jackson Burke Foundation, 2105.79.238. Minneapolis Institute of Art, Public domain.

Fig. 3.9: *Illustrated Scrolls of the Tale of Genji*, scene from the "Azumaya" chapter (chapter 50), first half of the twelfth century, handscroll, ink and color on paper, entire scroll: H. 22.6 cm x L. 117.7 cm. Tokugawa Art Museum, Wikimedia Commons.

Fig. 3.10: *Illustrated Scrolls of the Courtier Ban Dainagon*, attributed to Tokiwa Mitsunaga (active second half of the twelfth century), twelfth century, color and ink on paper, entire scroll: H. 31.5 cm x L. 2629.9 cm. Idemitsu Museum of Art, Wikimedia Commons.

Fig. 3.11: *Illustrated Scrolls of the Legends of Shigisan*, second half of the twelfth century, handscroll, ink and color on paper, first of three scrolls: H. 31.7 cm x L. 878.27 cm. Chōgosonshiji, Nara prefecture, Wikimedia Commons.

Fig. 3.12: *Scrolls of Frolicking Animals*, detail of wrestling frogs from the first handscroll, twelfth century, ink on paper, first scroll: H. 30.4 cm x L. 1148.4 cm. Kōzanji, Kyoto, Wikimedia Commons.

Fig. 3.13: Scene from the *Hells Scroll*, twelfth century, handscroll, ink and color on paper, entire scroll: H. 26.5 cm x L. 454.7 cm. Nara National Museum, Wikimedia Commons.

Fig. 3.14: *Scroll of Hungry Ghosts* (detail), twelfth century, handscroll, color on paper, entire scroll: H. 26.9 cm x W. 380.2 cm. Tokyo National Museum, Art Collection/Alamy Stock Photo.

Fig. 3.15: Lacquered wood case with design of carriage wheels in a stream, twelfth century, lacquered wood, *maki-e*, and mother of pearl inlay. H. 13.5 cm x L. 22.4 cm x W. 30.6 cm. Tokyo National Museum, Wikimedia Commons.

CHAPTER 4

Fig. 4.1: *Night Attack on the Sanjō Palace, from the Illustrated Scrolls of the Events of the Heiji Era* (*Heiji monogatari emaki*), Kamakura period, second half of the thirteenth century, handscroll, ink and color on paper, overall (including endpapers and *jiku*): 45.9 × 774.5 × 7.6 cm (18 1/16 × 304 15/16 × 3 in.), image: H. 41.3 cm × W. 700.3 cm (16 1/4 × 275 11/16 in.). Fenollosa-Weld Collection, 11.4000. Museum of Fine Arts, Boston. Photograph © 2026 Museum of Fine Arts, Boston.

Fig. 4.2: Armor (*yoroi*), early fourteenth to early fifteenth century, iron, leather, lacquer, silk, gilt copper. H. 69.9 cm x W 43.2 cm. Fletcher Fund, 1928, 28.60.1a–s. Metropolitan Museum of Art, New York, Public domain.

Fig. 4.3: Great South Gate of Tōdaiji, Nara, 1199, *daibutsu-yō* architectural style (wood with tile roof). H. 25.46 meters. Photo by author, 2023.

Fig. 4.4A: Kongō Rikishi, Ungyō, Unkei, Kaikei, Jōkaku and Unkei's eldest son Tankei 1203, assembled wood technique with color. H. 838.0 cm. Great South Gate, Tōdaiji, Public domain.

Fig. 4.4B: Kongō Rikishi, Agyō, Unkei, Kaikei, Jōkaku and Unkei's eldest son Tankei, 1203, assembled wood technique with color. H. 836.3 cm. Great South Gate, Tōdaiji, Wikimedia Commons.

Fig. 4.5: Chōgen, attributed to Unkei, first half of the thirteenth century, wood with color. H. 82.5 cm. Shunjō-dō, Tōdaiji, Public domain.

Fig. 4.6: Fudō Myōō, the Immovable Wisdom King (Achala Vidyaraja), Kaikei, early thirteenth century, Japanese cypress with lacquer, color, gold, cut gold leaf (*kirikane*), and inlaid crystal eyes. H. 53.3 cm x W. 42.5 cm. Mary Griggs Burke Collection, Gift of the Mary and Jackson Burke Foundation, 2015, 2015.300.252a, b. Metropolitan Museum of Art, New York, Public domain.

Fig. 4.7: Zen-style window, Zenkōji, Nagano City. Photo by author, 2023.

Fig. 4.8: Tōfukuji Sanmon, Kyoto, 1425, *zenshū-yō* architecture, two-story gate with wood frame. H. 22 meters. Tōfukuji, Kyoto. Photo © PlusMinus, Wikimedia Commons.

Fig. 4.9: Tōfukuji Sanmon (detail), 1425, *zenshū-yō* architecture, two-story gate with wood frame. H. 22 meters, Tōfukuji, Kyoto. Photo by author, 2023.

Fig. 4.10: *The Illustrated Miraculous Origins of the Yūzū Nenbutsu School* (detail), early fourteenth century, handscroll, ink, color, and gold on paper, entire scroll: H. 30.3 x L. 1373.5 cm. Mr. and Mrs. William H. Marlatt, John L. Severance, and Edward L. Whittemore Funds, 1956.87. Cleveland Museum of Art, Public domain.

Chapter 5

Fig. 5.1: Kinkakuji, original building: 1398, reconstruction: 1955, three stories with wood frame, Rokuonji, Kyoto. Photo by author, 2023.

Fig. 5.2: Kinkakuji roof (detail), original building: 1398, reconstruction: 1955, three stories with wood frame, Rokuonji, Kyoto. Photo by author, 2023.

Fig. 5.3: Kinkakuji pond and stroll garden, Rokuonji, Kyoto. Photo by author, 2007.

Fig. 5.4: Dry landscape garden, Daisen-in, late sixteenth century, Daitokuji, Kyoto, Wikimedia Commons.

Fig. 5.5: Sekka-tei Teahouse, Hōrin Jōshō (1593–1668), seventeenth century, twentieth-century restoration, *sukiya-zukuri* architectural style with nandina bamboo alcove posts and bush clover shelves, Kinkakuji, Kyoto. Photo by author, 2007.

Fig. 5.6: *Seasonal Landscapes*, Kano Hideyori (active mid-sixteenth century), mid to late 1500s, hanging scrolls, ink on paper. Overall: H. 153.6 cm x W. 53.9 cm. Leonard C. Hanna, Jr. fund, 1988.13. Cleveland Museum of Art, Public domain.

Fig. 5.7: *Landscape*, follower of Sesson Shūkei, sixteenth century, six-panel folding screen, ink on paper. H. 167.6 cm x W. 356.2 cm. Bequest of Hope Skillman Schary, 1981, 1982.244.16. Metropolitan Museum of Art, New York, Public domain.

Fig. 5.8: Ryōanji Kuri main building interior, Higashiyama style of the Muromachi period late fifteenth century, Ryōanji, Kyoto. Photo © Tedmoseby, Wikimedia Commons.

Fig. 5.9: Shoji screens and veranda, Kobe. Photo by author, 2010.

Fig. 5.10: *Catching a Catfish with a Gourd*, Josetsu, before 1451, hanging scroll, ink and light color on paper. H. 111.5 cm x W. 75.8 cm. Taizō-in, Myōshinji, Kyoto, Wikimedia Commons.

Fig. 5.11: *Amanohashidate*, Sesshū Tōyō, c. 1501–1506, hanging scroll, ink and light color on paper. H. 89.5 cm x W. 169.5 cm. Kyoto National Museum, Wikimedia Commons.

Fig. 5.12: Photograph of Amanohashidate. Photo © Chensiyuan, Wikimedia Commons.

Fig. 5.13: *Splashed Ink Landscape*, Sesshū Tōyō, 1495, hanging scroll, ink on paper. H. 147.9 cm x W. 32.7 cm. Tokyo National Museum, Wikimedia Commons.

Fig. 5.14: *Splashed Ink Landscape* (detail), Sesshū Tōyō, 1495, hanging scroll, ink on paper. H. 147.9 cm x W. 32.7 cm. Tokyo National Museum, Wikimedia Commons.

Fig. 5.15: Noh Costume (Nuihaku) with Blossoming Trees and Flowers, 1675–1699, embroidery, silk and applied gold leaf on silk ground. H. 164 cm x W. 138 cm. Purchase from the J.H. Wade Fund, 1974:36. Cleveland Museum of Art, Public domain.

Fig. 5.16: Noh Mask of Okina, 1400s, polychromed wood and hemp. H. 20.4 cm x W. 16.1 cm. Purchase from the J.H. Wade Fund, 1977:33. Cleveland Museum of Art, Public domain.

Fig. 5.17: Noh Mask: Waka-onna, Muromachi period, polychromed wood. H. 19.8 cm. John L. Severance Fund, 1972:69. Cleveland Museum of Art, Public domain.

Fig. 5.18: *Hyakki yagyō emaki* (*Night Procession of One Hundred Demons*), first half of the sixteenth century, attributed to Tosa Mitsunobu (d. early 1520s), Muromachi period, handscroll, ink and color on paper. H. 33 cm x L. 747.1 cm. Daitokuji, Kyoto, Wikimedia Commons.

Fig. 5.19: *Birds and Flowers of the Four Seasons*, Kano Motonobu, first half of the sixteenth century, originally eight sliding door panels, right side of panel, hanging scrolls, ink and color on paper, each H. 174.5 cm x W. 139.5 cm. Daisen-in, Daitokuji, Kyoto, Wikimedia Commons.

Fig. 5.20: "At the Pass" (Sekiya), illustration to Chapter 16 of *The Tale of Genji*, Tosa Mitsunobu, early sixteenth century, album leaf, ink, color, and gold on paper. H. 24.1 cm x W. 18.0 cm. Harvard Art Museums/Arthur M. Sackler Museum, Bequest of the Hofer Collection of the Arts of Asia, 1985.352.16.A, Public domain.

Fig. 5.21: Ginkakuji (Silver Pavilion), 1489, two stories with wood frame, Jishō-ji, Kyoto, Wikimedia Commons.

Fig. 5.22: Jar with loops, Bizen ware, sixteenth century, stoneware with natural ash glaze. H. 31.59 cm. Mary Griggs Burke Collection, Gift of the Mary and Jackson Burke Foundation, 2015.79.283. Minneapolis Institute of Art, Public domain.

Fig. 5.23: Scenes in and around Kyoto, early seventeenth century, folding screen, ink, color, and gold on paper. H. 170.18 cm x W. 375.92 cm. Mary Griggs Burke Collection, Gift of the Mary and Jackson Burke Foundation, 2015:79:95. Minneapolis Institute of Art, Public domain.

Chapter 6

Fig. 6.1: Himeji Castle, 1601–1613, Himeji, Japan. Photo by author, 2023.

Fig. 6.2: Himeji Castle detail of triangular cut in wall, 1601–1613, Himeji, Japan. Photo by author, 2007.

Fig. 6.3: Chinese lions (*karashishi*), Kano Eitoku, second half of the sixteenth century, folding screen, color, gold leaf, and ink on paper. H. 224.2 cm x W. 453.3 cm. Museum of the Imperial Collections, Tokyo, Wikimedia Commons.

Fig. 6.4: *Cypress Trees Screens*, Kano Eitoku, c. 1590, pair of folding screens, color, and gold leaf on paper, each H. 170 cm x W. 230.4 cm. Tokyo National Museum, Wikimedia Commons.

Fig. 6.5: *Pine Forest*, Hasegawa Tōhaku, second half of the sixteenth century, left half of a pair of folding screens, ink on paper. H. 156.0 cm x W. 356.0 cm. Tokyo National Museum, Wikimedia Commons.

Fig. 6.6: *Drying Fishnets in the Four Seasons*, Kaihō Yūshō (attributed to), c. 1610, one of a pair of folding screens, ink, color, and gold on paper, overall H. 168.1 cm x W. 377.2 cm. H. de Silver Fund and Ella C. Woodward Memorial Fund, 59.7.1. Brooklyn Museum. Photo © Brooklyn Museum, Creative Commons.

Fig. 6.7: *Crows*, artist unknown, early seventeenth century, pair of six panel screens, ink and gold on paper. H. 156.3 cm x W. 353.8 cm. Photo: Seiji Shirono. Eugene Fuller Memorial Collection, 36.21.2. Seattle Art Museum.

Fig. 6.8: Nanban screen, attributed to Kano Sanraku, early seventeenth century, pair of folding screens, ink, gold, and colors on silk, each H. 166.8 cm x W. 357.0 cm. Suntory Museum of Art, Wikimedia Commons.

Fig. 6.9: Black Seto tea bowl named "Iron Mallet," late sixteenth century, stoneware with black glaze (Mino ware, Black Seto type). H. 9.3 cm x diameter of rim 12 cm. Mary Griggs Burke Collection, Gift of the Mary and Jackson Burke Foundation, 2015, 2015.300.272. Metropolitan Museum of Art, New York, Public domain.

Fig. 6.10: Tea Garden, Kōkoen, Himeji, Japan. Photo by author, 2023.

Fig. 6.11: Red Raku tea bowl, style of Hon'ami Kōetsu (copy of the Kaga Kōetsu tea bowl), eighteenth century, earthenware with red slip under clear lead glaze (Raku ware). H. 9.5 cm x Depth 13 cm. The Howard Mansfield Collection, Gift of Howard Mansfield, 1936, 36.120.492. Metropolitan Museum of Art, New York, Public domain.

Fig. 6.12: *Nuihaku* (Noh Costume), sixteenth century, silk with resist dyeing, impressed gold leaf, and embroidery. H. 160.6 cm x W. 133.1 cm. Purchased with funds provided by Mrs. Charles H. Worcester, 1928.814. Art Institute of Chicago, Public domain.

Fig. 6.13: *Tōsei gusoku* armor, sixteenth to early seventeenth century, iron, silk, leather, wool, *maki-e*, copper, plating, red lacquered, blue-stringed suit. Suntory Museum of Art. Photo © Slimhannya, Wikimedia Commons.

Fig. 6.14: Portrait of Honda Heihachirō Tadakatsu (1548–1610), early seventeenth century, hanging scroll, ink and color on silk. H. 124.0 cm x 64.0 cm. Honda Takayuki Collection, Tokyo, Wikimedia Commons.

Chapter 7

Fig. 7.1: Nijō Castle entrance gate, Kyoto, 1624–1626. Photo by author, 2018.

Fig. 7.2: Nijō Castle entrance gate (detail), Kyoto, 1624–1626. Photo by author, 2018.

Fig. 7.3: Recreation of Ninomaru Palace room interior, 1624–1626, *shoin-zukuri* style of architecture. Nijō Castle, Kyoto, Wikimedia Commons.

Fig. 7.4: Ninomaru Palace garden, originally created in the seventeenth century. Nijō Castle, Kyoto. Photo by author, 2018.

Fig. 7.5: Ryōanji dry landscape garden, earliest descriptions date to 1680s, Ryōanji, Kyoto. Photo © Cquest, Wikimedia Commons.

Fig. 7.6: *The Old Plum Tree*, Kano Sansetsu, c. 1646, four sliding door panels, ink, color, gold, and gold leaf on paper, overall H. 174.6 cm x W. 485.5 cm. The Harry G. C. Packard Collection of Asian Art, Gift of Harry G. C. Packard, and Purchase, Fletcher, Rogers, Harris Brisbane Dick, and Louis V. Bell Funds, Joseph Pulitzer Bequest, and The Annenberg Fund Inc. Gift, 1975, 1975.268.48a–d. Metropolitan Museum of Art, New York, Public domain.

Fig. 7.7: *Hikone Screen*, c. 1624–1644, folding screen, ink and color on paper with gold leaf background, each panel H. 94 cm x W. 48 cm. Hikone Castle Museum, Wikimedia Commons.

Fig. 7.8: *Daruma Looking at His Reflection*, Suzuki Harunobu, c. 1762–1770, color woodblock print. H. 28.9 cm x W. 21 cm. Clarence Buckingham Collection, 1925.2064. Art Institute of Chicago, Public domain.

Fig. 7.9: *Two Lovers,* Hishikawa Moronobu, c. 1675–1680, woodblock print, leaf from an album of *shunga*. H. 22.9 cm x W. 33.7 cm. The Francis Lathrop Collection, Purchase, Frederick C. Hewitt Fund, 1911, JP676. Metropolitan Museum of Art, New York, Public domain.

Fig. 7.10: *The Actors Ichikawa Danjūrō II and Ichikawa Monnosuke I,* Torii Kiyonobu 1715–1725, hand-colored woodblock print. H. 31.6 cm x W. 15 cm. Gift of Mr. and Mrs. Harold G. Henderson, 1967.627. Art Institute of Chicago, Public domain.

Fig. 7.11: *Standing Courtesan in Kimono with Fern and Wheel Pattern*, Kaigetsudō Ando, c. 1710, hanging scroll, ink, color, gold, and shell white on paper. H. 80 cm x W. 29 cm Bequest of Richard P. Gale 74.1.29. Minneapolis Institute of Art, Public domain.

Fig. 7.12: Imari plate, Hizen ware, c. 1770, Imari plate with a vase of flowers, made for the European market, hard-paste porcelain with colored enamels over transparent glaze and gilded, diameter 26 cm. The Hans Syz Collection, Gift of Stephan B. Syz and John D. Syz, 1995, 1995.268.37. Metropolitan Museum of Art, New York, Public domain.

Fig. 7.13: Incense box in the shape of a rooster, Nonomura Ninsei, c. 1665, Kyōyaki ware, stoneware with overglaze enamels, box is H. 7.3 cm x W. 3.8 cm x Depth 6.7 cm. The Putnam Dana McMillan Fund, The Louis W. Hill, Jr. Fund and gift of the Asian Art Council, 2000.141A, B. Minneapolis Institute of Art, Public domain.

Fig. 7.14: *Poem Scroll with Deer* (detail), Tawaraya Sōtatsu, 1610s, handscroll, ink, gold, and silver on paper. Overall: 34.3 x 1041.9 cm. Photo: Seiji Shirono. Gift of Mrs. Donald E. Frederick, 51.127. Seattle Art Museum.

Fig. 7.15: Writing box decorated with cranes in reeds, Hon'ami Kōetsu, early seventeenth century, black and gold lacquer on wood, lead and pewter plates. 8.1cm x 21.8 cm x 23.2 cm. Photo: Paul Macapia. Gift of Mrs. Donald E. Frederick, 50.67. Seattle Art Museum.

Fig. 7.16: Jar, Hon'ami Kōetsu, c. 1620, clay, red and green glaze (Kyoto ware). H. 14 cm x diameter 17.8 cm. H.O. Havemeyer Collection, Bequest of Mrs. H.O. Havemeyer, 1929, 29.100.615a.b. Metropolitan Museum of Art, New York, Public domain.

Fig. 7.17: *Waves at Matsushima* (left screen), Tawaraya Sōtatsu, early seventeenth century, folding screen, ink, color, gold, and silver on paper, each H. 166 cm x W. 369.9 cm. Gift of Charles Lang Freer, F1906.231-232. National Museum of Asian Art, Smithsonian Institution, Washington, DC, Creative Commons.

Fig. 7.18: *Waves at Matsushima* (right screen), Tawaraya Sōtatsu, early seventeenth century, folding screen, ink, color, gold, and silver on paper, each H. 166 cm x W. 369.9 cm. Gift of Charles Lang Freer, F1906.231-232. National Museum of Asian Art, Smithsonian Institution, Washington, DC, Creative Commons.

Fig. 7.19: Dish with Design of Landscape with Blossoming Trees, Ogata Kenzan, 1699–1712, glazed stoneware. H. 2.6 cm x D. 11.2 cm x L. 19.1 cm. Gift of Mr. and Mrs. Richard Barancik, 1975.544. Art Institute of Chicago, Public domain.

Fig. 7.20: *Red and White Plum Blossoms*, Ogata Kōrin, first half of the eighteenth century, pair of two-panel folding screens, color and gold leaf on paper, each screen H. 156 cm x W. 173 cm. MOA Museum of Art, Atami, Wikimedia Commons.

Fig. 7.21: *Shinobazu Pond*, Odano Naotake, 1770s, hanging scroll, ink and color on silk. H. 132.5 cm x 98.5 cm. Akita Museum of Modern Art, Wikimedia Commons.

Fig.7.22: *Large Perspective Picture of the Kaomise Performance on the Kabuki Stage*, Okumura Masanobu, c. 1740, hand colored woodblock print. H. 46.8 cm x W. 68 cm Clarence Buckingham Collection, 1925.2285. Art Institute of Chicago, Public domain.

Fig. 7.23: *Parakeets Among Hydrangeas and Poppies*, Sō Shiseki, after 1770, hanging scroll, ink and color on silk, image H. 34.29 cm x W. 57.47 cm. Mary Griggs Burke Collection, Gift of the Mary and Jackson Burke Foundation 2015.79.191. Minneapolis Institute of Art, Public domain.

Fig. 7.24: *Orchid Pavilion Gathering: Autumn Harvest Festival*, Ike Taiga, c. 1763, one of a pair of folding screens, ink and color on paper, image H. 160.7 cm x W. 356 cm. Mary Griggs Burke Collection, Gift of the Mary and Jackson Burke Foundation, 2015, 2015.300.163.1, .2. Metropolitan Museum of Art, New York, Public domain.

Fig. 7.25: *Snow Landscape*, Yosa Buson, c. 1770s, hanging scroll, ink and color on paper, image 174.6 x 67.3 cm. Bequest of Mrs. A. Dean Perry, 1997.111. Cleveland Museum of Art, Public domain.

Fig. 7.26: *Perfuming a Robe as Visual Parody of the Four Accomplishments, Autumn*, Suzuki Harunobu, 1767, color woodblock print. H. 27.9 cm x W. 20.9 cm. Gift of Ruth Lathrop Sikes in memory of her brother Bruce Sikes, 1967, P.13.948. Minneapolis Institute of Art, Public domain.

Fig. 7.27: *Snow-Covered Pines* (right screen), Maruyama Ōkyo, second half of the eighteenth century, pair of six-fold screens, ink and gold on paper, each screen H. 155.5 x W. 362 cm. Mitsui Memorial Museum, Tokyo, Wikimedia Commons.

Fig. 7.28: *Two Crows*, Matsumura Goshun, late eighteenth to early nineteenth century, hanging scroll, ink and color on silk, image H. 49.85 cm x W. 43.97 cm. Gift of the Clark Center for Japanese Art & Culture 2013.29.1001. Minneapolis Institute of Art, Public domain.

Fig. 7.29: *Saboten gunkei-zu fusuma-e* (Cactus and Domestic Fowls), Itō Jakuchū, 1789, sliding doors (*fusuma*), ink and color on gold, each panel H. 177.2 cm x W. 92.2 cm. Saifuku-ji, Osaka, Wikimedia Commons.

Fig. 7.30: *White Elephant and Black Bull*, Nagasawa Rosetsu, between 1789 and 1801, left screen of a pair of folding screens, ink and gold paint on paper. H. 155.3 cm x W. 359.0 cm. The Etsuko and Joe Price Collection, Wikimedia Commons.

Fig. 7.31: *Gama Sennin (Hou Xiansheng) and His Three-Legged Toad*, Soga Shōhaku, eighteenth century, hanging scroll, ink on paper. H. 200.8 cm x W. 55.2 cm. Gift of Charles Lang Freer, F1904.192. Freer Gallery of Art Collection, Washington, DC, Public domain.

Fig. 7.32: *Portrait of Bodhidharma*, Hakuin Ekaku, mid-eighteenth century, hanging scroll, ink on paper, image H. 117.5 cm x 54 cm. Gift of Florence and Herbert Irving, 2015, 2015.500.9.3. Metropolitan Museum of Art, New York, Public domain.

Chapter 8

Fig. 8.1: Minka houses, Saiko Iyashi no Sato Nenba, open air museum (reconstruction of a former farming village), Fujikawaguchiko-machi. Photo by author, 2023.

Fig. 8.2: Interior of Minka house, Saiko Iyashi no Sato Nenba, open air museum (reconstruction of a former farming village), Fujikawaguchiko-machi. Photo by author, 2023.

Fig. 8.3: *The Jewel River of Bush Clover in Ōmi Province*, Utagawa Kunisada, 1847–1852, color woodblock print triptych, left sheet. H. 37.4 cm x W. 24.9 cm. Gift of Mrs. Elaine C. Norden in memory of her sister, Miss Esther M. Cleveland, P.70.90. Minneapolis Institute of Art, Public domain.

Fig. 8.4: Light brown-ground Ryūkyūan robe with ikat stripes, early twentieth century, banana fiber, cotton; two-color warp ikat. H. 107.95 cm x W. 102.87 cm. The John R. Van Derlip Fund and the Mary Griggs Burke Endowment Fund, 2019.20.182. Minneapolis Institute of Art, Public domain.

Fig. 8.5: Light blue-ground Ryūkyūan robe, nineteenth century, ramie, *bingata* (stencil resist with applied pigments). H. 132.72 cm x W. 121.92 cm. The John R. Van Derlip Fund and the Mary Griggs Burke Endowment Fund, 2019.20.146. Minneapolis Institute of Art, Public domain.

Fig. 8.6: "Fancy-Free Type" from the series *Ten Types in the Physiognomic Study of Women* Kitagawa Utamaro, 1792–1793, color woodblock print with mica, image H. 38 cm x W. 24.8 cm. Bequest of Richard P. Gale, 74.1.143. Minneapolis Institute of Art, Public domain.

Fig. 8.7: *Cherry and Maple Trees*, Sakai Hōitsu, early 1820s, one of a pair of six-panel screens, ink, color, and gold leaf on paper, each H. 158.5 cm x W. 342 cm. Purchase, Mary and James G. Wallach Foundation Gift, Rogers and Mary Livingston Griggs and Mary Griggs Burke Foundation Funds, and Brooke Russell Astor Bequest, 2018.55.1, .2. Metropolitan Museum of Art, New York, Public domain.

Fig. 8.8: *Portrait of Ōzora Buzaemon*, Watanabe Kazan, 1827, hanging scroll, ink and color on paper, image H. 221.8 cm x W. 117.8 cm. Leonard C. Hanna Jr. Fund, 1980.177. Cleveland Museum of Art, Public domain.

Fig. 8.9: *Ichikawa Ebizo IV as Takemura Sadanoshin*, Tōshūsai Sharaku, 1794, color woodblock print. H. 36 cm x W. 23.6 cm. Bequest of Edward L. Whittemore, 1930.205. Cleveland Museum of Art, Public domain.

Fig. 8.10: *The Earth Spider Generates Monsters at the Mansion of Lord Minamoto Yorimitsu*, Utagawa Kuniyoshi, color woodblock print triptych, 1843, overall H. 37 cm x W. 75 cm. The Pearl and Seymour Moskowitz Collection, S2021.5.591a-c. National Museum of Asian Art, Smithsonian Institution, Washington, DC.

Fig. 8.11: "Mishima, Morning Mist" from *Tōkaidō Hōeidō* series, Utagawa Hiroshige, c. 1832–1833, color woodblock print, No. 12 in the series. H. 23.13 cm x W. 36.2 cm. Gift of Louis W. Hill, Jr., P.77.39.7.1L. Minneapolis Institute of Art, Public domain.

Fig. 8.12: "Under the Wave off Kanagawa" from *Thirty-Six Views of Mount Fuji*, Katsushika Hokusai, 1830–1833, color woodblock print. H. 26 cm x W. 37.7 cm. Bequest of Richard P. Gale, 74.1.230. Minneapolis Institute of Art, Public domain.

Fig. 8.13: "Fireworks at Ryōgoku" from *One Hundred Famous Views of Edo*, Utagawa Hiroshige, 1858, color woodblock print. H. 33.8 cm x W. 22.5 cm. Gift of Louis W. Hill, Jr., P.75.51.378. Minneapolis Institute of Art, Public domain.

Fig. 8.14: "Oiwa" from the series *One Hundred Ghost Tales*, Katsushika Hokusai, 1831–1832, color woodblock print. H. 25.6 cm x W. 16.1 cm. Clarence Buckingham Collection, 1943.603. Art Institute of Chicago, Public domain.

Fig. 8.15: Gyokuran and Taiga, from the *Kinsei kijin den*, Mikuma Katen (1730–1794), 1790, woodblock printed book, approximately H. 25 cm x W. 17 cm. Spencer Collection, New York Public Library, New York Public Library Digital Collections, Public domain.

Fig. 8.16: *Night Scene in Yoshiwara* aka *Courtesans Showing Themselves to the Strollers through the Grille*, Katsushika Ōi, active c. 1818–1854, hanging scroll, ink and color on paper. H. 26.3 cm x W. 39.8 cm. Ōta Memorial Museum of Art, Tokyo, Wikimedia Commons.

Fig. 8.17: *Fūryū: The Great Battle of the Frogs*, Kawanabe Kyōsai, 1864, color woodblock print triptych, each sheet H. 36 cm x W. 24.5 cm. The Miriam and Ira D. Wallach Division of Art, Prints and Photographs: Print Collection, New York Public Library. "Fashionable Battle of Frogs," New York Public Library Digital Collections, Public domain.

Chapter 9

Fig. 9.1: Akasaka Palace, Katayama Tōkuma, 1909, steel-reinforced masonry, Wikimedia Commons.

Fig. 9.2: Illustration of the Museum at the Second National Domestic Industrial Exhibition in Ueno from the series *Famous Places in Tokyo*, Utagawa Hiroshige III (1843–1894), 1881, color woodblock print triptych. H. 34.9 cm x W. 71.4 cm. Gift of Lincoln Kirstein, 1959, JP3267. Metropolitan Museum of Art, New York, Public domain.

Fig. 9.3: Rokumeikan, Josiah Conder, 1883, "Renaissance villa" style of architecture, Wikimedia Commons.

Fig. 9.4: Kaichi School, Matsumoto, Tateishi Seijū, 1876, two stories with step tower, wood frame, Wikimedia Commons.

Fig. 9.5: *Salmon*, Takahashi Yuichi, 1877, oil on paper. H. 140 cm x W. 46.5 cm. University Art Museum, Tokyo University of the Arts, Wikimedia Commons.

Fig. 9.6: *Harvest*, Asai Chū, 1890, oil on canvas. H. 69.6 cm x W. 98.2 cm. The University Art Museum, Tokyo University of the Arts, Wikimedia Commons.

Fig. 9.7: Japanese Pavilion at the World's Columbian Exposition, Kuru Masamichi, 1893, Wikimedia Commons.

Fig. 9.8: Stacked food box (*jūbako*) with Taro Plants and Chrysanthemums, Shibata Zeshin, mid-nineteenth century, lacquered wood, gold and silver *hiramaki-e*, *takamaki-e*, and colored *togidashimaki-e*. H. 41.9 cm x W. 22.9 cm x depth 24.4 cm Mary Griggs Burke Collection, Gift of the Mary and Jackson Burke Foundation, 2105, 2015.300.289a–g. Metropolitan Museum of Art, New York, Public domain.

Fig. 9.9: Vases with Hen and Rooster, Namikawa Sōsuke, c. 1890–1900, *musen* and cloisonnė enamels worked in gold and silver wire; gilt copper rims and feet. H. 42.7 cm Nasser D. Khalili Collection of Japanese Art. Photo © John-Pierre Dalbéra, Wikimedia Commons.

Fig. 9.10: *Twelve Falcons*, Suzuki Chōkichi, 1893, cast bronze, lacquer, casting, gilding, and inlay, each H. 41 cm to 52 cm. National Museum of Modern Art, Tokyo. Photo © Daderot, Wikimedia Commons.

Fig. 9.11: Textile Hanging with Hō-ō Bird, 1895–1910, silk embroidery with woven silk border, overall H. 271 cm x W. 218 cm. Nassar D. Khalii Collection of Japanese Art, Wikimedia Commons.

Fig. 9.12: *Merciful Mother Kannon,* Kano Hōgai, 1883. Hanging scroll, ink, color, and gold on silk. H. 163.9 cm x W. 84.6 cm. National Museum of Asian Art, Smithsonian Institution, Freer Collection, Gift of Charles Lang Freer, F1902.225.

Fig. 9.13: *Orchids*, Okuhara Seiko, 1870, fan, ink on mica paper. H. 25.4 cm x W. 42.55 cm x Depth 1.59 cm. Gift of the Clark Center for Japanese Art & Culture, formerly given to the Center by Marjorie Bissinger 2013.29.349. Minneapolis Institute of Art, Public domain.

Fig. 9.14: *Twenty-Four Things We Like About Civilization, No. 1 Beef*, 1877, Toyoharu Kunichika, color woodblock print, one of a series. H. 36 cm x 24.5 cm. Collection of the author.

Fig. 9.15: *Concert of European Music*, Hashimoto Chikanobu, 1889, color woodblock print triptych. H. 36.8 cm x W. 73.7 cm. Gift of Lincoln Kirstein, 1959, JP3276. Metropolitan Museum of Art, New York, Public domain.

Fig. 9.16: *The Enlightenment of Fudō Myō-ō*, no. 5 from the series *Kyōsai rakuga*, Kawanabe Kyōsai, 1874, color woodblock print. H. 36 cm x W. 24.6 cm. Photo: Art Research Center, Ritsumeikan University, Israel Goldman Collection, London.

Fig. 9.17: *Eshinbun Nipponchi, No. 1*, 1874. Kawanabe Kyōsai and Kanagaki Robun. Satirical magazine cover, Wikimedia Commons.

Fig. 9.18: *Fujiwara Yasumasa Playing the Flute by Moonlight*, Tsukioka Yoshitoshi, February 1883, color woodblock print triptych, each sheet H. 35.56 cm x W. 24.77 cm The Mary Griggs Burke Endowment Fund 2017.106.149A-C. Minneapolis Institute of Art, Public domain.

Fig. 9.19: *View of Takanawa Ushimachi Under a Shrouded Moon*, Kobayashi Kiyochika, 1879, color woodblock print. H. 20.2 cm x W. 32.3 cm. National Museum of Asian Art, Smithsonian Institution, Robert O. Muller Collection, S2003.8.1179.

Fig. 9.20: *Use of Electricity During the Siege of Pyongyang*, Kobayashi Kiyochika, 1894, color woodblock print triptych. H. 37.5 cm x W. 71.8 cm. Bequest of William S. Lieberman, 2005, 2007.49.328. Metropolitan Museum of Art, New York, Public domain.

Fig. 9.21: *Kusunoki Masashige*, Takamura Kōun and others, 1893–1900, bronze. H. 8 meters including pedestal. Imperial Palace, Tokyo, Wikimedia Commons.

Fig. 9.22: *Maiko*, Kuroda Seiki, 1893, oil on canvas. H. 80.4 cm x 65.3 cm. Tokyo National Museum A-11258, Wikimedia Commons.

Fig. 9.23: *Two Divinities Dancing*, Tomioka Tessai, 1924, hanging scroll, ink and color on silk. H. 169 cm x W. 86 cm. Tokyo National Museum, Wikimedia Commons.

Fig. 9.24: Murin-an Garden, Kyoto, Ogawa Jihei VII (Ueji), 1894–1902. Photo © Oilstreet, Wikimedia Commons.

Chapter 10

Fig. 10.1: *Fallen Leaves* (right screen), Hishida Shunsō, 1909, pair of six-panel screens, ink and color on paper. H. 157 cm x W. 362 cm (each screen). Eisei-Bunko Museum, Tokyo, Wikimedia Commons.

Fig. 10.2: *Grand Canyon*, Yoshida Hiroshi, 1925, color woodblock print. H. 24.9 cm x W. 37.2 cm, Wikimedia Commons.

Fig. 10.3: *Butterflies*, Fujima Takeji, 1904, oil on canvas. H. 44.5 cm x W. 44.5 cm. Private collection, Wikimedia Commons.

Fig. 10.4: *Nude Beauty*, 1912, Yorozu Tetsugorō, oil on canvas. H. 160 cm x W. 97.5 cm. National Museum of Modern Art, Tokyo, Wikimedia Commons.

Fig. 10.5: *A Road Cut Through a Hill*, Kishida Ryūsei, 1915, oil on canvas. H. 56 cm x W. 53 cm. National Museum of Modern Art, Tokyo, Wikimedia Commons.

Fig. 10.6: *Mount Yakedate*, Yasui Sōtarō, 1941, oil on canvas. H. 52 cm x W. 46 cm. Museum of Modern Art, Kamakura, Public domain.

Figure 10.7: *Historic Spot of Rome* (left screen), Takeuchi Seihō, 1903, pair of six-panel screens, ink and color on silk (no size indicated). Umi-Mori Art Museum, Hiroshima prefecture, Wikimedia Commons.

Fig. 10.8: *Mother and Child*, Uemura Shōen, 1934, color on silk, framed. H. 168 cm x W. 115.5 cm. National Museum of Modern Art, Tokyo, Wikimedia Commons.

Fig. 10.9: *Spring Dawn over the Holy Mountain of Chichibu*, Yokoyama Taikan, 1928, Hanging scroll, ink and gold wash on silk. H. 67.2 cm x W. 113.5 cm. Household of Princess Chichibu, Wikimedia Commons.

Fig. 10.10: *Woman Looking at a Mirror*, Itō Shinsui, July 1916, color woodblock print, edition 120/150. H. 44.5 cm x W. 29.1 cm. Gift of Ellen and Fred Wells 2002.161.205. Minneapolis Institute of Arts, Public domain.

Fig. 10.11: *The Actor Morita Kan'ya XIII as Jean Valjean*, Yamamura Kōka, 1921, color woodblock print, edition 150. H. 40.2 cm x W. 27.3 cm. Based on the play *Les Misérables* performed at the Yūraku Theater, December 1920. Gift of Ellen and Fred Wells 2002.161.53. Minneapolis Institute of Arts, Public domain.

Fig. 10.12: *Komagata Embankment* from the series *Twelve Scenes of Tokyo*, Kawase Hasui early summer 1919, color woodblock print. H. 23.9 cm x W. 36.5 cm. Margaret McMillan Webster estate 51.40.1. Minneapolis Institute of Arts, Public domain.

Fig. 10.13: *Portrait of Hagiwara Sakutarō*, Onchi Kōshirō, 1943, first edition, color woodblock print. H. 55.4 cm x W. 44 cm. Gift of Yamaguchi Kikuo and Yamaguchi Harue, P01630. National Museum of Modern Art, Tokyo, Public domain.

Fig. 10.14: *Female Nude Seated in Water*, Ichijō Narumi, 1906, color lithograph, ink on card stock. H. 13.8 cm x W. 8.8 cm. Published by the Japanese Postcard Club. Museum of Fine Arts, Boston. Leonard A. Lauder Collection of Japanese Postcards, 2002, Wikimedia Commons.

Fig. 10.15: Tokyo Station Marunouchi Building, Tatsuno Kingo, 1914, steel framing with red brick. Wikimedia Commons.

Fig. 10.16: Heian Jingū, Kyoto, Itō Chūta, 1895, cypress wood with red lacquer. Photo by author, 2010.

Fig. 10.17: Vase, Hamada Shōji, twentieth century, glazed stoneware. H. 22.07 cm x W. 23.65 cm x Depth 23.65 cm. Gift of Stephen Addiss and Audrey Seo 2007.99.18. Minneapolis Institute of Art, Public domain.

Fig. 10.18: Front Cover of *MAVO*, No. 3, September 1924. Editors Okada Tatsuo and Murayama Tomoyoshi, art magazine. Spencer Collection, New York Public Library, New York Public Library Digital Collections, Public domain.

Fig. 10.19: *Suzhou (Shoshū), China* (title variations: *Sochu, China*; aka Su-chou or Soochow), Yoshida Hiroshi, 1940, color woodblock print. H. 27.1 cm x W. 40.6 cm. Wikimedia Commons.

Chapter 11

Fig. 11.1: Monju Bosatsu (Bodhisattva Manjusri) from *Two Bodhisattvas and Sakyamuni's Ten Great Disciples*, Munakata Shikō, 1939, woodcut, scroll mounted, image H. 37.25 cm x W. 12 cm. Purchased with funds provided by Mr. and Mrs. Charles J. Rosenbloom, 57.41.12. Carnegie Museum of Art, Pittsburgh.

Fig. 11.2: *Plastic Pumpkin*, Kusama Yayoi, 2016. This is one of many examples of the plastic pumpkin theme, Public domain.

Fig. 11.3: Gutai Pinacotheca, original 1962 photograph. 2018 photo © Matvisser, Wikimedia Commons.

Fig. 11.4: *Phase—Mother Earth*, Sekine Nobuo, 1968, earth. Photo © Osamu Murai, Wikimedia Commons.

Fig. 11.5: Hiroshima Peace Memorial Museum, Tange Kenzō, 1955, steel-framed reinforced concrete and glass. Wikimedia Commons.

Fig. 11.6: Mito Art Tower, Isozaki Arata, 1990. Photo © Korall, Wikimedia Commons.

Fig. 11.7: Team Disney Orlando, Isozaki Arata, 1991, postmodern architectural style. Lake Buena Vista, Florida, Wikimedia Commons.

Fig. 11.8: Hyogo Prefectural Museum of Art, Andō Tadao, 2002, Kobe, Japan. Photo © 664highland, Wikimedia Commons.

Fig. 11.9: "Calamity's Intense Heat" from the *Jiji manga*, Kitazawa Rakuten, July 17, 1921, tear sheets, manga, H. 51.2 cm x W. 38.9 cm, full-color Sunday supplement to the newspaper *Jiji shinpō*. Courtesy of The Ohio State University's Billy Ireland Cartoon Library and Museum, PN6790.J32 J55 no. 23.

Fig. 11.10: Collection of Japanese anime and manga examples, private collection. Photo by author.

Fig. 11.11: *Momotarō's Divine Sea Warriors*, Directed by Seo Mitsuyo, 1945, anime. Public domain.

Fig. 11.12: On the set of *Gojira* (*Godzilla*), 1954, feature-length film, Tōhō Studio, Tokyo A behind-the-scenes photograph from the filming of *Gojira* (*Godzilla*), showing crew members operating the Godzilla suit. Public domain.

Fig. 11.13: Scene from *Spirited Away*, Miyazaki Hayao, 2001, anime. Studio Ghibli, Public domain.

Fig. 11.14: Theatrical release poster of the 1954 film *Seven Samurai*, Kurosawa Akira, 1954 feature-length film. poster made by the Tōhō Kabushiki kaisha (Toho Company, Ltd.), Wikimedia Commons.

Fig. 11.15: *Bathing* – Shizu'ura, Shizuoka prefecture, 1936. Photo © Domon Ken, Public domain.